THE COMPLETE COOKBOOK OF AMERICAN FISH AND SHELLFISH

THE COMPLETE
COOKBOOK
of AMERICAN
FISH AND
SHELLFISH
SECOND EDITION

by John F. Nicolas

 Van Nostrand Reinhold
New York

Library of Congress Catalog Card Number 89–33710
ISBN 0–442–23504–6

Printed in the United States of America

Van Nostrand Reinhold
115 Fifth Avenue
New York, New York 10003

Van Nostrand Reinhold International Company Limited
11 New Fetter Lane
London EC4P 4EE, England

Van Nostrand Reinhold
480 La Trobe Street
Melbourne, Victoria 3000, Australia

Nelson Canada
1120 Birchmount Road
Scarborough, Ontario M1K 5G4, Canada

16 15 14 13 12 11 10 9 8 7 6 5 4 3 2 1

Library of Congress Cataloging-in-Publication Data

Nicolas, John F.
    The complete cookbook of American fish and shellfish / John F.
Nicolas.—2nd ed.
      p.   cm.
    Includes index.
    ISBN 0–442–23504–6
    1. Cookery (Fish)   2. Cookery (Shellfish)   I. Title.
TX747.N54   1990
641.6'92—dc20   89–33710
                                                                    CIP

My special thanks go to a woman of incredible determination and courage. Her knowledge of the culinary world has been a true inspiration. Her refined taste for all seafoods well prepared, her constructive evaluations of new recipes, and her intuitive suggestions were invaluable. She has brought thunder, lighting, tidal waves, and rainbows into my life. To you, Barbara, with all my love for ever . . .

CONTENTS

FOREWORD

Today, the architects—the chefs and cooks—of modern cuisine are making all efforts to produce healthy and good tasting food. John F. Nicolas, in his newly revised book, *The Complete Cookbook of American Fish and Shellfish,* has enhanced this effort. As I have known John F. Nicolas for over twenty years and have collaborated professionally with him on many occasions, I know that his new book will teach, advise, and provide new ideas in an area that is popular and healthy. Because of this, I can recommend this book to every professional, novice, and simple hobby cook.

Fritz Sonnenschmidt, C.M.C.
President
Mid Hudson Culinary Association
ACF Chapter

PREFACE

The rapid growth of the U.S. fish industry has brought a progressive but undeniable change to the way we eat. As we see the evolution of a fish-eating society, seafood restaurants abound all across America. The demand for quality fish and shellfish is constantly on the rise.

The second edition of *The Complete Cookbook of American Fish and Shellfish* takes into account our ever growing knowledge in seafood. Consumers have acquired a taste for almost anything that swims in our oceans and lakes.

Fish like catfish, monkfish, various species of sharks, and mollusks such as urchins, mussels, squid were all looked upon disdainfully in the 1970s and early 1980s when the first edition of this book appeared. These fish and shellfish are now an integral part of the second edition of the book, which includes about 500 recipes, many of them culinary wonders, covering a wide spectrum of tastes. French, Italian, Chinese, Japanese, Spanish, American, and Cajun innovative seafood specialties abound in *The Complete Cookbook of American Fish and Shellfish,* and it is hoped that the recipes will be of value to the reader.

It has been my great fortune to experience a unique professional environment for the past twenty years that has widened my knowledge of the culinary world to the highest level. I have been able to appreciate at an early age the true meaning of "freshly caught fish," and excell in the preparation of seafood dishes during my college education in the Paris Hotel School, France, to become the recipient of the Curnonsky award and Cointreau Cup, and other awards while competing against the best of European cooking schools. Five years in the Bahamas gave me a wonderful opportunity to familiarize myself with a tropical world of varied species of fish and shellfish and many Caribbean seafood specialties.

The Gaspe Peninsula, where I combined work and pleasure while fishing for Atlantic salmon and rainbows, motivated me to write a fish cookbook mostly about salmon. A decade ago, fresh salmon was rare and seasonal on the U.S. markets. The professional and consumer interest in strictly a salmon cookbook would have been limited. That is how the idea of the first edition of *The Complete Cookbook of American Fish and Shellfish* came to light.

The past eighteen winters by the Gulf of Mexico were delightful gastronomic experiences. Pompano, stone crab, grouper, sea trout, shrimp, and many other specialties were created in my kitchens under the best circumstances. Eighteen summers in the New England states gave me the opportunity to discover many intriguing species of fish along the Atlantic Coast. Tilefish, blue crabs, soft- and hard-shelled crabs, monkfish, skate, mussels, squid, and other fish went through rigorous testings in my kitchens. All of this seafood offers a great deal of possibilities in our kitchens when treated with care and savoir faire.

Abalone, Surimi, catfish recipes, and scores of new seafood appetizers have been added to this second edition. Seafood and nutrition go hand in hand. The recipes in this edition include the number of calories per serving. The

Appendix lists the recipe names and their number of calories per serving in ascending order.

Overall, the new edition of *The Complete Cookbook of American Fish and Shellfish* is a comprehensive and informative book with a whole new concept in fish cookery. As fish and all kinds of seafood are appreciated more, this book will hopefully stimulate the reader to acquire the knowledge of how to identify, use, cook, and present the bounty of our seas.

An innovative computer program called MICRO CUISINE has been created to manage all the recipes on diskettes. The easy-to-use data base software allows the user to count calories, adjust quantities, create personalized recipe files, and help find and organize all the recipes included in the second edition of *The Complete Cookbook of American Fish and Shellfish*. MICRO CUISINE has become the "The Program of Choice" at home and in the food service industry.

For additional information, please contact:
John F. Nicolas
Culinary Software Development
P.O. Box 975
Far Hills, N.J. 07931

ACKNOWLEDGMENTS

For their generous assistance, the author is especially grateful to:

The National Fisheries Institute
The National Marine Fisheries Service
The Atlantic States Marine Fisheries Commission
Texas Department of Parks and Wildlife
Florida Department of Natural Resources
California Department of Fish and Game
South Carolina Department of Wildlife and Marine Resources
Maryland Department of Natural Resources

This project has been a collaborative effort. For their inspiration and encouragement, I want to thank Pamela Scott, Editor, Hospitality Management, at Van Nostrand Reinhold; Paul Lukas, Editorial Supervisor; Cynthia Zigmund, Associate Editor, Architecture, Design, and Hospitality Management; and Maryellen Costa, Project Manager at Spectrum Publisher Services.

INTRODUCTION

In the United States, fish and shellfish continue to appear more frequently on our tables. To meet this growing need, over 4,000 seafood wholesalers and processors are serving consumers who have developed a penchant for almost anything that swims. Statistics compiled by the National Marine Fisheries Service indicate that the consumption of commercially caught fish and shellfish has increased dramatically during the past years and is still rising. In 1963, per capita consumption was 10.7 pounds (4.84 kg); in 1971, it rose to 11.5 pounds (5.2 kg); and in 1972, 12.4 pounds (5.6 kg). By 1976, per capita consumption reached 12.9 pounds (5.84 kg), and jumped to a record of 14.7 pounds (6.66 kg) in 1986. Due to our changing eating habits, expectations are that consumption may approach 30 pounds (13.6 kg) by the turn of the century.

During the past few years, the real changes in American fish consumption have occurred at the retail level. One of the big reasons for the dramatic growth of the fishing industry is the ability to rush fresh fish overnight from sea to markets in all parts of the country.

As a result, major grocery-store chains across the United States, especially in the Midwest where fresh fish was in short supply, are distributing large varieties of fresh seafoods daily. There is also a growing network of fish specialty chains. Companies and corporations as well are taking a new look at fish farming including the production of imitation fish products, particularly Surimi.

Fish is an excellent source of protein, minerals, and vitamins. The variety of seafoods available and their versatility in preparation are other factors responsible for their increased acceptance. We are constantly reminded that eating too much meat can be hazardous to our health, whereas eating more fish can help increase life expectancy. The per capita consumption of fish and shellfish in the Nordic countries is high and so is their longevity. Also, it is known that the Greenland Eskimos' coronary death rate is by far the lowest in the world. Their diet features fish such as salmon, which is rich in Omega-3 fatty acids, a nutritional substance that lowers the incidence of heart disease.

In 1986, six countries accounted for 55 percent of the world catch. Japan led with 13 percent, followed by the U.S.S.R., China, Chile, the United States, and Peru, the last two with 5.6 percent and 5.5 percent of the total catch, respectively.

As we depend more and more on the foods found in our oceans, lakes, and rivers, we must realize the dangers threatening our fish and shellfish. Pollution and overfishing are major threats to the balance of life in our seas; the leaping pink *Salmonidae* can no longer struggle in our polluted waters; *Homarus Americanus* is losing the battle against greedy fishermen; some mollusks have become health hazards; and the red tide is persistent in taking a share of our ocean crop.

The rapid rise in demand for seafood has drained American waters and put a burden on the nation's fishing fleet. As a result, 64 percent of all fish sold in the United States is imported, which makes this nation the world's number two importer of fish, after Japan. We are also the number two exporter of fish, after Canada, selling mostly salmon and crab to Japan. Imports, however, far exceeded exports; in 1986, over $4 billion of fish products came in while $1 billion went out.

Our taste for fish and our preoccupation with health have brought the business of seafood to an annual revenue of over $16 billion—compared with $14 billion for chicken, which is cheaper than fish, and $44 billion for beef.

In 1976, the United States Congress signed into law Bill No. 94-265, which extended American fishing rights from 12 to 200 miles off our shores, thus restricting foreign fishing. Primarily to protect New England and Pacific Northwest fishermen, this bill keeps foreign fishing fleets out of their waters. Above all, it helps to alleviate the depletion of our seafood stock and balance our marine resources.

As the fishing boom expands, statistics indicate that commercial landings of lobsters, scallops, tuna, flounders, and other fish are declining alarmingly. Still, demand for fishery products keeps climbing even though prices of some species of fish and shellfish have reached a range of $7 to $10 per pound.

The decline of our fish stock is not always due to pollution or overfishing however. Natural fluctuations that occur among marine resources, and environmental influences such as changing wind strengths and shifting currents, can affect the food sources for fish. Nevertheless, a large variety of fish and shellfish continues to be available throughout the country. Yet, because fishermen are especially sensitive to the decline in fish stock, they are now selling what was once considered "junk fish," which in fisherman's language is a fish that has or had no market value. For example, haddock and Alaskan crab were once classified as junk fish. Until recently, monkfish (lotte) was considered "trash fish" and was dumped back; now it is being served in first class restaurants. Squid, salmon, shark (dogfish), skate wings, and other species of fish with abysmal names like blowfish, sea robin, or orange roughie are marketed successfully. Other species of fish such as mahi, tilapia, ono, and opah will become trendy in the years to come.

Happily, the potential catch of underutilized species is staggering. In U.S. waters alone, squid, Pacific mackerel, Pacific pollock, small red crab, and Jonah and cancer crabs could yield as much as the *total* yearly United States fish catch. Future fish yields, therefore, while requiring caution, can be seen in a more optimistic light.

U.S. fishermen harvest over 3.4 billion pounds for human food. Although some species are on the decline, our continental shelf is far from empty. New England fishermen caught over 32 million pounds of American lobsters in 1986. The oyster yield was 56 million pounds of meat, salmon landings were 230 million pounds, and scallops yielded 7 million pounds of meat. Shrimp, the most valuable U.S. seafood, remains with tuna the highest in volume, 387 million pounds each. Our favorite flounder family yielded 230 million pounds, but landings of haddock, halibut, and cod declined driving their prices up as the demand keeps increasing. If the laws governing our seas are obeyed, there is no reason why we cannot continue to enjoy our favorite fish and shellfish at reasonable cost.

PART
ONE

PURCHASING
AND
PREPARATION

Seafood and Health

Only recently has light been shed on the nutritional and dietary values of seafood, which are significant. We now realize that fish and shellfish not only satisfy our appetite and taste, but also provide valuable proteins and minerals.

For example, there is growing evidence that eating fish rich in unsaturated fats is the healthiest thing you can do for your heart. Omega-3 fatty acids in fish can significantly increase your high Density Lipoproteins (HDLs), which fight cholesterol buildup, while diminishing your Low Density Lipoproteins (LDLs), which can cause heart disease.

NUTRITION: A KEY TO GOOD HEALTH

Fish and shellfish can furnish most of the nutrients that are required by the body—and in generous amounts. When properly prepared, fish and shellfish can be delicious and satisfying, thus contributing to the simple enjoyment of eating.

The Nutritional Characteristics of Fish and Shellfish

There are many reasons why the nutritional characteristics of seafood should be of vital interest to the consumer. Dieticians must provide balanced and appealing meals, at reasonable prices, for large numbers of people. Certainly, fishery products are highly nutritious and an excellent source of dietary essentials. Moreover, the cost per pound of edible flesh from most fish is no more, and is often less, than that of many cuts of meat from domestic animals. However, the cost per pound of popular fish and shellfish like flounder, sole, shrimp, and scallops has increased considerably over the past years as the demand keeps rising and the supply keeps decreasing.

Consumers are more and more concerned about the caloric content of foods. The fat content of fish varies greatly among species, but those with low amounts of fat are particularly suited for weight-control diets. Moreover, the fat in fish contains a high proportion of polyunsaturated fatty acids. Because polyunsaturates in the diet help to decrease the incidence of atherosclerosis,

3

heart specialists are particularly interested in the nutritional quality and composition of fishery products. Many doctors now recommend generous portions of fish in the diet to increase the intake of polyunsaturated fatty acids, while ensuring an adequate intake of protein.

Fishery products are also easily digested. Thus, they are valuable in the diets of young children and elderly people, where ease of digestibility is critically important.

Custom-Tailored Diets

Like people, fish come in many sizes and shapes, and can be classified as lean, medium, or fat. By properly selecting fat or lean species of fish, you can tailor your diet to your particular needs. Of course, fat is only one major component of fish; the others are protein, minerals, and water. In general, an inverse relationship exists between the fat and water content in the fish, and these two components account for approximately 80 percent of the weight of the fish.

Most fish and shellfish contain low amounts of fat and high amounts of protein. Some examples of low-fat, high-protein fish are tuna, halibut, cod, flounder, haddock, pollock, herring, rockfish, carp, whiting, crabs, scallops, and shrimp. Tuna and halibut are particularly good sources of protein. Some fish that contain both high amounts of fat and protein are anchovies, oysters, mackerel, salmon, and sardines.

For many centuries, fish and shellfish were considered easily digestible. Recent research proves that 90 to 100 percent of fish protein is digestible. This digestibility of seafood protein is considered slightly higher than that of beef and chicken. As a result, fishery products are included in many special diets for people with digestive disorders. For example, fish and shellfish are used liberally in diets recommended for convalescent ulcer patients.

Since fishery products contain low amounts of connective tissue and fibrous components, they are especially suitable for low bulk, bland diets. Here, the goal is to minimize the amount of undigested food in the digestive tract and still provide a nutritionally adequate diet. Often, fishery products are included in diets for people with digestive disorders to provide a wider variety of main dishes that are flavorful and appealing, but still suited to special dietary needs.

Fish and Shellfish: Excellent Sources of High-Quality Protein

Scientific studies have shown that fish and shellfish contain protein of excellent quality, clearly placing them in a unique and enviable class. There is no mystery surrounding the attributes of the protein in fish. Simply stated, the protein in fish and shellfish contains generous amounts of compounds called amino acids, which are needed to construct body protein. Moreover, fish protein can be easily and almost completely digested.

A serving of 4 ounces (120 grams) of lean fish will supply almost half the total amount of protein required daily by the body. The other half can be supplied easily by a normal intake of nonanimal protein. Although total protein content varies between lean and fatty fish, the amino acid composition and quality of the protein is remarkably constant. Thus, the quality of the protein is high whether it comes from lean or fatty fish.

Fish is often referred to by food faddists as brain food. Unfortunately, there is no basis for this claim. In fact, no such thing as brain food exists. However, as pointed out, fish is a particularly good source of high-quality protein. When included in a balanced diet, fish provides nourishment to all body tissues but shows no special preference for any particular part of the body.

Certain shellfish contain protein that is especially high in quality. Oysters, for example, are extremely beneficial for humans and are frequently used in therapeutic diets. Although the protein content of oysters is low, compared to that of most other fish and shellfish, the quality of oyster protein is superior to that of most fish and beef. While oysters are excellent food, there is no scientific basis for the popular view that generous amounts increase sexual potency.

Oil in Fish and Shellfish

Increasing attention has been given recently to the relationship between the amount and type of fat in the diet and the incidence of heart disease. This relationship has been established conclusively, and evidence does suggest that a high intake of animal fat is a predisposing factor contributing to heart disease. Because the fat in fish and shellfish has a unique chemical nature, fishery products are often recommended in diets designed to minimize the risk of heart disease.

Among vulnerable groups, two dietary modifications are often recommended to reduce the incidence of heart disease. The first is to reduce the fat content and the total caloric content of the diet. The second is to substitute the polyunsaturated fatty acids for some saturated fatty acids. Studies have shown that the ingestion of oil containing large amounts of polyunsaturated fatty acids tends to suppress the blood cholesterol level and lower the incidence of atherosclerosis. Few people, however, want to consume oil directly, although fish oil is currently available in capsule form. A much more palatable method is simply to include generous portions of fishery products in the diet. For example, some salmon average nearly 15 percent oil. A 6-ounce (180 gram) serving can furnish nearly 1 ounce (30 grams) of oil rich in polyunsaturated fatty acids. Fish not only contain high proportions of polyunsaturated fatty acids, but they also contain relatively small amounts of cholesterol. Certain cuts of beef and some egg products contain up to ten times as much cholesterol per ounce as is found in fish and shellfish.

Reducing the total intake of calories in the diet, however, is often as important to health as including liberal quantities of polyunsaturated fatty acids. In this case, fish that are low in oil will reduce the total caloric intake and still provide adequate protein to meet the body's requirements. Low-fat fish and shellfish normally contain less than 100 calories per 4-ounce (120 gram) serving. (For more details, see Table 1-1.) On the other hand, a 4-ounce serving of good quality beef may supply well over 300 calories. For those who are calorie conscious, seafood offers a distinct advantage over meats that are high in fat.

Table

1-1. Seafood Nutrition Chart

Based on 100 Grams Raw Edible Portion

Species	Calories per 100 grams	Protein gm per 100 grams	Fat gm per 100 grams	Cholesterol mg per 100 grams	Sodium mg per 100 grams	Iron mg per 100 grams
Saltwater Fish						
Anchovy (raw)	131	20.35	4.84	N/A	104	3.25
Bluefish	124	20.04	4.24	59	60	0.48
Blue Runner (Crevalle)	98	20.7	1.7	N/A	83	N/A
Butterfish	146	17.28	8.02	65	89	0.50
Bonito	111	20.5	2.5	37	N/A	12.15
Cod						
Atlantic Cod	82	17.81	0.67	43	54	0.38
Pacific Cod	82	17.90	0.63	37	71	0.26
Croaker	104	17.78	3.17	61	56	0.37
Crevalle Jack	94	18.8	1.9	N/A	N/A	8.0
Cusk	87	18.99	0.69	41	31	0.83
Dolphin	85	18.50	0.70	73	88	1.13
Eel (mixed species)	184	18.44	11.66	126	51	0.50
Flounder (mixed species)	91	18.84	1.19	48	81	0.36
Golden Kingklip	74	14.7	0.3	N/A	N/A	N/A
Greenland Turbot	99	16.9	3.5	N/A	N/A	N/A
Grouper	92	19.38	1.02	37	53	0.89
Haddock	87	18.91	0.72	57	68	1.05
Halibut	110	20.81	2.29	32	54	N/A
Hawaiian Fish						
Ahi (Bigeye Tuna)	108	23.38	0.95	45	37	0.73

MahiMahi (Dolphin Fish)	94	19.3	1.1	N/A	170	N/A
Oho (Hawaiian Wahoo)	124	24.1	2.3	N/A	82	N/A
Opakapaka (Pink Snapper)	102	21.9	0.9	N/A	54	N/A
Herring						
Atlantic	158	17.96	9.04	60	90	1.10
Pacific	195	16.39	13.88	77	74	1.12
Ling	87	18.99	0.64	N/A	135	0.65
Lingcod	85	17.66	1.06	52	59	0.32
Mackerel						
Atlantic Mackerel	205	18.60	13.89	70	90	1.63
King Mackerel	105	20.28	2.00	53	158	1.78
Pacific Jack Mackerel	157	20.07	7.89	47	86	1.16
Spanish Mackerel	139	19.29	6.30	76	59	0.44
Monkfish	76	14.48	1.52	25	18	0.32
Mullet	117	19.35	3.79	49	65	1.02
Ocean Catfish	103	17.60	3.60	N/A	100	N/A
Ocean Perch						
Atlantic Ocean Perch	94	18.62	1.63	42	75	0.92
Pacific Ocean Perch	91	18.50	1.40	N/A	70	N/A
Orange Roughy	126	14.70	7.00	20	63	0.18
Pollock						
Atlantic	92	19.44	0.98	71	86	0.46
Alaskan	81	17.18	0.80	71	94	0.23
Pompano	164	18.48	9.47	50	65	0.60
Porgy (Scup)	105	18.88	2.73	N/A	42	0.53
Redfish	117	18.50	4.80	N/A	81	N/A
Rockfish (mixed)	94	18.75	1.57	35	60	0.41
Sablefish	195	13.41	15.30	49	56	1.28

Table

1-1. Seafood Nutrition Chart *(continued)*

Based on 100 Grams Raw Edible Portion

Species	Calories per 100 grams	Protein gm per 100 grams	Fat gm per 100 grams	Cholesterol mg per 100 grams	Sodium mg per 100 grams	Iron mg per 100 grams
Salmon, (Raw)						
Chinook Salmon	180	20.06	10.44	66	47	0.71
Coho Salmon	146	21.62	5.95	39	46	0.70
Pink Salmon	116	19.94	3.45	52	67	0.77
Sockeye Salmon	168	21.30	8.56	62	47	0.47
Sardines						
Atlantic Canned in oil, drained	208	24.62	11.45	142	505	2.92
Pacific Canned in tomato sauce, drained	178	16.35	11.98	61	414	2.30
Sea Bass (mixed species)	97	18.43	2.00	41	68	0.29
Sea Trout (mixed)	104	16.74	3.61	83	58	0.27
Shad	197	16.93	13.77	N/A	51	0.97
Shark (mixed species)	130	20.98	4.51	51	79	0.84
Skate (ray)	89	19.60	0.70	N/A	90	7.50
Snapper (mixed)	100	20.51	1.34	37	64	0.18
Sole (mixed)	91	18.84	1.19	48	81	0.36
Spot	123	18.51	4.90	N/A	29	0.32
Striped Bass	97	17.73	2.33	80	69	0.84
Swordfish	121	19.80	4.01	39	90	0.81
Tilefish	96	17.50	2.31	N/A	53	0.25

Tuna						
Albacore	177	25.30	7.60	N/A	40	N/A
Bluefin	144	23.33	4.90	38	39	1.02
Skipjack	103	22.00	1.01	47	37	1.25
Yellowfin	108	23.38	0.95	45	37	0.73
Whitefish	134	19.09	5.86	60	51	0.37
Whiting (mixed)	90	18.31	1.31	67	72	0.34
Freshwater Fish						
Burbot	90	19.31	0.81	60	97	0.90
Carp	127	17.83	5.6	66	49	1.24
Catfish (channel)	116	18.18	4.26	58	63	0.97
Lake Trout	148	20.77	6.61	58	52	1.50
Lake Whitefish	140	18.50	7.20	N/A	52	N/A
Pike						
Northern	88	19.26	0.69	39	39	0.55
Walleye	93	19.14	1.22	86	51	1.30
Rainbow Trout	118	20.55	3.36	57	27	1.90
Shad	197	16.93	13.77	N/A	51	0.97
Smelt	97	17.63	2.42	70	60	0.90
Tilapia	98	18.50	2.40	N/A	52	N/A
Shellfish						
Abalone	105	17.10	0.76	85	301	3.19
Clams (raw, mixed species)	74	12.77	0.97	34	56	13.98
Crab (raw)						
Blue Crab	87	18.06	1.08	78	293	0.74
Dungeness Crab	86	17.41	0.97	59	295	0.37
King Crab	84	18.29	0.60	42	836	0.59
Snow Crab	90	18.50	1.18	55	539	N/A
Crayfish	89	18.66	1.06	139	53	2.45

Table

1-1. Seafood Nutrition Chart (*continued*)

Based on 100 Grams Raw Edible Portion

Species	Calories per 100 grams	Protein gm per 100 grams	Fat gm per 100 grams	Cholesterol mg per 100 grams	Sodium mg per 100 grams	Iron mg per 100 grams
Lobster						
Northern Lobster	90	18.80	0.90	95	N/A	N/A
Spiny Lobster	112	20.60	1.51	70	177	1.22
Mussels (Blue)	86	11.90	2.24	28	286	3.95
Oysters						
Eastern & Gulf	69	7.06	2.47	55	112	6.70
Pacific	81	9.45	2.30	N/A	106	5.11
Scallops (mixed)	88	16.78	0.76	33	161	0.29
Shrimp (mixed)	106	20.31	1.73	152	148	2.41
Snails (unspecified raw)	75	14.40	1.90	N/A	N/A	25.00
Squid	92	15.58	1.38	233	44	0.68

Data from USDA Handbook Eight (1987) Composition of Foods: Finfish and Shellfish Products.
*Data from Chemical and Nutritional Composition of Finfishes, Whales, Crustaceans, Mollusks, and their Products, Sidwell, NDAA Technical Memorandum NMFS F/SEC-11, U.S. Department of Commerce, 1981.

Vitamin Content

Fish products are good sources of several vitamins. The 13 common vitamins can be divided into two major groups, fat-soluble vitamins and water-soluble vitamins. In fishery products, fat-soluble vitamins are found in the oil; water-soluble vitamins are found in the water content. In the history of the study of vitamins, it was recognized early that fish liver oil was a rich and natural source of fat-soluble vitamins, especially vitamins A and D. The flesh of fish, however, contains relatively small amounts of fat-soluble vitamins.

Fish oil generally has a higher content of fat-soluble vitamins than the fat of animals. In turn, fatty fish contain more of these vitamins than lean fish. Some fatty fish are excellent sources of vitamin D; lean fish contain very small amounts. The vitamin A content of the flesh of most fish is relatively low. It has been noted, however, that swordfish and whitefish contain high amounts of vitamin A.

As for water-soluble vitamins, four of the eight members of the vitamin B family can be supplied in adequate amounts by fish and shellfish. These four vitamins are B_6, B_{12}, biotin, and niacin. The remaining four B vitamins are found in fishery products, but generally not in appreciable quantities. Larger amounts of B vitamins are usually found in high-fat fish rather than low-fat fish. Also, the B vitamin content of fish and animal is about the same.

Seafood is a Valuable Source of Many Essential Minerals

Fish contain relatively large amounts of phosphorus, potassium, and iron. Conversely, fish contain relatively low amounts of sodium and chlorine.

With the advent of low-sodium diets, attention has focused on the sodium content of fish and shellfish. Occasionally, doubt is expressed about the advisability of using fish in low-sodium diets prescribed for people suffering from hypertension. This doubt is unfounded, even in the case of saltwater fish. With the exception of most shellfish, fish are low in sodium and can be used freely in low-sodium diets. Fresh oysters and soft clams are also low in sodium. Other shellfish often contain higher amounts of sodium and are not recommended for low-sodium diets. Also, if salt is added during processing, sodium levels will exceed the maximum permissible level. Since fish vary considerably in flavor and texture, they add variety and diversification to low-sodium diets.

Fishery products are also noted for a high content of microminerals, or trace minerals, such as iodine and fluoride. Because trace minerals perform vital functions, fish and shellfish are viewed with special interest. Most essential trace minerals are present in seafood in amounts at least equivalent to those in meat, however, and usually in much higher amounts than in vegetables and dairy products.

FISH AND SHELLFISH CONTRIBUTE TO THE ENJOYMENT OF EATING

Over 150 varieties of fish and shellfish—either fresh or processed—are available to the consumer. With this multiplicity of choice, it is possible to please even the most discriminating palate. Seafood, however, is a most delicate food and must be handled with care from the time it is caught until it is placed on the table. Natural goodness and taste are easily lost if improper preservation and processing techniques are used. While meats tend to improve with aging, fish and shellfish are best when fresh. The methods used in cooking fish and shellfish are especially important. Good fish can be easily spoiled if improperly cooked. Essentially, fish should be cooked only until the flesh "sets" and is easily flaked from the bones.

Fish can be baked, broiled, boiled, or fried. Of course, certain types of fish are more suited to particular methods of cooking. For example, fatty fish are considered better for broiling and baking; lean fish are more appropriately broiled, boiled, or steamed. The important point is that overcooking must be avoided to preserve the natural texture and flavor. Fish and shellfish can be delicious and prepared with ease. They are more than a substitute for meat and can be used as an appetizer (see Chapter 15), a first course, or the main attraction. Even the connoisseur can find the right seafood to suit a particular purpose and taste. When cooked and flavored with appropriate herbs and spices, and consumed with vintage wine, seafood can be a truly enjoyable experience in eating.

2

Buying, Handling, and Storing Seafood

Meat must be aged to improve in taste, flavor, and tenderness. Fish and shellfish are perishable foods. As soon as they are exposed to warm air temperatures, they deteriorate rapidly. Fresh seafood, handled properly from landing to cooking, has an unmistakably good flavor and odor. Any error in handling and storing results in poor quality seafood.

BUYING QUALITY FRESH FISH

When buying fresh fish make certain that:

1. The flesh is firm and elastic, not separating from the bones. In buying fillets and steaks, look for a fresh-cut appearance and color that resembles freshly dressed fish.
2. The gills are bright red in color.
3. The odor is fresh and mild. A fish just taken from the water has practically no "fishy" odor.
4. The eyes are bright, clean, transparent, and full.
5. The skin is shiny and bright in color.
6. The scales adhere tightly to the skin.

HANDLING AND STORING FISH AND SHELLFISH

Seafoods spoil more rapidly than any other food product and should be handled and stored with utmost care. Freshly caught fish or shellfish that is brought to the pan quickly is in a class by itself. The flavor of seafood diminishes if processing, storing, or cooking are mishandled.

Fresh fish should be cleaned and gutted to preserve freshness. The removal of the intestines, liver, heart, and gills will eliminate the major sources of bacterial contamination. This is the most important step in retaining the freshness of fish. Occasionally, the gills are not removed when fish are cleaned by distributors. However, the complete removal of gills is necessary to preserve the full freshness of fish. Red snapper, which has a delicate meat, will spoil three to four times faster if the gills are not removed completely within a few hours of the catch.

Fresh fish should be refrigerated on ice at 35°F to 40°F (1.5°C to 4.5°C) as soon as they are received. Seal the fish if necessary before placing on ice. Use a separate refrigerator, if available, or at least a section of the refrigerator avoiding contact with other foods. Fish should not be exposed to air unnecessarily as oxidation may alter the flavor. Fillets of fish lose their flavor more rapidly than whole fish and should be processed without delay. Purchase whole fresh fish if available. Eviscerate as soon as possible and process into fillets, steaks, sticks, or other forms shortly before cooking. This method of preparation guarantees the full flavor of fish. For more details on preparing various types of fresh fish and shellfish, see Chapter 5.

The source of supply is an important factor when purchasing fish and shellfish. It is, therefore, necessary to select a reliable fish dealer. Beware of fish sections in many supermarkets that display smelly and stale fish and shellfish. There is no bargain in buying stale fish at any price. Numerous supermarkets in the United States have the reputation of selling the best quality meat and the worst quality seafood.

One can never achieve a culinary triumph with poor quality fish. A freshly cooked fish has a sweet taste; if the fish has been stored improperly, it will have a "fishy" taste. A strong rancid flavor indicates that the raw material was poorly handled before or during the freezing process. Rancidity is caused by oxidation of the fish oil. As a rule, fish containing less than 5 percent oil freeze and preserve better than those that contain higher oil percentages. (Refer to Table 2-1.) Mackerel, lake trout, shad, and smelt are likely to become rancid faster than yellow perch, halibut, red snapper, or lobster. The Atlantic salmon, king salmon, and silver salmon keep exceptionally well when frozen, even though their oil content is very high. Yet the comparatively lean pink salmon, called humpback in British Columbia, becomes rancid and discolors after a relatively short period of freezing. This species of salmon is mostly canned.

Different environmental conditions can cause a particular fish to have different flavors. Apart from the problems caused by water pollution, several species of fish found in northern waters have a palatability superior to the same species caught in southern waters. A bass or perch caught in muddy warm water is inferior to the same species caught in clear cold water. The same applies to hatchery trout, which seldom have the delicate flavor of wild brook trout.

Refrigerated smoked fish should not be placed in contact with ice. Smoked fish, especially trout, salmon, finnan haddie, and herring, should always be well sealed with wax paper and foil to contain their penetrating odors.

Table 2-1. Freezer Storage Life

Types	Species	Months
fat fish	mackerel, salmon, (king, silver) tuna, herring, et cetera	3
lean fish	haddock, cod, redfish, red snapper, swordfish, et cetera	6
	lobsters, crabs (meat)	2
	shrimp	6
	oysters, scallops, clams (shucked)	3 to 4

The Handling of Frozen Fish

Fish to be frozen should be wrapped and sealed in moistureproof and vapor-proof material. Do not freeze fish that are wrapped only in wax paper or polyethylene materials. Fresh fish may be frozen in a block of ice or by glazing, both of which prevent moisture loss. To freeze fish in a block of ice, place the fish in a container large enough to hold the fish and cover with water. Then freeze until solid.

Glazing is as effective as block freezing and takes less freezer space. To glaze fish (dressed, steaks, or fillets), place in a single layer on a tray, wrap, and freeze. As soon as the fish is frozen, remove from the freezer, unwrap, and dip quickly in ice-cold water. A glaze will form immediately. Repeat the dipping process three or four times. A thick coat of ice will result from each dipping. If necessary, return the fish to the freezer between dippings if the glaze does not build up after two or three consecutive dippings. Handle the fish carefully to avoid breaking the glaze. When glazed, wrap the fish tightly in freezer wrap or aluminum foil and return to the freezer. Glazing may need to be repeated if the fish is not used within one or two months.

Commercially packaged frozen fish products should be placed in a freezer, in their original moistureproof and vaporproof wrapper, immediately after purchase to maintain quality. Store at 0°F (–18°C) or lower. At temperatures above this level, chemical changes cause the fish to lose color, flavor, texture, and nutritive value. Storage time should be limited in order to enjoy the optimum flavor of frozen fish. It is good practice to date the packages for easy rotation.

The Handling of Shellfish

Fresh shellfish should be stored at approximately 33°F to 34°F (1°C to 2°C) and used within a day or two. Never store in water.

Clams and oysters in the shell are alive when the shells are tightly closed or close when lightly tapped. Gaping shells indicate that the shellfish are dead and not edible. Shucked oysters should be plump and have a creamy color and mild odor.

Cooked crabs and lobsters in the shell must be bright red with no disagreeable odor.

Fresh shrimp have a mild odor and meat that is firm in texture. Cooked shrimp have a red-colored shell and the meat has a reddish tint.

Scallops have a sweet odor and should be free of excess liquid when packaged.

To freeze shellfish, process the same way as frozen fish. Specific instructions for oysters and blue crabs follow.

To prepare oysters for freezing:

1. Wash shell thoroughly.
2. Open and remove meat. Place meat in a strainer and save liquid. Wash meat with a cool, 2 percent salt solution and remove loose shell particles.
3. Place in container with liquid and salt solution to cover meat. Label and freeze immediately.

To prepare live blue crabs for freezing:

1. Boil whole crabs for freezing. Boil whole crabs for 15 to 20 minutes in 5 percent salt water. Cool rapidly.
2. Pick meat from body and claws. Keep lump meat, claw meat, and flake meat separate, if desired.
3. Pack in moisture and vaporproof containers. Label container and freeze immediately.

Frozen Fish and Shellfish
Storage Life

Fish products of good quality, that were handled correctly from catch to freezer, should remain in good condition for the period indicated in Table 2-1 (at temperatures ranging from 0°F to −10°F or −18°C to −23°C). Good quality fish products, frozen under the best conditions, will not be discolored or display freezer burns (a very white, dry appearance around the edges). Ice crystals inside the package indicate moisture loss from fish flesh, which could be the result of thawing, refreezing, or insufficiently low temperatures. For complete details on fatty fish and lean fish, see Table 1-1.

Cooked Seafood

Cooked seafood can be stored in the refrigerator or freezer. If stored in the refrigerator, cover the seafood and hold no longer than two to three days. If stored in the freezer, package the seafood in a moisture and vaporproof material and hold no longer than three months.

Canned Fish Products

Canned seafood should be stored in a cool dry place for no longer than one year.

Thawing Fish Products

Schedule thawing so that fish or shellfish will be cooked soon after thawing. Thawed seafood should be held no longer than one day before cooking.

Place the package of frozen seafood in the refrigerator to thaw. Allow 18 to 24 hours per pound for thawing a package. If quicker thawing is necessary, place the package under cold running water. Allow 1 to 2 hours per pound. Do not thaw fish at room temperature or in warm water, as it loses moisture and flavor. Thawed seafood should not be refrozen. Some frozen seafoods, such as breaded frozen fish products, can be cooked without thawing. Any leftover, uncooked fresh seafood, scallops, oysters, clams, fish fillets, and sticks can be breaded and frozen. The breading preserves the freshness of the seafood. In addition, frozen fish fillets can be cooked without thawing, if additional time is allowed. The cooking time for frozen seafoods is double that for the same product, fresh or thawed.

HOW QUALITY IS LOST

The primary causes of quality breakdown in fish products are oxidation, dehydration, enzymatic action, and bacterial growth. When oxidation occurs, the oil or fat in the fish flesh can cause the fish to become rancid. Do not expose fish products to air unnecessarily, and wrap tightly before freezing. Dehydration is caused by improper packaging. Excessive drying out in frozen fish is known as freezer burn. Enzymatic action in the flesh of fish causes deterioration. Low temperatures slow enzymatic action and preserve the original quality. Bacterial growth increases mainly when the storage temperature is too high and when sanitation in handling fish is poor.

▬ Emergencies

If power failure occurs but is not expected to exceed 24 hours, keep the freezer closed to prevent thawing. When power is restored, turn the thermostat to the highest setting until the freezer temperature is reduced to 0°F to –10°F (–18°C to –23°C).

If the freezer is likely to be off for more than 24 hours, use dry ice to keep the food frozen until power is restored. Once fish products are thawed, they should not be refrozen.

HOW MUCH TO BUY

The amount of fish or shellfish to purchase varies according to portion size, the type of recipe, and the marketing form of the fish product. On the average, allow approximately 5½ to 7 oz. (150 to 200 g) of boneless fish per serving. Table 2-2 is a fish and shellfish buying guide with the approximate amount listed for 6 servings.

Table 2-2. Buying Guide for Fish and Shellfish

Type	Quantity for 6 Servings
Fish, whole	4½ lb. (2.040 kg)
Fish, dressed or pan dressed	3 lb. (1.360 kg)
Fish, fillets or steaks	2 lb. (900 g)
Fish, portions	2 lb. (900 g)
Fish, sticks	2 lb. (900 g)
Fish, canned	1½ lb. (680 g)
Clams, in the shell	3 doz.
Clams, shucked	1 qt. (11)
Crab, cooked meat	1½ lb. (680 g)
Lobsters, live	7 lb. (3.170 kg)
Lobster, cooked meat	2 lb. (900 g)
Oysters, in the shell	3 doz.
Oysters, shucked	1 qt. (11)
Scallops, shucked	2 lb. (900 g)
Shrimp, headless	3 lb. (1.360 kg)
Shrimp, cooked meat	2 lb. (900 g)

Marketing of Fish Products

Each year, about three billion pounds of fish and shellfish are caught commercially for food in the United States. The ocean's harvest is brought into United States ports nearly every day of the year. The highest landings occur generally from June through September, peaking in the last two months. Many species of fish and shellfish are then available at their lowest prices. Many shrewd food operators take advantage of the large supply of popular fish products and stock for months ahead.

Fresh fish is sold on the market in a number of forms:

1. Whole or round
2. Drawn
3. Dressed or pan dressed
4. Steaks
5. Fillets

Whole or round fish are marketed just as they come from the water. Before cooking they must be scaled and eviscerated. The fins are removed but the head and the tail may or may not be removed, depending on the type of recipe and the presentation of the dish.

Drawn fish are marketed with only the entrails removed (see Fig. 3-1). They need to be scaled and washed before cooking.

Dressed and pan-dressed fish are both scaled and eviscerated. Usually, head, tail, and fins are removed to ready them for cooking (see Fig. 3-2). Smaller pan-dressed fish usually have the head and tail left on when readied for cooking.

Steaks are cross section slices of larger dressed fish. They are ready to cook as purchased (see Fig. 3-3).

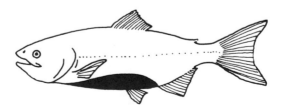

Figure 3-1. Whole drawn fish.

EDIBLE PORTIONS OF FISH AND SHELLFISH

The edible portion of fish products varies with the market form, the variety of fish, and the production area. Among all fish available commercially, salmon has the best yield. The edible portion of drawn salmon is 70 to 75 percent. Table 3-1 illustrates approximately how much of the market form of each fish product is edible.

Fillets are the sides of dressed fish, cut lengthwise away from the back bones (see Fig. 3-4). Fillets are usually boneless, may be skinned, and require no preparation before cooking. Butterfly fillets are the sides of the fish held together by the uncut belly skin or by the back, and are usually boneless. For more details on butterfly fillets, see p. 130.

Figure 3-2. Dressed or pan-dressed fish.

Figure 3-3. Fish steaks.

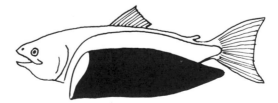

Figure 3-4. Fillet of fish.

Table
3-1. Edible Fish Products

Fish	Production Area	Edible Percentage
Whole or round	all	43 to 47
Drawn (eviscerated only)	all	46 to 50
Dressed (eviscerated, head fins removed)	all	65 to 69
Steaks	all	84 to 88
Fillets	all	100
Sticks and portions	all	100
Shellfish, live in shell		
Clams:		
Hard	New England	14.5
	Chesapeake	10
	Middle Atlantic	14
	South Atlantic	9.5
	Pacific	25
Soft	New England	22.7
	Chesapeake	18.5
Surf	Middle Atlantic	20
Oysters:		
Eastern	New England and Middle Atlantic	11
	South Atlantic	6.3
	Gulf	6.5
Pacific		11.3
Cooked in shell		
Crabs:		
Hard	Atlantic and Gulf	10 to 18
Dungeness	Pacific	22 to 26
Lobsters	New England	35 to 37
Shucked		
Clams, oysters, bay and sea scallops	all	100
Headless, raw shrimp	South Atlantic and Gulf States	50 to 60
Cooked meat		
Crabs, lobsters, and shrimp	all	100

HOW FROZEN FISH PRODUCTS ARE MARKETED

Frozen fish products are marketed as steaks, fillets, fish portions, and fish sticks. Fish portions are pieces of fish cut from the frozen fish block into uniform portions weighing no less than 1½ ounces (42 g) and up to 6 ounces

(170 g). Fish sticks are pieces of fish cut from frozen fish blocks into uniform portions, usually about 1 inch (2.5 cm) wide and 3 inches (7.5 cm) long. They weigh up to 1½ ounces (42 g).

HOW SHELLFISH ARE MARKETED

Fresh shellfish, such as oysters, clams, and some varieties of crabs, should be alive when purchased in the shell. Shucked shellfish are those that have been removed from their shells. Clams, oysters, and scallops are often shucked. The term *shrimp* refers to the fresh whole (heads on) shrimp that are sold mainly near product points. *Headless shrimp* are the edible portions with the heads removed. The term *green shrimp* describes raw shrimp, in the shell, with or without the head. *Peeled shrimp* are headless; *deveined* shrimp have the intestinal track or black vein removed.

Cooked shrimp are available fresh, frozen, dried, or canned and are usually sold peeled, deveined, and ready-to-use. Shrimp in the shell are marketed by size—jumbo, large, medium, and small—or by the number to the pound—21–25's indicates 21 to 25 shrimp to the pound, U 10's means under 10 shrimp to the pound.

Oysters are sold live in the shell, shucked, breaded, frozen raw headless, frozen fried, or canned (whole or as stew). Live oysters in the shell can be purchased by the barrel, part barrel, bushel, half bushel, etc. They are marked by size.

Crabs are sold in several forms. If purchased live, they should be alive and active at the time of cooking. Crabs cooked in the shell should be bright in color and free of disagreeable odors. Cooked crabmeat is available fresh or frozen and is picked from the shells. Canned crabmeat is ready to serve or use as purchased.

Scallops are marketed shucked or breaded. The large adductor muscle that opens and closes the shell is the only part of the scallop that is marketed as scallop meat. Breaded scallops are available frozen raw or frozen fried. Shells can be purchased for serving scallops and other fish en coquille (in the shell).

The six principal species of clams available on the market are butter, hard, little, razor, soft, and surf clams. They can be purchased live in the shell, shucked, breaded raw or cooked, or canned.

Lobsters can be purchased live in the shell or as fresh or frozen cooked meat. Frozen meat is marketed in 14 ounce (400 g) cans and packed in a salt-water solution. Live lobsters keep best when covered with seaweed or heavy paper. Excessive cold can make them appear inactive and sleepy when they are not. Lobster must be live when cooked. The flesh of dead meat flakes and falls apart. Fresh meat is firm and white with pink tinges. If the tail of a boiled lobster springs back when straightened out, it indicates that the lobster was alive before cooking. The shells of live lobsters vary in color, depending on their habitat, from dark bluish green or nearly black to mottled shades of brown and dark green. During cooking, the shells turn bright red. The moulting season for lobsters occurs generally in late July and early August. At that time, lobsters shed their hard shells and start new ones. In the soft-shell stage, lobsters are extremely perishable, lose weight, and have less meat than hard-shell lobsters.

THE SEAFOOD MARKET'S UNIQUE CHARACTERISTICS

An average of 62 to 65 percent of the frozen seafood distributed in the United States goes to restaurants, institutions, and service operations. Only 35 to 38 percent is distributed through retail outlets. About 90 percent of frozen trout goes to the institutional market. On the other hand, frozen fillets are split almost evenly between the institutional and the retail trades. By way of contrast, the institutional trade received only about 26 percent of frozen poultry products and 40 percent of all frozen foods distributed in the United States.

The range of frozen seafood products marketed in the United States is extensive. It is interesting to note that it was in Gloucester, Massachusetts, in the mid-1920s, that Clarence E. Birdseye developed and perfected a method of quick freezing that has had a tremendous impact on the entire food market. Only a little over 20 years ago, Birdseye developed frozen fish sticks, which have had a revolutionary effect on fish marketing. John Kaylor, veteran food technologist at the NMFS Atlantic Fishery Products Technology Center in Gloucester, points out that many of the 6,000 or more items now sold at many supermarkets, especially fish products, were unheard of as recently as five or ten years ago.

Valuable information pertaining to a specific fish or shellfish listed in this book can be found in Chapter 4. It includes the availability fresh, the best average weight, the market size, the quality, and the disposition for most species of fish and shellfish sold commercially.

The landings of fish and shellfish vary considerably; some months are more productive than others. Wind storms cut into fishing time; migratory fish, such as whiting, mackerel, and bluefish show up only in warm weather months; and at times one species experiences a population explosion and another species goes into decline. Purchases of fresh fish and shellfish should be planned accordingly.

The National Marine Fisheries Service created the Fishery Market News service. Fishery Market News reports current information on prices, market conditions, production, imports, exports, cold storage holdings, and market receipts of seafood products in major fish trading centers in the United States. Information is collected by market reporters, and reported to, compiled, and disseminated by Market News offices in Boston, New York, New Orleans, Terminal Island, and Seattle. Each office issues the information in two-to-four-page reports. The information aids United States buyers and sellers of fish products in making intelligent marketing decisions. The reports also establish an equal bargaining basis for everyone in the marketing system. The triweekly report or the weekly summary can be ordered from the National Marine Fisheries Service in Washington, D.C. In some parts of the country, automatic telephone message devices are used for rapid relay of current information on fish and shellfish landings, exvessel prices, and other market conditions. Telephone numbers for these Automatic Telephone Message Centers are:

Boston, Mass.—617-542-7878
Gloucester, Mass.—617-283-1101
New Bedford, Mass.—617-997-6565
New York, N.Y.
   a. Landings/prices—212-620-3577
   b. Frozen prices—212-620-3244
Hampton, Va.—804-723-0303
Chicago, Ill.—312-353-8484.

UNITED STATES INSPECTION PROGRAMS

Bringing the harvest of the seas to consumers is often a complex operation. The Department of Commerce, The National Oceanographic and Atmospheric Administration (NOAA), and the National Marine Fisheries Service (NMFS) provide inspection programs to meet various needs. Fish and shellfish are naturally nutritious, appetizing, and varied. But unless these products are properly handled during processing and distribution, they will not retain their goodness and quality.

According to Gene Cope, Consumer and Trade Education Specialist, Fishery Product Inspection and Safety Division, NOAA, "Unlike other food areas that fall under the watchful eye of mandatory federal inspection programs, the fish industry has been given scarcely a supervisory glance." He adds that the only reason for this is that such an inspection program was never deemed necessary. Whether it is confidence in product quality or in a company's reputation that has led to this consenting opinion is guesswork. For those who purchase fish products without inspection or grading markings, the trust in a particular processing plant or distributor is commendable. There is no denying that quality products induce repeat business. Indeed, there is no reason to doubt quality if past product quality has always been satisfactory. Processing plants take pride in offering the best fish products available, despite the absence of federal watchdogs. The objectives and guidelines of most distributors of fish products are often as stringent, and more so, than federal regulations. But the option of federal inspection does exist for fish products, and the public should be aware of this alternative. The United States Department of Commerce (USDC) inspection and grading seal offers a product guarantee with no guesswork involved.

Inspection and Grading

There are two separate but related parts to the federal inspection program—inspection and grading. Inspection is the examination of fish products by inspectors to make certain that the products are safe, pure, and properly labeled. The plant, equipment, and food-handling personnel must also meet adequate and appropriate hygienic standards. Products that pass inspection may bear the Federal Inspection Mark or statement, "Packed Under Federal Inspection," on the brand labels.

Figure 3-5. The Inspection Mark identifies fish products certified by federal inspectors to be safe, clean, wholesome, and properly labeled. The United States Grade Shield indicates the quality level of graded products. All products that bear Grade Shields have been federally inspected.

Grading is an added step in which the quality level of certain products is determined and certified by the inspector. In general, high volume fish products for mass feeding and direct consumer markets are subject to grading. Graded products bear a United States Grade Shield that shows their quality level.

Types of Inspection

There are three types of inspection: contract inspection, lot inspection, and miscellaneous inspection.

Contract inspection enables processing plants to have inspectors oversee preparation, processing, and packaging operations. Inspectors monitor the quality of raw materials and examine samples of the finished products. Producers and packers primarily use this service.

Lot inspection is performed on specific lots of a product. Lots are usually located in processing plants, warehouses, cold storage plants, or terminal markets. Primary users are brokers, buyers, and others with a financial interest in the product.

Miscellaneous inspection and consultation services include plant surveys, sanitation evaluation, new product evaluation, and label and product inspection reviews. Processors, packers, and brokers use these services.

The Roles of Inspectors

Inspectors fill five roles that are tailored to the type of inspection desired by applicants. In general, these roles are:

1. Sanitation expert—pinpoints unsanitary conditions in the plant and recommends ways to correct them.
2. Quality control adviser—makes certain that the quality of the raw materials

and all ingredients will produce a wholesome product. Helps establish procedures that result in a uniform product.

3. Quality control assessor—samples and grades the finished product.
4. Observer—keeps a careful watch on the overall operation of the plant.
5. Reporter—reports noted problems to plant management for resolution.

Inspection Benefits Consumers

Inspection services make an important contribution to the four principal areas of consumer concern about food products: quality, health, hygiene, and economy. Grade marks identify the product quality levels to enable wise consumer choices. Inspection assures the safety and purity of fishery products. It also assures that the product was produced, processed, and packaged under sanitary conditions. Finally, inspection helps consumers select foods that are truthfully and informatively labeled and packaged.

United States Grade Standards for Fish Products

United States Grade Standards are an important aid to orderly and efficient fish marketing. As a part of voluntary federal inspection, grading provides useful standardized information for trade transactions in fish products.

Are Grade Standards Desirable?

Grade standards identify the relative value, utility, and quality of each unit of fish product. For example, a product marked "Grade A" is of higher quality than "Grade B" or "Grade C" products. Fishermen, wholesalers, processors, distributors—all those involved in the production of fish products—use grade standards to buy and sell products of known and accepted quality. Consumers can rely on grading as a guide to quality products.

Products that Bear Standards

The National Marine Fisheries Service assigns United States Grade Standards to many high-volume fish products for direct mass consumer markets. These standards cover such products as: frozen fish fillets and fillet blocks; frozen raw fish portions and fish steaks; frozen raw breaded and precooked fish portions and fish sticks; frozen raw headless shrimp and raw breaded shrimp; and frozen raw and precooked breaded scallops.

What Grade Standards Do

Grade standards reflect different quality levels of products; form a basis for sales and purchases; provide guidelines for in-plant quality control; and establish a basis for official inspection.

The Meanings of Grade Standards

Grade A means the top or best quality. Grade A products are uniform in size, practically free of blemishes and defects, in excellent condition, and possess good flavor for the species. Grade B indicates good quality. Grade B products may not be as uniform in size or as free of blemishes or defects as Grade A products. Grade B can be termed a general commercial grade, suitable for most purposes.

Grade C means fairly good quality. Grade C products are just as wholesome and generally as nutritious as higher grades. Grade C products have a definite value as a thrifty buy when appearance is not an important factor. Consumers will not find products labeled Grade B or Grade C in the marketplace because these products are usually marketed without any grade designation.

Inspection Reinforces Grading

Product grading is more valid when done by a neutral and unbiased party. The National Marine Fisheries Service provides voluntary federal inspection on a fee-for-service basis, paid by the plant under inspection. Officially graded and certified products from such plants are eligible to carry the inspection mark and/or the prefix U.S. on their grade marks (U.S. Grade A, for example). Products that bear only the inspection mark must be at least Grade B, and most are Grade A. Consequently, knowledgeable consumers consider inspection an added service by concerned processors on behalf of consumers.

Grading by Eye at Time of Purchase

Grade standards help maintain fish product quality from the seas to the kitchen. Knowledgeable consumers also check for the following indications of proper handling at the time of purchase. Packages of frozen fish should be solid, not soft. They should be stacked well below the frost line or load line of the store's display freezer. Containers and wrapping should be intact. Packages should be free of "drip" or ice, which may indicate that the contents have thawed and been refrozen. Cello-wrap packages should not be discolored or show other signs of freezer burn. Breaded fish products should remain separated in the package. If poor quality products are purchased inadvertently, they should be returned to the store at once.

Consumer interests are a major concern of the fish industry. Much care and attention go into the production and distribution of fish products. Grade standards, inspection, and wise purchasing habits help consumers buy wholesome and nutritious seafood products at their best.

Federal Inspection Marks

Federal inspection marks are official marks approved by the Secretary of Commerce and authorized for use on brand labels of fish products. When displayed on product labels, these marks signify that federal inspectors from the Department of Commerce inspected, graded, and certified that the products met all the requirements of the inspection regulations and were produced in accordance with official United States Grade Standards or approved specifications.

They Serve Two Functions

The distinctive inspection marks signify two distinct but related functions in guiding the consumer to safe, wholesome products, produced in a sanitary environment and packed in accordance with uniform quality standards under the supervision of the United States Department of Commerce's voluntary inspection service. The inspection marks are "U.S. Grade" and "Packed Under Federal Inspection."

Fish Products That Bear Federal Inspection Marks

Many brand-name fish products carry either one or both inspection marks on their labels. The following is a list of fish and shellfish products, made from a variety of species, that bear inspection marks:

    frozen raw fish fillets, portions and sticks
    frozen fried fish fillets, portions and sticks
    fresh and frozen whole or dressed fish
    frozen raw breaded shrimp
    frozen whole cooked crabs and crabmeat
    fried fish and seafood cakes
    raw and fried fish dinners
    fried clams and clam cake dinners
    fried scallops and fried scallop dinners
    raw breaded scallops
    frozen fish steaks
    raw peeled and deveined shrimp
    cooked crabmeat, legs and claws
    fish and shellfish in sauce dinners

4

A Comprehensive
Survey of American Fish
and Shellfish

FISH

Saltwater Fish

Anchovy

The anchovy is a small marine species of the herring family. It has a long snout and a large mouth. It is blue green on top and silvery on the sides and belly. The northern anchovy is usually 5 to 6 inches (12 to 15 cm) long with a maximum length of 9 inches (22 cm), and ranges from Baja California to Washington. The striped anchovy is abundant from Delaware Bay through the West Indies.

Anchovies are not usually eaten fresh or whole, but they contribute a distinctive rich flavor to a variety of foods when pickled and salted. The fillets are usually cured in salt and olive oil. Anchovy paste is also available commercially. Most of the anchovy production is cured in fillets and canned.

Bluefish

Other name. Blue runner.

Appearance. The bluefish has a stout body with a bluntly pointed snout and sharp canine teeth. The coloration is blue green on the top fading to near silver on the belly. The bluefish is a dogged fighter with an insatiable feeding habit. Due to their exceptional appetites, they are capable of tripling their size in a single year (see Fig. 4-2).

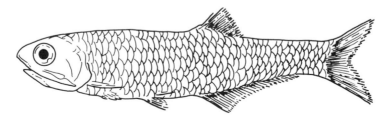

Figure 4-1. Anchovy.

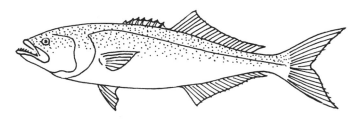

Figure 4-2. Bluefish.

Source. New England to the Gulf states.
Availability fresh. From May to November, bluefish are abundant in the northeast; in the winter months, in the Gulf states.
Average weight. Three to six pounds (1.360 to 2.7 kg).
Quality. Bluefish has a dark meat with a delicate flavor. However, the meat is fatty (10 to 14 percent).
Disposition. Bluefish do not freeze well. Commercially, they are sold mostly fresh, in fillets. Poor handling will render the flesh unpalatable, with an oily and strong flavor.

Butterfish

Other names. Dollarfish, harvest fish.
Appearance. The butterfish is a small silvery fish with a very thin, deep body (see Fig. 4-3).
Source. It is common on the northeastern coast.
Availability fresh. The fishing season in Chesapeake Bay runs from May through November. Butterfish are abundant in the coastal waters of New England during summer. The supply gradually disappears in November and the winter months.
Trade size.

   Small—5 or less to a pound
   Mixed—5 to a pound and over
   Large—¾ pound (340 g) and over

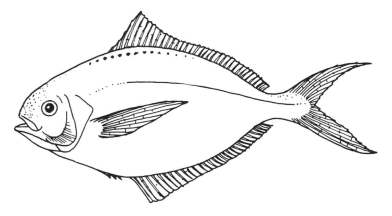

Figure 4-3. Butterfish.

A Comprehensive Survey of American Fish and Shellfish   **29**

Quality. A fatty, fine flavored fish of excellent food value. Butterfish is one of the best pan fish found on the Atlantic coast.

Disposition. Fresh, frozen, and smoked.

Cod

Other names. Atlantic cod, codfish.

Appearance. The Atlantic cod, a member of a large family of marine fish, is considered one of the most abundant fish in the United States. The cod is a heavy-bodied fish with three dorsal fins and a broad, nearly square tail. Cod vary in color from shades of gray to green, brown, or reddish tints, depending on the background (they are capable of changing color to match their surroundings). The back and sides are covered with roundish brown or red spots and there is a distinct, lighter colored lateral line (see Fig. 4-4).

Cod are differentiated from haddock by this pale lateral line, and from pollock by the large barbel and the projected upper jaw.

Source. Cod range in Atlantic waters from Newfoundland to New England, the chief ports being Boston, New Bedford, Gloucester, and Provincetown, Massachusetts, and Portland, Maine.

Availability fresh. Fishing for cod is a year-round industry. However, cod are most abundant from March to September. The price is usually higher from October to March.

Average weight. Ten pounds (4.5 kg). The best size is 6 to 8 pounds (2.7 to 3.6 kg).

Trade size.

Scrod—1½ to 2½ pounds (680 g to 1.130 kg)
Market—2½ to 8 pounds (1.130 kg to 3.6 kg)
Large—8 to 20 pounds (3.6 kg to 9 kg)
Extra large—over 20 pounds (9 kg)

To conserve the "beef of the sea," an international law is now in effect banning the use of otter trawl nets with a mesh size smaller than 4½ inches (11.25 cm). The law affects both the cod and haddock fisheries. Another step that is certain to help the repopulation of Atlantic cod is the 200-mile (320-km) limit law extending American fishing rights.

In 1986, the annual landing of Atlantic cod was over 66 million pounds; the Pacific cod recorded a harvest of 105 million pounds.

Quality. Cod is an excellent food fish with flaky, lean (0.5 percent fat) white meat.

Disposition. Fresh and frozen

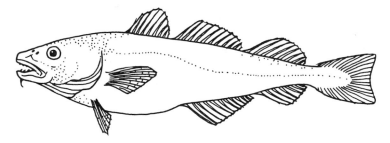

Figure 4-4. Cod.

Fillets—raw and breaded (raw and cooked)
Steaks
Specialties—breaded (raw and cooked) cakes and patties; croquettes; fish
   and chips; in sauce
Canned—cakes, flaked and salted
Salted
Smoked
Sun-dried (in hot sauce)
Lutefisk (alkaline-cured fish)

Scrod

In New England, fish called scrod may be immature cod or haddock weighing
1½ to 2½ pounds (680 g to 1.140 kg). Sometimes the term is applied to cusk of
about the same weight, or to pollock weighing 1½ to 4 pounds (680 g to 1.8
kg). When fishermen use the word, they are usually referring to gutted small
haddock.

Pacific Cod

Other names. Cod, sea bass, true cod, gray cod.
Appearance. The Pacific cod is a close relative of the Atlantic cod, and one of
the 59 members of the *Gadidae* family of cod species. Several Pacific fish called
cod are not true cod but only related. These are rockfish (rock cod), greenlings
(tommy cod), sablefish (black cod), and lingcod (cultus cod). The practice of
placing cod in the common names of many species serves to confuse the
different species and families.

   The presence of three, soft-rayed, well-separated dorsal fins, the single
barbel on the lower jaw, and two anal fins distinguish the Pacific cod from its
relatives. These fish range in color from brown to gray, fading to white to
grayish white on the sides (see Fig. 4-5).
Source. From California to northern Alaska.
Average weight. From 5 to 10 pounds (2.3 to 4.5 kg).
Quality. The Pacific cod has a mild flavor with very soft, white meat that
flakes apart easily when cooked. The meat is marketed as fresh and frozen
fillets, and frozen portions and sticks. Some of the catch is also marketed as
whole fresh fish or smoked, dried fillets. Fresh Pacific cod is available all year
in the markets of the Northwest, where it is labeled as true cod to distinguish it
from other fish that have cod in their names.

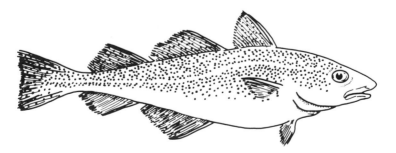

Figure 4-5. Pacific Cod.

Salted Cod

The amount of salt used to cure cod varies greatly with the weather conditions, the humidity, the time of year, and the type of curing or brine. The results range from a lightly salted, moist cod to a heavily cured, dry fish. Excessively cured cod has little moisture and requires a longer time to soak. The flavor, therefore, is often impaired.

Croaker

Other names. Atlantic croaker, crocus, hard head, king billy.

Appearance. A member of the drum family, the croaker is a small pan fish characterized by a lateral line that extends onto the caudal fin, barbels on the lower jaw, and a concave tail. The upper part of the body is covered with many small dark specks (see Fig. 4-6).

Source. Available from Texas to Massachusetts, but abundant in Virginia, North Carolina, New Jersey, and Chesapeake Bay.

Availability fresh. Although available all year, the biggest landings occur from March to October.

Average weight. The market size is between ½ to 2 pounds (225 to 900 g).

Trade size. (round)

> Pins—under ½ pound (225 g)
> Small—½ to ¾ pound (225 to 340 g)
> Medium—¾ to 1½ pounds (340 to 680 g)
> Large—1½ pound and up (680 g and up)

Quality. A good quality, lean pan fish, ideal for frying and broiling. It has a high food value, containing 17 percent protein in a 3-ounce (85 g) serving, which is nearly 25 percent of the recommended daily amount for adults. It is also exceptionally high in potassium, a vital trace element.

Disposition. The moderately priced croaker is available fresh or frozen, and pan ready. A new product, called "flaked croaker," comes in 3 or 4 ounce (85 to 110 g) raw and precooked breaded portions. It is being readily accepted by the American consumer.

Cusk

Other names. Tusk, torsk.

Appearance. The cusk is a cold-water ground fish with an elongated body, a small barbel on the lower jaw, one long dorsal fin, and a rounded tail. The

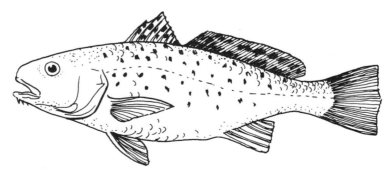

Figure 4-6. Croaker.

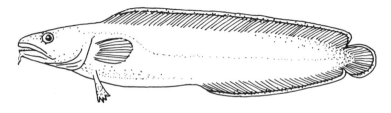

Figure 4-7. Cusk.

coloration varies from greenish brown to pale yellow fading to a cream color on the ventral side (see Fig. 4–7).

Source. Mostly New England states, rarely as far as New Jersey.

Availability fresh. February to July.

Average weight. Cusk can reach 30 pounds (13.5 kg). The best weight is 5 to 10 pounds (2.270 to 4.5 kg).

Trade size. (drawn weight)

> Scrod—1½ to 3 pounds (680 g to 1.360 kg)
> Medium—3 to 7 pounds (1.360 to 3.170 kg)
> Large—7 to 15 pounds (3.170 to 6.8 kg)
> Jumbo—15 pounds (6.8 kg) and up

Quality. The cusk, marketed under the name deep sea whitefish, has a soft, white delicate lean flesh.

Disposition. Fillets, fresh and frozen.

Dolphin

Other names. Dorado, mahimahi.

Appearance. This is not the friendly mammal we all know, but the brilliant color-changing, rainbowlike fish called mahimahi in Hawaii. Two commonly known relatives are the pompano dolphin, which reaches a length of 2 feet (60 cm) and a weight of 5 pounds (2.270 kg), and the slender dorado, which can exceed 50 pounds (22.650 kg), although most catches are between 5 to 15 pounds (2.70 to 6.8 kg) (see Fig. 4-8).

Source. Dolphins are found in areas influenced by the warm waters of the Gulf Stream. They have been caught as far north as Nova Scotia, but only rarely. Commercial landings of dolphin center around Hawaii, where an average of 100,000 to 120,000 pounds are caught each year.

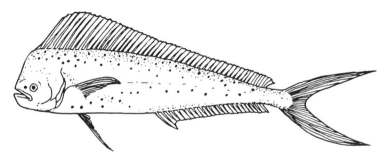

Figure 4-8. Dolphin.

A Comprehensive Survey of American Fish and Shellfish   **33**

Quality. Dolphin is a gourmet's delight, probably among the top ten of the best fin fishes. On most restaurant menus, the fish is sold under the Hawaiian name, mahimahi.

Disposition. Dolphin is usually marketed fresh, in fillets.

Eel

Other names. American eel, silver eel.

Appearance. The American eel is a catadromous fish, spending the major part of its life in fresh water and returning to sea to spawn. It is closely related to the European eel, *Anguilla Vulgaris.*

The eel is elongated, almost snakelike in appearance. The dorsal fin originates far behind the pectorals, a characteristic that distinguishes it from the conger eel on which the dorsal fin originates slightly behind the tip of the pectorals. The eel has a pointed snout and a large mouth. Its color varies with the habitat and the spawning season, ranging from gray to olive to black (see Fig. 4-9).

The reproduction of the American eel and the European eel has remained a mystery for many years. It is now known that adult eels travel from estuaries, tidal marshes, rivers, and lakes to spawn thousands of miles away, south of Bermuda and a thousand miles east of Florida and the Bahamas. Eels die after their single spawning. The larvae return to the coastal waters after a journey lasting one year or more.

Quality. The eel is not America's favorite food fish. But in Europe and Japan, the demand for eels exceeds the supply. Eel farming is a well-organized business in Japan. In the United States there is a market for eel around the Christmas holidays, particularly among families of European origin.

Availability fresh. All year, but abundant during November and December.

Source. The principal points are the St. Lawrence River in Canada, Cape Charles, Virginia, and Chesapeake Bay. Eels are shipped live by aerated trucks to major fish markets on the East coast, Chicago, and New York.

Disposition. Dressed frozen and smoked.

How to Skin an Eel

Eel should be skinned before cooking. To remove the skin, tie a string around the head and secure the string to a nail. Cut the skin around just below the head. Peel back the skin, using a pair of pliers if necessary. In a quick motion, tear off the skin the entire length of the eel. Remove the head, cut the fish open, and clean. Remove the fins with a pair of scissors. Depending on the recipe, fillet the eel or cut into sections.

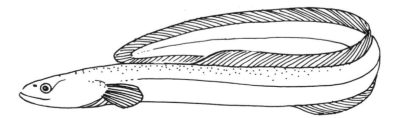

Figure 4-9. Eel.

Flounder

Flounder, an important year-round food fish, is one of a large variety of flatfish. They are abundant in Atlantic, Gulf, and Pacific coastal waters. The most common flounder are:

blackback or winter flounder
fluke or summer flounder
yellowtail flounder
dab or plaice
starry flounder

Most food operators list the above species under the general term *fillet of sole;* establishments of good reputation, however, often specify the type of flounder served on the menu since the taste, texture, and flavor vary.

The Title 50 Code of Federal Regulations lists the following species for the United States Standards for grades of frozen flounder: blackback, yellowtail, dab or plaice, starry flounder, and fluke.

In general, the fluke is considered one of the finest table fishes. The winter flounder or blackback is also an excellently flavored fish, with thick fillets. The yellowtail, slimmer than the winter flounder, is marketed in large quantities and has a good flavor. The fillets are quite thin and the meat is flaky. The dab, once considered unpopular and undesirable, has a sweet flesh with a distinctive flavor and texture. It has thick layers of flesh on both upper and lower sides.

Blackback

Other name. Winter flounder.
Appearance. This species, best known to anglers, is a righteye fish. It has a small mouth like the yellowtail flounder, but differs in its straight lateral line with no arch over the pectoral fin, its thicker body, and widely spaced eyes (see Fig. 4-10).
Source. Blackback occur from Labrador to Georgia, commonly from the Gulf of St. Lawrence to Chesapeake Bay. The centers of abundance include the coastal waters of Massachusetts, Rhode Island, Connecticut, New York, and New Jersey.

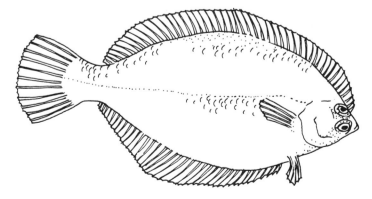

Figure 4-10. Blackback.

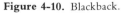

Availability fresh. During the fall and winter months.
Average weight. Usually 1 to 2 pounds (450 to 900 g), sometimes reaching 5 pounds (2.270 kg).
Trade size. (round)

Small—under ¾ pounds (under 340 g)
Medium—¾ to 1½ pounds (340 to 680 g)
Large—1½ pounds (680 g) and up

Quality. Winter flounder is an excellent table fish. It has white, firm, delicately flavored meat.

Fluke

Other name. Summer flounder.
Appearance. The fluke is considered one of the finest table fish. It is easily recognized by its large mouth and sharp teeth, and the eyes on the colored left side. The fluke usually has ocellated spots on its body (see Fig. 4-11).
Source. Ranges from Main to South Carolina, but mainly off New England.
Availability fresh. Throughout the year. In some states, the angler's catch surpasses the commercial catch.
Average weight. Usually 2 to 4 pounds (900 g to 1.8 kg).
Trade size. (round)

Medium—1½ to 2 pounds (680 to 900 g)
Large—2 to 4 pounds (900 g to 1.8 kg)
Jumbo—4 pounds (1.8 kg) and up

Quality. One of the finest table fish, with lean white meat. Although the summer flounder is a fast grower (11 inches, 27.5 cm, when a year old), the commercial harvest has declined markedly. Fishermen have noticed a decrease in the size of the flounder and in their catches, a sign of a high fishing rate.

Yellowtail Flounder

Other name. Rusty dab.
Appearance. This righteyed species is characterized by its small mouth, pointed snout, and thin body, which has a definite arch in the lateral line over the pectoral fin. The body shape is nearly oval. Its color varies from grayish olive

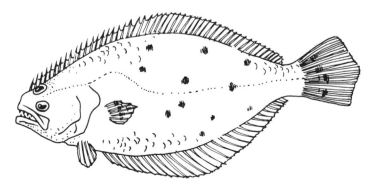

Figure 4-11. Fluke.

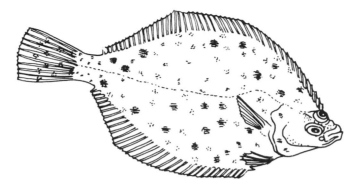

Figure 4-12. Yellowtail Flounder.

green to reddish brown, with large irregular rusty spots. The tail fin is yellow, hence its name (see Fig. 4-12).

Source. The species is found from Labrador to Virginia.

Availability fresh. Abundant from June to December.

Average weight. Usually 1 pound, (450 g); seldom exceeds 2 pounds (900 g).

Trade size. (round)

Small—under 1 pound (450 g)
Large—1 pound (450 g) and over

Quality. This is an excellent very lean food fish.

American Plaice

Other names. Dab, sanddab.

Appearance. This species is distinct from the European plaice. The American plaice is plain reddish to gray brown in color, lacking the red spotting of the common European plaice (see Fig. 4-13).

Source. The species is abundant on both sides of the Atlantic, occurring from Cape Cod to the Grand Banks.

Average weight. Ranges from 2 to 3 pounds (907 g to 1.350 kg).

Trade size. (round)

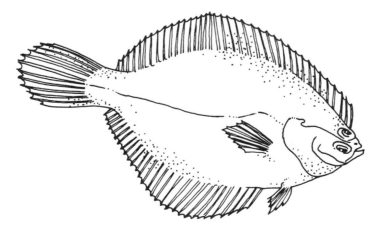

Figure 4-13. American Plaice.

Small—under 2 pounds (900 g)
Large—2 pounds (907 g) and up

Quality. This species, once neglected, is an excellent pan fish. It has a thick layer of flesh, free from bones, on both the upper and lower sides. The meat is sweet and lean with a distinctive flavor and texture.

Starry Flounder

Appearance. This species is easily recognized by the alternating pattern of orange white and dark bars on the fins. The fish has a small mouth and a nearly straight lateral line. Although a lefteyed form, it may have the eyes on the right side. The body is rough, covered with spinous plates on the eyed side. It is dark brown to black with mottlings on the eyed side (see Fig. 4-14).

Source. Central California to Alaska.

Average weight. Usually 5 to 10 pounds (2.270 to 5.4 kg), reaching a weight of 20 pounds (10.8 kg).

Quality. Excellent food fish.

Disposition. Fresh and frozen

Fillets—raw or breaded (raw and cooked)
Steaks, breaded raw
Specialties—breaded (raw and cooked), stuffed, cooked
Salted
Other—au gratin, in sauces

Other Flatfish of Commercial Importance

On the Pacific coast, the California halibut and the arrowtooth halibut are both available commercially. The California halibut weighs an average of 4 to 10 pounds (1.8 to 4.5 kg) and is sold mostly in fresh boneless fillets.

The arrowtooth halibut occurs in California and Alaska. It is sometimes marketed as turbot or French sole, and is sold mostly whole, frozen and gutted.

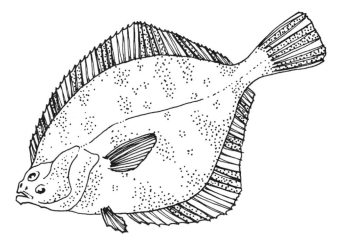

Figure 4-14. Starry Flounder.

The imported turbot, closely related to the brill (known in French as *barbue*), is a flatfish at least as superior as the English Dover sole. These two fish are not related to the Pacific "turbots" that are inferior in quality. On the United States market, turbot is available frozen whole in quartered fillets and steaks.

Grouper

Other name. Red grouper.
Other varieties.

Black grouper
Yellow fin grouper
Nassau grouper
Gag

All are marketed without distinction as to species.
Appearance. The red grouper is one of the most common species in southern Florida and the tropical American Atlantic. It has dark bars on its head and body, and sometimes scattered spots. The grouper is a member of the sea bass family (see Fig. 4-15).
Source. Abundant in Florida and the Gulf states.
Availability fresh. April to December.
Average weight. Ranges from 4 to 6 pounds (1.8 to 2.7 kg). In the Gulf states markets, 5 to 15 pounds (2.270 to 6.8 kg).
Quality. Excellent lean fish. Red grouper is one of the most important commercial groupers in the United States.
Disposition. Fresh and frozen

Fillets—raw and breaded raw
Steaks—raw
Specialties—fingers, breaded raw

Haddock

Haddock, which was once considered junk fish when other species of fish were abundant, increased in popularity between 1925 and 1930, when an estimated 1 billion pounds were harvested in the United States. The smallest catch

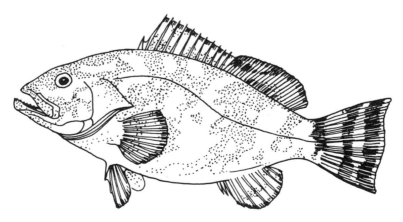

Figure 4-15. Red Grouper.

A Comprehensive Survey of American Fish and Shellfish   **39**

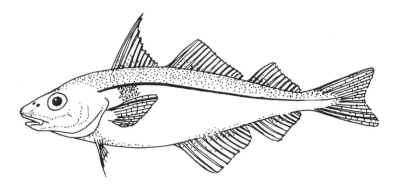

Figure 4-16. Haddock.

occurred in 1972 (11.8 million pounds). Due to overfishing, haddock landings are near historic lows, declining in 1986 to 11.0 million pounds.

Appearance. The haddock is closely related to the cod, and belongs to the same family of fish as the pollock and hake. The haddock is usually smaller than the cod, with a dark lateral line and a black patch on the shoulder known as the "Devil's thumb print" or "St. Peter's mark" (See Fig. 4-16).

Source. Haddock are found only in the North Atlantic. They range principally from Cape Cod to Georges Bank and the Great Banks off Newfoundland.

Availability fresh. All year, but abundant during the months of March and April with supply falling off in November. The smaller supplies during the winter months usually cause a rise in price.

Average weight. Ranges from 3 to 4 pounds (1.360 to 1.8 kg).

Trade size.

    Scrod—1½ to 2½ pounds (680 g to 1.140 kg)
    Large—2½ pounds (1.140 kg) and up

Trawl nets with a mesh size smaller than 4½ inches (10.25 cm) have been banned in a conservation measure designed to protect young fish not yet of marketable size. As a result, snapper haddock and small scrod are not available.

Quality. Very lean white meat of excellent quality.

Disposition. Fresh and frozen

    Fillets—raw or breaded (raw and cooked)
    Specialities—au gratin, dinners, patties, et cetera
    Smoked
    Canned (finnan haddies)

Finnan Haddie

The smoked haddock, known as finnan haddie, became a popular item accidentally when a fire in a fish market in Findon, Scotland, smoked some fillets of haddock—hence the name finnan haddie. Today, one must be cautious when buying smoked haddock as the substitution of other fish and the addition of coloring and unnecessary preservatives result in poor quality smoked fish.

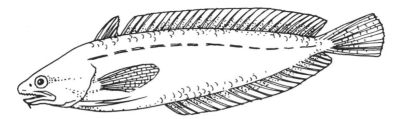

Figure 4-17. King Hake.

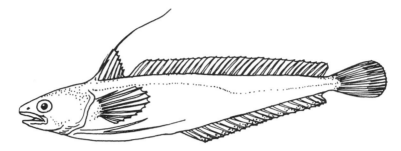

Figure 4-18. Squirrel Hake.

Hake

Other names. Ling, Boston hake, white hake, black hake, mud hake, king hake. Commercially, four species are recognized (but not separated) on the market: squirrel, white, long finned, and spotted. Squirrel hake and white hake make up most of the catch.

Like many ground fish, hake is sometimes substituted for haddock or even cod, especially when salted.

Appearance. The hake is a member of a large family of marine ground fish. It has two dorsal fins and one long anal fin. Most species have one elongated, filamentlike ray on the first dorsal fin, except for the king hake (also known as spotted hake). Like the Atlantic cod, the hake has a barbel on the lower jaw; the upper jaw projects beyond the lower (see Figs. 4-17 and 4-18).

Source. From the Gulf of St. Lawrence to North Carolina. Also abundant on the Pacific coast, but not used much as food fish.

Availability fresh. June, with peak harvest in August and September.

Average weight. Ranges from 1 to 8 pounds (450 g to 3.6 kg).

Trade size. Scrod or red hake—½ to 2 pounds (225 to 907 g) White hake (small—2 to 6 pounds (907 g to 2.7 kg); (large—6 pounds (2.7 kg) and over).

Quality. A white meat of good quality. The flesh is lean and softens quickly if not strictly fresh.

Disposition.

Fresh and frozen fillets and steaks
Salted
Smoked

Halibut

Other names. Atlantic or eastern halibut, North Pacific halibut.

Appearance. The halibut, the largest member of the flatfish family, has a large

A Comprehensive Survey of American Fish and Shellfish **41**

mouth and sharp curved teeth. The eyes are on the right side of the head. The tail is concave; the anal fin is shorter than the dorsal and starts at the pectoral fin. The English thought highly of halibut and served it on holy days, calling it "holy-day-butte" (*butte* was the Middle English word for flatfish or flounder) (see Fig. 4-19). Over the years, holy-butte evolved into halibut.

Source. East and west coasts of the United States. Atlantic or eastern halibut are caught off the coast of New England. North Pacific halibut are taken off Alaska and the shores of Washington.

Availability fresh. All year, but most abundant from March to August.

Average weight. Ranges from 10 to 60 pounds (4.5 to 27.2 kg). Some specimens weigh from 150 to 200 pounds (68 to 90 kg) or more.

Trade size. (eastern, drawn)

> Snapper—under 7 pounds (3 kg)
> Chicken—7 to 12 pounds (3 to 5.4 kg)
>   Medium—12 to 60 pounds (5.4 to 27.2 kg)
>   Large—60 to 125 pounds (27.2 to 56.6 kg)
> Whale—125 pounds (56.6 kg) and over
> (western, drawn)
> Chicken—5 to 10 pounds (2.27 to 4.5 kg)
>   Medium—10 to 60 pounds (4.5 to 27.2 kg)
>   Large—60 to 80 pounds (27.2 to 36.2 kg)
> Whale—80 pounds (36.2 kg) and over

Quality. Halibut is an excellent source of high-quality protein and minerals, but low in sodium, fat, and calories. The true halibut, which has a white, tender flesh with a mild flavor, should not be confused with other species of flatfish that are sometimes sold as halibut.

Disposition. Fresh and frozen

> Fillets—raw and breaded (raw and cooked)
> Steaks, raw
> Cheeks
> Specialties—au gratin, patties, and in sauce

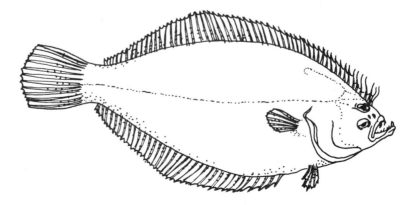

Figure 4-19. Halibut.

Preparation. Halibut can be cooked in a variety of recipes (see Sole). Halibut steaks are broiled, poached, or grilled, and served with a hot sauce.

Herring

Herring, other than those canned for sardines, have never been consumed to any extent in the United States. The New England Fisheries Development Program, prepared by the New England Fisheries Steering Committee, states that a major problem faced by the industry has been the holding quality of the fish, which has made it impossible for our fleets to fish more than 4 to 5 hours from port. The New England Program addressed this problem by developing, testing, and demonstrating the technology needed to assure quality fish when landed. As a result of these program efforts, herring has gained in popularity in the United States.

A Sex Sorter!

Herring roe is highly marketable. During the roe-bearing season, a large amount of herring are "firmed" in brine (the roe must be firmed before removal from the female). Since the firming process renders the flesh inedible, males were wasted. Now a sex sorter has come to the rescue of the fishing industry. This unique machine separates roe-bearing females from males; as a result, 50 percent more fish are being used as fresh fillets for the market instead of waste or fertilizer.

The machine, designed by Canadian engineers, has a separation efficiency of 95 percent and a production rate of 2 tons (1.8 metric tons) per hour. An added advantage is that when the roe-bearing season is over, the sex sorter can be used as an automatic feeder for filleting, or for scaling such small fish as smelt, anchovy, and perch. It is estimated that a $20 million industry would exist for herring if they were all processed for human consumption.

Herring are processed in many forms. Several European countries export various types of preserved, pickled, smoked, or cured herring that are available at consumer levels.

Bismarck herring. Herring fillets cured in vinegar, salt, onions, and sugar.
Rollmops. Fillets of Bismarck herring wrapped around pickle slices and secured with wooden picks. They are usually preserved in vinegar and spices.
Schmaltz herring. A fat herring that is skinned, cut into sections, pickled, and preserved in a brine.
Soused herring. A British term to describe herring pickled in vinegar, white wine, and spices.
Matjes herring. A juvenile herring, bigger than the sardine, that is skinned, filleted, and cured in sugar, salt, vinegar, and spices. This is a European specialty, mainly Dutch.
Kipper. A butterflied herring, brined and cold smoked. Marketed fresh, frozen, or canned. The fish, gold in color, is usually artificially colored.

Other forms of herring are available commercially, such as herring in sour cream, hard salt herring, marinated herring roe, and pickled herring.

Lingcod

Other names. Blue cod, buffalo cod, cultus cod.

Appearance. As the Indian name *cultus* (meaning "false") indicates, lingcod is not a true cod but one of a number of species commonly called greenlings. For such a highly prized fish, its appearance is both deceiving and detracting. Its highly variable coloration is closely associated with its habitat. Basically, lingcod has subdued coloration ranging from a mottled brown to bluish green with cream colored undersides. The spots or blotches are brown, green, or tan, outlined in orange or light blue. The lingcod has a large protruding mouth armed with large caninelike teeth.

Source. Lingcod range from Baja California, to northwest Alaska, but are most abundant in the cold waters of the north.

Availability fresh. All year. In California, best from April to October; farther north, the fishing is best from October to May.

Average weight. Ranges from 5 to 20 pounds (2.270 to 9.10 kg). Some fish can weigh up to 40 pounds (18 kg).

Quality. Fresh lingcod is available along the Pacific coast, but sold frozen in other areas of the country. It is a fine eating fresh fish and is marketed dressed, in fillets, and in steaks. Smoked lingcod is another delicacy found in the markets.

The uninitiated sometimes avoid lingcod due to the unusual green or bluish green color of the flesh. The color is not harmful and disappears when cooked, producing a delicate, white, tender flesh very low in fat. Some of the preferred methods of preparation for lincod fillets and steaks are broiling, butter sauteing, and poaching. Whole fish can be baked or poached. For broiling, small fish can be split down the middle and the backbone removed. An increasingly popular method of preparing lingcod is to pan- or deep-fat-fry for "fish and chips." Most of the lingcod produced now goes into the rapidly expanding commercial fish and chips market.

Mackerel

Mackerel are commercially important in the United States (landings totaled 94.8 million pounds in 1986). The Atlantic mackerel is superior in quality, followed in order by the Spanish, king, Pacific, and Pacific Jack mackerel, which is lowest in quality and sells rather cheaply in cans.

Spanish Mackerel

Appearance. Spanish mackerel is a member of a large family including tuna and other mackerel. They are beautifully colored fish. Their slender graceful bodies are dark blue on the upper part, paling to almost silver on the belly. Many small yellowish or olive oval spots occur above and below the wavy lateral line (see Fig. 4-20).

Source. Spanish mackerel are found from Massachusetts to the Gulf coast, and as far as Brazil. They are abundant from Florida to Chesapeake Bay. On the Pacific coast, they range from San Diego, California, to the Galapagos Islands.

Availability fresh. In New York, from November to May; in southern Atlantic states, from June to September; and in the Gulf states, during the winter months.

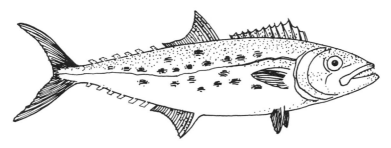

Figure 4-20. Spanish Mackerel.

Average weight. From 1½ to 4 pounds (680 g to 1.8 kg). The best size is 1½ to 2 pounds (680 to 900 g).
Trade size.

Small—½ to 1 pound (225 to 450 g)
Large—1½ to 3 pounds (675 to 1.360 g)

Quality. A fatty fish with excellent flavor. The flesh is firm and much lighter than the dark meat of the Boston mackerel.

Atlantic Mackerel.

Other names. Boston mackerel.
Appearance. The Atlantic mackerel has a smooth, tapering head, streamlined body, and brilliant coloration. A distinguishing characteristic is the series of 23 to 33 wavy dark bands above the lateral line. There are also 4 to 6 finlets behind the dorsal and anal fins (see Fig. 4-21).
Source. The Atlantic mackerel is an important commercial fish on the Atlantic coast. Most mackerel fishing is done off New England but some occurs in the Middle Atlantic region. Massachusetts ports receive most of the commercial catch.
Availability fresh. The run is from April to early December, with heaviest landings in midsummer. Spawning season occurs during May and June, at which time the flesh may not be as good. Mackerel caught in gill nets are "drowned"—they have a mark around the neck, are considered inferior, and sell for less.
Average weight. From ½ to 2½ pounds (225 g to 1.140 kg).
Trade size.

Small or spike—under ½ pound (225 g) round
Tinker—½ to 1 pound (225 to 450 g)

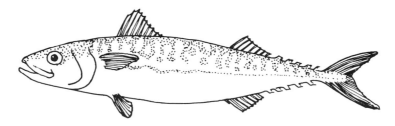

Figure 4-21. Atlantic Mackerel.

Medium—1 to 2½ pounds (450 g to 1.140 kg)
Large—2½ pounds (1.140 kg) and over

Quality. A fatty fish (7 percent polyunsaturated fat) with dark meat high in protein, vitamins, and minerals. Best when consumed fresh.

King Mackerel

Other name. Kingfish.

Appearance. The king mackerel lacks the yellow spotting of the Spanish mackerel, but has a similar shape with fewer spines on the first dorsal fin. Kingfish range from 5 to 25 pounds (2.270 to 11.30 kg) and over.

Source. Florida to Massachusetts. The largest catch occurs in Florida and the other Gulf states.

Availability fresh. November to March.

Trade size.

Small—under 5 pounds (2.270 kg)
Medium—5 to 8 pounds (2.270 to 3.6 kg)
Large—8 to 12 pounds (3.6 to 5.4 kg)
Jumbo—12 pounds (5.4 kg) and up

Quality. A fatty fish with fine flesh. It has an excellent flavor like the smaller Spanish mackerel.

Disposition.

Fillets and steaks, frozen
Canned, paste and spreads
Smoked

Monkfish

Other names. Anglerfish, goosefish, baudroie.

Appearance. The anglerfish is all mouth, with a large number of teeth. The body is flat with a thin slippery skin. Its most unusual feature is the first dorsal spine, which is terminated by a small flap of skin. The anglerfish moves this spine back and forth to attract small fish on which it feeds insatiably. The flipperlike pectoral fins are another characteristic. The fish occurs mainly off New England and is caught principally by cod hunters (see Fig. 4-22).

Marketing. Anglerfish is marketed headless and skinned. The flesh is white and very firm. On the market it is known as "bellyfish." Anglerfish can be baked, broiled, or deep fried in fingers.

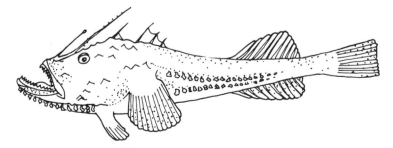

Figure 4-22. Monkfish.

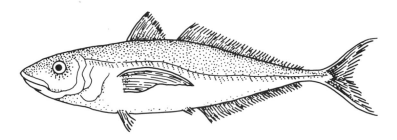

Figure 4-23. Pacific Jack Mackerel.

Pacific Jack Mackerel

Other name. California horse mackerel.
Appearance. The Pacific Jack mackerel should not be confused with the Pacific mackerel. It has no detached finlets behind the dorsal and anal fins. The Pacific mackerel resembles species of mackerel found in American Atlantic waters. The curved and the straight laterals of the Pacific Jack mackerel have enlarged scutes (see Fig. 4-23).
Source. From Baja California to southern Alaska. It is commercially important with landings of 23.7 million pounds in 1986.
Availability fresh. This species of fish is mostly canned. Only a small percentage is sold fresh.
Average size. From 1 to 2½ pounds (450 g to 1.140 kg).
Quality. The Pacific Jack mackerel lacks the quality of other members of the mackerel family. Most of the harvest is canned or smoked.

Mullet

Other names. Striped mullet, Florida mullet, black mullet.
Appearance. These versatile fish, sometimes called jumping mullet, are moderately sized. The bodies are elongated and rather stout. They have a dark bluish color on the top and silvery sides. The head and mouth are small. Mullet have large scales with dark centers that give an appearance of dark horizontal stripes (see Fig. 4-24).
Source. Mullet are the most important food fish in the South Atlantic and Gulf states, with an annual harvest of 30.5 million pounds. Florida produces about 75 percent of the mullet caught in the United States. They also occur in southern California.

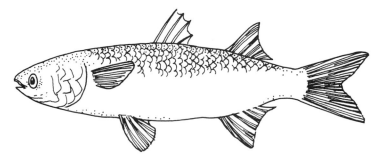

Figure 4-24. Mullet.

Availability fresh. In the Gulf states, all year; abundant from April to November, with the heaviest run usually in September.

Average weight. From 2 to 3 pounds (900 g to 1.360 kg), occasionally up to 6 pounds (2.7 kg).

Trade size.

Small—1 to 2 pounds (450 to 900 g)
Medium—2 to 3 pounds (900 g to 1.360 kg)
Large—3 pounds (1.360 kg) and over

Quality. This is the favorite fish of commercial fishermen. The tender, firm-textured flesh has a mild nutlike flavor. The iodine content of mullet is hundreds of times higher than that of the best grade beef. It is also rich in minerals. Fatter mullet are smoked; lean mullet are marketed fresh, whole or in fillets.

Disposition. Fresh and frozen

Roe
Fillets
Split for curing
Smoked

Ocean Perch

Other names. Atlantic coast: redfish, rosefish, deep sea perch, red perch. Pacific coast: longjaw rockfish.

Appearance. Ocean perch range in color from orange to flame red, occasionally grayish or brownish red, with a lighter red on the belly. The eyes are large and black, contrasting with the brightly colored body. The ocean perch has spiny projections on the sides of the large head as well as on the back fin. The Pacific coast rockfish numbers about 50 varieties, very similar in appearance to their relatives in the Atlantic but with numerous color variations (see Fig. 4-25).

Source. Ocean perch are found in the deep offshore waters of the Atlantic from southern Labrador to the Gulf of Maine. In the Pacific, they range from the Bering Sea to southern California.

Availability fresh. Almost the entire catch is filleted and frozen. Ocean perch is sometimes available fresh during the peak season of May, June, and July.

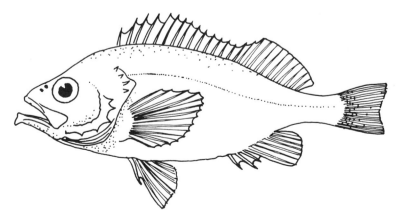

Figure 4-25. Ocean Perch.

Average weight. From ½ to 2 pounds (225 to 900 g). Specimens over 5 pounds (2.270 kg) have a coarse texture and are unpalatable.

Trade size. Mixed, round—½ to 3 pounds (225 g to 1.360 kg).

Quality. Excellent food fish, with firm, lean, white flaky flesh.

Orange Roughy

Orange roughy is a relatively new fish to gain popularity in the United States, and has been available only since 1982. It is native to New Zealand waters and is air freighted to New York, Boston, and other major United States cities.

This large-headed fish averages 3½ pounds and, as its name implies, is orange colored. It is exported to the United States as frozen, skinless fillets, and is sold mainly to restaurants. Its meat is white, firm, and mild flavored (see Fig. 4-26).

Pollock

Other names. American pollock, Boston bluefish.

Appearance. Pollock are ground fish related to the cod and the haddock. The white lean flesh of pollock is in class with the hake and the cusk. Pollock is used as a substitute for cod and haddock in salting.

The head of the pollock is more pointed than the haddock's, the lower jaw projects, and the white lateral line is never black. Pollock usually have a deep olive or brownish green color above, paling to yellowish or smoky gray on the sides, and to silvery gray on the belly (see Fig. 4-27).

Source. American pollock range in cold Atlantic waters from Nova Scotia to Virginia.

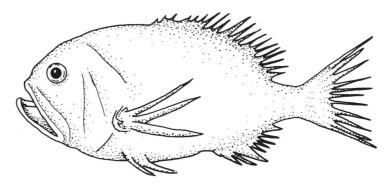

Figure 4-26. Orange Roughy.

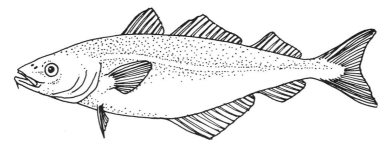

Figure 4-27. Pollock.

A Comprehensive Survey of American Fish and Shellfish   **49**

Availability fresh. About 80 percent of the annual pollock landing occurs during October, November, and December.

Average weight. From 4 to 12 pounds (1.8 to 5.4 kg).

Trade size. Scrod—1½ to 4 pounds (680 g to 1.8 kg).

Quality. A lean fish with a good texture when fresh. However, the flesh softens quickly and becomes fibrous. The fish rates high nutritionally with easily assimilated protein, vitamins, and minerals. Pollock fillets hold up well under freezing.

Alaskan Pollock

Other names. Pacific pollock, Snow cod, Walleye pollock.

Appearance. Alaskan pollock is similar to the American pollock. The meat of Alaskan pollock is mostly processed into imitation shellfish products (see Fig. 4-28).

Source. Alaskan pollock supports the world largest single species food fishery. It is very abundant off the Alaskan coast where it is fished by several nations.

Availability fresh. The predominant product form is skinless, boneless, frozen fillets.

Average weight. 2 pounds (900 g) or under.

Quality. The meat is lightly colored, flavored, and flaky. The major part is currently being used to produce imitation shellfish products, processed into blocks of surimi, a jelly-like fish paste. Surimi is later processed into imitation shellfish products, fish sausages, and other products (see section on Surimi).

Pompano

Other names. Cobblerfish, butterfish, palmenta.

Appearance. The Florida pompano is the only commercially important species. It is a thin, deep-bodied fish with a deeply forked caudal tail and dorsal fins. It has a silvery body, shading to metallic blue above and to golden yellow ventrally. Some experts contend that the Florida pompano is a member of the butterfish family rather than the Pacific or the California pompano family (see Fig. 4-29).

Source. Commercial landings of Florida pompano occur from Virginia to Texas, but most of the United States catch is from Florida waters.

Availability fresh. Pompano are caught all year round but major fishing occurs in March, April, and May.

Average weight. Ranges from 1½ to 4 pounds (680 g to 1.8 kg).

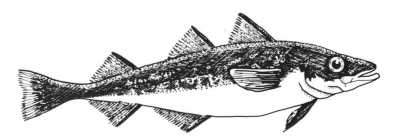

Figure 4-28. Alaska Pollock.

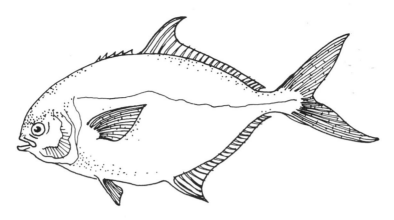

Figure 4-29. Pompano.

Trade size.

> Gulf states market (round): ½ to 4 pounds (225 g to 1.8 kg).
> New York market (round):
>> Small—under ¾ pound (under 340 g)
>> Medium—¾ to 1¼ pounds (340 to 565 g)
>> Large—1½ to 3 pounds (680 g to 1.360 kg)

Quality. Florida pompano is incomparable in taste to any other salt-water or fresh-water fish. Pompano has a firm white flesh and is moderately fat. It is easy to fillet, to handle, and to cook, and it freezes well. It is distributed frozen in fillets.

Porgy

Other name. Scup.

Appearance. Porgies or scup are members of the vast perch family. The porgy has a body about half as deep as it is long. The color is dull silver and iridescent, darker above than below, and white on the belly. The head is silvery with dusky blotches, and the eyes are rather small. The front dorsal fin points forward. The scales are rather large, thick, and firmly attached, and the tail is crescent shaped.

Source. Porgies or scup range in Atlantic coastal waters between Cape Cod, Massachusetts, and Cape Hatteras, North Carolina.

Availability fresh. The major scup population moves northward in the spring and south in the fall. They are abundant from April to June in New England; as they migrate south in the fall they are caught in the Middle Atlantic states.

Average weight. The average size is 1 to 2 pounds (450 to 900 g).

Trade size. (whole dressed)

> Small—under ½ pound (225 g)
> Medium—½ to 1 pound (225 to 450 g)
> Large—1 to 2 pounds (450 to 900 g)

Quality. Porgies or scup are known as the saltwater pan fish and are tender and fine eating.

Disposition. Usually whole dressed; seldom filleted.

Preparation. Porgies are best sautéed meunière and pan fried. See cooking techniques, Chapter 6.

Redfish

Other names. Channel bass, red drum, red bass.

Appearance. The upper half of the body is reddish bronze and the large scales are silvery around the edges and coppery in the center. One or more black dots appear at the upper base of the tail.

Source. Abundant in the South Atlantic and the Gulf states where annual landings average 3 million pounds.★

Availability fresh. All year, but abundant from November through February.

Average weight. From 2 to 8 pounds (900 g to 3.6 kg). Above 10 pounds (4.5 kg), the fish loses in quality.

Trade size. (Gulf states market round or drawn)

> Rats—1½ to 3 pounds (680 g to 1.3 kg)
> Medium—3 to 8 pounds (1.3 to 3.6 kg)
> Bulls—8 pounds (3.6 kg) and up

Quality. Excellent eating fish with a light firm meat.

Disposition. Fillets, frozen.

Red Snapper

Other name. Mexican snapper.

Appearance. Bright and gaudy best describes the red snapper's coloration. There is a rosy red hue on the upper part of the body, fading to a pink, then a white stomach. A very distinguishing feature are the eyes, which are always red (see Fig. 4-30).

Source. Red snapper range along the Atlantic and Gulf coasts; they are abundant in the Gulf of Mexico.

Availability fresh. All year, but abundant during the summer months.

Average weight. From 2 to 8 pounds (900 g to 3.6 kg). Some species, weighing over 15 to 20 pounds (6.7 to 9 kg), are available and make incomparable buffet displays served cold.

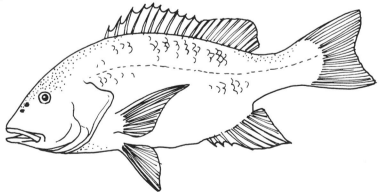

Figure 4-30. Red Snapper.

★As a result of the craze for Blackened redfish, a cajun recipe popularized in New Orleans, Louisiana, landings of redfish have reached an all-time low.

Trade size. (drawn)

Small—under 2 pounds (900 g)
Medium—2 to 5 pounds (900 g to 2.270 kg)
Large—5 pounds (2.270 kg) and over

Quality. Delicate, lean white meat with excellent taste. The red snapper is the most important commercial snapper in the United States. Do not discard the head of the snapper as it makes an unexcelled base or stock for fish fumet, chowder, bouillabaisse, etc. The throat flesh is the most delicate and the richest tasting part of the entire fish; it is taken from the ventral side of the head, reaching down to the border of the gill flaps.

At least three distinct families of fish, including the mangrove or gray snapper that takes on a reddish color when dead, have been sold as red snapper. They include the "hambone" or blackfin snapper, silk snapper, red grouper, yellowfin grouper, and black hind.

Surimi*

Surimi, pronounced sir-ree-mee, is a Japanese term applied to a new form of seafood made from mild white fish, such as Alaska Pollock, that is shaped and flavored to resemble shellfish. Surimi seafood, whether shaped like crab legs, crab meat or shrimp tails, appeals to today's seafood consumer.

Surimi is prepared under strict controls at sea or on shore. The fillet portion of fresh caught fish, mostly Alaska Pollock, is minced, washed, and strained to yield a concentrated fish paste. Small quantities of salt, sugar and/or sorbitol are added to stabilize the protein. The paste is frozen for transportation to further processing plants where it becomes raw material for unique food products.

Mild white fish such as the abundant Alaska Pollock is the foundation fish for most surimi presently used in the United States, because of its favorable gelling qualities, light color, mild flavor, and good texture.

How is Surimi Processed?
Surimi is blended with binders such as starch or egg white. Real shellfish, a shellfish extract or artificial shellfish flavoring is added to make it taste like shellfish. Then it is fabricated into the shape, texture, and color of shellfish.

What Are the Most Common Surimi Seafood Products?
The first Surimi seafood product available in the United States was the imitation crab leg. It was soon followed by crab flavored chunk and flake Surimi seafood. These two were later combined in the popular "salad style," a blend of flaked and chunk forms that closely resembles picked crab meat. Shrimp, scallop and lobster-flavored and shaped Surimi seafood are also available. Breaded Surimi seafood includes scallop and shrimp look-alikes.

What Are the Nutritional Attributes of Surimi Seafood?
Surimi seafood is nutritionally similar to ocean white fish which it is usually made from. Surimi is low in fat and cholesterol; it is a good source of high quality protein. Salt and sugar levels vary according to brand.

---

*This information was provided by Surimi Seafood Education Center, Washington DC.

Figure 4-31. Surimi. (Courtesy Surimi Seafood Education Center, National Fisheries Institute, 2000 M St., N.W., Ste. 580, Washington, D.C. 20036)

How Is Surimi Seafood Best Stored?

Frozen Surimi seafood will keep in the freezer for several months. Follow the directions on the package. Store the unfrozen product in the coldest part of the refrigerator and use in a day or two, just as you would any other perishable product.

How Can Surimi Seafood Be Used?

Surimi seafood is precooked, so once it is thawed it is ready to eat. Serve it chilled in salads or with your favorite dip. Serve Surimi seafoods with cocktail sauce or tartar sauce for quick appetizer ideas.

In hot dishes, add Surimi seafood during the last minutes of cooking time, just long enough to heat through. Overheating will toughen Surimi seafood just as it does other types of shellfish. Surimi seafood heats well in the microwave; it takes only seconds to become hot enough to serve. Heat breaded Surimi seafood products according to package directions or deep fry at 350°F (180°C) until golden. Drain and serve hot with lemon wedges or a sauce.

It is expected that new surimi seafood products will be available in the future as pasta fillers, sausages, and snacks.

Rockfish

More than fifty varieties of rockfish live along the coasts of Washington, Oregon, and California. Many of them are excellent for eating.

Appearance. The rockfish family, as a group, is distinguished by stout, heavily constructed bodies. The heads are large and broad and usually have prominent ridges and spines. The fins are heavily spined; the scales are large and ridged. Rockfish vary greatly in coloration, ranging from black or drab green to bright orange or crimson. Some varieties have large stripes and others are spotted (see Fig. 4-32).

The following rockfish are among the best for eating and the most commercially important.

1. The orange rockfish is a light olive gray color with prominent orange red coloration. This fish is distinguished by three yellow orange stripes radiating from the eyes across the head, and reddish orange streaks along the upper part of the body. It ranges from California to southwestern Alaska and is caught in deep waters. It reaches 30 inches (75 cm) in length.

2. The yellowtail rockfish is not as colorful as some others but is excellent for eating. It is usually grayish brown, mottled and streaked with dark brown, washed with dusky green, and showing yellow on the fins. It ranges from southern California to Vancouver Island, lives moderately deep, and reaches about 26 inches (65 cm) in length.

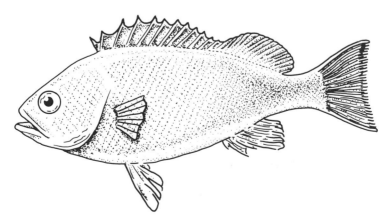

Figure 4-32. Pacific Rockfish.

3. The bocaccio is important commercially in California. It is light green to dark brown in color, flushed with clear pale red, and often has intense black spots on the body. Bocaccio means large mouth and that aptly describes this fish. Its large mouth shows red on the protruding lower jaw with black on the tip. The bocaccio ranges from southern California to Queen Charlotte Sound. It reaches a length of about 34 inches (85 cm). The bocaccio freezes well.
4. The red rockfish is also known as red snapper, red rock, cod, or rasphead rockfish. It is deep red in color, paling to lighter red, and has whitish streaks along the lateral line of the body. In large specimens coming from deep water, the body and head are often blotched and dotted with black spots. It ranges from southern California to the Gulf of Alaska and reaches a length of 3 feet (90 cm). This very popular, good eating fish is often sold as red snapper although it is not related to the true Atlantic red snapper.

Quality and uses of rockfish. Rockfish have firm, white, fine textured flesh and a mild flavor. Most of the commercial catch is filleted and sold fresh. However, some are sold whole dressed, and some are filleted and frozen for shipment to other areas of the United States. Rockfish fillets can be used in the same way as other fish fillets, adapting readily to pan frying, deep-fat frying, broiling, and baking; it can also be used in chowders.

Sablefish

Other name. Black cod.
Appearance. The sablefish is not a true cod but a member of the skilfish family. This family is noted for a lack of ridges or spines on the head. Sablefish are streamlined fish, having rather compressed bodies with wide separation of the dorsal fins, some spines on the fins, and slender tail sections. They have a slatey black to greenish color on the top surface, shading to lighter gray on the belly.
Source. Sablefish range from the Bering Sea to California. Alaskan and Washington waters account for about two thirds of the annual catch of approximately 7 million pounds.
Availability fresh. Almost the entire catch is frozen.
Average weight. Range up to 40 pounds (18 kg) in weight, but the average size is about 8 pounds (3.6 kg).
Quality. Most of the harvest is dressed, frozen, and taken to fish-curing plants for preparation into smoked products. Smoked sablefish have long been considered a delicacy and there is an increasing demand for them. These fish are particularly suited to smoking because of their moderately high fat content and mild, delicate flavor. The smoked product is usually sold in chunks and is

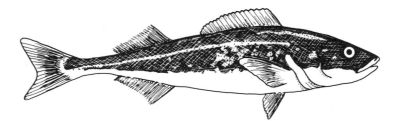

Figure 4–33. Sablefish.

available at seafood markets, supermarkets or delicatessens. The fish can be steamed or used in casseroles or salads (see finnan haddie, page 40).

Salmon

Man can learn more from salmon than from any other species of fish. The cultural, ecological, and economic importance of this magnificent fish has been demonstrated by several governments, associations, and foundations. The programmed death mechanism of the Pacific Northwest salmon may one day help researchers to understand the aging of man. Several species of Pacific salmon go from a youthful vigor to a quick death after reaching their spawning grounds and depositing their eggs. It is known that a flood of adrenocorticotropic hormone kills the fish. Recent studies on coronary disease in Atlantic salmon have been most rewarding, giving relevant clues to human heart disease.

Many questions remain unanswered about the migration of salmon. The young parrs leave their native rivers, following a migratory route several thousand miles away from home, only to come back two or three years later to their river of birth. For many years, man has polluted and barred the rivers to salmon. Unlike other species of fish, salmon cannot tolerate pollution and seek clean, unpolluted water. The return of Atlantic salmon to several American rivers is a strong indication of environmental improvement. The day may come when the Hudson River will see the return of salmon. Several reports show that sturgeon, bass, shad, and many other fish have returned to the New York river as pollution has been controlled in some areas. As long as demand exceeds the supply, salmon will remain the most prized species of fish on the United States market.

Varieties of Salmon in the United States

The United States is the only country in the world with six different species of salmon available commercially (five of which are found in the Pacific). The Atlantic salmon is the only species caught in the Atlantic. The Northwest Pacific species occur mainly in Alaska, Washington, Oregon, and California. Some species are also available commercially in British Columbia, Canada.

The common names of salmon are:

1. King salmon in Alaska, chinook in British Columbia
2. Silver salmon or coho
3. Red salmon in Alaska, sockeye in British Columbia
4. Pink salmon or humpback
5. Chum salmon or keta

The six species of salmon are anadromous: the alevins remain in fresh water an average three to six months, leave for the ocean's fertile feeding grounds, and come back at maturity (after two to seven years depending on the species). Three species are important sport fish: the Atlantic, king, and silver salmon. All the species are caught commercially, the pink yielding the highest catch, followed by the red, the king, the silver, the chum, and the Atlantic (caught mostly in Canada).

Salmon Management

A campaign against pollution has been undertaken in many states to improve the salmon habitat. Artificial propagation is also an important tool of salmon management. Hatcheries in Oregon and Washington release silver, chinook, and sockeye fingerlings to supplement the natural runs of adult salmon. Even Atlantic salmon are released by hatcheries into lake systems where living conditions are suitable. The mature fish become the so-called landlocked salmon.

There is yet another salmon, the small land-locked sockeye or kokanee found in the large lakes of Idaho. Commercially it is of little value.

Another fish, much like salmon, is the anadromous rainbow trout known as steelhead. It is recognized commercially by the trade. The steelhead occurs mainly in the Pacific Northwest. This excellent fish is included in the trout section.

In New England, cohos are raised in hatcheries and sold commercially when they reach a weight of 2 to 5 pounds (900 g to 2.270 kg) that is ideal for the trade. The fish are sold under the name blueback.

A General Review of Salmon

Producing states. Alaska, California, Oregon, and Washington.
Availability fresh. From May to November, depending on species.
Disposition.

Canned
Frozen raw fillets and steaks
Breaded raw steaks
Smoked
Caviar with roe
Salted
Pickled
Mild cured

Frozen specialties:

Roe in rice wine mash
Patties
Steaks, breaded and cooked

Canned specialties: spreads and pastes

Chinook Salmon

Other names. King, blackmouth.
Appearance. The color is greenish on the back with profuse black spotting. The sides and belly are silvery, and the inside of the mouth is black or dusky (see Figure 4-34).
Source. Pacific Northwest (central California to Alaska).
Availability fresh. May to October.
Average weight. From 5 to 30 pounds (2.270 to 13.60 kg).
Quality. A fatty fish (10 to 13 percent) with excellent flavor. The color of the flesh ranges from deep salmon to almost white.
Note: The chinook accounts for about 20 percent of the total salmon landings in the Pacific and is one of the most commercially valuable fish in the world.

Coho Salmon

Other name. Silver salmon.
Appearance. The color is metallic blue along the back fading to silvery on the

sides and belly. The silver salmon has irregular black spotting along the back. The mouth is black with a white gum or tooth line (see Fig. 4-35).

Source. Southern Oregon to southeastern Alaska. Coho salmon planted in the Great Lakes have shown tremendous promise. The silver salmon is also raised in New England hatcheries and sold commercially as blueback.

Availability fresh. June to September.

Average weight. From 3 to 12 pounds (1.360 to 5.4 kg). Hatchery-raised salmon usually weigh 2 to 3 pounds (900 g to 1.360 kg).

Quality. A fatty fish (10 to 12 percent) of good quality, with light to dark pink flesh.

Note: This species represents about 20 percent of the total salmon landings in the Pacific.

Sockeye Salmon

Other names. Red salmon, blueback.

Appearance. The back is greenish blue with silvery sides and belly. Sockeye salmon have no black spotting (see Fig. 4-36).

Source. Columbia River to Bristol Bay, Alaska.

Availability fresh. June and July.

Average weight. From 3 to 12 pounds (1.360 to 5.4 kg).

Quality. A fatty fish with an oil content of 10 to 13 percent. The excellent flavor and deep red meat are particularly suitable when richness and color are important.

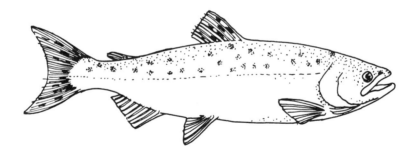

Figure 4-34. Chinook Salmon.

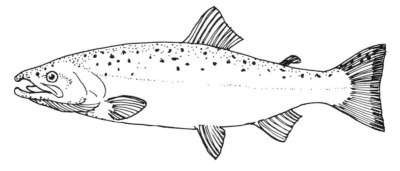

Figure 4-35. Coho Salmon.

A Comprehensive Survey of American Fish and Shellfish   **59**

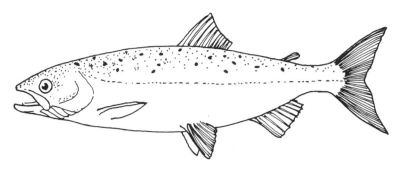

Figure 4-36. Sockeye Salmon.

Pink Salmon

Other name. Humpback.

Appearance. The pink salmon has a bluish green back and numerous black blotches on its sides. A prominent hump appears on the backs of males at spawning time. This is the smallest of the Pacific salmon.

Source. Southern California to northwestern Alaska.

Availability fresh. June to November. Pink salmon is mostly canned.

Quality. A lean, good flavored fish with soft pink flesh.

Chum Salmon

Other names. Keta, dog.

Appearance. The back is metallic blue with a slight purplish sheen. The belly and sides are silvery. The coloring of the chum salmon is similar to that of the chinook, but it has no spots (see Figure 4-37).

Source. Puget Sound to southern Alaska.

Availability fresh. August to October, but this species is mostly canned.

Average weight. From 5 to 10 pounds (2.270 to 4.5 kg).

Quality. A lean fish with poor flavor. The flesh is yellow to white.

Atlantic Salmon

Appearance. A migratory fish with a well-shaped body and a wide tail. The snout is slender and elongated. The adult fish has a grayish brown back with scattered black spotting, a silvery side, and a brilliant white stomach. Upon ascending the spawning areas, the fish takes on a brighter color.

Source. Canada, (Nova Scotia, Gaspe Coast), Iceland, Norway, Ireland, and Scotland.

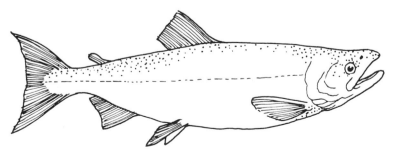

Figure 4-37. Chum Salmon.

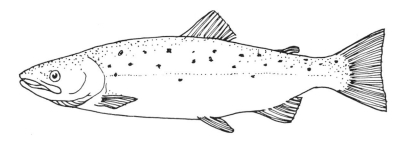

Figure 4-38. Atlantic Salmon.

Availability fresh. From Canada, June to October. Farmed Atlantic salmon from Norway is also available fresh all year round.
Average weight. 5 to 15 pounds (2.270 to 6.75 kg).
Quality. The flesh is the most delicate and tasty with a pink color and a fat content ranging from 12 to 15 percent.

Truly the king of fish and the fish of kings, the Atlantic salmon is known for its superb quality. It is universally acclaimed as the most famous freshwater gamefish, putting up a savage battle (see Fig. 4-38).

Unlike the Pacific salmon, the Atlantic salmon travels up river to spawn several times, returning to the ocean after each spawning. A few large salmon, with four to five years of ocean feeding, have been caught commercially and by sport fishermen.

The many attempts to establish the Atlantic salmon in tributary streams of the Pacific have met with little success. The return of the Atlantic salmon to northeastern tributaries is an indication of good management by the United States Department of Fisheries.

Although commercial landings of Atlantic salmon are negligible in the United States, they represent a yearly landing of 2 to 3 million pounds in Canada. Most Atlantic salmon sold on the United States market is smoked, and demands a high price.

Sardine

Other names. Maine sardine, Atlantic herring, Pacific sardine, Norwegian sardine.
Appearance. Maine sardines are the immature young of the Atlantic herring. They have an elongated body and are greenish blue in color, with a silvery cast on the sides and belly. The tail is deeply forked and has a single dorsal fin directly over the small ventral. The scales are large and loosely attached, a characteristic of all fish belonging to the herring family (including shad) (see Fig. 4-39).

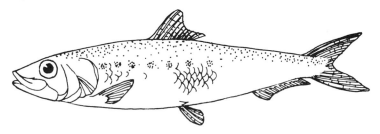

Figure 4-39. Sardine.

Source. Atlantic herring are found from Virginia north to Labrador and Greenland. The largest number are caught north of Cape Cod, with the Maine coastline the center of the industry.

The Pacific sardine, also known as the pilchard or Pacific sea herring, occurs off the coast of California to the Bering Sea. Pacific sardines are used for fish meal, oil, or bait; a substantial amount is used as food. The Norwegian sardine is known as the brisling or sprat and is commonly available on the United States market. Sardines are so called because they were first found and caught in great abundance around the island of Sardinia, in the Mediterranean.

Availability fresh. Small quantities of sardines are marketed fresh during the winter months when there is a surplus; the major harvest is canned.

Average size. Sardines reach about 3 to 4 inches (7.5 to 10 cm) in length by the end of a year.

Quality. Sardines are recognized by nutrition experts as excellent sources of high-quality protein, minerals, vitamins, and other nutrients. The following is an excerpt from a book by Dr. Benjamen S. Frank, *No Aging Diet,* that emphasizes the importance of sardines in the diet.

> To achieve the most youthful, healthy appearance along with good health itself, we need one to one and a half grams of nucleic acid per day. It does not matter much whether they come from sardines or soybeans, providing we avoid excessive cholesterol and calories. Sardines, for example, are richer in minerals than soybean and my experience shows that they have a remarkable ability to lower cholesterol. Besides they are lower on the food chain than bigger fish like tuna, and are therefore less likely to contain man-made pollutants like insecticides. Big fish eat smaller fish, smaller fist eat still smaller fish, each with some pollutants stored in its body. The smaller the fish the closer it is to the bottom of the food chain where there are less pollutants to eat.

Dr. Frank quickly points out that many people cannot stomach sardines. For those who can, he adds, "Four days a week eat a three ounce, 85 g can of small sardines. One other day a week have salmon, canned or fresh, and still another day have shrimp, lobster, squid, clam, or oysters as a main course. On the remaining day eat any other kind of fish. In other words, eat seafood seven times a week, and especially sardines to grow younger." The no aging diet conscious Americans who want to keep their youthful vigor should rely more than ever on their can openers or keys, and enjoy the unpolluted Atlantic herring, pilchard, brisling, or sprat. Chapter 15 offers a number of ways to enjoy sardines besides the common sandwich.

Sardine canning. Large quantities of sardines are sold in cans in the United States. They are packed in olive oil, cottonseed oil, or mustard or tomato sauce. Only the very small sardines (2 to 4 inches; 5 to 10 cm) are packed in oil. The Norwegian brisling is the finest quality. Boneless and skinless Portuguese sardines are also favored. Large quantities of Maine sardines are available at lower prices and are packed in soybean or cottonseed oil. Pacific sardines, similar to the Mediterranean pilchard, have not been canned since 1968. The California State Legislature, in an effort to conserve the resource, established an indefinite moratorium on sardine fishing.

Sea Bass

Several species are caught commercially, the most common being the Northeast black sea bass and the Pacific white sea bass. The California black sea bass is also valuable commercially. The larger fish can weigh 700 pounds (317 kg) or more, and are sometimes called jewfish; they do not have the same quality as the Florida species. The California black sea bass has a white, flaky flesh with a fine flavor.

Black Sea Bass

Appearance. The black sea bass has a high back, a flat-topped head, moderately pointed snout, and one sharp spine near the uppermost point of each gill cover. The caudal fin is rounded. Like many fish that inhabit rocky bottoms, the color is variable ranging from smoky gray to dusky brown (see Fig. 4-40).
Source. From Cape Cod to North Carolina. Abundant in the Middle Atlantic states.
Availability fresh. All year, but mainly in the spring when the fish move inshore.
Average weight. Black sea bass are not large fish; they average 1½ pounds (680 g). Some specimens reach 5 pounds (2.270 kg).
Trade size.

   Pins—3 to 4 to a pound
   Small—1 to 1½ pounds (450 to 680 g)
   Medium—1½ to 2½ pounds (680 g to 1.140 kg)
   Large—over 2½ pounds (1.140 kg)

Quality. Excellent for eating; the flesh is firm, white, and delicately flavored. The black sea bass should be handled with great care because of its stiff sharp dorsal spines. Remove the fins before attempting any preparation.

White Sea Bass

This fish is not a true sea bass; it is closely related to the West Coast corvinas and the East Coast weakfishes. It is known as white corvina in Mexico.
Appearance. The body color is gray to blue on the back, silvery on the sides,

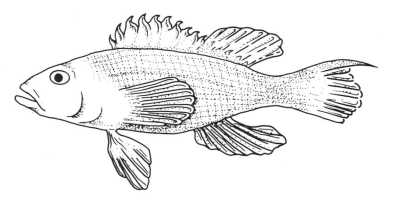

Figure 4-40. Black Sea Bass.

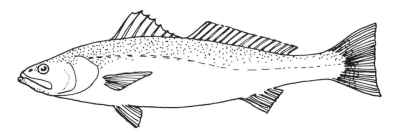

Figure 4-41. White Sea Bass.

and white on the belly. The dorsal fins are in contact. The lateral line is spotted and slightly curved (see Fig. 4-41).

Source. From Alaska to Chile, but uncommon north of San Francisco.

Availability fresh. Abundant from May to September.

Average weight. Can reach 40 pounds (18 kg), but averages 10 pounds (4.5 kg).

Quality. The white sea bass is in a class with the weakfish and the sea trout.

Disposition.

Fillets, fresh and frozen
Smoked

Shad

Other names. American shad, white shad. The shad is anadromous, spending most of its life in the ocean and returning to fresh water to spawn. The South Atlantic shad dies after spawning.

Appearance. The American shad has a greenish color with metallic luster above, and silvery sides. A dark or dusky spot above and at the rear edge of the gill cover is often followed by smaller spots. The lower jaw is enclosed by the upper when the two are pressed together. This characteristic distinguishes the shad from others of the herring family, especially the alewive and the hickory shad (see Fig. 4-42).

Source. Shad naturally range from the St. John's River in Florida to the St. Lawrence River in Canada. Shad from the Connecticut River and other East Coast rivers have been stocked in streams. On the West Coast, where the fish is now abundant, it ranges from the Mexican border to Cook Inlet in Alaska. American shad was introduced to the Pacific coast in 1871.

Availability fresh. Early February in the St. John's River to July in the St.

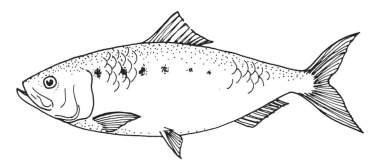

Figure 4-42. Shad.

Lawrence River and in Alaska. In the northeastern states, shad is most abundant in March, April, and May.

Average weight. From 3 to 4 pounds (1 kg 350 to 1 kg 800). Some specimens reach 7 pounds (3 kg 170) or more, although they are rare.

Quality. A fatty fish of exceptional quality (about 9 to 9.5 percent fat). In season, shad is in greater demand than any other fish.

Trade size.

> Shad: Skip—¾ to 1½ pounds (340 to 680 g)
> Cut (drawn)—2 pounds (900 g) and over
> Buck (round)—1½ pounds (680 g) and over
> Roe—3 pounds (1 kg 350) and over.
> Shad roe (per pair):
>> Small—under 8 ounces (225 g)
>> Medium—8 to 10 ounces (225 to 285 g)
>> Large—10 to 14 ounces (285 to 400 g)
>> Jumbo—14 ounces (400 g) and over

It is as easy to scale a shad as it is challenging to bone it. (See Chapter 5 for details on boning shad.) The annual yield of shad has decreased at an alarming rate. Problems similar to those of salmon are threatening their existence. Attempts to propagate shad in hatcheries have not been successful. Effective management and pollution control will only stabilize the annual yield of shad.

Disposition.

> Over 90 percent fresh (boned)
> Canned
> Smoked Roe

Note: Boneless shad fillets can be prepared in many ways. They may be fried whole or in portions, after carefully dredging them in seasoned flour and placing them, skin side down, in a pan or skillet containing half oil and half butter. Once the fillets have firmed, they can be turned.

Broiling is probably one of the most popular ways to cook shad. The shad fillets should be broiled between hinged racks for easy handling. A marinade improves the delicate flavor of shad.

The shad roe is best when brined in salt and water for 24 hours. Shad roe has a tendency to lack taste if not carefully seasoned. The roe should be cooked at low temperature until firm.

Shark

Commercial shark fishing used to be a booming business when the demand for natural vitamin A was high. Shark liver is a good source of vitamin A, but since the synthetic form was discovered, the demand for natural vitamin has diminished.

Today, more and more people are discovering what Europeans have known for years, that shark meat is a highly acceptable food product. Many species of shark are marketed as food fish, including: the sand shark (commonly known as dogfish), the dusky, sharpnose, bonnethead, blacktip, and the most popular of all, mako shark, whose flesh has a similarity to swordfish.

Several European nations have effectively exploited shark, especially the dogfish or spiny dogfish, as food fish. It is used for all types of hors d'oeuvre and for fish and chips. In the United States, mako shark and dogfish are the most common sharks. Mako shark is often used as a substitute for swordfish. The appearance, taste, and texture are similar.

How to Prepare and Test the Quality of Shark Meat

Some appealing features of shark meat are its lack of bones, firm texture, and versatility of preparation. Like any fish, shark meat is best when purchased fresh. If it is to be stored longer than 24 hours, it should be wrapped in airtight wrappers and stored in the freezer. Shark meat can be prepared much like any other fish. It lends itself well to kebabs as the flesh is firm and will not fall off the skewers. Chunks of fresh shark meat can be enjoyed in gumbos, soups, or creoles. Shark can be broiled, baked, fried, poached, grilled, or smoked, and served with a sauce. The cooked fish can be combined with other ingredients to create salads or au gratin seafood dishes.

Smell and color are the primary standards for judging shark meat quality. There should be no ammonia smell and the flesh should be bright red in color. The unpleasant smell associated with dogfish is linked to the production of ammonia during the autolytic spoilage process. To avoid this danger, the fish must be particularly fresh when processed, and it should be frozen and stored at very low temperatures, particularly if the product is held for long periods in cold storage.

Skate

Ironically, skates, which are considered almost universally as junk fish, are sometimes disguised as a substitute for scallops, proving that their succulence is on a par with the United States sea scallop. Skates, gliding through water with sweeping motions of their wings, look strange enough to be regarded suspiciously as human food (see Fig. 4-43). Their relatives, the stingrays, are

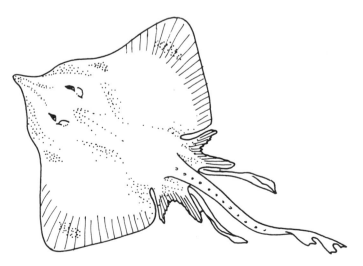

Figure 4-43. Barn Door Skate.

armed with one or two long, venemous spines on the tail, and can be very dangerous. They should not be confused with skates.

Skate wings have an excellent food value, like scallops, and are considered a delicacy in Europe. Pieces of skate wings, pan fried or deep fried, and cut like scallops, are a gourmet delight.

Skates can be caught profitably by our fishermen. Since consumers already have a taste for scallops, skate may appear on the United States markets if the demand arises.

In quality, a skate is similar to a dogfish; it has poor keeping qualities. The fish should be frozen or marketed fresh as soon as possible after capture. If the fish has any ammonia smell when thawed, it is unacceptable.

Sheepshead

Appearance. The two unique features of the saltwater sheepshead are the 5 to 6 distinct, dark vertical bars on the sides and the broad, strong incisor teeth (see Fig. 4-44).
Source. The largest landings occur in the Gulf states. Sheepshead are also caught off the southern Atlantic coast in smaller quantities.
Availability fresh. April to November.
Average weight. From ¾ to 8 pounds (340 g to 3.6 kg). Best size is 3 to 4 pounds (1.360 to 1.800 kg).
Trade size. Gulf states market—1 to 5 pounds (450 g to 2.270 kg).
Quality. The meat of the sheepshead is white, flaky, well flavored, and tender.

Smelt

Other names. Icefish, frostfish, candlelight fish.
Appearance. Smelt resemble midget salmon in appearance and are distantly related to the salmon family. The smelt is a small, slender, silvery fish with olive green coloring along the back. The average size of smelt varies from 7 to 8 inches (17.5 to 20 cm). Smelt have a large mouth for their size and the lower jaw projects beyond the upper. The tip of the tongue has large, fang-like teeth

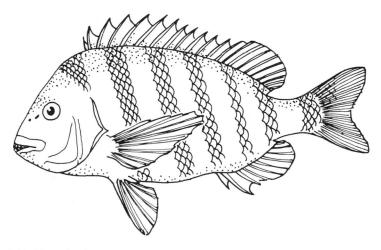

Figure 4-44. Sheepshead.

that, along with the large mouth, distinguish smelt from similar small fish. Smelt have large scales that come off readily (see Fig. 4-45 and 4-46).

Source. Originally anadromous, like their relatives, smelt have adapted to fresh-water habitats, living in cold lakes and streams in many parts of the United States. The Columbia River, with its tributaries in the West, the Gulf of St. Lawrence to the Virginia Capes in the East, and the Great Lakes area in the Midwest all support smelt. Smelt were first introduced into the Great Lakes area in 1906.

Availability fresh. Lake-dwelling smelt are caught during the spawning runs in mid-March and April. The sea smelt are best during the winter months. The peak seasons occur in September in Maine, December in New York, June in Seattle, and June to September in California.

Average weight. Although smelt can weigh up to 1 pound (450 g), most are much smaller, ranging from 15 per pound to 4 to 7 per pound.

Trade size. Great Lakes (round)

> Medium—over 10 per pound
> No. 1—7 to 10 per pound
> Jumbo—4 to 6 per pound

Salt water, East coast (round)

> Small—15 and over per pound
> Medium—12 to 14 per pound
> No. 1—8 to 10 per pound
> Jumbo—4 to 6 per pound

Seattle (round, drawn)

> Silver—5 to 12 per pound
> Eulachon—5 to 8 per pound

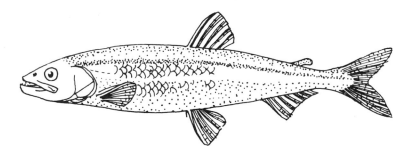

Figure 4-45. Eastern Smelt.

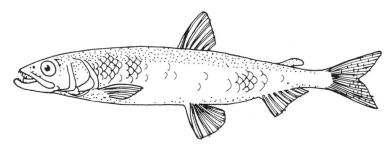

Figure 4-46. Alaska Smelt.

Quality. Smelt have a fatty, rich mild flavor. If consumed fresh, the lake or sea smelt make the most delicious pan fish.

Sole

Sole are one of the most clearly defined and distinctive orders of fish. The order also includes such flatfish as halibut and flounder. The underside of these fish is usually white; the top is pigmented, resembling the bottom on which the flatfish lives. An interesting fact is that the eyes of these fish can be raised slightly and moved independently, thus increasing vision. In size and other characteristics flatfish vary greatly.

Description. Atlantic coast sole include two main species:

1. The gray sole is also called witch flounder. This sole, which grows up to 25 inches (62.5 cm), is noted for its fine flavor and is commercially important.
2. The lemon sole is called winter flounder or blackback when it weighs less than 3½ pounds (1.590 kg). Its usual length, when caught inshore, is around 18 inches (45 cm). These two Atlantic sole share characteristic small mouths, straight lateral lines on the body, and eyes on the right side (see Fig. 4-47).

Pacific Coast sole of commercial importance include the following:

1. The petrale sole, also known as brill sole. It averages about 17 inches (42.5 cm) in length and 2½ pounds (1.140 kg) round weight. It has a wide body, small scales, large mouth, and slightly curved lateral line, and is olive brown in color.
2. The English sole is also known as the lemon sole, but is an entirely different species than the Atlantic lemon sole. It is noted for its fine flavor. Smaller than the petrale, the English sole averages about 15 inches (37.5 cm) in length and slightly over ¾ pound (340 g) in weight. It is distinguished by a small mouth, a slender shape, and a pointed head. Other Pacific sole include the rex, California dover, and rock. The Pacific rex sole and rock sole are small flounders. The rex sole has the finest flavor. These two species are not caught in abundance and, due to their small size, are usually pan fried whole.

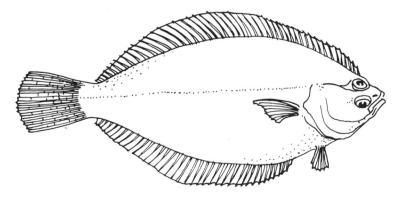

Figure 4-47. Atlantic Sole.

Source. Most sole live along the continental shelf and slope. Some come into shoal waters and are found in bays or close inshore. The lemon sole of the Atlantic range from as far north as Labrador, south as far as Georgia, with the greatest abundance off the coast of New England. The gray sole of the Atlantic live in moderately deep water from the Gulf of St. Lawrence and the Southern Grand Banks, as far south as Cape Hatteras. The Pacific petrale or brill, and the English or lemon sole, range from southern California to Alaska.

Quality. Sole are fine eating fish. The flesh is firm, lean, white, and delicate in flavor. Most sole are filleted and can be purchased either fresh or frozen. Fillets vary in weight from 2 to 4 ounces (55 to 110 g) and occasionally reach 8 ounces (225 g). Some sole are dressed and sold whole for stuffing.

Dover Sole

Appearance. This species *(Microstomus Pacificus)* should not be confused with the imported Dover sole *(Solea vulgaris* or *Solea Solea)* that is imported from waters of the Channel Islands and the North Sea (see Fig. 4-48).

Large eyes and a small mouth characterize this righteye Pacific species. It is uniformly light to dark brown on the eyed side. The slender body has numerous small scales and is covered with a heavy slime (see Fig. 4-49).

Source. Southern California to northwestern Alaska.

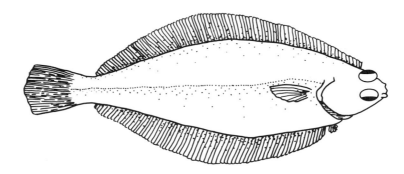

Figure 4-48. Dover Sole.

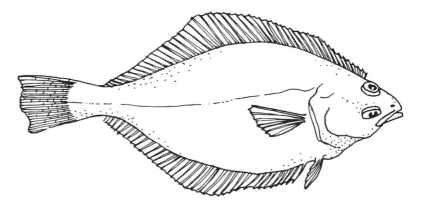

Figure 4-49. California Dover Sole.

Average weight. From 2 to 6 pounds (900 g to 2.720 kg), sometimes reaching 10 pounds (4.5 kg).
Quality. The flesh is considered delicious.

Note: European waters do not abound with such a variety of flatfish, and the term *fillet of sole* is applied strictly to the English Dover sole, so abundant in the Channel Islands and the North Sea. It is the most adaptable fish for innumerable sophisticated recipes, unsurpassed by even the salmon.

Spot

Other names. Lafayette, goody.
Appearance. A member of the croaker family, spot is a good pan fish not very well known in the trade. The spot has 12 to 15 yellowish oblique bars above the lateral line and a yellowish black spot directly behind the gills (see Fig. 4-50).
Source. Massachusetts to Texas, with the largest production around the Middle Atlantic states.
Availability fresh. In the Middle Atlantic states, July to October. In the South Atlantic states, mainly North Carolina, June to November.
Trade size.

Small—4 to a pound (450 g)
Medium—3 to a pound (450 g)
Large—¾ to 1 pound (340 to 450 g)

Quality. Lean, flaky, and tender meat.

Squid

Other names. Inkfish, cuttlefish, calamari.
Appearance. The squid and octopus belong to the same family. Squid have ten arms and usually a long, cigar-shaped body with fins at the end; octopuses have eight arms and more of a stubby body. Squid have no back bone but rather a pen that is located beneath the mantle of the body. Two fins, located near the terminal end, are about half as long as the mantle and are slightly lobed in front. Squid are ordinarily a milky, translucent color, but when

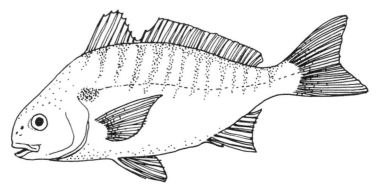

Figure 4-50. Spot.

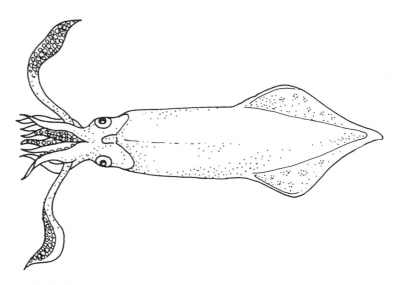

Figure 4-51. Squid.

aroused, intense and varied colors ripple over the body, turning rapidly to red, pink, brown, blue, and yellow, even several hours after they are caught.

Squid are able to control their coloration in order to hide from prey and predators alike. An inklike fluid is contained in a sack in the mantle and ejected at will. The siphon or funnel that ejects the ink is also instrumental in the squid's rapid movements (see Fig. 4-51).

Source. Squid occur on both the Atlantic and Pacific coasts and in the Gulf of Mexico. The ones most sought by commercial fishermen are found along the Pacific coast and the usual range is from Puget Sound to San Diego. Their year-round habitat is the deeper offshore water, except when spawning.

Availability fresh. February to June in the Monterey Bay area; November through February in southern California.

Quality. Squid is considered a gourmet or specialty item and has long been popular with Mediterranean, Oriental, and Mexican cooks. It is high in protein and phosphorus, and contains traces of calcium, thiamine, and riboflavin. The white meat is very lean. Squid, the poor man's lobster, may well become the rich man's delight. The inexpensive squid is readily available on the markets. Many consumers may be startled at the thought of eating squid, but after the initial bite, prejudice dissolves.

Filled with spinach and rice, or in cold salads, paella, fish soups, and chowders, or fried or simmered with tomatoes, squid is a highly nutritious seafood certain to gain popularity in the United States.

Striped Bass

Other names. Rockfish, striper.

Appearance. This fish, a member of the sea bass family, is one of the most valuable fish on the coast of North America. The striped bass is easily recognized by its 7 or 8 prominent, dark, longitudinal stripes. The body is elongated and slightly compressed (see Fig. 4-52).

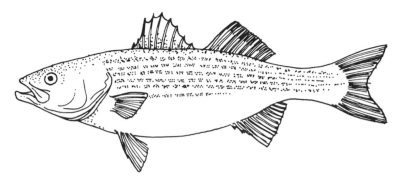

Figure 4-52. Striped Bass.

Source. The species is most abundant in Chesapeake Bay, although it ranges from Canada to the St. John's River in Florida, and to the Gulf of Mexico, California, and Washington. The striped bass is not caught commercially on the Pacific coast but is considered a sport fish.*

Availability fresh. All year, but abundant in October, November, February, March, and April.

Average weight. From 1 to 15 pounds (450 g to 6.8 kg). Some specimens reach 40 to 50 pounds (18 to 22 kg) or more, but these are rare.

Trade size. (round)

Small—2 to 5 pounds (900 g to 2.270 kg)
Medium—5 to 10 pounds (2.270 to 4.5 kg)
Large—10 to 15 pounds (4.5 to 6.8 kg)
Jumbo—over 15 pounds (6.8 kg)

Quality. Its excellent quality, white, flaky flesh is in high demand. Striped bass is a medium fat fish that is adaptable to numerous culinary techniques.

Swordfish

Appearance. The swordfish is shaped like an oversized mackerel. The body is thickest in the shoulder area and tapers to the tail, which is reinforced by a keel on either side. The long upper jaw and snout form a flat, sharp, double-edged sword that can be as much as one-third of the total length of the fish. Swordfish vary in color from a dark, metallic purplish cast on the upper surfaces of the body to almost white on the sides and lower body (see Fig. 4-53).

Source. Swordfish are found in tropical waters around the Americas. In Pacific waters, they range from Chile to California and around the Hawaiian Islands; in Atlantic waters, from the West Indies to the Grand Banks. Swordfish tend to form schools. However, when they are plentiful, individuals are usually scattered. They seem to prefer temperatures in excess of 60°F (15°C).

Availability fresh. From June to October, with the largest landings in August.

---

*Overfishing and pollution have had devastating effects on the East coast striped bass resulting in bans on commercial fishing—new ventures in striped bass farming have become successful and profitable.

Figure 4-53. Swordfish.

Average weight. From 100 to 200 pounds (45 to 90 kg), with specimens reaching over 400 pounds (180 kg).
Trade size.

Pups—under 100 pounds (49.8 kg)
Large—over 110 pounds (49.8 kg and up)

Quality. The meat is firm with medium fat, and of good quality. Center cuts are the best.
Disposition.

Steaks, fresh and frozen
Smoked.

In 1971, a swordfish scare went into effect when the Federal Drug Administration (FDA) advised the public to stop eating the fish, when over 90 percent of samples tested showed an excessive mercury content that could damage the human nervous system. Despite arguments that the fish, by nature, has always contained a minute level of mercury, to this date, no one has been known to suffer damage from swordfish consumption. Today, swordfish is *safe* for eating. In 1987, United States landings accounted for 9.4 million pounds, and imports represented about 9 million pounds.

Note: The mako shark and other similar species of shark are often used as a substitute for swordfish. Mako shark steak has a firm flesh and is palatable. Fresh swordfish steak has a light pink color; mako shark steak flesh has a deeper color.

Tilefish

Tilefish is an excellent food fish that has gained in popularity in recent years. In 1882, the species almost became extinct. A temporary flood of cold water through the warm zone left several thousand square miles covered with dead tilefish. Today, there is an average annual yield of 6 million pounds. Tilefish are most abundant off the New England and Middle Atlantic States (see Fig. 4-54).

Quality. The flesh of tilefish is firm, of the same quality as snapper or grouper. Many fishermen agree with the slogan: "If you like lobster, you will love tilefish."

Trade size.

Kitten—under 4 pounds (1.8 kg)
Medium—4 to 7 pounds (1.8 to 3.2 kg)
Large—7 pounds (3.2 kg) and up.

Tuna

At the rate tuna fish were being caught in recent years, no one could have foreseen the decline of one of the most abundant species. But suddenly, the most sought after species, the bluefin, is vanishing.

For a long time we have enjoyed one of the cheapest sources of protein from our seas. We consume well over a million pounds of tuna daily in the United States. In 1986, tuna landings totaled 556 million pounds and imports exceeded 640 million pounds in the United States. American fishermen are well equipped to catch huge amounts of tuna, especially on the Pacific coast. Tuna vessels cost over $5 million and can store more than 2,000 tons of tuna.

The United States and Japan process and market over 40 percent of the total world harvest. Fishermen, marine biologists, and marketers all agree that tuna, particularly the bluefin, may become extinct unless something is done in the near future. However, it is difficult to accept this warning. In the United States, tuna has been so pervasively advertised and marketed that nearly all of us take the supply for granted.

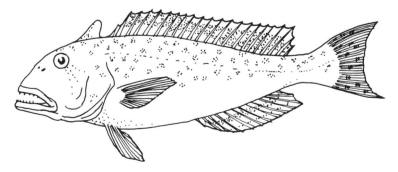

Figure 4-54. Tilefish.

In addition to the shortage of tuna, fishermen are facing other problems. Seiners and superseiners, operating off the East and Pacific coasts, are endangering another species. Too many friendly porpoises, the tuna's traveling companions, are killed in the giant nets. This has prompted several protection agencies to curtail tuna fishing until a compromise is reached.

Eight species of tuna are hunted in the oceans. These are: albacore, yellowfin, bluefin, skipjack, bigeye, blackfin, little tuna, and bonito. The first four are of commercial importance in the United States.

Quality. Tuna supplies a rich source of protein, vitamins, and minerals. It is easily digested, and can be used straight from the can or combined with other foods. It is economical—there is no waste in the compactly packed and compressed cans.

Grades. Only the canned albacore can be labeled as "white meat." The remaining species must be labeled "light meat." Bonito, little tuna, blackfin, and bigeye cannot be labeled "tuna" since they are members of the mackerel family.

Canned tuna is labeled:

Fancy—solid meat only
Standard—75 percent solid meat
Grated or flaked—all small pieces

In 1986, the U.S. pack of canned tuna was 636.8 million pounds. Albacore tuna was 25 percent of the tuna pack. Lightmeat tuna (bluefin, skipjack, and yellowtail) comprised the remainder.

Processing and Canning. The following information was supplied by the marketing services of Castle and Cooke Foods, San Francisco, California.

> After the tuna is caught and taken to the cannery, it is cleaned, then graded according to size and then precooked. The purpose of the pre-cook is to expell the strongly flavored natural oil of the tuna, to make it possible quickly and fully to remove the skin and dark meat of the tuna, and to separate the entire fish into four boneless loins of solid meat. After cooling, the loins go to the can-filling section on the production line. After the cans are filled by machine, measured amounts of salt and oil and/or vegetable broth are placed in the can, which then passes into the closing machines where vacuum is established in the can and it is sealed hermetically.

Only a small amount of tuna is consumed fresh in the United States. During the summer months, fresh tuna is available in East and West Coast markets.

Processed tuna comes in 3¼ to 3½, 6½ to 7, 9¼, and 12½ to 13 ounce cans. Larger cans are sold for institutional use.

Albacore

Albacore vary from other tuna in flavor and in the whiteness of their flesh. They are also known as "longfins" and can be recognized by their long, sabre-sharp pectoral fins. They are further distinguished by the metallic, steely blue color on the top and sides of the body, a silvery color on the bottom, and by the absence of stripes. The usual weight ranges between 10 and 60 pounds

(4.5 to 27.2 kg). Albacore range from southern California to mid-Mexican waters, sometimes reaching as far north as Puget Sound in the summer (see Fig. 4-55).

Yellowfin

Probably the favorite of the tuna fishing fleet, these tuna are light fleshed. They are considered perhaps the most commercially valuable of the top four species. Yellowfin are distinguished by elongated, yellowish dorsal and anal fins, and yellowish coloring on the sides. They vary in weight from 30 to 150 pounds (13.5 to 68 kg). The choicest for canning weigh 40 to 100 pounds (18 to 45 kg). Yellowfin tuna are found from the Gulf of California south to the waters off northern Chile (see Fig. 4-56).

Bluefin

This species has light flesh and varies in commercial weight from 15 to 80 pounds (6.8 to 36 kg). Bluefin are distinguished by the deep blue or green color on the top and sides of the body. Unlike most fish, the high metabolic rate of the bluefin tuna maintains its body temperature warmer than the water.

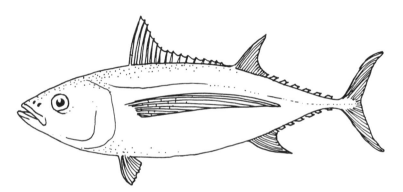

Figure 4-55. Albacore.

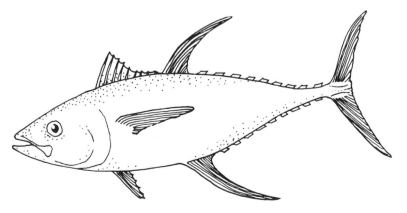

Figure 4-56. Yellowfin Tuna.

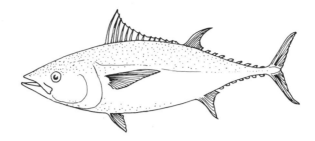

Figure 4-57. Bluefin.

Bluefin are found from Alaska to lower California. This species is also found in the Atlantic Ocean (see Fig. 4-57).

Skipjack

Skipjack are also known as striped tuna. They have light flesh and are distinguished by parallel, black-to-dusky stripes on the lower sides of the body. Skipjack tuna are dark metallic blue on the top and sides, shading to a silvery color on the bottom surfaces: They are the smallest of these four tuna, weighing from 4 to 24 pounds (1.8 to 10.8 kg). Skipjack are found in the same tropical waters as the yellowfin (see Fig. 4-58).

Turtle

The term *turtle* is generally applied to all species, but mainly to the sea turtle. A tortoise is a land or fresh-water species. The terrapin is a variety of turtle found in the coastal swamps of the eastern seaboard and the Gulf (see Fig. 4-59).

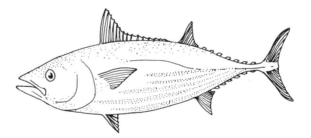

Figure 4-58. Skipjack Tuna.

Figure 4-59. Turtle.

The most prized turtle, the green turtle, produces a soup of sublime quality that is available mostly in cans. Turtle meat is also sold canned. Green turtle steaks resemble veal and have a fine flavor. The fresh meat, which remains a southern specialty, is rarely sold in northeastern markets.

Commercial fishing for green turtles centers around South Florida, especially Key West. Green turtles are also found along the coasts of the Bahamas, Jamaica, and other islands.

The once highly prized diamond terrapin has now become very scarce.

Sea Trout

Other names. Weakfish, speckled trout, gray sea trout, squeteagues, summer trout.

Appearance. A member of the drum family, the weakfish is a slim, shapely, colorful fish with dark olive green above, and with lustrous purple, lavender, green, blue, gold, or copper tints on its back and sides. It is marked above the lateral line with many small black, dark green, or bronze spots. The lower surface is white to silvery. The large mouth is armed with two sharp canine teeth. The name *weakfish* refers to its delicate mouth structure (see Fig. 4-60).

Source. Weakfish range from the eastern coast of Florida to Massachusetts, occasionally straying northward.

Availability fresh. Abundant during the summer off the coast of New York, New Jersey, and Virginia. In the autumn, they move south to offshore waters.

Average weight. From 1 to 3 pounds (450 g to 1.360 kg), with a few reaching 5 or 6 pounds (2.270 to 2.720 kg).

Trade size. (round or dressed)

Pin—under ½ pound (225 g)
Small—¾ to 1¼ pounds (340 to 560 g)
Medium—1¼ to 3½ pounds (560 g to 1.590 kg)
Large—over 3½ pounds (1.590 kg)

Quality. Sea Trouts are known for their tasty, tender flesh. They are usually available whole or pan dressed because of their small size; occasionally, however, fillets from larger fish are available.

Whiting

Other names. Silver hake, silver perch.

Appearance. The whiting is a slender, soft-rayed fish with a streamlined body,

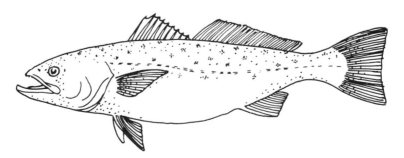

Figure 4-60. Sea Trout.

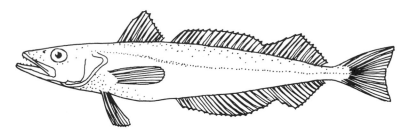

Figure 4-61. Whiting.

two dorsal fins, and sharp teeth. The upper fins are transparent. The body is gray, turning to silver below the lateral line (see Fig. 4-61).

Source. Whiting occur along the New England coast off Georges Bank, the Middle Atlantic coast, and Chesapeake Bay.

Availability fresh. In New England, north of Cape Cod, whiting appear from May until October. The peak supply is landed in July and August along the Middle Atlantic states.

Average weight. Males average ½ pound (225 g), females 3 to 5 pounds (1.360 to 2.270 kg).

Trade size.

Snapper—½ to 1½ pounds (225 to 680 g)
Small—1½ to 2½ pounds (680 g to 1.140 kg)
Medium—2½ to 5 pounds (1.140 to 2.270 kg)
Large—over 5 pounds (2.270 kg)

Freshwater Fish

Buffalofish

Other names. Bigmouth buffalo, Black buffalo, rooter, prairie, Smallmouth buffalo or suckermouth.

Appearance. The buffalo has a large deep body, laterally compressed. Because of its terminal mouth, body shape and color, and long dorsal fin, buffalo easily might be confused with carp. In fact, buffalofish is used interchangeably in all carp recipes. The color is a dull brown to olive on the upper sides and white on the ventral side (see Fig. 4-62).

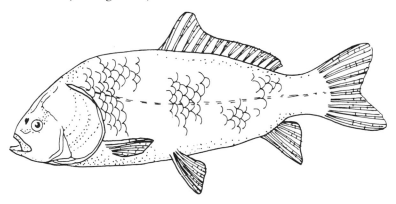

Figure 4-62. Buffalofish.

Source. Large quantities are caught in the Mississippi River and tributaries, mainly in Louisiana. The fish also inhabits the Great Lakes.

Availability fresh. February through August.

Quality. Soft, delicate, white lean meat that flakes easily when cooked. Whiting is also sold as "deep sea fillets," along with cod and haddock. This species was not always desired as a food fish. Its popular acceptance began in the 1920s and since then annual landings increased from about 10 million pounds to a record high of 132 million pounds in 1957. Annual landings have decreased considerably in the last three years.

Disposition. Fresh and frozen

> Headed and dressed
> Fillets—raw and breaded (raw and cooked)
> Smoked

Average weight. Best size is 8 to 10 pounds (3.6 to 4.5 kg).

Trade size.

> Medium—2 to 4 pounds (907 g to 1.8 kg)
> No. 1—4 to 8 pounds (1.8 to 3.6 kg)
> Jumbo—8 pounds (3.6 kg) and over

Quality. The smallmouth buffalo is considered superior in flavor. This medium fat, firm fish is preferred to carp and has fewer troublesome bones.

Disposition. Fresh and frozen fillets, and smoked.

Carp

Other names. European carp, German carp, mirror carp, leather carp.

Appearance. The carp has an elongated body with two pairs of barbels on the upper lip. Its color is olive green on the back and yellowish on the belly (see Fig. 4-63).

Source. The Great Lakes, mainly Michigan, Huron, and Erie. Carp fishing in the Mississippi is also important.

Availability fresh. In Chicago markets, April is the biggest month, although large quantities are sold in December, February, March, May, and June.

Average weight. From 2 to 8 pounds (907 g to 3.6 kg). Carp grow to a weight of 30 pounds (13.6 kg) or more, but the best size range is 3 to 5 pounds (1.360 to 2.270 kg). This size has a better flavor during the cold months.

Trade size. (round)

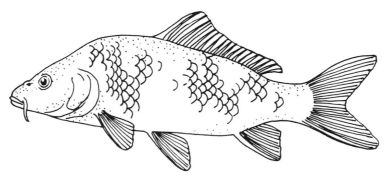

Figure 4-63. Carp.

Medium—2 to 4 pounds (907 g to 1.800 kg)
No. 1—4 to 8 pounds (1.800 to 3.6 kg)
Jumbo—over 8 pounds (3.6 kg)

Large quantities are shipped and sold alive, or frozen as fillets. Smoked carp is also available.

Quality. Carp is a lean, firm fish, palatable when raised in clean waters. The carp is not highly esteemed due to its muddy taste. Carp raised under controlled conditions, however, have a good flavor and can be cooked in various ways.

Catfish

In the United States, catfish has become one of the greatest success stories in the fish industry. Until recently, channel catfish was strictly a regional food with a reputation as a "thrash" fish consumed by poor Southerners. Fortunately, that reputation has faded. Consumers, chefs, and nutritionists are now finding the white flesh of farmed-raised channel catfish healthy and tasty, with a mild sweet buttery flavor. As a result, catfish can be found in supermarkets across the nation; it is a bargain in nutritional value as well as price. In addition, catfish is low in calories, and a good source of protein. In 1970, 5.7 million pounds of farmed catfish were shipped; last year over 300 million pounds were shipped. Mississippi is by far the number one producer of farmed catfish, followed by Alabama, Arkansas, and Louisiana.

Many food operators in first class restaurants also feature catfish on their menus. Farmed catfish can be cooked in the same manner as other firm delicate fish like sole, cod, sea bass, red snapper, and halibut.

Appearance. All catfish have long barbels about the mouth that are used to locate food. Catfish are scaleless, and have heavy, sharp pectoral and dorsal spines. Channel catfish are easily distinguished from other catfish by their deeply forked tails, relatively small heads, and small irregular spots on the sides (see Fig. 4-64).

Source. Mississippi valley, Arkansas, Alabama, Louisiana, Minnesota, Ohio, and Missouri.

Average weight. From 2 to 10 pounds (1.350 to 4.5 kg). Farmed catfish, which have an average weight of 2 pounds (900 g), are always sold in fillets. Generally, only wild catfish are sold whole.

Quality. Channel catfish is an excellent food fish. The tender, white, nutritious

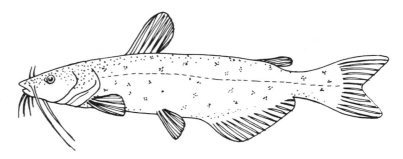

Figure 4-64. Channel Catfish.

flesh can be prepared in a variety of ways. While sea catfish are not considered food fish, the flesh is edible. Because farmers use floating food pellets which force the catfish to feed at the surface, the flavor of pond-raised catfish is the opposite of the oily, muddy, fishy taste of river dwelling catfish.
Disposition.

Fresh, whole, dressed, skinned
Frozen
Steaks
Specialties—breaded with cornmeal (raw or cooked)
Smoked

Caviar

Genuine caviar is the roe of the sturgeon, but the roe of whitefish, lumpfish, salmon, herring, pike, perch, and other fish is also known as caviar. In the wholesale trade, caviar is qualified by the name of the fish from which the roe has been processed; purists recognize only sturgeon caviar. Although the word *caviar* brings Russia to mind, it does not appear in the Russian language; in Russia it is known as *Ikra*.

Caviar is derived from the Turkish word *Khavyah*. The precious roe was brought to Italy by knights of the Holy Army. In Italy it was named *Caviala*. From Italy, caviar was introduced to all the European countries. Shakespeare mentioned it in *Hamlet,* saying, "T'was Caviare to the General!" Savarin's *Dictionaire de Commerce,* written around 1711, makes it clear that it was not despised at the highest tables of France.

What is Caviar?

What is this novelty that has such irresistible appeal for gourmets throughout the world? It is the salted roe of a species of fish called sturgeon. Sturgeon are caught in the Caspian and Black Seas, as well as in other locations. Until industry and pollution came along, the sturgeon was found in rivers running into the Atlantic and Baltic, the Rhine, and in North American lakes. Today all caviar comes from Iran, Russia, and Rumania.

Most fish containing roe are caught during the spawning season. The anadromous sturgeons leave the deep ocean waters and seek shallow river beds in order to spawn. At this time, the roe is oily, unpalatable, and unsuited for consumption. Fish caught during this period are placed in submerged floating cages. Unable to find food, they use up the reserve of fat that is stored in the roe, thus making the roe less oily. When roe is right for salting, it is extracted from the live fish. The sturgeon is then released.

Of the varieties of sturgeon that produce caviar, the beluga is the largest, sometimes reaching 2,500 pounds (1,132.5 kg) and producing up to 130 pounds (58.9 kg) of roe. The next largest is the ocictrova, or osetra, weighing around 400 pounds (180 kg) and producing 40 pounds (18 kg) of roe. The smallest of the sturgeon family is the sevruga, which weighs 60 pounds (27.2 kg) and from which only 8 pounds of roe can be harvested.

The size of the roe, even from the same species, does not denote quality. The roe is taken from the fish, carefully sieved, all tissues and membranes are removed, and it is then steeped in a salt solution. The strength of the solution is carefully controlled since the extent of salting determines the quality of the caviar. The amount of salt used depends on the grade of the sturgeon roe being prepared, the weather, the condition of the roe, and the market for which it is destined. Only after the salt has been added to the sturgeon roe does it become caviar; therefore, there is no such thing as unsalted caviar. For the United States market, only salt is used as a preservative; in European countries, salt and borax may be used. Caviar prepared with salt and borax tastes sweeter; the Food and Drug Administration does not accept borax as a food additive.

Top quality caviar is known as malosol. This word does not denote a type of caviar, it means "little salt" and it is used in conjunction with the words beluga, osetra, or sevruga. The best caviar is prepared from sturgeon caught between March and April, when the water is cool and the fish roe are firm and fresh. Fall fishing does not produce as fine a quality caviar because the hotter weather causes the roe to lose its firmness.

Caviar prepared in Russia or Iran, and qualified for the malosol grade, is packed in puds weighing 41 pounds (18.5 kg) and sent to the consumer in refrigerated containers. Nonrefrigerated caviar, for example processed caviar, has a shelf life of about 3 months, and is usually vacuum-packed in 1-to-5-ounce glass jars. After 3 months, white specks may appear; the spots are fat and crystallized salt and are absolutely harmless although not always eye appealing.

Caviar made by one special process is known as paiusnaya or "pressed" caviar. After cleaning the eggs (roe) in the usual way, the caviar is packed in linen bags and hung to drain. This destroys the natural shape of the roe, as they are crushed together. The caviar is then packed in puds holding 50 to 100 pounds (22.7 to 45 kg). Pressed caviar has a much saltier taste than malosol caviar and it looks very much like a solid mass. It is a great favorite in Russia and is greatly prized among connoisseurs.

The color of caviar ranges between gray and black. Color is no indication of quality, although some eggs are more attractive than others.

All fresh caviar keeps best at a temperature between 28°F and 32°F (−2°C and 0°C) for several weeks. Caviar that has been exposed to the air should be eaten within a few days as it will deteriorate rapidly. Any container that has been opened should be covered and kept under refrigeration.

The nutritional value of caviar has been debated for years. It has been reported that caviar contains over 40 nutrients, one of which, a vitamin called actylcholine, has been identified as one of the major brain chemicals. Tests have shown that actylcholine produces a greater tolerance to alcoholic beverages, with no hangover. Could this explain why caviar-eating Russians show a remarkable capacity for alcohol? Some people claim that caviar is an aphrodisiac just as others make that claim for oysters eaten raw on the half shells. There is no evidence to prove it.

As the world supply of caviar dwindles at an alarming rate, the price goes up and up. Caviar is now the costliest food on our planet. The scarce sturgeon roe has become the epicurean status symbol. Most caviar consumed in the United States comes from Iran; much of the caviar consumed in Russia also comes from Iran because of the polluted Volga. "Today, a sturgeon in the Volga is like a Czar in the Winter Palace" said a reporter. One fact is clear. We will have to treat caviar with a growing reverence. At $300 to $400 a pound who would not.

Chub

Other names. Bluefin, blackfin, tullibee.
Appearance. The chub is a member of the whitefish family. It has a larger head than the whitefish and a more slender body.
Source. Lakes Superior and Michigan.
Availability fresh. From June to December, with the peak harvest in November and December. Almost the entire catch is smoked as a substitute for whitefish. Only one species, the blackfin, is highly esteemed as a fresh fish.
Average weight. From ⅓ to 2½ pounds (150 g to 1.140 kg).
Trade size.

    Small—over 7 per pound (450 g)
    Medium—5 to 7 per pound
    Large—3 to 4 per pound

Quality. The chub has a very soft flesh; it is excellent when smoked.

Frogs' Legs

Two types of frogs are consumed in the United States—the wild, common uncultivated frog and the cultivated bull frog. Wild common frogs are plentiful in the southern United States. They are not sold commercially. The bull frog, a cultivated product, is the best grade with white tender meat.
Source. Middle West, Florida, Louisiana, Mississippi, and California.
Availability fresh. April to October.
Trade size.

    Small—9 to 12 pairs to a pound
    Medium—6 to 8 pairs to a pound
    Large—4 to 5 pairs to a pound
    Extra large—2 to 3 pairs to a pound

Quality. A white, delicately flavored, tender lean meat.

Lake Herring

Other names. Cisco of Lake Erie, blueback.
Appearance. Several species of lake herring occur mainly in the Great Lakes. Superficially, lake herring resemble sea herring in appearance. They have large scales and the overall coloration is silvery with a pink-to-purple iridescence (see Fig. 4-65).

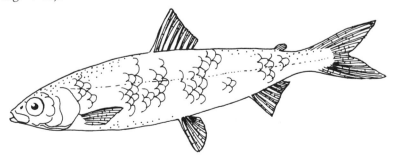

Figure 4-65. Lake Herring.

A Comprehensive Survey of American Fish and Shellfish   **85**

Source. Lakes Superior, Michigan, Huron, and Ontario.
Availability fresh. All year, with the peak harvest in November and December.
Average weight. From ½ to 1 pound (225 to 450 g).
Trade size.

Regular—4 per pound
Large—3 per pound

Quality. Lake herring are fatty fish of excellent quality. The large specimens are often sold as whitefish. Smoked lake herring, also called ciscoes, are usually sold as smoked whitefish.
Disposition. Smoked, fresh, or frozen.

Lake herring production has been declining rapidly in the Great Lakes for many years. The only remaining viable stocks are in the Canadian portion of Lake Superior. In 1986, United States production was less than 300,000 pounds, and the Canadian production approximately 1.2 million pounds. Fifteen years ago, the combined production of Canada and the United States was over 10 million pounds.

Northern Pike

Other names. Lake pickerel, grass pike.
Once this fish was featured in many gourmet dishes created by the greatest European chefs. Quenelles de brochet, known as pike dumplings, are considered a sublime recipe in French cooking. But like many species of high quality, the supply of pike has been depleted. In the United States it has been removed from the commercial species list in many states and reserved exclusively for sport fishermen. In 1986, less than 20,000 pounds were produced in the United States, and less than 400,000 pounds in Canada.
Appearance. Pike have a long body, laterally compressed. The mouth, shaped into a moderately broad and rounded snout, is armed with sharp canine teeth. The dorsal and anal fins are placed far back on the body near the tail. The basic color arrangement of the northern pike is a pattern of light spots on a dark ground, in contrast to their cousins, the muskellunge, which have a pattern of dark markings on a lighter background (see Fig. 4-66).
Trade size. (round)

Regular—½ to 1½ pounds (225 to 680 g)
Jumbo—1½ pounds (680 g) and over

Quality. The meat is lean, firm, and flaky, and of excellent quality.

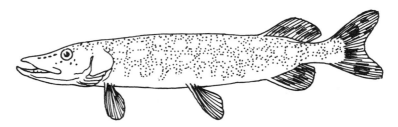

Figure 4-66. Northern Pike.

Sheepshead

Other names. Freshwater drum, white perch, gasperou, gray bass.

Appearance. The freshwater sheepshead is a relative of the marine drum, producing audible sounds of varying amplitude by twanging muscles against its air bladder. Like the saltwater drum, the freshwater species has a strongly arched back. The lower jaw is shorter than the upper. The fish is silvery, somewhat darker above than below.

Source. The freshwater drum is widely distributed. The species is abundant from the Great Lakes, except Lake Superior, to the Gulf and eastern Mexico, with large numbers found in the Mississippi and Red rivers. The largest landings occur mainly in the Great Lakes (Lakes Erie, Huron, and Ontario).

Availability fresh. April, May, and June.

Trade size.

> Small—¾ to 1½ pounds (340 to 680 g)
> Medium—1½ to 5 pounds (680 g to 2.270 kg)
> Large—over 5 pounds (2.270 kg)

Quality. The meat is white and lean, with large coarse flakes. In quality, the fish is similar to the marine species known as black drum. The smaller species, ¾ to 3 pounds (340 g to 1.360 kg), have the finest flavor. The larger ones have a coarse texture.

Steelhead

The migratory rainbow trout is known as a steelhead. It resembles the lake-dwelling form in color when it comes from the sea, but as it proceeds up river and nears spawning time, it becomes dark and spotted. The red band appears, and the fish looks like the mature nonmigratory form, although its body is generally slimmer. It grows to 36 pounds (16.3 kg).

Source. Oregon, Washington, and California.

Lake Sturgeon

Other names. Shortnose sturgeon, common sturgeon, Atlantic sturgeon.

Appearance. Sturgeon originate far back in geologic history and are as primitive as paddlefish. Grayish green in color, it has a sharpened but flattened head, covered with bony plates, and a long pointed snout. Along its back and down its sides are raised scutes; otherwise the fish is scaleless. The heavy, torpedo-shaped body ends with a tail resembling that of a shark, curving upward in an arch that rises well above the hump of its back (see Fig. 4-67).

Source. On the West Coast, white and green sturgeon are caught mainly from

Figure 4-67. Lake Sturgeon.

A Comprehensive Survey of American Fish and Shellfish   **87**

the Columbia River. On the East Coast, a few sturgeon occur in Georgia, South Carolina, and Louisiana, and are sold mostly at the New York Fulton Market.
Best size. Small sturgeon, ranging from 8 to 10 pounds (3.6 to 4.5 kg), are best.
Quality. The flesh has a good quality, very firm and delicately flavored. The lake sturgeon is considered endangered in many areas of the United States and Canada. In 1986, only a few pounds (less than 1,000) were reported in the United States, and less than 30,000 pounds were produced in Canada.
Disposition. The major retail market in North America is for the smoked product. The white sturgeon is sometimes available in fresh steaks and fillets.

Lake Trout

Other names. Mackinaw, togue, longue, Great Lake trout.
Appearance. The lake trout, a member of the salmon family, is the largest trout in American waters. Lake trout vary widely in color with shades of gray and olive predominating. There are variations in the color of the flesh ranging from pale ivory to deep pink. These color differences probably are determined by environment as well as heredity. Much of the body is mottled with grayish white or white spots, and these profuse markings extend over the head and the deeply forked tail (see Fig. 4-68).

Several subspecies of lake trout appear to exist: one is found at moderate depths in the Great Lakes and inland lakes, and another, the siscowet, frequents the deeper waters of Lakes Superior and Michigan. The siscowet, generally considered too oily for ordinary use, is mostly smoked for market.
Source. Commercial fishing for lake trout occurs in the Great Lakes, except for Lake Erie. The catastrophic collapse of lake trout caused by the invasion of sea lamprey was brought under control after extensive research by state agencies of the United States and Canada, and with the cooperation of the Great Lakes Fishery Commission. Lake trout are being restocked in fresh-water lakes with young fish raised in fish hatcheries. Interest also centers on the hybrid splake, a cross between a female lake trout and a male brook trout, which has potential for the future of lake fishery.
Availability fresh. About 80 to 85 percent are caught from May to October.
Average weight. From 2 to 8 pounds (900 g to 3.6 kg).
Trade size.

> No. 1—2 to 4 pounds (900 g to 1.8 kg)
> Medium—4 to 8 pounds (1.8 to 3.6 kg)
> Large—8 to 10 pounds (3.6 to 4.5 kg)

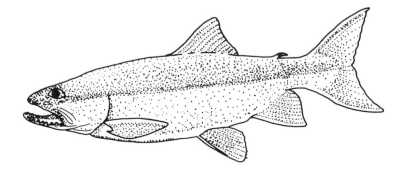

Figure 4-68. Lake Trout.

The 4 to 8 pound, pink fleshed trout are preferred, but the 2 to 4 pound size usually brings the top premium prices.

Quality. Lake trout rank with whitefish as a choice fish. Lake trout have a firm textured flesh that is rich in flavor. The white to pinkish flesh is high in protein and rather fatty.

Rainbow Trout

Appearance. This native American trout is high on the world's list of game fish. Rainbow trout are easily identified by the broad reddish band or "rainbow" that runs along the side of the fish from head to tail. The reddish band blends into a dark olive green on the back, and pure white or silver on the belly. Rainbows sometimes migrate to the ocean where they spend several years. By the time they return to their stream to spawn, they have acquired a grayish tinge from the salt water and are called steelheads (see Fig. 4-69).

Source. The rainbow is a native of the Pacific slope of the Sierras from California to Alaska. It has since been transported to nearly every state in the Union. Trout prefer clear, cool, unpolluted water, and usually are not found in waters lacking these qualities.

Availability fresh. We don't have to rely on the whims of nature to enjoy trout. Modern trout farms raise these tempting fish for our tables. Using modern scientific equipment, trout farms create the best environment and feeding conditions for fast growing, healthy trout. Selective breeding has produced strains of rainbow trout that grow bigger and faster than their wild counterparts. A farmed trout can be fed to yield a pink flesh. A substance derived from carotene, provitamine A, which has no influence on the taste of trout, can be added to the fish diet.

Average sizes. To meet the needs of professionals and consumers, trout are sold whole, weighing 5, 6, 8, or 10 ounces (140, 170, 225, or 280 g).

Trade forms. Because of modern freezing and shipping techniques, frozen rainbow trout are available nationwide almost anytime of the year. All trout are sold with the head and tail attached. Frozen trout are sold fresh frozen, boned, and boned and breaded. Boned trout have the backbone and ribs removed. Boned and breaded trout have the fins, backbone, and ribs removed. Frozen trout are usually sold in 8-ounce (225-g) packages. Each package contains two 4-ounce (110-g) trout. Fresh whole trout are also available on the market.

Quality. The flavor is excellent and the flesh delicate. Trout are highly prized

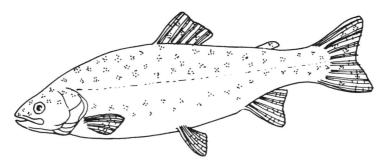

Figure 4-69. Rainbow Trout.

all over the United States, and satisfy the taste of a high percentage of consumers. A survey conducted by Quick Frozen Foods indicates that 90 percent of frozen trout go to the institutional market.

Whitefish

Other names. Lake whitefish, eastern whitefish, inland whitefish.

Appearance. The species, easily recognized by the small short head, is a member of the salmon and trout family. The whitefish is one of the most acclaimed fresh-water fish in the United States. The silver, thick flexible body can be curved gracefully and poached for cold presentation. The roes of females are the same quality as shad roe (see Fig. 4-70).

Source. The largest landings occur in the Great Lakes. Canadian imports of whitefish are also valuable.

Availability fresh. The largest catches occur from May to August.

Average weight. From 2 to 6 pounds (900 g to 2.720 kg). Best weight is 4 pounds (1.8 kg).

Trade size. (mostly drawn)

    No. 1—1½ to 3 pounds (680 g to 1.360 kg)
    Medium—3 pounds (1.360 kg)
    Large—3½ to 4 pounds (1.590 to 1.8 kg)
    Jumbo—4 pounds (1.8 kg) and over

Quality. Whitefish is one of the best fresh-water fish in the United States. The meat is fatty, white, and flaky, and has a fine flavor. Smoked whitefish, a gourmet delight, is available commercially. Smoked ciscoes, chubs, and tullibees are also sold under the name whitefish, but are of lower quality.

Yellow Perch

Other names. Lake perch, ringed perch, striped perch, coon perch.

Appearance. Yellow perch is generally classified as a pan fish. It is one of 19 species of perch, including the walleys, saugers, and darters. The perch has a moderately elongated body that is slightly compressed with a humpback appearance. The coloration is a golden yellow on the sides and white on the belly. Six to eight dark bands extend from the back to below the lateral line (see Fig. 4-71).

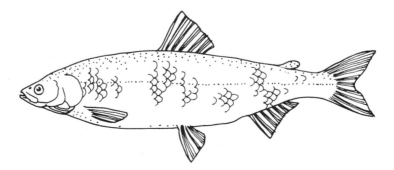

Figure 4-70. Whitefish.

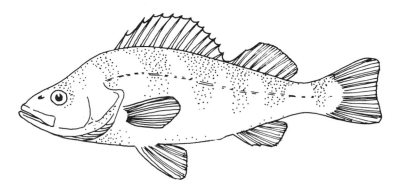

Figure 4-71. Yellow Perch.

Source. Lakes Erie and Michigan produce the major crop, although the yellow perch is widely distributed in lakes and streams from Nova Scotia to South Carolina and in the lakes of the western states.

Availability fresh. Most abundant from April to November.

Average weight. Seldom reach over 1 pound (450 g); usually, the weight varies from ¼ to ¾ pounds (110 to 340 g).

Trade size.

Small—over 4 per pound (450 g)
Medium—4 per pound
Large—3 per pound
Jumbo—½ to ¾ per pound (225 to 340 g)

Quality. Yellow perch is a lean, excellently flavored fish, with firm white meat.

Shellfish

American Lobster

One half of the popular American dish, "Surf and Turf," may be doomed to extinction. The beef is here to stay, but the outlook for the great American lobster is bleak. This lobster is one of the largest of all marine crustaceans; it may also be the meanest. Unquestionably, it is the most valuable, which is the reason it is being overfished to the point of diminishing return.

Although many of the 12,000 New England lobstermen flatly dismiss any suggestion that *Homarus Americanus* is in trouble, the lobster harvest has declined significantly. As a result, the value of lobsters keeps rising dramatically. The National Marine Fisheries Service in Massachusetts lists the lobster as an endangered species.

Lobsters are measured from the eye socket to the end of the carapace, rather than by overall length, because of the difficulty of straightening the tail for measurements. The legal size for lobster varies from 3⅙ inches in Rhode Island, to 3⅜ inches in Maine, New York, and Massachusetts. Ninety percent of the lobsters caught today fall within this size range.

The American lobster, also called the Maine lobster, which ranges from the Maritime Provinces of Canada to the coast of North Carolina, is most

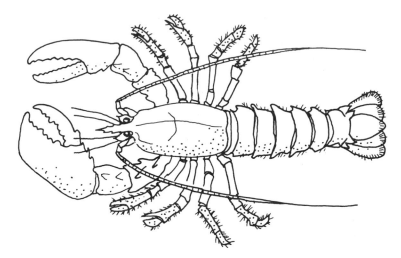

Figure 4-72. American Lobster.

abundant in the waters of Maine and Newfoundland. The average weight is 1 to 5 pounds (450 g to 2.270 kg). Some species grow to 20 pounds (9.1 kg) or more, and may be 50 years old. They make remarkable buffet show pieces. Seawater temperatures and available food affect the growth rate of lobsters tremendously (see Fig. 4-72).

Trade size.

> Select or quarter—1¼ to 3 pounds (560 g to 1.360 kg)
> Large—1½ to 2½ pounds (680 g to 1.140 kg)
> Jumbo—over 3 pounds (1.360 kg)
> Culls—lobsters with only one claw

Disposition. Fresh and frozen

> Cooked—meat or whole
> Specialties—breaded, raw and cooked; canned (deviled, dips, newburg, bisques, soups, spreads, meats, etc.)

The item marketed as lobster tail usually is a spiny lobster (for more details on spiny lobster, see p. 103).

Lobster: Eye-catching Merchandise in Tanks

An effective way to sell lobsters, guaranteed to be live, is to keep them in tanks. Specially constructed tanks are available in various sizes and shapes. Displaying the live seafood in a conspicuous place may create an immediate desire for a fresh lobster dinner. There is something exciting and intriguing about seeing fresh lobsters "swimming" in a tank. The patron selects a particular lobster and has a sense of personal participation in the preparation of dinner. An interesting fact about live lobsters in a tank is that they purify themselves after being in the tank for a few hours.

Questions Asked Most About Lobsters

1. What is tomalley?

Tomalley is the lobster's liver. It turns green when cooked and is considered a delicacy.

2. What is the coral?

Coral is the underdeveloped egg mass of a female lobster. It is the best part of the lobster. Cooking colors the tiny eggs a deep coral or red.

3. How old is a one-pound lobster?

No one knows exactly, but aquarium studies suggest 5 to 7 years.

4. Can a lobster be kept alive in fresh water with ice?

No. Fresh water is lethal. A lobster has salty blood and tissue, which require a seawater environment to maintain life.

5. How long can a lobster live out of water?

Several days if kept in a cool, moist environment. The lobster is a gill breather, and moisture is essential for survival.

6. How many one-pound lobsters are needed for a pound of lobster meat?

Five, on the average.

7. How does a lobster grow?

It sheds its hard shell and grows a new, larger one. Since the skeleton is on the outside, this molting is essential for growth.

8. How many times must a lobster molt before it reaches market size?

Between 20 and 30 molts take place before a lobster reaches market size.

9. Have people been poisoned by eating lobsters that were allowed to die before being cooked? Is it true that a dead lobster deteriorates very rapidly?

Lobsters are not poisonous if they die before cooking, but cooking should not be delayed. Lobsters that have been dead for several hours (usually 6 to 8) are easy to detect when cooked; the tail shrinks to less than half, and it is mushy and unpalatable. If the lobster is "beheaded" before or soon after death, the body meat will stay fresh much longer. Freezing slows deterioration and harmful chemical actions that follow death.

10. How can one tell if a boiled lobster was alive when cooked?

The tail of a dead lobster loses its elasticity and ability to curl under the body. When plunged into boiling water, a live lobster curls under its tail. It remains in that position during and after cooking.

Display Lobsters

Although large specimens are not common, they are available commercially and can be used for exclusive buffet displays. Consider, for example, a 27-pound (12.2 kg) lobster. The amount of meat that can be expected from its tail is about 1 pound, 6 ounces (620 g); the claws yield 4 pounds (1.8 kg) of meat. The result is a 19 percent yield of meat.

Crabs

Among the salt-water fin fishes, salmon, tuna, flounder, and sole dominate the markets. They are abundant and well accepted by the public.

But the bounty from the sea is surely the edible crab family. The blue crab is naturally number one. The tremendous king crab, once considered as junk fish, is also an American favorite. The Florida stone crab is often compared to the sweet, innocent, and delicious meat of the northern lobster.

And then there is the East Coast blue crab's counterpart, the Pacific dungeness, highly prized on the West Coast.

Edible crabs are evenly distributed around the United States. But we have eaten so many of these overfished delicacies that fishermen have had to invade the untouched deep oceans, only to discover that new species abound. Some examples are the snow crab or Tanner crab from Alaska and the Bering Sea, and the Jonah crab, cancer crab, and red crab.

Any of the crabs mentioned previously can be used interchangeably in recipes, unless otherwise specified.

The following crabs are commercially important in the United States:

Blue crab, including the hard crab and soft-shell crab
Dungeness crab
King crab
Stone crab
Snow crab
Green crab
Jonah crab
Red crab
Cancer crab

Blue Crab

This is one of the crabs harvested in large quantities in the United States. The edible blue crab is one of the most abundant crustaceans in the shore waters of the Atlantic, from New Jersey to Florida, and along the Gulf Coast to Texas. Blue crabs have been introduced to Europe where occasional specimens are found from France to Denmark, along the coast of Israel, and in the Nile River Delta. Chesapeake Bay is the major source, producing millions of pounds of hard, soft, and peeler crabs annually. Maryland and Virginia provide almost all the United States supply of soft-shell crabs.

A soft-shell crab is a blue crab that has just emerged from the old shell and has a new, soft, pliable shell. In Maryland, the minimum legal size for soft-shell crab is 3½ inches (8.75 cm) across the shell.

A peeler crab is a hard crab that has a fully formed soft shell beneath the hard outer shell. The recent development of obtaining soft crabs by shedding peelers in land tanks is becoming more widespread. It permits a more efficient handling of crabs.

A buckram is a blue crab with the soft shell that has toughened. A hard crab is a blue crab with a hard shell. There is also the green crab that has very recently shed its shell. Its meat is soft and watery, and it can not be kept legally.

Soft-shell crabs trade sizes.

Spiders (minimum legal size)—3½ inches (8.75 cm) point to point
Hotel prime—4 to 4½ inches (10 to 11.25 cm) point to point
Prime—5 to 5½ inches (12.5 to 13.75 cm) point to point
Jumbo—6 to 7 inches (15 to 17.5 cm) point to point

Marketing of blue crabs. Blue crabs are caught and marketed in both the hard-shelled and soft-shelled stages. Soft-shell crabs are considered a delicacy and

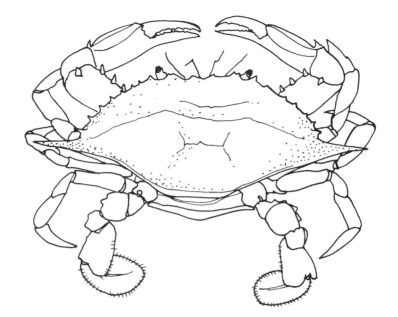

Figure 4-73. Blue Crab.

bring higher prices. The entire body of a soft-shell crab can be eaten after cooking. For details on cleaning soft-shell crabs, refer to Chapter 5.

Hard-shell crabs are either sold alive, or they are steamed and the meat picked from the shell, packed into containers, refrigerated, and sold as fresh crabmeat. Blue crabmeat is marketed as: lump meat—whole lumps from the large body muscles that operate the swimming legs; flake meat—small pieces of white meat from the body; flake and lump—a combination of the first two; and claw meat—a brownish tinted meat from the claws.

Pasteurization of blue crabmeat is another method of preparation for marketing. With pasteurization, the crabs are steamed, and the meat picked from the shell and packed immediately into cans. The cans are hermetically sealed and immersed in a hot-water bath. This method does not alter the taste or texture of the meat, and it is fresh and table ready. Pasteurized crabmeat must be refrigerated until ready to use. Blue crabmeat is seldom frozen or canned. All crabmeat provides excellent high-quality protein, vitamins, and minerals.

Alaskan King Crab

King crabs are the object of intense fishing by the United States in the northern Pacific Ocean and Bering Sea. King crabs are not true crabs like the dungeness crab of the Pacific coast, but are more closely related to hermit crabs. The legs of king crabs are jointed to fold behind the body, not jointed forward like the legs of true crabs. The legs and carapace are spiny, providing protection from predaceous fish (see Fig. 4-74).

King crabs grow as large as 24 pounds (10.8 kg) in 15 years, but commercially caught males average 7 pounds (3.180 kg) and are 8 or 9 years old. Crabs of this size measure about 3 feet (90 cm) with legs extended.

Source. King crabs are located in the eastern Bering Sea and along the entire

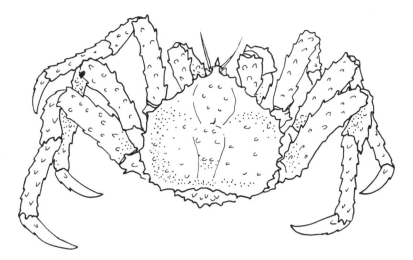

Figure 4-74. King Crab.

Pacific coast of Alaska, including the Aleutian Islands. Major Alaskan fisheries are centered at lower Cook Inlet, Kodiak Island, and the eastern Bering Sea. *Marketing of king crabmeat.* The prime meat of the king crab is in the claws, legs, and shoulders, and this is the only part that is used. These parts are separated, washed, cooked in boiling water, chilled, and washed again before being trimmed, processed, inspected, packaged, and quick frozen, ready for marketing. State law prohibits shipping live king crab out of Alaska. Crab legs may be partially split and sold frozen as "fancy ready split legs." Whole legs are frozen, trimmed, glazed, and marketed as "fancy whole legs." King crabmeat is also available freshly packed, frozen, or canned in 5, 6½, and 13 ounce sizes. The white, sweet, coarse meat is tender and delicate.

Green Crab

This crab has little commercial value. It grows to about 3 inches (7.5 cm) and is found on the East Coast from Maine to New Jersey. The body is dark green or green with yellow mottlings. In Europe, where green crabs are abundant, they are a popular food. In the United States, they are used mostly as bait and considered a nuisance by commercial fishermen since they destroy large quantities of soft-shell clams along the New England coast.

Dungeness Crab

This popular shellfish is found on the Pacific coast. The dungeness supports both a major commercial fishery and a considerable sport fishery.
Appearance. The dungeness crab has a flattened body that is covered by a hard, chitinous, reddish brown spotted shell and two of its ten legs have large pincers. This species is distinguished from other commercially important crabs by legs that are smaller and shorter than its body (see Fig. 4-75).
Source. It inhabits sandy and grassy bottoms below the tidal range, from as far north as Cook Inlet and Prince William Sound south to Magdalena Bay, Mexico.
Availability fresh. Supply starts in April, increases in May, and peaks in June.

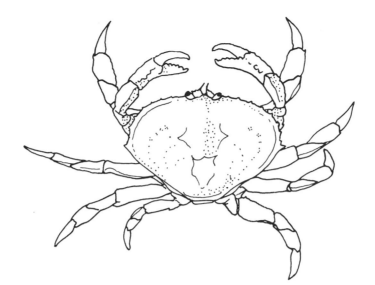

Figure 4-75. Dungeness Crab.

Average size. Commercial fishing regulations vary in different areas. But there is one specific regulation—only male crabs can be taken. The legal widths of the shells are set by states, and vary from 5¾ to 6½ inches (14.3 to 16¼ cm). The crabs reach legal size in 3 to 4 years and live about 8 years.

How is dungeness crabmeat marketed. Dungeness crabmeat is available by the pound, already cooked, with the picked meat from body and claws sold as one grade. Whole, cooked dungeness crab is also available, either fresh or frozen. Some of the crabmeat is canned, usually in 6½-ounce (200-g) cans. Dungeness crabmeat is an excellent source of easily digestable protein and vitamins (especially thiamine, niacin, and riboflavin), but low in fat and calories.

Snow Crab

Until recently, the crab fisheries of the Pacific coast and Alaska were based almost entirely on dungeness and king crabs. Now another crabmeat resource is being harvested—the snow crab.

Other names. Tanner crab, queen crab. The Food and Drug Administration has officially designated these species as snow crab for marketing and labeling purposes. Until recently, snow crabs were an underutilized resource, although their potential may be as great as that of the king crab.

Appearance. Snow crabs belong to the family of spider crabs, so called because their legs are long and slender in proportion to their rounded bodies. Like other crustaceans, snow crabs have hard shells and five pairs of jointed legs. The first pair of legs is always equipped with pincers, varying in size according to the species.

Source. Two species of snow crabs are important to the crab fishery of Alaska. They range throughout the central and southeastern waters off Alaska and down to Washington. Other species occur in waters off Washington and Oregon, and down to northern Mexico.

Availability fresh. Snow crab is only available fully cooked, either frozen or canned.

Trade size. Marketing is much the same as for the king crab. Frozen blocks of snow crabmeat are designated for the trade as:

Supreme—all leg meat
Premium—65 percent leg and 35 percent body meat
Regular—35 percent leg and 65 percent body meat
Salad—all body meat

Quality. Snow crabmeat has a delicate flavor, is tender and succulent, and low in calories. The meat from the legs is white with vivid red coloring on the surface; the body meat is white.

Disposition. The biggest proportion of snow crabmeat is packed in 7½-ounce (225-g) cans for consumer use.

Stone Crab

This member of the mud crab family is a very popular commercial crab on the west coast of Florida, especially Marathon and Key West.

Appearance. The stone crab has an oval-shaped, flattened shell with a purplish to brown or reddish brown color, and brownish mottlings. The large claws have a very hard shell with black tips.

Source. North and South Carolina and the east coast of Florida. Stone crabs reach their peak of abundance and size in Key West and the west coast of Florida. Commercial fishermen are allowed to keep only one claw of the crabs; then they must release their catch. Stone crabs will grow another claw within days, usually on the full moon or new moon. This method avoids the complete depletion of the limited stone crab fishery.

Availability. In Florida, where 90 percent of the stone crabs are harvested, the season starts on October 15 and ends on April 15.

Quality. The flesh of the stone crab is rich and very delicate, similar to the claws of northern lobster. It is the most prized of all crabs. Stone crab claws are sold frozen and cooked.

How is Crabmeat Marketed?

Crabmeat extracted from different species, mainly rock and hard-shell blue crabs, is sold cooked, chilled, or pasteurized, and by the pound, according to its body location.

Lumpmeat comes from the large muscles that operate the back fins. It is white and is considered the best grade.
Flakemeat comes from the remaining portion of the body. It is also white.
Claw meat comes from the crab claws. It is dark in color. Claw fingers are also available and are used primarily as appetizers for cocktails.
Body and leg meat, from the dungeness or Pacific crabs, is taken from both body and legs. It is a good grade of meat.

Canned crabmeat grades are: fancy, choice, passed A, and fair. Fresh hard-shell crabs sold commercially must be alive or they are unfit for consumption and should be discarded.

Norway or Icelandic Lobster or Lobsterette

This imported species is remotely related to the American lobster. The Norway or Icelandic lobster has a long tail, large protuberant eyes, and elongated

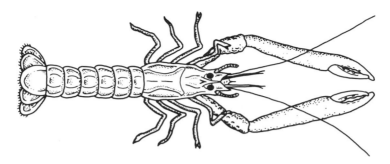

Figure 4-76. Lobsterette.

claws with sharp teeth. Its color varies from brick red to salmon red. The color does not change with cooking. This species is much smaller than the lobster and very rarely exceeds 9 inches (22.5 cm) in length when fully grown (see Fig. 4-76).

The Norway or Icelandic lobster is a delicacy and is known for its sweet flavor and tender texture. Only small amounts are sold on the United States markets. The frozen tails vary in size and are adaptable to a myriad of recipes.

Shrimp

"If there is anything out of the ocean with more virtues than shrimp, I'd be hard put to name it," said Craig Claiborne of the *New York Times*. Shrimp is the most valuable United States fishery, with an impressive harvest of over 400 million pounds (heads on) in 1986 that was worth a record $600 million. We consume over 1.5 million pounds of shrimp daily in the United States. One would think, based on these stunning figures, that the United States shrimp fishing industry would be self-sufficient. However, Americans love shrimp and 400 million pounds were not enough. Record imports of 400 million pounds of shrimp, mostly frozen and canned, came from 68 countries. *Appearance.* The shrimp is a ten-legged crustacean that acquired its name because of its size. The word *shrimp* was derived from the Middle English word *shrimpe,* meaning "puny person," and the Swedish *skrympa,* meaning "to shrink." Like other crustaceans, the shrimp's skeleton is on the outside of the body and, in order to grow, it casts off its shell and replaces it with a new one.

There are three species of southern shrimp that are commercially important; all three are members of the family, *Penaeidae.* They are:

1. The common shrimp or white shrimp
2. The brown shrimp (see Fig. 4-77)
3. The pink or white spotted shrimp (see Fig. 4-78)

The tiny, North Pacific shrimp and the northern shrimp are the same species. Another species, also called North Pacific shrimp, is caught in Washington, Oregon, and California. Of the three varieties, southern shrimp are usually the largest and North Pacific shrimp are the smallest.

Two other underutilized species are landed in significant quantities; the royal red shrimp in the deep waters of the continental shelf, and in the Gulf and South Atlantic region, and the rock shrimp, easily distinguished by its hard, rough sculptured shell.

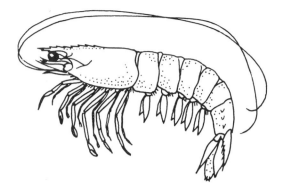

Figure 4-77. Pink Shrimp.

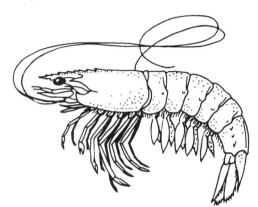

Figure 4-78. Brown Shrimp.

Color is not a very reliable means of distinguishing the species of shrimp. White shrimp are generally grayish white and are variously tinged about the tail. Brown shrimp are usually reddish brown in color, with tinges of blue or purple on the tail section. Pink or brown spotted shrimp vary greatly in coloration according to locality. Along the Atlantic coast, they are usually lighter in color than brown shrimp; on the Tortugas grounds, they are pink; and along the northern Gulf Coast, they are often lemon yellow. The brown spot on the side of the abdomen or tail is usually present. Royal shrimp are usually deep red all over, but sometimes are only grayish pink.

Source. The northern shrimp is found in the offshore waters of Maine and Massachusetts. The tiny, North Pacific shrimp is found along the coastlines of California, Oregon, Washington, and Alaska. The southern shrimp is taken from waters of the Gulf and South Atlantic states.

The Gulf states, principally Texas and Louisiana, account for over 80 percent of the total landings of shrimp. On the Pacific coast, Alaska and Oregon are the leading states.

Availability fresh. Shrimp are in season all year but are most expensive from January to April. During this season, they are in prime condition because the shells are harder and the flesh firmer. Peak landings occur in the Gulf states, from August to October; in the Middle Atlantic states, from May to August; in New England, from June to September; and on the West Coast, from July to September. The major harvest is frozen and beheaded.

Trade size. Shrimp are sold by weight and number per pound (count), and are usually frozen headless. The commercial count (number per pound) and descriptive size names, if used, conform to one of the following categories:

Commercial count (number of shrimp per pound)	Descriptive size name
under 10	extra colossal
10–15	colossal
16–20	extra jumbo
21–25	jumbo
26–30	extra large
31–35	large
36–42	medium large
43–50	medium
51–60	small
61–70	extra small
over 70	tiny

Quality. Shrimp are an excellent source of high-quality protein, vitamins, and minerals. They are low in fat and calories and are easily digested. The edible part of the shrimp is the tail section. Raw shrimp are often referred to as "green shrimp" at the retail level. Although raw shrimp vary in color, the cooked product is pink-white, and the flavor and nutritional values are the same. Regardless of size and variety, shrimp can be used interchangeably in most recipes.

Disposition. Commercially, shrimp are processed and sold in different forms:

Raw headless
Peeled and deveined, cooked or raw
Breaded raw or breaded cooked
Cooked whole
Cooked specialties—soups, sauces, gumbos, stuffed, croquettes, canned
Smoked and sun dried

The Elusive Rock Shrimp

The rock shrimp is an indisputable member of the shrimp family, although its tough, rigid exoskeleton is not dainty like the thin shell of its cousin, the common or pink shrimp. In addition to the hard shell, the texture of the meat of the rock shrimp is like that of a lobster. The flavor is somewhere between lobster and shrimp (see Fig. 4-79).

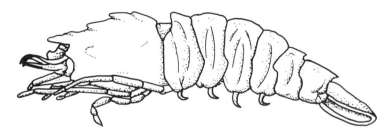

Figure 4-79. Rock Shrimp.

A Comprehensive Survey of American Fish and Shellfish **101**

This species of shrimp often escapes the attention of the average consumer in southwest Florida, where it is available in markets during the winter months. Rock shrimp are brought up in shrimper's nets along with regular shrimp. But rock shrimp are far more perishable than either the Florida spiny lobster or its southern shrimp relatives. Therefore, they are marketed frozen raw, as either whole or split tails.

The largest size available is usually 21 to 25 per pound. Rock shrimp are delicious broiled in the shell. However, the cleaning instructions are different when this method of cooking is used. To clean the whole rock shrimp tails for broiling, place the tails on a cutting board with the swimmerettes exposed. With a sharp knife, cut between the swimmerettes through the meat to the hard shell. Spread the shell until it lies flat, and wash thoroughly in cold water to remove all the sand vein.

Cooking rock shrimp. Rock shrimp cook faster than other shrimp and require very close attention to avoid overcooking. When overcooked, the meat becomes rubbery. To cook approximately 1½ pounds (680 g) of raw, peeled, deveined rock shrimp, add 2 tablespoons salt to 1 quart (1 l) of boiling water, and simmer for about a minute. Drain and rinse in cold water for two minutes. Remove any particles of sand vein. Serve with melted butter, with a sauce, or use in any shrimp recipe in chapter 14.

According to the National Marine Fisheries Service in Washington, evaluations of exploratory data on Florida's east coast indicate a resource of 5.7 million pounds of rock shrimp. The exploration of deeper waters in the west central Atlantic reveals the presence of many other shrimp in commercial concentrations. The royal red shrimp are the most abundant in depths of 200 to 250 fathoms (1 fathom equals 6 feet), and the estimated crop is over 1.5 million pounds. But existing gears are ineffective in depths over 150 fathoms.

Another deep-water shrimp, the small speckled shrimp, is probably more abundant than the red shrimp with which it is associated in distribution. As yet, its small size has attracted no commercial interest. In Europe, a similar tiny shrimp has been sold commercially for many years. It is called *bouquet* in France. The shrimp are cooked and served whole.

Imports from Spain and North Africa have introduced the giant scarlet prawn to the United States consumer. The day may come when United States shrimp trawlers will catch this species off the Gulf of Mexico and the Caribbean at depths of 350 to 500 fathoms. The deep red imported shrimp, also called shrimp royale, are sold frozen, headless raw. Their sizes vary from jumbo (7 shrimp per pound) to 24 extra small per pound. Spanish shrimp have a delicious taste and a firm white meat. The scarlet shell of this shrimp lends itself to colorful buffet presentations.

The tedious work of manually peeling shrimp is over. The peeling machine processes over one thousand pounds of shrimp an hour, and has revolutionized both the canning and freezing industry. Automated cooking and flash freezing has also greatly improved the transfer of shrimp to food operations and consumers throughout the country.

The Difference Between Prawns, Crayfish, and Shrimp

Often, common names are used loosely and inconsistently with the shrimp family. The prawn of Great Britain and other countries is essentially the same as the shrimp of the United States. In this country, shrimp includes all crustaceans of the *Natantia* group, regardless of size. Crayfish or crawfish are names given to both a fresh-water crustacean and the salt-water lobster.

Spiny Lobster

Other names. Crawfish, crayfish, sea crawfish, rock lobster.

Appearance. The spiny lobster is related to crabs, shrimp and crayfish. Unlike the American lobster, it lacks claws. In the western Atlantic, there are six species of spiny lobsters. It is beautifully marked with brown, yellow, orange, green, and blue mottled over the upper part and underside of the tail. Unfortunately, whole live spiny lobsters are uncommon; but they make remarkable buffet displays when presented whole (see Fig. 4-80).

Source. Commercially, important relatives of spiny lobsters occur in California, the Mediterranean, South Africa, and Australia. In the United States, they are abundant in the Caribbean Sea, in South Florida, as far as the Bahamas, Cuba, and British Honduras, and off the coast of California.

Availability fresh. The peak season occurs from December to May.

Average weight. The live spiny lobster averages 2 to 5 pounds (900 g to 2.270 kg).

Trade size. (tails)

   Small—6 to 9 ounce (170 to 255 g)
   Medium—9 to 12 ounce (255 to 340 g)
   Large—12 to 16 ounce (340 to 450 g)
   Jumbo—over 1 pound (450 g)

Quality. The spiny lobster offers a high-quality protein, with snow-white, lean meat. Large quantities of spiny lobsters are imported into the United States annually. The South African or Australian lobsters are considered best, followed by the California and Cuban species. Florida spiny lobster is considered fair (see Figs. 4-81 and 4-82).

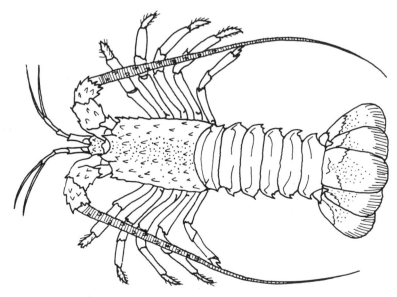

Figure 4-80. Spiny Lobster.

A Comprehensive Survey of American Fish and Shellfish   **103**

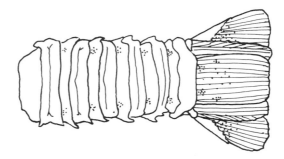

Figure 4-81. Western Australian Spiny Lobster Tail.

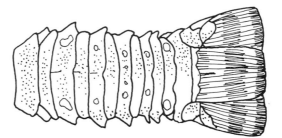

Figure 4-82. Florida or Cuban Spiny Lobster Tail.

Crayfish

Crayfish, crawfish, Dixie lobster, and mini-lobster are some of the names given to these creatures. This delicious fresh-water crustacean is highly prized in Louisiana, where over 90 percent of the nation's yield is produced and 85 percent is consumed. Crayfish are also found in West Coast markets, in Oregon and Washington. Minnesota, Wisconsin, and West Virginia also practice crayfish culture (see Fig. 4-83).

Researchers at Louisiana State University (LSU) have been working for several years to strengthen this industry. The wild crayfish crop has always been erratic, with bumper crops occurring only about two years in five. The red swamp crayfish, which makes up 90 percent of the commercial catch, is very adaptable to environmental conditions. About two dozen species are scattered over several states. For many years, crayfish culture has been practiced in southern Louisiana, yielding good returns ranging from 200 to 800 pounds (91 to 362 kg) per acre. Today, crayfish farm acreage numbers more than 40,000 acres. Rice fields for crayfish farming represent a multiple use of acreage. In 1987, several million pounds of crayfish were exported to France, Denmark, and other European countries.

Although marketing specialists are studying existing channels of commerce for crayfish, they are rarely found in eastern markets. There the demand is greater in gourmet restaurants.

Commercial crayfish farming has intensified due to increased demand, especially for Louisiana crayfish. In Europe, the supply cannot meet the

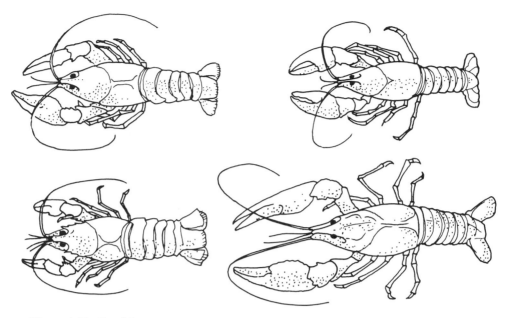

Figure 4-83. Crayfish.

demand. Europeans have many ways of preparing crayfish, and can transform them into culinary marvels.

Abalone

Abalone are marine gastropods or snails, and are related to chitons, clams, oysters, squid, octopuses, and other mollusks. The abalone is one of the most primitive in form and structure, and inhabits the temperate and tropical seas of the world. The greatest variety of species occurs off the coast of Australia. In the United States, abalone are found on the Pacific coast, mainly in California.

Appearance. This univalve (with the generic name *haliotis* from the Greek meaning "sea ear") has an ear-shaped shell that protects its body. The muscle adheres to rocks and in crevices where it feeds on algae (see Fig. 4-84).

Abalone have been exploited throughout the world for their shells and the eating quality of the muscles. The flavor of the muscle is unique. So is its texture—tough and rubbery. The meat must be tenderized and pounded with a wooden mallet. Abalone steaks are sliced across, parallel to the bottom of the foot, with each steak about ⅜ inch (½ cm) thick. Under no circumstances should abalone steaks be overcooked; they become rubbery and lose their culinary value. A thin abalone steak, sauteed in butter, is cooked about 30 seconds on each side, over intense heat. Connoisseurs often favor abalone in its raw state, cut into cubes and marinated.

Eight species of abalone appear on the West Coast: red, black, green, pink, thread, white, flat, and pinto.

   Red abalone. The largest of all abalone, it reaches over 11 inches (27.5 cm) in
      diameter. The outside color of the shell is dull brick red. It ranges from

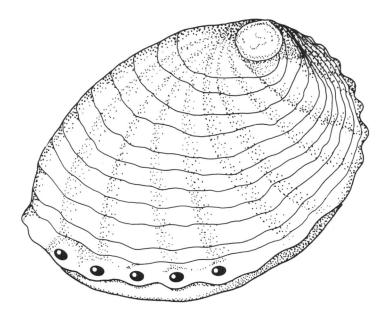

Figure 4-84. Abalone.

Sunset Bay, Oregon, to Baja, California. This is the most important commercial abalone. Almost the entire catch is sold fresh frozen to restaurants. Those sold fresh in fish markets command the highest prices.

Green abalone. Once very abundant around the Channel Islands, they are taken by skindivers and sportsmen in southern California. They frequently harbor a parasitic worm that is unsightly and tends to discourage the commercial market for them.

Black abalone. This species is of little importance to commercial fishermen because of its dark meat and small size.

Flat abalone. They range in size from 3 to 5 inches (7.5 to 12.5 cm). They are taken by commercial divers and, due to their small size, sell for high prices.

White abalone. Found in depths up to 150 feet, they are commercially included with the pink abalone. They occur off the coast of California. The body is typically colored yellow to orange, and the meat is quite tender.

Threaded and pink abalone and Pinto. They are the least common species and seldom appear in the commercial catch.

The best quality abalone are the red, white, and pink species.

California law prohibits the canning of abalone and shipping of fresh and frozen abalone out-of-state. In 1987, the commercial harvest in California was over 2 million pounds.

Clams

Along the Atlantic coast, the three species of clams that rank highest in commercial importance are: hard clams, surf clams, and soft-shell clams. The Pacific coast clams include: razor clams, butter clams, littleneck clams, Atlantic soft-shell clams (transplanted), and the geoducks (see Fig. 4-85).

Figure 4-85. Clams—Cherrystones and Little Necks.

Appearance. The bivalve shells that encase the clam's body are joined together at the back by a hinge ligament that is usually visible from the outside. The shells, while varying in shape, are composed of three layers. The outer layer is often varnishlike; the thick middle layer is somewhat chalky; and the inner layer, which is usually hard, is often iridescent or lustrous. Concentric rings are laid down on the shells as the clam grows. Shell colors vary because they are affected by the habitat (see Fig. 4-86).

The two most prominent features of the clam's body are the foot, or adductor muscle, and the siphon or neck. The muscular foot aids the clam in digging in the soft sand or mud and in opening and closing the valves. The retractable siphon is a tubelike extension that conducts water in and out of the clam.

Hard Clams

Other names. Quahog, quohog, quauhaug.

The hard clam is distributed along the Atlantic coast, from Florida to the Gulf of St. Lawrence. It is also found along the Gulf of Mexico to the Yucatan Peninsula. New York leads in production, accounting for approximately 45 percent. The next highest producer is New Jersey, followed by Virginia, Rhode Island, and Massachusetts.

Marketing. Hard clams are sold under three names corresponding to their size. The largest and cheapest clams are marketed as "chowders," and are used mostly for chowders, clam fritters, stuffed clams, et cetera. "Cherrystones," the medium sized and medium priced clams, are used to some extent in the half-shell trade. This size is used exclusively for baked clams and the popular New England clam bake. "Little necks" are the smallest and most expensive of

Figure 4-86. Clams—Soft Shell, Surf, Quahogs, and Ocean Quahogs.

the legal sized hard clams. They are used in the half shells and as steamed clams, the same way the blue mussel and the soft-shell clam are cooked.

Depending on traditional practices in a given locale, hard clams are marketed not only by size, but by the "piece," by count per volume, by weight per volume, or by weight or volume alone. This causes considerable confusion when the clams are shipped interstate. The Marine Fisheries Commission has recommended the adoption of a uniform minimum legal size and the standardization of clam count and/or weight of clams marketed in any given volume.

As with any fish or shellfish, pollution presents the greatest threat to the hard clam resource. The transplanting of clams to certified clean waters and depuration would undoubtedly increase the price of clams. The ultimate solution would be the control of pollution.

Soft-Shell Clams

Soft-shell clams are found from Labrador to North Carolina and in a number of scattered locations on the West Coast. New England states are the main producers. Unlike the hard and surf clams, these popular clams have elongated shells that are very thin and brittle. The soft-shell clams cannot close tightly because their long necks extend beyond the shells.

Surf Clams

The surf clams are also known as skimmer, beach, giant, sea, hen, or bar clams. This species makes up the largest volume caught along the Atlantic shores, but it is not as valuable as the hard or soft-shell clams. Practically all canned clams are surf clams.

Quality. Clams, one of our most delicious shellfish, have a nutritional value similar to mussels and oysters. They are high in protein and low in calories. They contain iodine, iron, and other minerals. A half-dozen cherrystones provides an excellent supply of protein, only 70 calories, and a level of iron comparable to that in a serving of beef liver.

Buying clams. Clams can be bought in three forms: in the shell, shucked, and canned. Clams in the shell should be alive when purchased. Hard clams with gaping shells that do not close when handled are dead clams and should be discarded. With other varieties, there will be some constriction of the siphon or neck when the clam is touched. Fresh clams in the shell, stored in the refrigerator at about 40°F (4.5°C), will live for several days.

Shucked clams, or clam meats that have been removed from the shells, are generally sold by the pint or quart. Shucked clams should be plump, with a clear liquor, and free from shell particles. Fresh shucked clams should be refrigerated or packed in ice. When properly handled, they will stay fresh for 7 to 10 days. Shucked clams are also packaged and quick frozen, making them available all year. Frozen clams should not be thawed until ready to use. Once thawed, they should not be refrozen.

Canned clams are packed in various can sizes, whole, minced, or as chowder. Clam juice, broth, and nectar are also available canned or bottled.

Clam specialties available commercially are: breaded (raw or cooked), strips, cakes and patties, stuffed, burgers, croquettes, sticks, cocktails, and chowders.

Note: For instructions on shucking clams, see Chapter 5.

The Geoduck Clam

Other names. King clam, gweduc, gooey-duck.

Appearance. The geoduck is mostly neck. Even the mantle bulges out of the shell, which is always too small to contain the entire clam. Geoducks are the most impressive clams in United States waters, and are believed to be second in size only to the giant clam found in the East Indies. The largest geoduck ever found weighed 13 pounds (5.9 kg). The average clam weighs 3 pounds (1.360 kg), and yields 1½ pounds (680 g) of meat.

Source. Geoducks are found all along the West Coast, but they are most abundant in Washington's Puget Sound. These giant clams live from 18 inches (45 cm) to 6 feet (1.80 meters) below the surface of the beach, or underwater, beneath the surface of the bottom.

Harvesting. Commercial harvesting is strictly by diving, using hand-operated equipment. Divers work at depths of 10 to 60 feet, with hoses that deliver water under pressure to them. This water jet is directed into the soil to dislodge the geoducks. Each diver collects 300 to 500 geoducks per day. According to a survey made by the State of Washington, millions of geoducks live beneath the sands in fairly deep water and could be harvested without endangering future supplies.

Uses. Geoduck meat is juicy and rich, and has a fine flavor. Enthusiasts say that geoduck steak compares in taste and texture to abalone, but is sweeter. These clams are marketed in numerous forms, including frozen breast and neck steaks, frozen and canned minced meats, frozen and canned chunks, and canned smoked chunks. They are also available fresh on request.

The steaks can be served pan fried or grilled; the minced clams are used in dips or chowder; and the canned chunks and smoked canned chunks are party snacks.

If the clams are purchased fresh, dipping them in hot water will open the shell and loosen the skin. The skin and stomach are discarded, and the clams are then washed thoroughly and rinsed in cold water. It is possible to cut three steaks from one geoduck—one from the breast and two from the neck. These are best breaded and fried. The remaining meat can be ground and used for clam fritters or chowder.

Sunray Venus Clam

Appearance. The shell of the sunray venus clam is elongated, compressed, and glossy-smooth with a thin, varnishlike, protective covering. Its color is dull pink to bluish purple with broken radial bands of darker color. The interior of the shell is a flat white with a blush of red over the central area.

Source. The sunray venus clam ranges from South Carolina to Florida and the Gulf states. Its attractive shell is popular with shell collectors and tourists. Commercial harvesting began in 1967; presently, the largest producing bed in Florida is off Port St. Joseph.

Average weight. Mature sunrays, from 4 to 5 years old, measure 5 to 7 inches (12.5 to 17.5 cm) in length.

Because of a plentiful supply of clams in general, processors of the sunray venus have encountered difficulty in marketing their higher priced, higher quality clam. Processors are conducting a consumer education program to convince shoppers that sunray venus clams are worth the extra pennies, partly because they come from sandy bottoms (no mud) and partly because they are hand-shucked and hand-packed and carry no grit. They are also sweeter and more tender than most other clams.

Uses. Sunray venus clams are currently available only in 5- and 10-pound (2.270- and 4.5-kg) frozen minced blocks. These raw meats are of high quality and useful for chowder, fritters, patties, dips, and clam loaf.

Ocean Quahog

Other names. Mahogany quahog, mahogany clam, black quahog.

Appearance. The ocean quahog has a black or chestnut shell that distinguishes it from all other mollusks of similar size and shape. Fresh ocean quahog meats, raw and cooked, vary in color from brown to gray.

Source. The ocean quahog was considered strictly a European species. But today, thanks to NMFS resource research, it is known to range from the Arctic Ocean to Cape Hatteras, North Carolina. Though ocean quahogs are found in depths of about 6 to 90 fathoms (1 fathom equals 6 feet or 180 cm), the best catches are made at depths of 18 to 24 fathoms. The clams are harvested year round with a hydraulic sea clam dredge.

Average size. Ocean quahogs average ½ pound (225 g) in weight, and 3½ to 4 inches (8.75 to 10 cm) in length.

Processing ocean quahog. For a long time, one disadvantage of ocean quahogs was the great amount of time and effort required for hand shucking, and the high costs that resulted. The ocean quahog has an extremely hard shell that is completely closed, with no easily accessible opening for a knife to penetrate. Even opening this clam with steam under pressure (a technique used commercially to open other species of clams) is unsatisfactory because of unpleasant effects on the meat. Now the clams are being opened with microwave energy. Experiments have shown that microwave opening of clams is feasible. This breakthrough should result ultimately in lower prices for the consumer.

Uses. Ocean quahogs are darker in color and have a stronger flavor and aroma than other clams. They are particularly suitable for Manhattan or New England chowders, and they can also be used successfully in poultry stuffing, patties, deviled clams, sausage, et cetera.

Mussels

At last, mussels have become a fashionable food in the United States, and found the popularity they rightfully deserve. European cuisines have been taking advantage of the virtues of mussels for years—steamed in wine and shallots in the French manner, stewed with garlic or in tomato-laced broth, as they are in Italy and Spain—and now, American cuisine is quickly catching up with the blue mussel growing industry. As the demand for mussels keeps growing, the raising of farmed mussels has become a successful venture especially in Maine. The Great Eastern Mussel Farms in Tenants Harbor, Maine, and other farms, produce top quality mussels for United States markets. Great Eastern has become one of the largest growers and harvesters of blue mussels in the United States. Their mussel culture is patterned after the traditional underwater-bed mussel farms of Europe, especially The Netherlands, France, and Spain.

Appearance. The mussel is a bivalve mollusk. The only edible species is the blue mussel. The shell is dark blue in color and the inside has shades of violet and white (see Fig. 4-87).

Source. Mussels are abundant on the New England coast. Farmed mussels represent a booming industry in Maine where the production is highest and the quality superior. Mussels are often found in clusters, attached to rocks, gravels, and sea walls by threads or beards that the mollusks secrete.

Availability fresh. The peak season occurs during fall, winter, and spring. Mussels spawn during late spring and early summer, at which time they are whitish and watery.

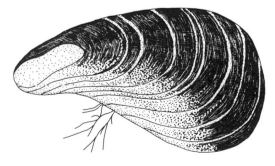

Figure 4-87. Mussel.

Quality. The mussel is high in protein and low in fat (2 percent). It is rich in vitamins and minerals, iron, calcium, and phosphorus.

Consumers should be wary when buying fresh mussels. Uncounted millions of mussels from the intertidal areas of the New England coast are not worth harvesting. They are slow growing, lack sufficient meat, and often contain a large number of crude pearls that make them unsuitable for marketing, either fresh or canned. Farmed mussels, calibrated, scrubbed, with a low insidence of pearls are by far the best.

What consumers should beware of is raw mussels whose shells are open. These "gapers," as they are called, can be contaminated with parasites and should not be eaten. Mussels which ramain closed after cooking are presumed to have been dead before cooking and therefore unfit for consumption.

Octopus

In the United States, octopus will probably be one of the last marine creatures to gain acceptance as food. Actually, they are in a class with squid and very much appreciated in Spain, Portugal, and the Orient, where large amounts are consumed.

Appearance. Octopuses are mollusks and, like squid, have an ink sack that they discharge when attacked. The globular body is extended by eight long arms covered with suction cups. Octopuses are well armed to capture shellfish like clams, abalone, and scallops that are part of their diets. No wonder octopus meat is sweet and has excellent food value (see Fig. 4-88).

Source. The common octopus is abundant on the West Coast from Alaska to Baja California. A different species occurs on the East Coast, where it ranges from New England to the Gulf of Mexico.

Marketing. Octopus is marketed fresh or frozen. It is usually gutted and dressed.

There are many European and Oriental recipes. The ink sack is sometimes used to season and flavor the dishes. Cooking methods used for squid are often applied to octopus.

Oysters

The American oyster is a bivalve mollusk belonging to the genus *crassostrea,* which has other members in various parts of the world. In the United States, the West Coast oyster, imported from Japan, is a representative of the genus; the eastern or Atlantic oyster is another.

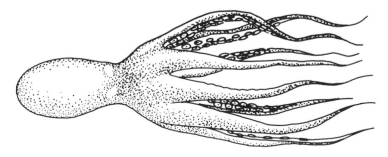

Figure 4-88. Octopus.

The four species of commercially important oysters are:

1. The Japanese or Pacific oyster
2. The European oyster
3. The eastern or Atlantic oyster
4. The olympia oyster

Appearance. True oysters are distinguished by dissimilar lower and upper shells. These shells, or valves, are hinged together by a complex elastic ligament. The upper valve is normally flat, while the lower is concave, providing space for the body of the oyster. The two valves create a watertight seal when the oyster closes, providing the shell is not damaged or broken. Near the center of the oyster's body is an adductor muscle, attached to both valves, which controls the opening and closing of the shell (see Fig. 4-89).

Japanese or Pacific oyster. This oyster grows in coastal waters from Alaska to northern California. The biggest production area is in the Puget Sound, Gray's Harbor, and Willapa Harbor areas of Washington. This oyster is grown from seed imported from Japan. The Pacific oyster is now the principal commercial species on the West Coast.

European oyster. The European or common oyster is established in Maine, and is grown experimentally on the West Coast.

Eastern oyster. Also known as the Chesapeake Bay oyster and Virginia oyster, it is the principal commercial oyster of the East Coast.

Olympia oyster. Also known as the western oyster, it is native to the Pacific coast. The yield of this species has declined because of predators, water pollution, and increased production costs. Some olympias are still available and it is hoped that conservation methods will increase the cultivation of this species.

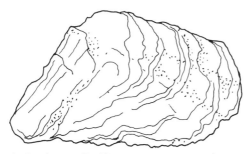

1. Japanese or Pacific oyster.

2. European oyster.

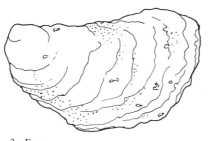

3. Eastern oyster.

4. Olympia oyster.

Figure 4-89. Oysters.

A Comprehensive Survey of American Fish and Shellfish   **113**

Oyster harvesting. A number of methods are used in harvesting oysters. In some areas, where there are natural oyster beds, no mechanical methods are allowed and the oysters are harvested by handpicking during low water or by manual tongs. If the oysters are plentiful, a tonger may take 25 to 30 bushels a day. In other areas, such as the public grounds of Chesapeake Bay and Connecticut, only hand-operated dredges are permitted. Privately owned or leased oyster beds are harvested by large machine-hoisted dredges, or by suction dredges that operate like a vacuum cleaner. Suction dredges are very efficient in carrying oysters and other materials up from the bottom to the conveyor on the deck of the dredge boat. In addition to harvesting oysters, the suction dredge helps to clear the beds of starfish, mussels, and other enemies of oysters. The escalator or scooptype harvester is effective in shallow waters.

Oyster farming has been practiced for several years in Delaware Bay and Chesapeake Bay to avoid the parasites that destroy oysters (the most destructive is the MSX). Today, oysters are produced under controlled conditions in commercial hatcheries. It is reasonable to anticipate that healthy oysters eventually will be abundant on the United States market, although production has been declining.

Marine waters producing oysters must have the same high quality as fresh drinking water; in all poor quality waters, the taking of oysters is prohibited. Several million acres of water are controlled by the Atlantic States Marine Fisheries Commission to ensure the production of healthy oysters.

The day is coming when a fast-growing oyster of uniform size and shape will be mass produced. It will be a great achievement! After all, is there anything better than a healthy, freshly opened oyster served on the half shell? *Availability.* Oysters are edible all year although they are at their peak from October to May. Spawning occurs during the warm summer months and, to most people, they are unpalatable at that time.

Trade size. (Eastern or Atlantic oyster, in shell)

Small (bluepoints)—320 to 400 per bushel
Half shell—280 to 320 per bushel
Medium—200 to 240 per bushel
Large (counts or box)—120 to 160 per bushel

Never allow oysters to reach room temperature. The best temperature is 39°F (4°C). Keep them away from sunlight. If properly handled, they will keep 7 to 10 days. Never allow oysters to freeze. Do not refrigerate in water. Discard any open oyster or any bad-smelling oyster. Such oysters are dead and are poisonous. Do not open oysters more than 5 minutes before serving on the half shell.

Northern oysters with broad, thin, tough shells are superior to the southern oysters, which have thick, spongy shells and an inferior flavor.
Quality. Nutritionally, the oyster is a gold mine, comparable to the food value of the truffle. The underground fungus and the oyster have a similar composition: 72 percent water, 8 to 10 percent protein, 4 percent fat, 12 to 14 percent carbohydrates, and 3 to 5 percent mineral substances. Oysters contain large amounts of iodine, phosphorus, calcium, and iron essential to a balanced diet. Oysters are highly recommended by doctors to patients with anemia.
Disposition. Fresh and frozen

Eastern—shucked, steamed, and specialties (breaded, raw and cooked, and pies, stews, stuffed, etc.)
Pacific—shucked and specialties (breaded, raw and cooked, and stews)
Western—shucked
Canned—regular (eastern and Pacific)
Specialties—smoked, stews, and stew bases

Scallops

Appearance. The scallop is a mollusk so named because of its fluted and scalloped shell. The shells of young scallops are particularly beautiful; the outside is delicately colored, sometimes having pink, white, or darker color variations (see Fig. 4-90).

Scallops, like clams and oysters, are mollusks having two shells. They differ, however, in that they are active swimmers. The scallop swims freely through the waters and over the ocean floor by snapping its shells together. This action results in the development of an oversized muscle called the "eye," and this sweetly flavored muscle is the only part of the scallop eaten by Americans. Europeans, in contrast, eat the muscle and the delicious pink roe attached to it. The creamy white muscle combined with the pink roe is as colorful as it is tasty.

Varieties of scallops. The New England sea scallop is the most commercially important scallop in the United States. It has a saucer-shaped shell and grows as large as 8 inches (20 cm) in diameter; the muscle or eye sometimes reaches 2 inches (5 cm) across.

The bay scallop is much less plentiful but greatly desired by scallop fanciers. It reaches a maximum size of about 4 inches (10 cm) in diameter with a muscle about ½ inch across. The bay scallop shell is similar to that of the sea scallop but is smaller and more grooved, and the edges are more serrated.

A new fishery has been developed for the calico scallop, located off Florida and in the Gulf of Mexico. The calico scallop is closely related to the bay scallop, although slightly larger. It gets its name from the mottled or calico appearance of the shells.

The discovery of a new and potentially important source of sea scallops in the cold waters surrounding Alaska is particularly interesting. This species,

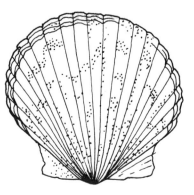

Figure 4-90. Scallop.

A Comprehensive Survey of American Fish and Shellfish **115**

found as far south as Oregon, is different than the sea scallop found in New England waters.

Source. On the East Coast, the largest source comes from the North and Middle Atlantic states. Most of the catch is landed in New Bedford, Massachusetts. Bay scallops are found from New England to the Gulf of Mexico. Scallops cannot close their shells tightly and die soon after being taken from the water. Because of their perishability, scallops are shucked aboard ship as soon as caught, and the meats are iced.

Availability fresh. All year, but best from April to October.

Average sizes. Bay scallops yield 5 to 6 pounds (2.270 to 2.720 kg) shucked per bushel; sea scallops yield 3 to 4 pounds (1.360 to 1.800 kg) shucked per bushel, or 9 pounds (4 kg) per gallon.

Quality. The tender, succulent meats of bay, sea, or calico scallops have no waste and can be used interchangeably. All scallop meats are excellent sources of protein, vitamins, and minerals, and are low in fat (0.1 percent).

Several commercial distributors often put scallops through a soaking process, placing the muscles in fresh water for several hours and thus depleting their delicate flavor. This process increases the bulk of the muscles by one-third and turns the creamy color very white. But from a culinary standpoint, the flavor is inferior. Always buy scallops from a reputable distributor who guarantees their freshness. The cream colored muscles are an indication of unquestionable freshness. Fresh scallops have a sweet nutty odor, reminiscent of fresh lobster. Many epicureans consider bay scallops the finest, although fresh, deep sea scallops are equally good.

In 1986, the relative volumes of landings were: 22.3 million pounds (weight of meat) of sea scallops; 2,261 million pounds of calico; and 2,131 million pounds of bay scallops.

Sometimes skate is sold in lieu of scallops, but it lacks the sweet odor of scallops. Mr. Smalleys, owner of Smalleys Seafood in Dunnellen, New Jersey, has encountered this practice only once in 40 years of business. His comment was, "Skate are too scarce to be stamped out into scallops, and they make a poor imitation."

Snails

The most commonly known snails are not the marine mollusks but the terrestrial variety. Most snails eaten in the United States are imported from France; they are canned and the empty shells are sold with the mollusks. Fresh snails found in the continental United States are as good as any others, providing they are prepared and cooked properly.

Periwinkles

Periwinkles are small, black or gray, snaillike marine mollusks, found fastened to rocks and seawalls in New England coastal waters. The tiny, live, unshelled mollusks are cooked in salted boiling water for 5 to 10 minutes, or until the black cap, used as a lid by the mollusk, can be lifted and removed easily.

Periwinkles are extracted with a needle or a sharp toothpick, and the sweet morsels are dipped in lemon butter and eaten "au naturel." They can be served as appetizers, on buffets, or with cold seafood trays.

Sea Urchins

The spiky hedgehogs of the sea have long been delicacies in European gourmet restaurants and in Japan. The Japanese and the French, who are the largest consumers in the world, use the roe for a delicious sushi item called uni, served in many sushi bars in the United States. In addition, since the early 1980s, sea urchins have become fashionable and are on the menus of first class gourmet restaurants in the United States.

Sea urchins are at their peak in spring. Only the roe is edible, and it makes a delicious first course when eaten raw from the shell, accompanied by a good dry white wine and French bread. The taste is very subtle and comparable with caviar or the finest oysters. Nothing more than a drop of lemon juice is needed. The roe is carefully scooped out with a small spoon.

Selecting sea urchins is a tricky business. The roe is at its best when the moon is full; when overripe, however, the roe is bitter. The quills on fresh sea urchins are important signs. Usually, they are sharp and green. If the quills are matted and dark brown, the urchins are old and should not be picked. Yet, of those that are not old, it is still difficult to tell which have the best roe. Whatever their size, then, pick the heaviest in that particular size. To serve, cut the sea urchins horizontally in half using a sharp knife or scissors. Do not rinse them. In addition to serving sea urchins in the shells, they can be pureed in sauces, or added to soups.

CHAPTER 5

The Basic Preparation of Fish and Shellfish

This chapter deals with the basic preparatory techniques for fish and shell-fish. It includes the following:

1. How to bone a shad.
2. How to bone a summer flounder or fluke.
3. How to clean blue mussels.
4. How to dress soft-shell crabs.
5. How to fillet a flounder.
6. How to fillet a whole dressed fish.
7. How to fillet imported Dover sole.
8. How to poach a whole fish for cold presentation.
9. How to shell, devein, and butterfly large shrimp.
10. How to prepare lobster for cold presentation.
11. How to shuck hard-shell clams.
12. How to shuck oysters.
13. How to clean squid.
14. How to make salmon steaks with salmon fillet.

HOW TO BONE A SHAD

The secret of boning shad has been guarded carefully and the technique has been handed down through generations in a few families. Boning a shad is a tedious process that very few professionals have mastered. Indeed, most chefs have no idea how to bone a shad. Surprisingly, in Europe, shad is very seldom boned. The French have partially solved the problem. When this author asked an eminent French chef why the "alose" (shad) was cooked whole with sorrel, a spinach-like sour tasting green, he replied that the sorrel softens the bones of the fish. In France the standard recipe for shad is "a l'oseille," with sorrel that is available fresh, frozen, or in cans.

In the United States, we are willing to pay high prices for boneless shad. With practice, one should be able to bone a shad in 10 minutes or less. Anyone can master the boning of shad using the following procedure. (The first four steps are preliminary and need not be illustrated for our purposes here.)

1. Clip off all fins with shears except for the caudal (tail) fin.
2. Scale the fish even if it was purchased scaled. The scales are removed easily but stick stubbornly to any surface. Wash the shad under cold water.
3. Cut through the flesh between and under the gill covers. Use a very sharp boning knife during the entire boning process.
4. Insert the knife point between the roe, if it is a female, and the body wall. Carefully cut away from the roe and toward the vent on the left side of the belly ridge. If the shad is a male, the process is the same even though the fish does not contain roe.
5. If you have been careful in cutting through the lower body wall (belly flap), the roe should be intact. The many small bones that are cut through the belly will be eliminated in the final trimming.
6. Lift out the roe. Wash off and soak in brine for several hours before cooking.
7. Cut off the head close behind the base of the pectoral (side) fins.
8. Cut off the belly ridge. You will feel the knife pass through the small bones that extend from the belly ridge up into the body wall.
9. Cut along the left side of the back bone and base of the dorsal fin; the cut must be made close and over the bones. As the knife passes along the vertical bones it will meet and cut through two rows of lateral bones that connect to the vertical bones. Then slide the knife along the rib cage and lift the fillet. Do not cut through the rib cage bones (This procedure is followed when boning any other fin fish.).

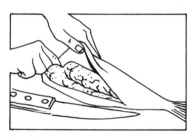

Step 5.

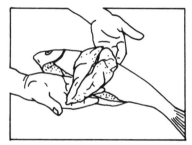

Step 6.

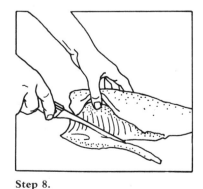

Step 8.

Figure 5-1. How to bone a shad: intermediate steps.

10. The same process is followed on the other side of the fish. The result is two fillets ready for boning and a bony carcass to be discarded.
11. Select a small board about 1 inch (2.5 cm) longer and wider than the fillet.
12. Start with the fillet from the right side of the fish. Blot the fillet dry with paper towels; place on the board. You will notice a row of bones that come to the surface along the lateral line of the center of the fillet.
13. Step 13 shows a diagrammatic representation of the right fillet ready for boning. The back is at the top of the picture, and the belly at the bottom. The head is to the left. Note the outcropping of the ends of three rows of bones that are exposed on the fleshy side of the fillet. The bones project down into the fillet and then curve and lay next to the skin. Examine this diagram in relation to your fillet. In some of the following steps, the fillet is turned so that the back (dorsal) side is at the lower side of the illustration. When this occurs, the terms *above*, *below*, *back* (dorsal) *side*, and *belly*

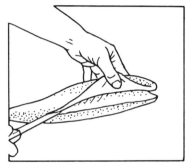

Step 9.

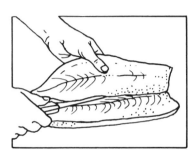

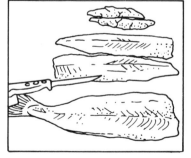

Step 10.

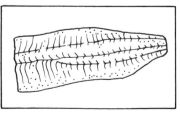

Step 12.

Step 13.

Figure 5-1. Continued.

(ventral) *side* refer to the right fillet as shown in this diagram. As you proceed in boning the fillet, refer occasionally to this diagram to orient yourself.

14. Place the fillet in the same relative position as the one illustrated. Start cutting on the belly (ventral) side of the center side (lateral) bones, to the skin but not through it. You will have to cut through some bones at the head end of the fillet (see diagram). Make another cut toward the back of the lateral bones. Again cut to the skin but not through it. These two cuts, one on each side of the lateral bones, are to be made the length of the fillet.

15. Pull out the lateral bones using a knife to loosen the strip from the skin if the cuts are not perfect.

16. Now feel the row of bones that poke out the length of this fillet on the back (dorsal) part, above the strip of lateral bones that already have been removed. This row of bones begins at the head end of the fillet, curves upward slightly, then straightens out and continues to the tail end of the fillet. Begin your cut about $\frac{1}{16}$-inch (2 mm) below this row of bones (toward the lateral strip). Cut straight down to (but not through) the skin from the head end of the fillet to about half way to the tail where you will feel your knife meet some bones. Do not cut through these bones.

17. At about half the distance toward the tail, the bones you have been following start curving under the flesh close to the skin toward the lateral strip. Let your knife ride over the bones by turning your blade toward the lateral strip. Cut in this manner to the tail end. The boneless strip of flesh you have just cut away from the bones will be connected to the skin almost the entire length. Fold it back toward the center of the fillet.

Step 14.

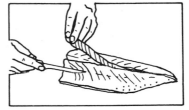

Step 15.

Step 16.

Step 17.

The Basic Preparation of Fish and Shellfish   **121**

18. The next cut begins at the head end of the fillet, about ¹⁄₁₆-inch (2 mm) above (dorsal to) the row of bones on which you have been working. Cut down deeply to where the bones curve outward and under the knife. Do not cut through them. As you cut toward the tail, the bones become shallower. Continue this cut about one-half the length of the fillet, toward the tail.

19. After cutting half the distance to the tail, the bones begin to curve out closer to the fleshy surface of the fillet. Turn the knife blade outward and let it ride over the bones. Cut over the bones, not through them. Feel the bones with your fingers since they are difficult to see.

20. Turn the boning board and fillet so that the head end is closer to you. Lay back the fleshy part closest to you and carefully cut it away from the bones. Let the knife ride over the bones. Cut out to, but not past, the end of the bones. Leave the edge of the flap of flesh attached to the skin beyond the end of these bones. Lay the fleshy portion out and away from the center of the fillet.

21. The back part of the fillet now has two boneless fleshy portions; between them is a section full of bones that must be removed next. As illustrated, cut at the head end outward from the center. Your knife must pass under the bones and between the bones and the skin. Be careful not to cut through the skin.

22. Continue separating the bones from the skin, working toward the tail end. After cutting two-thirds of the distance to the tail end, remove the entire bony portion with a quick tug. If this does not work, separate the bony strip with your knife until completely removed.

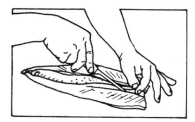

Step 18.

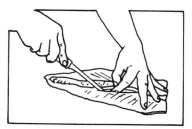

Step 19.

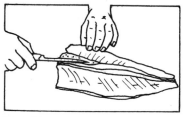

Step 20.

Step 21.

Figure 5-1. Continued.

23. Turn the boning board and fillet so the tail end is closest to you. One more row of bones projects out of the fleshy part of the fillet. It begins about one-quarter of the distance from the head end of the fillet to the tail end, on the line where the lateral (middle side) strip was removed. This row of bones curves outward and becomes parallel to the lateral line as it approaches the tail. (See diagram.) Run your finger along these bones to locate them. Begin your cut above (dorsal to) the bones at the lateral line as illustrated. As the knife passes toward the tail, the bones curve toward the lateral line and become shallower. Do not cut through them.

24. Let the knife ride over the bones. Fold back the flap of flesh as it is freed from the bones. Look closely, as the bones become finer as they approach the lateral line; the ends are actually fibers. Cut through the fibers toward the skin, leaving the fleshy section attached to the skin.

25. Begin the next cut at the head end about ⅛ inch toward the belly from the cut where the lateral strip was removed. Cut down into the fillet until you feel the bones with your knife; do not cut through them. Cut toward the tail to a point where you began the last cut. Continue the cut about ⅛ inch from your last cut on the other side of this row of bones. As the knife reaches about one-half the distance to the tail, turn the edge of the blade outward toward the edge of the fillet. Let the knife ride over the bones without cutting through them.

26. Continue to cut the fleshy section from the underlying bones, leaving it attached to the skin at the outer edge of the fillet, just beyond the ends of the bones. Lay the fleshy strip away from the bony portion.

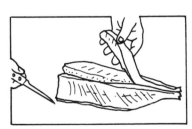

Step 22.

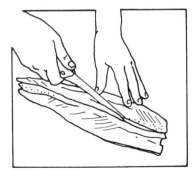

Step 23.

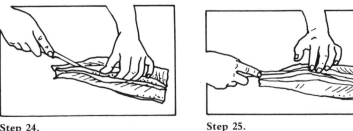

Step 24.

Step 25.

The Basic Preparation of Fish and Shellfish **123**

27. Turn the boning board and the fillet to the position shown in the illustration. Beginning at the head end, near the center of the fillet, start cutting under the bones, separating the bones from the skin.
28. Turn the boning board so that the belly (ventral part) of the fillet is away from you, and slide your knife between the bones and the skin. Continue cutting in this manner until the bony strip can be removed.
29. With the last bony section removed and with all the fleshy boneless flaps laid back, your fillet should look like the one illustrated. To the right are the three strips of bones taken from the fillet. At this point, fold the fleshy flaps back in place, trim the edge of the fillet evenly, and cut off the last ¼ inch (½ cm) to ½ inch (1 cm) at the tail section.
30. When the fillet is trimmed, it can be stored in a cold dry place, after being folded in wax paper. Do not let the fillet come in contact with water or ice. This will discolor the flesh, causing it to deteriorate.

Now you are ready to begin the same process with the left fillet. Don't give up—it takes practice to do the job well.

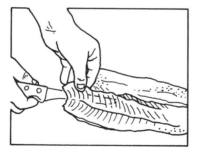

Step 26.

Step 27.

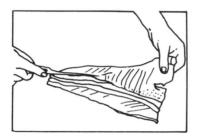

Step 28.

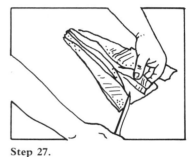

Step 29.

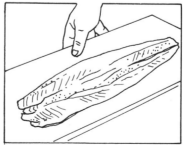

Step 30.

Figure 5-1. Continued.

HOW TO BONE A SUMMER FLOUNDER OR FLUKE

1. The illustration shows the dark side (as opposed to the white side) of a 5-pound (2.270 kg) summer flounder, also known as fluke.
2. With the dark side up, use a sharp flexible knife to make an incision along the spine bone of the flounder, from the gills to the tail.
3. Slide the blade of the knife between the backbone and the flesh of the fish, lifting one fillet, but making sure it remains attached to the bones.
4. Cut the other fillet in the same manner. The fillets from the dark side of a fluke are approximately double the size of the white side fillets.
5. Cut the bone, with scissors, at the base of the tail.
6. Cut the bone all around at the base of the fins, but not through the flesh.

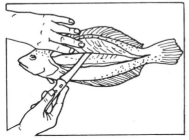

Step 1.

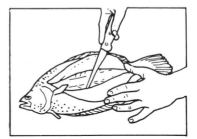

Step 2.

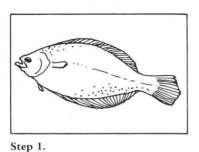

Step 3.

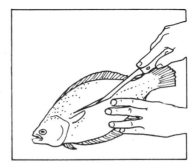

Step 4.

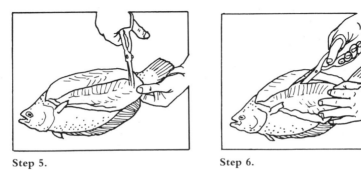

Step 5.

Step 6.

Figure 5-2. How to bone a summer flounder or fluke.

7. Slide the blade of the knife under the bone, starting from the tail end, and cut the flesh off the bone.
8. Cut off the bone at the base of the head. Clean and eviscerate the flounder.
9. Shown is a boneless flounder.
10. The fish can be stuffed with fish mousse, crabmeat, mushrooms, or other suitable stuffing.
11. Fold the uncut fillets over the stuffing.
12. Turn the fish over, showing the white side, and place on a buttered baking pan. See the recipe Summer Flounder Nicolas for complete instructions on page 246.

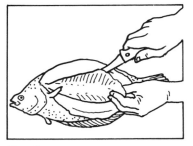

Step 7.

Step 8.

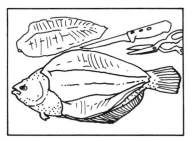

Step 9.

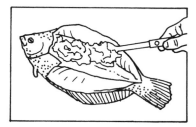

Step 10.

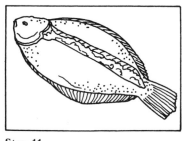

Step 11.

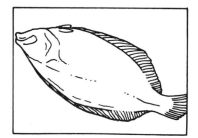

Step 12.

Figure 5-2. Continued.

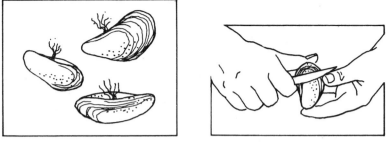

Step 1.   Step 2.

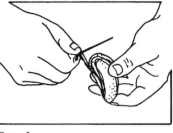

Step 3.

Figure 5-3. How to clean blue mussels.

HOW TO CLEAN BLUE MUSSELS

1. Live mussels usually keep their shells tightly closed; discard those with open shells.
2. Scrub each shell thoroughly to remove mud and grass.
3. Pull the beards that are attached between the shells. Wash mussels in cold water and use according to the recipe.

HOW TO DRESS SOFT-SHELL CRABS

1. Remove the apron, that is, the segmented abdominal part of the body underneath the carapace.
2. Lift each of the pointed ends of the carapace to remove the spongy parts.
3. Cut off the face of the crab about ½ inch (1.25 cm) behind the eyes. This part contains the sensory and respiratory organs and the digestive system, all unsuitable for consumption.
4. Shown is the muscular edible portion with the legs.

The Basic Preparation of Fish and Shellfish   **127**

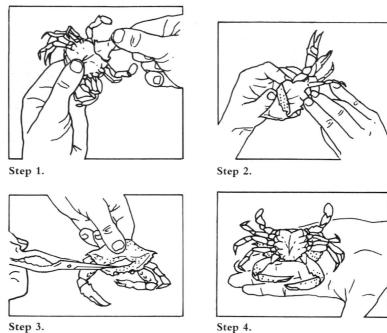

Step 1.   Step 2.

Step 3.   Step 4.

Figure 5-4. How to dress soft-shell crabs.

HOW TO FILLET A FLOUNDER

1. Shown are both the dark and white sides of the flounder.
2. Place flounder, dark side up, on a cutting board. Using a flexible boning knife, make an incision along the spine of the flounder, from the gills to the tail.
3. Slide the blade of the knife between the backbone and the flesh of the fillet, cutting the fillet away from the bone.
4. Remove the first fillet. Remove the second fillet in the same manner.
5. To skin the fillet, place the fillet skin side down. Grasping it by the tail end, cut the meat free by working in a seesaw motion as close to the skin as possible.
6. Turn the flounder over and repeat the process to remove the last two fillets. Save bones for preparation of fish fumet.

HOW TO FILLET A WHOLE DRESSED FISH

1. Slide a boning knife along the backbone, from head to tail, to remove first fillet.
2. Repeat process to remove second fillet.
3. Trim fillets, cutting off any bony edges and fins. Save backbone and head for fumet.

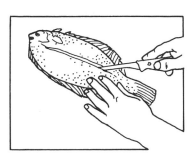

Step 1.

Step 2.

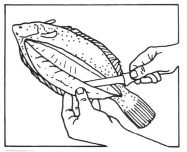

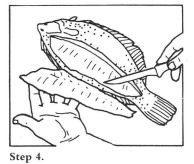

Step 3.

Step 4.

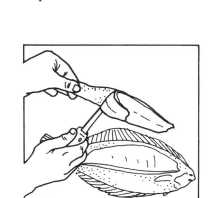

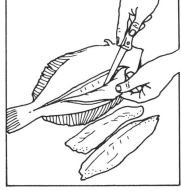

Step 5.

Step 6.

Figure 5-5. How to fillet a flounder.

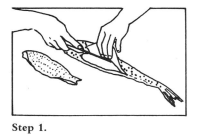

Step 1.

Step 2.

Figure 5-6. How to fillet a whole dressed fish.

129

Step 3.

Figure 5-6. Continued

HOW TO FILLET IMPORTED DOVER SOLE

1. Imported sole from the Channel Islands and the North Sea is a species of flatfish in great demand in Europe. It is available frozen in the United States. The skin is light to dark gray on one side and white on the other side. Contrary to most species of domestic flounder and sole, the skin of imported Dover sole is removed before filleting.
2. Cut off the fins with a pair of scissors. Place the fish with the white skin down on the working surface. Snip off the tail fin. Scrape off the skin starting at the tail end. Lift the skin and rip off with a tearing movement while holding the fish flat.
3. Following the same procedure, peel off the skin on the other side of the sole.
4. Cut off the head of the sole. Make an incision along the backbone. Slide the blade of a flexible knife between the backbone and the fillet. Remove the first fillet.
5. Remove the second fillet in the same manner. Turn the sole over and remove the third and fourth fillets. Save the bone for fumet.
6. Fillets of sole can be arranged and cooked in various manners, depending on the recipe and the presentation. Illustrated are some of the styles in which fillets may be portioned. *Top left:* the straight fillets are slightly flattened with a meat pounder to prevent curling while cooking. *Top right:* a butterflied sole ready for cooking. The fillets remain attached to the bones. The bottom fillets are uncut. Notice that the bone is cut in three places for easy removal when cooked. Sole in this style is usually breaded and fried. *Center:* paupiettes of sole are flattened fillets seasoned and rolled up. A quenelle forcemeat can be spread over the fillets before rolling. *Bottom left:* the fillets are cut into socalled gougeonnettes and are usually breaded and fried. *Bottom center:* fillets are folded in half and can be stuffed with a forcemeat. *Bottom right:* another way of folding fillets for poaching.

Step 1.

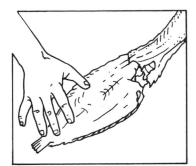

Step 3.

Step 2.

Step 4.

Step 5.

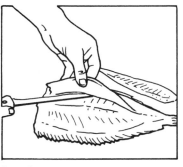

Step 6.

Figure 5.7 How to fillet imported Dover sole.

HOW TO POACH A WHOLE FISH FOR COLD PRESENTATION

The presentation of a cold decorated fish in an upright position is an elegant, easy method of displaying a whole "swimming" fish, in contrast to the common "nature morte" (lying on the side). The fish can be slightly curved before poaching to add another dimension to the final presentation. For best results, fish weighing 6 pounds (2.7 kg) or more should be poached, or at times baked, in the upright position.

The illustrations show a Lake Huron whitefish ready for poaching. The

The Basic Preparation of Fish and Shellfish **131**

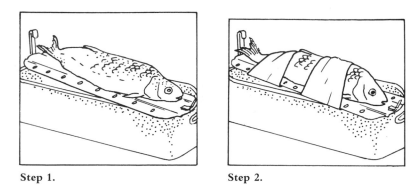

| Step 1. | Step 2. |

Figure 5-8. How to poach a whole fish for cold presentation.

soft texture of whitefish permits easy curving. (See pages 199 and 422 for Cold Whitefish Andalouse.)

1. Clean, scale, and wash the fish. Place in an upright position on the rack of a fish poacher.
2. To hold the fish safely, wrap cheese cloth around the rack and the fish. Tie the cloth loosely.

   Immerse the fish in court bouillon, making sure it is completely covered. Cook according to poaching directions in Chapter 6.

HOW TO SHELL, DEVEIN, AND BUTTERFLY LARGE SHRIMP

1. With a sharp knife, make a ¼-inch incision along the back, from head to tail.
2. Wash under cold running water to remove sand track (devein). Strip off shells and legs, leaving the tail intact. You now have a fantail shrimp.

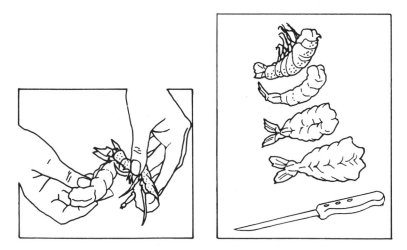

Figure 5-9. How to shell, devein, and butterfly large shrimp.

The tail is a convenient, decorative part of the shrimp. It is easily grasped by the cook for dipping in batter before frying, or by the diner for eating. Do not coat the tail with batter or breading.

When butterflying shrimp, use a large or jumbo shrimp. Shell and devein, leaving the tail intact as shown. With a sharp knife, cut along the back but not all the way through. Separate halves and spread open. The illustration shows, from top to bottom, headless unpeeled shrimp, fantail shrimp, and butterflied shrimp.

HOW TO PREPARE LOBSTER FOR COLD PREPARATION

1. Select a live lobster from 3 pounds (1.360 kg) up to 20 pounds (9 kgs), depending on the type of display desired.
2. Lay the crustacean flat on a rectangular board or on the rack of a fish poacher (poissonniere). Tie string around the lobster to prevent the tail from curling up while cooking. Secure the antennae. Boil in court bouillon no. 3, timing it 10 minutes per pound. (Lobsters exceeding 8 to 10 pounds should simmer for the same amount of time.) When cooked, remove from bouillon and cool at room temperature, then refrigerate.

HOW TO SHUCK HARD-SHELL CLAMS
▬ Clams on the Half Shell

1. Wash the shell clams thoroughly, discarding any broken shells or dead clams.
2. Hold the clam in the palm of the left hand. Place the sharp edge of a clam knife against the outside edge between shells. Exert a firm pressure with

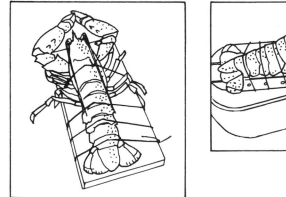

Figure 5-10. How to prepare lobster for cold preparation.

The Basic Preparation of Fish and Shellfish **133**

the left hand and fingers against the dull or heavy side of the knife blade, forcing the blade between the shells and severing the first muscle.

3. To pry open the shell, run knife around edge of the shell to cut the second muscle, located opposite the first. Do not damage the flesh of the clam.

4. Open clam and discard upper shell. Loosen clam from lower shell and examine for shell fragments.

5. Serve as shown. Cocktail sauce usually accompanies raw clams on half shells.

Other Uses

1. To open a large amount of hard-shell clams rapidly, rinse and clean the shells, and arrange in one layer on a tray or sheet pan; place in a 420°F (220°C) oven for 5 minutes. The clams will open partially. *The flesh should not be cooked.*

2. Cut the muscles, remove the meat, and save the juice.

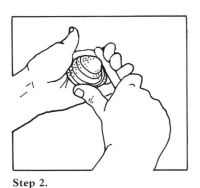

Step 2.

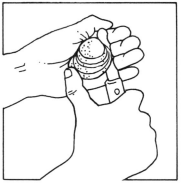

Step 3.

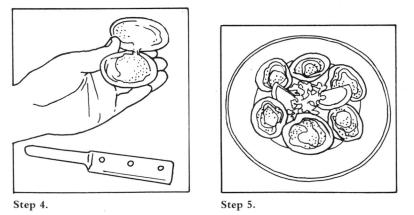

Step 4.

Step 5.

Figure 5-11. How to shuck hard-shell clams after rinsing and cleaning.

HOW TO SHUCK OYSTERS

1. Wash the shell oysters thoroughly.
2. Hold the oyster in the palm of your hand.
3. Place the edge of an oyster knife against the outside edge between the shells. With the fingers, exert firm pressure against the knife blade, forcing it between the shells.
4. To pry open the shell, run the knife around the edge of the shell to cut the muscle holding the valves together.
5. Loosen the oyster from the lower shell; examine for shell fragments.
6. Shown is an oyster on a half shell, ready to be served.

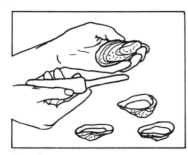

Step 2.

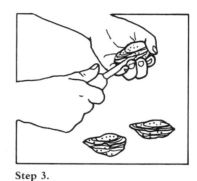

Step 3.

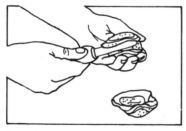

Step 4.

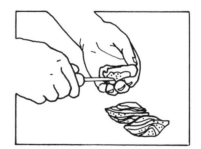

Step 5.

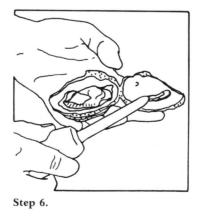

Step 6.

Figure 5-12. How to shuck oysters after washing thoroughly.

The Basic Preparation of Fish and Shellfish   **135**

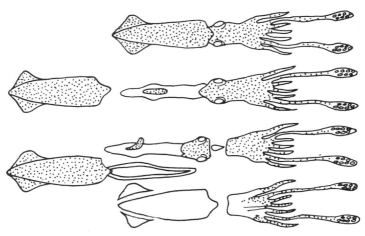

Figure 5-13. How to clean squid.

HOW TO CLEAN SQUID

See diagram above.

For Stuffing and Rings

1. Thaw squid if frozen.
2. Hold mantle with one hand. With other hand, grasp head and arms, and pinch quill at opening to separate from mantle.
3. While holding on to chitinous pen and head, remove pen, head, and intestines with pulling motion.
4. Starting with tail end, pinch fins, pulling fins and outer membrane from mantle. Peel off remaining membrane.
5. Wash mantle thoroughly under cold water. Keep whole for stuffing or cut into rings.

Preparing Tentacles and Arms

1. Squid have two tentacles and eight arms. Cut across head in front of eyes to retain arms.
2. Squeeze out round sack containing cartilage or beak.
3. Skin may be removed from arms more easily if they are first placed in boiling water for 2 to 3 minutes.

Preparing Squid for Strips and Pieces

1. From opening in mantle of squid, cut mantle with knife lengthwise. Spread inside of mantle open flat.
2. Pressing mantle with one hand, grasp head and arms and pull off intestines at the same time. Take out chitinous pen. With a knife, scrape away visceral remains adhering to the inside of mantle wall.

3. Turn mantle to other side and pull fins and outer membrane from mantle.
4. Wash squid under cold water. Cut mantle into strips or desired size pieces.

HOW TO MAKE SALMON STEAKS WITH SALMON FILLETS

In my kitchens, I have developed a revolutionary method for making salmon steaks with a salmon fillet. The end result is a completely boneless, skinless salmon steak.

The standard method consists in cutting the whole salmon across into steaks, with the skin and bones. When the fish steak is cooked, it is a tedious and time-consuming task to remove all the bones and skin from the steak. Very often, small bones can remain hidden in the steak, which can cause serious problems if the diner is not careful while eating the fish.

The following procedure, therefore, describes in detail how to make steaks with salmon fillets.

1. Fillet a whole dressed salmon, cutting along the back bone and base of the dorsal fin; the cut must be made close and over the bones. As the boning knife slides along the vertical back bone, it will meet a row of lateral bones. *Do not cut these bones.* Rather, pull them out of the fillet as shown, using a knife or a finger.
2. Slide the knife along the rib cage. Lift the boned fillet. The lateral bones end half way up the length of the salmon, so the tail end of the salmon fillet has no lateral bones.
3. The same process is followed on the other side of the salmon. The result is two boneless fillets, and a bony carcass with the head attached. Do not discard. Use for stock or fumet.
4. Holding the tail end of the salmon fillet, remove the skin, sliding the knife along the skin, using a seesaw motion for easy removal of the skin. Repeat the same process with other fillet.

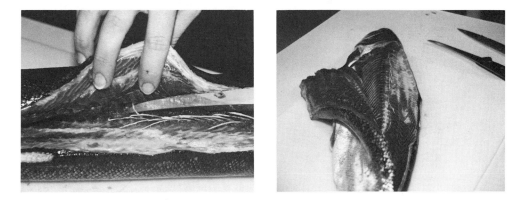

Step 1.   **Step 2.**

Figure 5-14. How to make salmon steaks with salmon fillets.

Step 3.

Step 4.

Step 5.

Step 6.

Step 7.

Figure 5-14. Continued.

5. Place the fillet on a board, with the skinned side up. Position the knife about one inch (2.5 cm) from the end of the fillet. Make a partial cut across, about three quarters down the thickness of the fillet, leaving the piece attached.

6. Make another cut across the fillet. This time the cut is complete as shown, leaving a butterflied piece of salmon fillet.

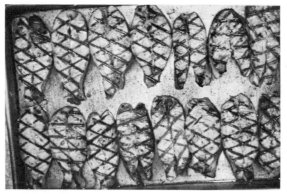

Step 8.

7. Open the butterflied piece of salmon. Make a 1 inch (2.5 cm) cut on the thin belly side of the salmon. The result is a perfect salmon steak, without skin and bones. To make more steaks, continue the same procedure with the remaining salmon fillet.
8. Here the salmon steaks have been broiled and are ready to be served with a sauce or other garnish.

6

Techniques for Cooking Fish

The shape, color, texture, and structure of fish and shellfish are so varied that they afford a multitude of cooking techniques, which are interesting and appealing to professionals, amateurs, and consumers. One important point is that any cooking method applied to fish or shellfish requires low heat. The nutritive value of seafoods is destroyed by intense heat and overcooking.

There are 15 cooking techniques detailed in this chapter including:

Au bleu
Au gratin
Baking and braising
Broiling
Deep frying
En papillotte
Glazing
Marinating and pickling
Microwaving
Pan frying and oven frying
Poaching or simmering
Sautéing (meuniè)
Smoking
Steaming
Stewing

These general techniques provide a basic understanding and a foundation for seafood cooking. Before beginning any dish, the reader should become familiar with them. Of course, the composition of each fish helps determine the best cooking method, particularly if the reader tackles recipes not included in this book. Several fish accept almost any cooking method; salmon, trout, sole, and shrimp are among the most versatile species. One can create at will with these fish and shellfish.

AU BLEU

This exclusive cooking technique of European origin is used mainly for trout and occasionally for pickerel. Fish cooked au bleu (in the blue style) must be live shortly before cooking.

The fish is dispatched with a blow on the head and gutted through the gills. Avoid overhandling of the skin. The viscous matter covering the fish takes on a bluish tint when it comes in contact with the hot vinegar that is poured over the fish before poaching in court bouillon. The hot liquid causes the flesh to curl up and sometimes split. If the fish are to be presented in an ordered manner, and this applies particularly to cold trout, it is preferable to tie the head and the tail of each fish before cooking so that they join together. A free fish that contacts boiling liquid will curl in different directions, resulting in a poor presentation. Fish au bleu, curled up from head to tail, can be decorated elegantly and served hot or cold.

How to Cook Trout Au Bleu

The best procedure is to immerse the trout, cleaned and tied, in a strong solution of vinegar and water to get a blue skin. Then the cooking process is continued in a court bouillon. Bring to a boil 2 quarts (2 l) of water and 2 cups (5 dl) of wine vinegar. In the meantime, prepare court bouillon no. 2 (see page 166). Gently lower the trout into the boiling water and vinegar until the skin becomes blue. Then transfer to the court bouillon and poach at 185°F (85°C) for 10 to 15 minutes.

Arrange on a serving platter and decorate with parsley and lemon baskets. Serve hot or cold.

Au Gratin

This method embraces many possibilities, since almost any fish is suitable for the golden brown dish called au gratin. The process consists of coating the prepared fish with cheese or breadcrumbs, or a rich fish sauce. The fish is then placed in the oven or under the broiler to brown.

The au gratin technique is classified into two types. One utilizes fresh uncooked seafood; the other has cooked or leftover seafoods as the main ingredient. The first cooking process requires perfect timing as the fish must cook and brown simultaneously. The clean whole fish or fillet is placed in a suitable buttered baking dish and covered with a small layer of duxelle (chopped mushrooms and chopped shallots). The addition of dry white wine is desirable for a large whole fish or fillets. A rich fish sauce coats the fish and the bottom of the baking dish. Allow extra sauce for a large fish (5 lb. or over) as the longer cooking time causes a greater reduction of the sauce. Sprinkle fresh breadcrumbs over the top of the fish and bake until the fish is fully cooked and browned. To obtain the best possible results, a large fish or fillet cooks best at 350°F (180°C); a small fish portion or fillet should be cooked at 375°F (190°C) to brown the sauce quickly and prevent overcooking of the fish. To speed up the au gratin process, the fish can be browned under a hot broiler for a few seconds. This is also advisable if the fish is cooked but not yet brown.

The second cooking method is commonly used for leftover seafood or freshly poached fish and shellfish. It is a fast technique that gives remarkable results, providing the garnishes and ingredients used are of good quality. The sauce, crowning touch to a dish au gratin, must be prepared and seasoned with great care. The cooked fish is boned, skinned, and flaked and then placed in a buttered baking dish. A fine duxelle is usually combined with the flaked fish.

Heat the fish in the oven for a while and pour a hot sauce over it. Sprinkle with grated cheese or breadcrumbs, and melted butter, and brown in a 375° to 400°F (190° to 205°C) oven.

Recipes of fish au gratin are easily created. Today, many canned fish have found an important role in the au gratin cooking technique. Among those fish, tuna and salmon are great favorites. Shellfish, such as crab, shrimp, and scallops, also suit our sophisticated tastes. Seafood Au Gratin a l'Americaine, Oysters Rockefeller Au Gratin, and Stone Crab Au Gratin are examples of the multitude of possibilities available with this technique.

Au gratin fish dishes have been designed recently to suit our hurried kitchen schedules. Fish recipes are increasingly turned into full meals; vegetables, potatoes, noodles, and cream soups for sauces are included in the recipes. These new dishes reflect the state of our society—everything must be done quickly and efficiently, with minimum cost, waste, and effort. Leftover fish florentine with spinach and cheese sauce, cooked salmon with eggplant and tomato sauce, or tuna with egg noodles, broccoli, and canned mushroom soup are just a few examples of high protein dishes that are important to our diet and easy to prepare in a short time. Thrifty cooks can create many fish dishes au gratin from basic casseroles.

Baking and Braising

Baking and braising applies to whole fish, lean or fat. Baking is a form of dry heat cooking used for fish with a high fat content; the braising method, which combines dry and moist heat, is commonly used for whole lean and fat fish (salmon, large lake trout, bass, bluefish, etc.).

Depending on the recipe, the fish can be stuffed or filleted, and the cooking liquid can differ with each recipe. Usually, a rich fumet combined with a dry white wine is poured over the fish, to cover half or less, before baking or braising. A fatty fish can be baked without any liquid. In this case, it is preferable to cover the fish with strips of bacon to prevent drying. Bake at a moderate temperature and baste frequently.

Broiling

The broiling method is particularly suitable for fish with a high fat content, although lean fish are also broiled. Whole small fish, fish fillets, and fish steaks are ideal individual portions for broiling.

A lean fragile fillet of fish, like lemon sole, brook trout, sea trout, or flounder, is coated with flour and dipped in oil before broiling, to prevent drying while cooking. Even a fish with high fat content should be lightly oiled prior to broiling. Since butter has a tendency to burn under intense heat, a combination of half oil and half butter is recommended.

To facilitate the handling of fish, hand racks are commonly used. They eliminate breakage but permit turning of the fish that is held between the racks. Shellfish, particularly sea scallops and shrimp, can be broiled on skewers.

Broiled seafood should be served as soon as cooked. It is customary to garnish broiled fish and shellfish with lemon wedges or lemon baskets and a bunch of fresh parsley. A partially broiled fish, baked just before serving time, retains more moisture than a fish fully cooked on the broiler.

Maitre d'hotel butter, anchovy butter, or ravigotte butter (see Chapter 11) are excellent accompaniments to broiled seafoods.

Note: The broiling method is done on a grill (charcoal, electric, gas, or other) with the source of heat coming from above or below. Today, many cooks divert from this method by cooking fish and shellfish on a sheet pan under a top broiler; the method is improperly called broiling. To be broiled, foods must be cooked on a grill.

Deep Frying

In the United States, the consumption of deepfried fish and shellfish is greater than for seafood cooked by any other method. Deep-fat frying is a popular cooking process suitable for small whole fish, fish fillets or steaks, shellfish, or frozen breaded fish products. It is a speedy method much appreciated by food operators. Seafoods to be fried are invariably coated, breaded, or dipped in batter. To accentuate the flavor in many recipes, fish is marinated prior to breading. Frozen breaded fish and shellfish can be purchased all year round and are profitable menu items sold under various titles.

Most often, fried fish is served with tartar sauce, although many other cold sauces are favored by seafood lovers. Simple, unsophisticated, tasty cold sauces meet the approval of many gourmets, and tartar sauce is only one among many. For more details on cold sauces, see Chapter 11.

Any fish or shellfish to be fried should be processed, cleaned, seasoned, sometimes marinated, and then breaded or dipped in batter. Usually, boneless fish fillets or sticks are dipped in a semi-liquid batter and cooked immediately in hot fat. Fish and shellfish to be breaded are coated in flour, dipped in beaten eggs, and rolled in preferably fresh bread crumbs. Commercially prepared crumb mixtures are also available in different forms.

Fish fried in batter does not have as crispy a surface as breaded fish. However, fast food chains are presently selling a popular fish and chips dish with a cooked batter that has a remarkably lasting crust. Perhaps culinary secrets still exist.

The fish frying method offers many advantages, providing a few factors are considered:

1. The quality of the frying medium, vegetable oil or shortening, should be without reproach; a decomposed fat increases the frying time of fish and causes a greater absortion of fat. Clean, strained fat is important for proper frying.

2. The temperature of the deep fryer should be between 350° and 375°F. It is generally recognized that the shorter the cooking time the higher the temperature. For example, freshly breaded soft-shell crabs or bay scallops cook best at 375°F for 3 to 4 minutes; the outside crust browns rapidly and the inside remains moist and tender. If the cooking time is longer, the deep-frying temperature should be lower. A thick fillet of gray sole, dipped in batter, should fry best at 350°F, until golden brown and cooked

in the center. At higher temperatures, the outside surface burns, damaging the fish and preventing the penetration of heat. The result is uncooked burned fish.

3. The cooking time varies with the size and volume of the fish, the temperature of the deep fryer, the temperature of the fish, and finally the condition of the fat. These factors are of great importance when determining the proper cooking time for frying seafoods.

4. Do not overload the deep fryer, particularly when frying frozen breaded fish. A fast temperature recovery deep fryer with a thermostat is strongly recommended to keep a constant temperature when frying frozen seafood. This also applies to any large amount of fresh fish to be fried.

   When using a conventional deep fryer, always determine the temperature of the fat with a thermometer, if the fryer is not equipped with one. A drop of water will not tell the temperature, and guessing can be deceiving.

5. Change the fat as soon as it shows any sign of poor frying: an abnormal absorption of fat into the fish, a dark burnt color, and unpleasant odors are indications that fat should be replaced. Fat kept in excellent condition will always give a quality fried fish with minimum effort.

Caution: reusing cooking oil may be economical, but it also exposes humans to possible health hazards. A fifteen-year study of fats and oils used in frying has shown that once the products decompose, harmful chemical changes occur. The longer cooking oil is kept at high heat and exposed to oxygen, the more dangerous it becomes. A word of caution: be wary when oil appears to flow more slowly in a pan, or becomes darker.

Oil Absorption in Deep Fat Frying

We often hear that deep-fried foods are too greasy, too fattening, or unhealthy because of the high absorption of oil. An experiment conducted by this author shows that an 8-ounce (226-g) deep-fried serving of fish or shellfish absorbs less oil than a portion of salad seasoned with an oil and vinegar dressing or other oil-based dressing. The experiment was carried out under normal conditions, with 2 gallons (8 l) of fresh oil. Five pounds of freshly breaded, headless medium shrimp were deep fried at 370°F (188°C), frying 1 pound (450 g) at a time to avoid an overload. The cooking time for each load was 3½ minutes.

After the oil cooled and was strained, a measurement showed that only 5 fluid ounces (2 dl) of oil were absorbed by the fried shrimp. Considering an 8-ounce (226-g) serving of shrimp, this represents a mere tablespoon of oil per serving.

Consequently, providing all five measures described for deep frying are taken into consideration, deep-fried fish and shellfish definitely are not hazardous to our health. The absorption of oil is minimal if the fish or shellfish are breaded with care and cooked under the proper conditions.

The Breading of Fish and Shellfish

The primary objective of breading is to provide a crispy protective covering to fried seafoods. The products used in breading are flour, eggs, and breading agents that include bread crumbs, cracker meal, corn meal, and other commercially prepared products. The breading procedure is done in three steps:

1. Coat the seasoned fish or shellfish thoroughly in flour.
2. Immerse in beaten eggs, or mixture of eggs and water or milk, to cover the entire surface.
3. Drain and cover with crumbs or any other breading agent. Finally, shake off any excess breading and fry without delay. Clams and oysters contain a high degree of moisture and must be fried immediately after breading or they become soggy and sticky. In general, moist seafood should not be breaded too far in advance.

En Papillotte

This is a clever way to seal a combination of flavors in a bag! The technique is quite simple and is applied to small whole fish or fillets. The raw or precooked fish is enclosed in a heart-shaped sheet of parchment paper. Garnishes, herbs, and seasonings are added to contribute to the development of an incomparably subtle flavor.

The dimension of the heart-shaped parchment paper should correspond to the size of the whole fish or fillet(s) to be cooked. The portion of fish is placed on one side of the heart, with butter, lemon juice, seasonings, herbs, garnishes, and any other ingredients listed in the recipe. The other side of the heart is folded over from the center, covering the fish; the edges are then sealed tightly. The parchment is greased on the outside to prevent burning, and placed in a 400°F (205°C) oven.

As the fish cooks, some steam will puff the bag and the parchment paper will brown. As soon as the fish is cooked, slide the bag onto a plate and serve immediately. At the table, supply a sharp knife to cut the paper. The opening of the bag will release a delicious aroma and the fullest flavors any recipe can possibly give. This cooking method adds drama to conventional recipes and is quite appropriate for noble fish such as pompano, salmon, and king crab.

Fish and shellfish can also be enclosed in puff pastry or other dough. The excellent recipe Mousseline of Salmon Royale is a typical example of fish en feuillete, instead of en papillotte. The golden brown, crusty pastry seals in the flavor of fish and adds a new dimension to fish and shellfish cooking (see Chapter 7).

Glazing

The most intriguing technique adaptable to seafood is glazing. For glazing, whole fish, fillets, or shellfish are baked with fish fumet and white wine. Small fillets can be folded and stuffed with a color-contrasting mousse (fillet of sole with salmon mousse or jumbo pink shrimp stuffed with pike mousse). Other garnishes, especially chopped shallots, mushrooms, tomatoes, and chopped parsley, are often included in the recipes to add flavor.

The cooked fish is transferred to a warm serving platter and the strained cooking liquid is reduced to $\frac{1}{2}$ to $\frac{2}{3}$ of its volume in a heavy saucepan. Heavy cream is added and the reduction continues until the sauce thickens. At this time, a cream sauce and fresh butter are stirred into the sauce. The addition of hollandaise sauce contributes to the glazing ability of the sauce.

This marvelous sauce is poured over the fish and, when placed under a hot broiler, glazes instantly. Many chefs do not add a cream sauce to the reduced stock, but just use the essence of the reduced fumet with heavy cream. Continuous boiling reduces the sauce to the desired thickness. Bits of fresh butter are stirred into the sauce and a small amount of hollandaise sauce increases the glazing power of the fish sauce. Under a hot broiler the sauce will glaze in 5 to 10 seconds. This glazing technique is unique to fish and is found in several recipes in this book. The concentration of fish flavors in the sauce transforms any glazed fish into a culinary marvel.

Marinating and Pickling

Several species of fish profit from marinating or pickling. The objective of this technique is to preserve the fish and add an aromatic flavor that varies with the type of herbs and species used. Herring, mackerel, salmon, and other fish acquire a new taste and flavor when marinated or pickled. Generally, fish with a high fat content are best for marinating or pickling.

A short marinade for any fish or shellfish consists of chopped onions, chopped shallots, parsley, crushed thyme, bay leaves, lemon juice, and soy sauce. Small fish fillets, fingers, or shellfish are marinated for an hour or two before cooking. The marinade is blended thoroughly with the seafood. To accentuate the flavor of marinated fish and shellfish, monosodium glutamate is sometimes added to the marinade.

Marinades consisting of white wine, salt, pepper, and herbs are called cooked marinades, as whole fish or fillets are cooked in it. Such fish include herring, mackerel, trout, and others. For further details, refer to the chapters covering these fish.

The major ingredient for pickling fish is vinegar. A large variety of fresh- and saltwater fish can be pickled. The pickling method has the advantage of conserving fish for a great length of time. Canada, Iceland, and the Scandinavian countries produce large amounts of pickled fish. Haddock, herring, and cod are native to the cold waters of these countries and preserve better in a brine or pickling solution than in a freezer. These fish are usually prepared on board ships and can be purchased commercially.

Fish acquire a new dimension especially when treated according to specific recipes. Such is the gravlax, a Swedish salmon delicacy that is easily prepared by marinating fillets of salmon with dill, onion, salt, sugar, spices, and lemon juice. The fish is marinated for several days (2 to 3) and served, thinly sliced, as an appetizer with brown bread and a mustard sauce. Gravlax is always part of a Swedish smorgasbord (see recipe in Chapter 12).

Mackerel cooked with white wine, carrots, onions, and spices improves considerably in flavor. The recipe for mackerel in white wine is given in Chapter 12.

A typical recipe of South American origin is ceviche. This is a marinating method of preserving fish for a short period of time, usually from 3 to 4 days. The fish is literally "cooked" by the citric acid of fruit (lemon or lime). For a complete recipe for ceviche, see page 390.

Microwaving

As a quick method for cooking and defrosting seafoods, microwaving is becoming more and more popular.

To defrost a pound of fish, unwrap and place on trivet in dish. Turn over after 4 minutes on the defrost cycle. Shield ends with foil. Continue the defrost cycle for 4 more minutes.

To defrost whole fish allow 2 to 3 minutes per pound, 4 to 5 minutes for shellfish, and follow the same method for defrosting, turning fish or shellfish after first half of time.

To cook, cut fresh or thawed fish into equal portions to facilitate even cooking. Season and place in shallow microwave-proof dish with thinner parts overlapping in the center to make an even layer. Cover with plastic wrap. Allow approximately 3 minutes per pound cooking time at highest setting for boneless fish and 2 to 3 minutes per pound for shellfish. Rotate dish halfway through cooking time. Allow 3 to 5 minutes covered "standing time" to finish cooking. Microwaved fish and shellfish can be accompanied with a hot sauce.

Pan Frying and Oven Frying

The pan-frying method is used for small whole fish, fish fillets, steaks, and shellfish. The surface of the seafood is seasoned and coated with flour or crumbs to provide a crisp golden brown color. The three-step breading method used for deep frying can also be used for pan-fried seafood.

Pan-fried fish or shellfish are cooked in a heavy frying pan or skillet containing a small amount of butter. Cook at low temperature to brown one side; turn to complete cooking and browning. Another pan-frying method, very popular in France, is called *A l'Anglaise*. This is a variation of the standard pan-frying technique that is used primarily for fish fillets. A flavored mixture (l'Anglaise) is prepared by beating whole eggs with salt, ground white pepper, and a small quantity of oil. Cover the fish fillets with flour; shake to remove any excess. Dip the fillets into the egg mixture. Drain well, then roll in breadcrumbs, patting the fillets with the palm of the hand to make the breadcrumbs stick. With the blunt edge of a knife, mark out squares on one side of the fish fillets. Melt some butter in a heavy skillet and pan fry the fillets with the marked sides down. Cook gently to brown, turn over carefully, and cook until the fish is flaky.

Pan-fried fish and shellfish are served with lemon wedges, butter mixtures, or hot sauces.

Oven frying produces a product similar to pan frying. Place fish fillets on a shallow, well-greased baking pan. Pour melted butter or fat over the fish and bake in a 450°F (230°C) oven until fish flakes easily when tested with a fork. Fish cooked in this way do not require turning or basting, and the cooking time is short (see Table 6-1). This method is ideal when serving fish to large groups.

Poaching or Simmering

Poaching or simmering, improperly called boiling, is a cooking technique widely used for fish. The selection of the cooking liquid, called court bouillon

Table

6-1. Chart for Poaching Fish

Whole Dressed		Steaks, Fillets, Pieces	
Served Hot	**Served Cold**	**Served Hot**	**Served Cold**
5 minutes per pound of clean fish. Take out of court bouillon. Serve hot.	3 minutes per pound of clean fish. Cool in court bouillon. Serve cold.	10 minutes per inch (2.5 cm) thickness. Take out of court bouillon. Serve hot.	5 minutes per inch (2.5 cm) thickness. Cool in court bouillon. Serve cold.

(see Chapter 8), is determined by the type of fish to be poached. A fresh-water fish, lacking flavor, is poached in a court bouillon containing a generous amount of seasoning and herbs; the salt-water fish requires a milder court bouillon.

A poissonnière, an oblong fish poacher with a rack, allows easy handling of a whole fish when poaching (see Fig. 6-1). The most common fish poached in a poissonnière are salmon, northern pike, sea trout, red snapper, weakfish, sea bass, grouper, and striped bass. Any of these fish can be poached whole, in steaks, in pieces, or in fillets. The diamond-shaped poacher with a rack, called a turbotière, is used to poach the imported turbot and the brill (see Fig. 6-2). These two flat fish are no longer in much demand in the United States.

Notes: Weigh clean dressed fish, steaks, fillets or pieces or measure at the thickest point.

Start poaching in cold court bouillon.

Time fish when court bouillon reaches 180°F to 185°F (82°C to 85°C).

If served hot, take out of court bouillon after cooking time is elapsed.

If served cold, allow to cool in court bouillon.

The following points should be remembered when poaching fish:

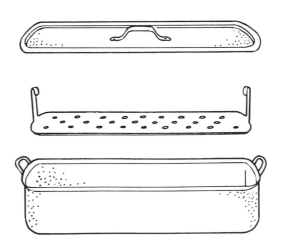

Figure 6-1. Poissonnière.

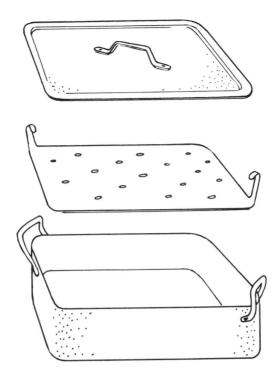

Figure 6-2. Turbotière.

1. All fish should be poached starting with cold court bouillon to preserve the full nutritional value.
2. The cooking time for whole fish to be served cold is 3 minutes per pound of clean drawn fish. In this case, allow the fish to cool in the court bouillon; it will retain more moisture and flavor. The cooking time starts at the simmering point, 180°–185°F (82°C–85°C). To keep an accurate temperature, use a thermometer.

    If the fish is to be served hot, allow 5 minutes per pound of clean drawn fish and remove from the court bouillon when the time has elapsed. A 10-pound, clean striped bass takes 50 minutes to poach if served hot. The cooking time would be 30 minutes if the fish were served cold.
3. To time the poaching of small pieces of fish, like steaks or center cut pieces and fillets, a different approach is necessary. Measure the thickness of the fish pieces at their thickest point and allow 10 minutes per inch (2.5 cm) thickness if served hot (5 minutes if served cold). The timing starts after the court bouillon has reached 180°–185°F (82°–85°C). For example, immerse a one-inch thick salmon steak in cold court bouillon. Bring the temperature of the court bouillon to 180°–185°F and poach 10 minutes. Remove from the cooking liquid and serve hot. If the salmon steak is to be served cold, cut the time by half and let the fish cool in the court bouillon.

When served cold, poached fish can be decorated elaborately (see Chapter 16). Cold fish is accompanied by one or several cold sauces (see Chapter 11). Hot poached fish is invariably served with a hot sauce and usually with parsleyed boiled or steamed potatoes.

Sautéing (Meunière)

This excellent cooking technique is used for small fish, shellfish, fish fillets, and fish steaks. The fish are seasoned, floured, and pan fried in a small amount of clarified butter. For whole fish that take longer to cook than fillets or steaks, use half clarified butter and half oil to prevent burning. Brown the fish on one side, then turn to complete the cooking process. Transfer the fish to a warm serving platter. Sprinkle some chopped parsley on the fish. In a clean frying pan, melt some butter and pour in a small quantity of lemon juice. When the butter is brown and bubbly, pour over the fish and serve immediately.

The hazelnut flavor of the bubbling butter gives a delicious flavor to any sauteed fish. The cooking technique is simple and quick, and highly favored by many fish experts.

To complement the flavor of fish meunière, recipes sometimes call for almonds, hazelnuts, and pine nuts. These add a new twist to this fine cooking method.

Smoking

The smoking method is probably as old as fire. The preservation of fish by smoking is a process that transforms such fish as salmon, trout, sturgeon, eel, mullet, and other species into delicacies. The salt and smoke impart a delectable flavor even to unpopular species of fish. The fatter the fish, the better for smoking. The oily sea herring is preferable to lake herring. Salmon is one of the best smoked fish, commanding high prices on the market, due to the high oil content of some species (10 to 15 percent).

Since salt–smoke cure is a drying and flavoring process, it is not recommended for lean fish; they tend to dry up and lose their flavor.

Basic Cures for Smoking

Dry salt
2 cups (450 g) coarse pickling salt
1 cup (210 g) brown sugar
2 tbsp. cracked black pepper
½ oz. (15 g) sodium nitrate

Combine the salt, sugar, seasonings, and sodium nitrate. Rub well into the exposed surfaces of the fish. Small fish or fillets are left up to 6 hours in the curing mixture; large whole fish or fillets are generally cured for up to 12 hours. Other spices may be added to develop a particular flavor, such as cayenne, curry, caraway or cumin seeds, dill, fennel, or tarragon.

Brine
1 gal. (4 l) water
1 cup (225 g) coarse or iodized salt
1 tbsp. cracked peppercorns
1 bay leaf

Dissolve salt in water. Add spices and immerse fish in the brine according to the instructions specified in the smoking process that follows.

Preparing Fish for Smoking

Clean fish, scale, and wash well. Wipe dry. Whole dressed fish, fillets, and butterfly pieces with the skin on are the most suitable cuts for smoking.

Smoking Procedures

There are two typical smoking methods, hot smoking and cold smoking. Both methods require curing in brine and smoking.

How to Hot Smoke Fish

Fish processed by hot smoking are fully cooked and should be consumed within a few days, refrigerated, or frozen.

To hot smoke fish, split them into fillets, wash in cold fresh water, and soak in the brine for 30 minutes. Drain and transfer the fish to a curing mixture consisting of: 4 cups (910 g) salt; 2 cups (450 g) light brown sugar; 2 tbsp, crushed black peppercorns; 1 tbsp. crushed bay leaves; and 1 gal. (4 l) water. Allow the fish to steep in the brine for 2 to 4 hours, depending on the size, thickness, amount of fat, and degree of curing desired. Rinse the fish in fresh water and hang in a cool breezy place to dry for 2 to 3 hours. Place fish in smoke house; build up a dense smoke keeping the temperature from 160°F (54°C) to 180°F (65°C) for up to 4 hours. The fish is now completely smoked.

How to Cold Smoke Fish

The cold smoking of fish is primarily a commercial process for treating a large amount of fish. The fish are not cooked but cured in a brine and thoroughly dried at a temperature of 85°F (30°C) to 90°F (33°C) for a prolonged period. The preservation of smoked fish depends on the length of time the product is smoked and the amount of salt used. To cold smoke fish, you can use the dry salt method or the brine method.

With the dry salt method fish are cleaned, filleted (if large), and placed in brine for 30 minutes. The fish are then removed from the brine and rinsed in cold water. Drain off excess moisture. Next, place each fish or fillet in a shallow wooden box containing iodized salt. Dredge the pieces of fish and pick up as much salt as will cling to them. Place in even layers in another suitable wooden box. Leave the fish in salt for 6 hours, if split, or 12 hours, if whole, in a dry cool place. Rinse the fish in cold water and dry in a shady place until a fine shiny skin has formed on the surface. Under average conditions this will take 3 hours. Use an electric fan if necessary. The fish should not be smoked while moist; the smoke will steam the fish, impairing its color. Place the fish in a smokehouse not exceeding a temperature of 90°F (33°C). Use a thermometer to check the temperature of the smokehouse. For quality smoked fish, smoking should be done progressively, starting with light smoking and continuing more intensively. The smoking time should be proportionate to the size and shape of fish. A 10-to-12 pound (4.5-to-5.3-kg) salmon, split into fillets, will take about 48 hours of smoking; whole Idaho trout, about 12 hours. Fish exceeding 15 pounds (6.7 kg) need about 3 days of smoking. A few trial runs are helpful to determine the best timing.

The brine method for cold smoked fish differs from the dry salt process in so far as the fish are only placed for 12 hours in the curing salt mixture, then transferred to brine for 30 minutes. Before smoking, do not wash the fish but dry thoroughly as described for the cold smoking dry salt method. Follow the same cooking procedure.

Each country has curing and smoking processes similar to those described here. The species of fish may differ; the wood used for smoking is usually a hardwood native to the country (maple, hickory, oak, and apple). Scandinavians are experts in turning the silver baltic herring into a golden delicacy. What smoked herring is to Scandinavians, hamburgers are to Americans. These fish are treated with great reverence in Denmark, Norway, and Sweden. For many years, the Scots have had their particular way to smoke the champion of fish—Atlantic salmon. Here is a superb recipe for smoking salmon in the Scottish way.

Scottish Smoked Salmon

For a 10-to-12-pound (4.5-to-5.3-kg) salmon.

salt cure:
2 cups (450 g) coarse or iodized salt
2 cups (425 g) dark brown sugar
2 tbsp. cognac or brandy

Any fatty fish of good size can be smoked according to this method, but the colorful fatty flesh of salmon yields spectacular results. Anadromous fish like shad, stripped bass, steelhead, or lake whitefish are excellent substitutes. The fish should be fresh and whole.

Scrape or scale the fish. Split through the back into butterfly style to clean. Cut off the head and remove the bones. Salmon smoked according to the old Scottish method is not washed. The blood particles may or may not be washed out. Dry the fillets carefully if washed. Pour the brandy or cognac over the fillets. Rub well all over with the salt cure. Lay the fish skin down in a suitable wooden box. Rub the cure mixture into the raw flesh and fold the fish with the cure inside. Place a board on the fish with a 25-to-35-pound (11.3-to-13.5-kg) weight. According to Warren Gilker, a Director of the Atlantic Salmon Association (A.S.A.), Scottish fishermen would place a "killick" (an anchor weighing 28 lb., 12.68 kg) over the salmon fillets to leach the moisture from the fish tissue and replace it with salt, thus inhibiting the spoiling action of bacteria. This method is still used today. Mr. Gilker, a salmon smoking expert, has shown that the Scottish method gives unsurpassable results.

Hang the fish in a dry, cool shaded place, spreading it with sticks to permit even drying, until a filmy skin or pellicle forms. Cold smoke for approximately 48 hours.

How to Preserve Smoked Fish

Smoked fish does not last indefinitely even under proper refrigeration. Smoked fish prepared without the addition of sodium nitrate to the curing mixture should be consumed within a week or stored in a freezer. Most commercially prepared smoked fish have one or more preservatives and can be kept under refrigeration for two weeks or sometimes longer. Some experts contend that smoked fish have a tendency to lose their flavor if frozen for a long period of time. Smoked fish are at their best when freshly smoked; refrigeration or freezing impairs the flavor.

Steaming

Contrary to the poaching process, in which the cooking liquid is usually discarded after the fish is poached, the steaming method utilizes a small amount of liquid, usually fish fumet and wine, that is used to prepare the sauce served with the fish. Place the fish in a suitable buttered pan, season with salt and pepper, and barely moisten with a strong fish fumet and white wine. Cover tightly with aluminum foil and cook in a moderate oven. When cooked, transfer the fish to a serving dish. The cooking liquid is reduced and used in the preparation of the sauce.

A new approach is gradually being introduced through the *nouvelle cuisine*. The fish to be steamed is placed on a bed of seaweed that provides a novel flavor to the fish while cooking. The Japanese use seaweed extensively and new culinary techniques are certain to develop using seaweed, adding a new dimension to fish cookery.

Another approach to steaming consists of cooking the fish in a tightly covered pan, with the fish resting on a steaming rack out of contact with the cooking liquid. The steam generated from the boiling liquid cooks the fish, which retains its natural juices and flavors. Allow 5 to 10 minutes per inch thickness measured at the thickest point.

Stewing

Of the many seafoods available on the market, a great number can be transformed totally by the stewing method. Specialty dishes like bouillabaisse [pronounced boo-yah-bays] and matelotes [mah-teh-lot] are seasoned with red or white wine, herbs, and spices. Bouillabaisse, the controvertial French specialty, is surely an individual dish. Despite the tremendous variety of edible seafoods available in the United States, it is hard to copy the genuine Marseille bouillabaisse. Our waters do not offer the ugly John Dory with its delicate flesh, or the bony gurnet, or the hogfish, all native to Mediterranean waters. Those fish and many others are part of the elaborate concoction that is bouillabaisse. In the United States, several substitutes are available to make a bouillabaisse Marseillaise. Depending on the region, such seafoods as red snapper or mutton snapper, American lobster, crawfish, sea bass, striped bass, redfish, other firm lean salt-water fish, mussels, and clams are often used.

Matelotes are not great American favorites. The typical French specialties no longer hold the edge in France either, although good restaurants feature matelotes of eel, perch, bream, sole, and other firm fleshed fish. In the United States, many recipes relying on the stewing technique can be turned into excellent dishes: chowders made with clams, oyster stew, codfish stew, and others. Unlike the French type of fish stews, especially matelotes that invariably contain red or white wine, American fish stews do not contain any wine. The thickening agents are mostly flour and butter, a mixture called beurre manie, or potatoes.

The following chart (Table 6-2) is a guide for cooking fish. Fish products require little time to cook. When the flesh loses its translucent appearance, becomes opaque, and flakes easily when pierced with a fork, the fish is cooked. Always test the thickest part—it takes the longest to cook.

Table

6-2. Cooking Guide for Fish

Method of Cooking	Market Form	Amount for 6	Cooking Temperature	Approximate Cooking Time in Minutes
Baking	Dressed	3 lb. (1 kg 360)	350°F (180°C)	45 to 60
	Pan-dressed	3 lb. (1 kg 360)	350°F (180°C)	25 to 30
	Fillets or steaks	2 lb. (900 g)	350°F (180°C)	20 to 25
	Frozen fried portions	12 por. 3 oz. (85 g) each	400°F (205°C)	15 to 20
	Frozen fried sticks	24 sticks 1¼ oz. (30 g) each	400°F (205°C)	15 to 20
Broiling	Pan-dressed	3 lb. (1 kg 360)		10 to 15
	Fillets or steaks	2 lb. (900 g)		10 to 15
	Frozen fried portions	12 por. 3 oz. (85 g) each		10 to 15
	Frozen fried sticks	24 sticks 1¼ oz. (30 g) each		10 to 15
Charcoal broiling	Pan-dressed	3 lb. (1 kg 360)	Moderate	10 to 15
	Fillets or steaks	2 lb. (900 g)	Moderate	10 to 15
	Frozen fried portions	12 por. 3 oz. (85 g) each	Moderate	8 to 10
	Frozen fried sticks	24 sticks 1¼ oz. (30 g) each	Moderate	8 to 10
Deep-fat frying	Pan-dressed	3 lb. (1 kg 360)	360°F (182°C)	3 to 5
	Fillets or steaks	2 lb. (900 g)	360°F (182°C)	3 to 5
	Frozen raw breaded portions	12 por. 3 oz. (85 g) each	360°F (182°C)	3 to 5
Oven frying	Pan-dressed	3 lb. (1 kg 360)	450°F (230°C)	15 to 20
	Fillets or steaks	2 lb. (900 g)	450°F (230°C)	10 to 15
Pan frying	Pan-dressed	3 lb. (1 kg 360)	Moderate	8 to 10
	Fillets or steaks	2 lb. (900 g)	Moderate	8 to 10

154

Table
6-2. Cooking Guide for Fish *(continued)*

Method of Cooking	Market Form	Amount for 6	Cooking Temperature	Approximate Cooking Time in Minutes
	Frozen raw breaded or frozen fried portions	12 por. 3 oz. (85 g each)	Moderate	8 to 10
	Frozen fried sticks	24 sticks 1¼ oz. (30 g) each	Moderate	8 to 10
Poaching	Dressed	3 lb. (1 kg 360)	Simmer	See poaching technique
	Fillets or steaks	2 lb. (900 g)	Simmer	
Steaming	Fillets or steaks	2 lb. (900 g)	Boil	5 to 10

CATEGORIES OF SEAFOODS

This chart groups together fish and shellfish of similar flavor, richness, and color. The different seafoods in each category have a similarity in taste and can be prepared the same way. If a recipe calls for a fish that is not available in your area, you can use another from the same group in its place.

▬ Fin Fish

White meat, very light, delicate flavor.

Cod, Cusk, Dover Sole, Haddock, Lake Whitefish, Orange Roughy, Pacific Halibut, Pacific Sanddab, Petrale Sole, Rex Sole, Southern Flounder, Spotted Cabrila, Summer Flounder, Witch Flounder, Yellowtail Flounder, Yellowtail Snapper.

White meat, light to moderate flavor.

American Plaice/Dab, Arrowtooth Flounder, Butterfish, Catfish, Cobia, English Sole, Lingcod, Mahi Mahi, Pacific Whiting, Red Snapper, Rock Sole, Sauger, Snook, Spotted Sea Trout, Starry Flounder, Tilefish, White King Salmon, White Sea Trout, Whiting, Winter Flounder, Wolfish.

Light meat, very light, delicate flavor.

Alaska Pollock, Brook Trout, Giant Sea Bass, Grouper, Pacific Ocean Perch, Rainbow Trout, Smelt, Tautog, Walleye, White Crappie, White Sea Bass.

Light meat, light to moderate flavor.

Atlantic Ocean Perch, Atlantic Salmon, Black Drum, Buffalofish, Burbot, Carp, Chum Salmon, Crevalle Jack, Croaker, Greenland Turbot, Jewfish, King Salmon, Lake Chub, Lake Herring, Lake Sturgeon, Lake Trout, Mako Shark, Monkfish, Mullet, Northern Pike, Ocean Pout, Perch, Pink Salmon, Pollock, Pompano, Rockfish, Sablefish, Sand Shark, Sculpin, Sculp/Porgie, Sheepshead, Silver (Coho) Salmon, Spot, Striped Bass, Swordfish, Vermilion Snapper.

Light meat, more pronounced flavor.

Atlantic Mackerel, King Mackerel, Spanish Mackerel.

Darker meat, light to moderate flavor.

Black Seabass, Bluefish, Sockeye (Red) Salmon, Tuna.

Shellfish

Crabs

Alaska King Crab, Blue Crab, Dungeness Crab, Jonah Crab, Red Crab, Soft Shell Crab, Snow Crab, Stone Crab.

Lobsters

American Lobster, Rock Lobster, Slipper Lobster, Spiny Lobster.

Bivalves

Clams: Butter Clam, Geoduck Clam, Hard or Quahog Clam, Littleneck Clam, Pismo Clam, Razor Clam, Soft Clam/Steamer, Surf or Skimmer Clam.

Scallops: Bay Scallop, Calico Scallop, Sea Scallop.

Oysters: Eastern/Atlantic Oyster, Gulf Oyster, Olympia Oyster, Pacific Oyster, South American Oyster.

Mussels: Blue Mussel, California Mussel, Green Shell Mussel.

Shrimp

Brown Shrimp, California Bay Shrimp, Northern Shrimp, Pink Shrimp, Rock Shrimp, Red Shrimp, Tiger Shrimp, White Shrimp.

Univalves

Abalone, Conch, Snails.

Others

Octopus, Squid, Crawfish (Freshwater Crayfish).

PART
TWO   **COOKERY**

CHAPTER 7

The Marriage of Batters and Pastries in Seafood Cooking

New delights are realized by combining seafoods with light pastries or batter coverings. The results are always visually pleasing and tempt the palate if prepared with care. There are a myriad of elegant ways to serve fish and shellfish using batters and various pastries. These basic preparations are indispensable to cooking.

Batters seal in the flavors of deep-fried fish and shellfish. Puff pastries are ideal containers for seafood with sauces; vol-au-vent and bouchées are particularly suitable. Other pastry delicacies, like fleurons, are irresistibly French. Turnovers, tart shells, ravioli, pastry shells, and patty shells are some of the many interesting variations to combine with seafood.

Deep-fried fish products acquire a Japanese flavor in tempura batter. Seafood pizzas and crusty pastries bring Italy to mind. The very adaptable barquettes and tartlets make wonderful appetizers with almost any seafood. Beer batter adds another dimension to deep frying, and pie crusts are perfect for specialties like seafood quiches and tarts. Above all, these basic preparations, most of which are made with starch, blend so well in so many seafood dishes that they deserve a chapter of their own.

BATTERS

Batters are mixtures of light to heavy consistency, made with flour and varying amounts of such liquids as water, milk, beer, or carbonated water. Beaten egg whites add lightness to some batters. Beer adds little flavor to seafoods fried in batter, but the bubbles contribute a light and crisp texture to the cooked batter. Batter-fried seafood is not feasible for large servings. If the cooked product cannot be served within five minutes of frying, the crisp outer crust becomes soft and the steam from the cooked seafood turns the batter soggy.

Beer Batter

| 9 | oz. flour |
| 1 | tsp. salt |

159

2	oz. oil
1	egg
¾	cup beer
1	cup water
2	egg whites

Combine all the ingredients except the egg whites. Beat well until the batter is smooth. Whip the egg whites medium stiff, and fold into the batter. Use without delay.

Brioche Dough

1	envelope active dry yeast
1	tsp. sugar
2	oz. lukewarm water
½	cup bread flour
9	oz. bread flour
3	beaten eggs
¾	tsp. salt
6	oz. softened butter

Dissolve the yeast and sugar in the water. Add the flour and blend well. Cover with a towel and allow to double in size in a warm place. Meanwhile, beat half the remaining flour with the eggs and salt. Add the yeast mixture and butter and knead in the remaining flour. Let rise at room temperature for 3 hours

Punch the dough and refrigerate for 12 hours, covered with a wet towel.

Cream Puff Dough

1	cup water
½	cup butter
1	cup sifted flour
4	eggs

Heat the water and butter to a rolling boil in a saucepan. Stir in the flour all at once. Stir vigorously over low heat until the mixture no longer sticks to the pan and forms into a ball. Remove from heat. Beat the eggs in thoroughly, one at a time. Beat the mixture until smooth.

Spoon the cream puff mixture into a pastry bag fitted with a plain tube and pipe onto an ungreased baking sheet. Bake until puffed, golden brown, and dry.

Use as directed by specific recipe.

Crêpe Batter

4	oz. flour
1	egg
½	tsp. salt
1	cup milk
2	tbsp. melted butter

Combine the flour, egg, and salt in a mixing bowl. Stir in the milk until the batter is smooth. Add the melted butter.

Heat up lightly greased crêpe pans. Pour a thin layer of batter in the pan. Spread to cover the whole bottom surface. Brown on both sides.

Save and refrigerate for future use.

Flaky Pie Crust Dough

1	lb. flour
8	oz. shortening
5	oz. water
½	tsp. salt

Combine all ingredients and blend until the dough is mixed well and can be shaped into a ball.

Use for seafood quiches and turnovers.

Pie Crust Dough

1	lb. flour
8	oz. softened butter
1	egg
1	oz. water
½	tsp. salt

Combine all ingredients in a mixing bowl. Mix well until the dough is smooth and can be formed into a ball.

Use for barquettes (small boat-shaped crusts), tart shells for quiches, and tartlets (individual small round tarts).

The Marriage of Batters and Pastries in Seafood Cooking   **161**

Pizza Dough

1	package dry yeast
1	tsp. sugar
1	cup lukewarm water
2½	cups flour
1	tsp. salt
¼	cup oil

In an electric mixing bowl, dissolve the yeast in the water and sugar. Add the flour, salt, and oil, and mix the dough for about 10 minutes. Cover the dough with a cloth, and allow to rise in a warm place until double in bulk.

Use for seafood pizzas and pissaladieres.

Tempura Batter

1	cup flour
1	cup cornstarch
1	tsp. baking powder
2	tbsp. sesame oil
1	tbsp. white vinegar
1	egg
1¼	cups cold water

Combine all dry ingredients. Add the oil, vinegar, egg, and water and whisk until batter is smooth. Chill before using.

Dip the prepared seafoods in the cold batter, coating the pieces completely. Drop in a deep fryer at 360°F (185°C) and fry for 2 to 5 minutes, according to size and shape.

Use for fried seafood tempura, vegetables tempura, gougeonnettes of fish (small fish sticks), and thin fish fillets, scallops, etc.

Puff Pastry

This magic pastry is probably the most intriguing and spectacular of all pastries. Puff pastry is created by a series of rollings, foldings and chillings, and finally baking. Excellent puff pastry dough is available commercially, for hotels and restaurants, in 15-pound (6.8 kg) portions; at the consumer level, 1-pound (½ kg) blocks or other forms such as cooked or uncooked patty shells can be purchased.

Puff pastry is a mixture of flour, salt, and water rolled several times between layers of butter or shortening that make it puff when baking. The dough is rolled and chilled several times, which makes it a time–consuming process.

The use of butter can present problems, however, even to the experienced baker. Butter can become too hard or too soft, resulting in an unpuffed pastry of poor quality. Shortening that is specially processed for use in puff pastry is recommended; it does not have the fine flavor or taste of butter, but it certainly eases the preparation, blends well into layers when rolled in the dough, and results in a feathery light, cooked pastry.

Puff Pastry

1	cup ice water
½	tsp. salt
4½	cups high gluten flour
1¼	lb. chilled butter

Combine the water and salt. Reserve half a cup of flour. Place the remaining flour in a mixing bowl. Cut a quarter pound of the butter into small pieces and toss into the flour. Add just enough water to form a ball. Cover and chill.

Pat the rest of butter together. Kneed in the remaining flour. Form into a square block, and set aside.

Place the chilled dough on a board. Cut a large cross at the top, opening up the ball of dough into a clover-shaped square with 4 inch ears. Sprinkle with flour and roll the 4 inch ears to

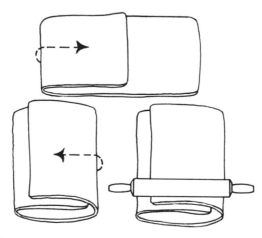

Figure 7-1. Puff Pastry.

The Marriage of Batters and Pastries in Seafood Cooking **163** half inch thickness. Place the butter block in the middle. Fold each ear over to form a package. Roll into a rectangle. Fold rectangle into 3 parts (see Fig. 7-1). Chill an hour. Repeat same process five times. Use according to the recipe.

Use for vol-au-vent—large puff pastry shells to serve 6 to 8 persons; patty shells—individual puff pastry shells; fleurons— crescent shaped puff pastry used as garnish with fish; bouchées— appetizer puff pastry shells; and turnovers—for quenelles (see Mousselines of Salmon in Chapter 9).

8

Court Bouillons and Fumets

Auguste Escoffier, the wizard of French culinary art, was correct when he said, "Stock is everything in good and well-flavored cooking. If one's stock is of good flavor, what remains of the work is easy; if on the other hand, flavor is lacking, or merely mediocre, it is quite hopeless to expect anything approaching a satisfactory result."

Stocks are often the basis of sauce preparation; their reductions are called fumets. The essence of quality dishes comes from the flavors of stocks or fumets and their abundance of protein. Fatty fish, such as salmon, mackerel, and shad, have a distinctive flavor and usually do not require the addition of foreign flavors to improve their taste. On the other hand, bland fish like sole, flounder, and most ground fish, which are usually lean, are best when spiked with rich sauces containing wines and cooked with well-flavored court bouillons. Freshwater fish, which by nature lack character, cannot be seasoned lightly if the results are to reach professional standards.

The pH scale of most fish is close to 7 (representing neutrality between acidity and alkalinity), which offers a wealth of culinary possibilities. For the same reason, wines play a predominant role in fish cookery. Some of the most glorious seafood recipes contain wine combined with stock or fumets. Since lean fish do not hold up well on their own, rich stocks, fumets, and wine sauces must come to their rescue. Cooks and chefs have learned to take advantage of the neutrality of lean, bland fish. Sole and flounder, America's favorite fish, have been transformed into many different specialties, some of which could be called marvels. Above all, stocks, court bouillons, or fumets can contribute greatly to the success of any seafood dish.

COURT BOUILLON

Fish and shellfish poached in plain water acquire no flavor unless enhanced by the addition of vegetables, herbs, and seasonings. This is the purpose of court bouillon (short broths).

In most cases, court bouillon is prepared in advance to develop its flavor, especially if the fish must be cooked in half an hour or less. There is no single standard recipe for court bouillon, as fish differ in flavor, size, and color. Marine species, which usually have more flavor than freshwater species, are poached in mildly seasoned court bouillons that contain a small proportion of vegetables, seasonings, and herbs. Freshwater fish need a flavorful court bouillon to improve their taste. This applies particularly to lake-dwellers like whitefish, lake trout, or rainbow or so-called brook trout. In comparison with the migrating steelhead, which spends most of its life in salt water, the freshwater-cultured rainbow trout has much to gain from a strongly flavored court bouillon. Both fish belong to the same family, but the steelhead is comparable to salmon with its pink color and rich flavor. The court bouillon used to poach farmed rainbow trout would impair its taste.

Occasionally, it is unnecessary to alter the taste of fish. In this case, salted water should be used to poach fish and shellfish. For example, fresh cod steaks can be poached in this manner. The plain fish is not very palatable, but served with a contrasting, flawless rich sauce, the cod is delightful to taste. Lobster is also at its best when cooked in salted boiling water; lemon butter accentuates the sweet rich taste of this prized crustacean. Details for poaching fish and shellfish are described in Chapter 6.

Court Bouillon No. 1

5	qt. water
1	cup white vinegar
2	oz. salt
1	lb. sliced carrots
1	lb. sliced onions
½	tsp. thyme
2	bay leaves
2	oz. parsley stems
1	oz. peppercorns

Combine all ingredients in a suitable pot. Bring to a boil and simmer for 45 minutes to an hour. Strain and cool. Refrigerate if not used within a few hours. Yields 5 quarts.

Use for poaching salmon, steelhead striped bass, and all marine fish having a fat content over 5 percent.

Court Bouillon No. 2

4	qt. water
1	qt. dry white wine
1	lb. leeks
2	lb. sliced onions

2	oz. parsley stems
1	tsp. thyme
2	bay leaves
½	oz. peppercorns
2	oz. salt

Combine all ingredients except wine. Simmer for 30 minutes. Strain, then add the wine. Cool and refrigerate if not used within a few hours.

Use to poach pike, lake trout, whitefish, and most freshwater fish suitable for poaching.

Court Bouillon No. 3

4	qt. water
1	qt. milk
2	oz. salt
2	lemon slices

Combine all ingredients in a suitable pot. Yields 5 quarts.

Use to poach smoked fish (finnan haddie, smoked hake, etc.) and other fresh fish without altering the flavor.

Fish Stock or Fumet

2	oz. butter
3	lb. lean fish bones
3	qt. water
2	bay leaves
1	tsp. thyme
2	large sliced onions
2	celery ribs
1	lb. sliced carrots
1	tsp. peppercorns
2	tsp. salt

Melt the butter in a kettle. Stir in the cleaned bones. Add the remaining ingredients and simmer for 30 minutes. Strain through a fine china cap.

Fish fumet is obtained by reducing a stock to achieve a richer flavor. Depending on the use of the fumet, the addition of wine is sometimes desirable. The reduction of fish stock is not necessary if a large quantity of fish bones is included in the stock. The bones provide a richer stock that approximates a fumet. If the fish stock gells under refrigeration, it can be called fumet. In culinary language, fish stock and fish fumet are synonymous. They both serve the same purpose. Yields 2 quarts.

9

Quenelles and Mousses

Many highly respected fish recipes stem from great achievements in finesse and are the ultimate in fish cookery. These recipes often start with basic elements known as quenelles and mousses: ground forcemeats from clean, boneless, and skinless raw or cooked fish or shellfish, combined with cream, eggs, jelly, and other ingredients, and seasoned to perfection.

Formerly, the making of quenelles and mousses involved detailed preparation due to the lack of modern equipment. Fish was forced through fine sieves, separating sinews and bones from the flesh. Today, food processors can turn a piece of fish into a velvety mousse in record time. The prepared forcemeat is put through a food mill to eliminate any sinews or bones.

BASIC RECIPES FOR QUENELLES AND MOUSSES

Pike, a lean, white, firm fish, is one of the most suitable fish for forcemeat, known in French as farce. This fish is now scarce in the United States, but other fish and shellfish like salmon, whiting, sole, trout, shrimp, and lobster are excellent candidates for quenelles and mousses.

Quenelles and Mousses

9	oz. boneless fish
2	egg whites
1	cup heavy cream
½	tsp. salt
¼	tsp. ground white pepper
⅛	tsp. cayenne

If using fish: skin and debone. If using shellfish: shell and devein.

Cut the fish or shellfish in cubes. Blend in a food processor with egg whites and cream. Season with salt, pepper, and cayenne.

This recipe can be used for mousses, quenelles (dumplings), and soufflés, and for stuffing large fish that are to be braised whole.

Note: The addition of panada improves the texture and lightness of quenelles and mousses. However, the delicate flavor of the seafood is impaired. For this reason, quenelles, mousses, or soufflés made with forcemeat are often accompanied by sauces prepared with rich fumets.

Serves: 6
Calories per serving: 115

Panada for Quenelles

½	cup milk
2	oz. butter
5	oz. flour
2	egg yolks

Boil the milk with the butter in a saucepan. Add the flour and mix well with a wooden spoon to obtain a smooth paste. Dry the panada over low heat. Remove from heat.

Mix in the egg yolks one at a time. Cool the panada and mix well with the forcemeat. This recipe is used for mousses, quenelles, mousselines, fish pâtés, or as a stuffing to fill the cavity of whole fish to be cooked.

Serves: 8
Calories per serving: 112

Shrimp Quenelles

9	oz. shelled shrimp
4	oz. sole fillet
2	egg whites
1	cup heavy cream
¾	cup salt
¼	tsp. ground white pepper
⅛	tsp. cayenne pepper
1½	cups shrimp sauce

Clean and devein the shrimp. Cut the fillet of sole into 1-inch (2.5 cm) pieces. Mix the shrimp and sole in a food processor to form a paste. Add the egg whites and heavy cream while mixing continuously. Season with salt and peppers.

Use a tablespoon to shape the quenelles into oval shapes. Butter a baking dish large enough to hold the quenelles. Cover with salted boiling water. Simmer for 3 minutes. Turn the quenelles over and let stand for 3 more minutes. Drain on absorbent paper, arrange on a serving dish, and cover each quenelle with shrimp sauce.

Serves: 6
Calories per serving: 258

Specialty recipes like Quenelles of Pike Sauce Normande, Mousse of Salmon, Sauce Americaine, and Mousseline of Trout Royale, are variations of the standard recipes. Their preparation is tailored to acquire new flavors, and sometimes new presentations are used. These recipes allow cooks and specialty chefs to demonstrate their talents and savoir faire.

Quenelles

Quenelles, poorly translated as dumplings, are oval-shaped fish or shellfish forcemeats poached in water or fumets, or simply steamed. Mousseline is another term used for quenelles. They are served with a sauce as garnish, with other fish, or even in soups. Their size varies depending on their use.

How to Shape Quenelles

Oval-shaped scoops, similar to ice cream scoops, are ideal for shaping fish forcemeat into quenelles. But the most common method consists of dipping a large soup spoon in hot water and scooping up a heaping amount of the forcemeat. Using another spoon, round the mixture to make a neat, egg-shaped quenelle. Cook according to directions in the specific recipe.

Test and sample any quenelle to determine its taste and texture, as all fish are different. Results can also vary if the raw seafood has been frozen. An adjustment in seasoning may be required; and sometimes the addition of egg whites will improve the texture of the product.

Mousses

Seafood mousses are classified into two categories: hot and cold mousses. Mousses to be served hot are cooked in various molds—ring, fish-shaped, or individual portion molds. They are prepared from the basic recipe for fish forcemeat, with or without panada. The cooked dish is always served hot with an appropriate sauce. Many variations of mousse recipes exist, with the addition of such garnishes as truffles, pistachio nuts, and mushrooms. The same recipe is used to make fish pâté, but it is served cold. For more details, see the recipe for Pâté of Salmon.

Cold seafood mousses offer another dimension in fish cooking. Freshly poached fish, shellfish, and smoked fish can be mixed into a fine smooth paste. Fish jelly and whipped cream are invariably added to the recipe.

As these preparations are always served cold, the seasonings must be balanced carefully; cold mousses often require more seasoning than hot mousses, both in variety and quantity. A poorly seasoned cold mousse is unpalatable and deceiving. Resourceful cooks and chefs know many ways to improve the taste of a cold mousse. A good quality fish jelly is definitely of great help. Mayonnaise, white wine, cold cream sauces or veloutes, lemon juice, and herbs are choice ingredients to overcome the neutrality of cooked fish.

Cold Fish Mousse

1	lb. cooked fish
1	tbsp. unflavored gelatin
1	cup liquid aspic jelly
1	tsp. salt
¼	tsp. ground white pepper
¼	tsp. worcestershire
1	tsp. chopped dill
½	cup mayonnaise
¼	cup dry white wine
½	cup heavy cream

Use poached fish or shellfish such as salmon, trout, sole, pike, halibut, shrimp, or lobster.

Skin and bone the fish or shellfish. Dissolve the gelatin in aspic. Blend the fish or shellfish in a food processor gradually adding the fish aspic. Add the seasonings, mayonnaise, and white wine, and combine well. Cool on ice.

Whip the cream to a medium consistency. Fold into the fish mixture. Pour into molds and allow to set in refrigerator.

Fish mousse can also be used as a filling in various garnishes for seafood dishes or barquettes, tomatoes, cucumbers, artichoke bottoms, or mushroom caps.

Serves: 6
Calories per serving: 258

Cold Lobster Mousse

1	cup strong aspic jelly
14	oz. cooked lobster meat
2	oz. cooked coral

2	oz. béchamel sauce
6	oz. whipped cream
8	tomato slices

Grind cooked lobster and cooked coral through a fine meat grinder plate.

Mix with béchamel and reduced aspic jelly. Fold in whipped cream. Adjust seasoning. Pour into mold and chill.

Unmold on a serving plate or platter. Garnish with sliced tomatoes.

Serves: 8
Calories per serving: 125

Mousse of Salmon and Trout

1	cup aspic jelly
8	slices truffle
5	oz. smoked salmon
4	oz. velouté sauce
1	tbsp. unflavored gelatin
½	cup fish stock
4	oz. whipped heavy cream
4	oz. beluga★ caviar
5	oz. smoked trout fillet
4	oz. velouté sauce
1	tbsp. unflavored gelatin
½	cup fish stock

Line two molds with aspic jelly and decorate with truffle circles. Cut smoked salmon into pieces and puree with warm velouté. Dissolve gelatin in stock, and add to mixture while food processor is working. Fold in cream, adjust seasoning, and put into a mold. Mold should be half filled with smoked salmon mousse. Place a layer of caviar over salmon mousse.

Prepare trout mousse, following the same procedure. Place on top of salmon mousse and caviar and chill. Unmold and serve.

★Golden whitefish caviar or salmon caviar can be substituted for beluga caviar.

Serves: 8
Calories per serving: 153

Salmon Mousse

16	oz. cooked salmon
2	oz. veloute sauce
16	oz. aspic jelly
6	oz. whipped cream

Reduce the aspic jelly to 8 oz. Puree the salmon with veloute sauce and reduced aspic jelly. Fold in the whipped cream. Season with salt and pepper. Pour into a mold and chill.

Serves: 8
Calories per serving: 159

Shrimp Mousse

1	oz. butter
1	oz. chopped onion
1	oz. chopped carrot
1¼	lb. medium shrimp
3	oz. cognac
3	oz. dry white wine
¾	cup veloute sauce
2	oz. shrimp butter
1½	cups liquid aspic jelly
1	cup whipped heavy cream
½	tsp. salt
¼	tsp. ground white pepper
6	slices truffles

Melt the butter in a saucepan. Add the onion and carrot and cook over low heat for 5 minutes. Shell and devein the shrimp. Rinse under cold water, and add to vegetables. Cook until the shrimp are pink. Pour in the cognac and ignite. Add wine and simmer for 5 minutes. Puree the shrimp mixture in a food processor. Transfer to a mixing bowl. Blend in the shrimp butter, and stir in half of the aspic. Fold in the cream. Season with salt and pepper. Pour the cold mousse into a decorative mold. Refrigerate for 2 hours.

To unmold, dip the mold in lukewarm water, invert on a chilled platter. Decorate with truffle slices and glaze with remaining cold aspic.

Serves: 8
Calories per serving: 234

Variations with Mousses

Interesting variations can be prepared by mixing several kinds of fish and shellfish to make mousses in combinations; for example, ½ brook trout mousse and ½ salmon mousse (chinook or sockeye). The color contrast is eye catching. Other combinations, such as ⅓ salmon mousse, ⅓ sole mousse, and ⅓ crabmeat mousse, are possible. Remember, any leftovers of cooked shellfish or poached fish can be transformed into splendid decorative creations.

Smoked fish mousses are also delicacies. For a standard recipe for smoked fish mousse, refer to Smoked Salmon Mousse in Chapter 12.

Cold fish soufflés are unusual presentations easily accomplished in soufflé molds of various sizes. Simply surround a soufflé mold with a paper collar extending at least 1 inch (2 ½ cm) above the rim of the mold. Fill mold with cold soufflé mixture. Chill until set and remove the paper. Decorate the top with radish slices, olives, or other suitable garnish.

CHAPTER 10

Fish Soups, Stews, and Matelotes

Combinations of seafoods, vegetables, herbs, stocks, and wines are many and varied. All over the world, fish soups, stews, or matelotes, are typical specialties of imaginative cooks and chefs: for example, bouillabaisse in France, clam chowders on the eastern coast of the United States, conch chowder in the southern states, and cioppino on the Pacific coast. These creations often depend on the regional availability of fresh fish and shellfish, and the ingredients in the recipes may vary during the year.

A chowder, fish soup, or stew, prepared with strictly fresh fish and shellfish, easily can make the reputation of an establishment, if prepared with the utmost care. Those who live near water learn to explore the nature of fish, and inevitably take advantage of their quality and freshness. Some of the best fish soups are found in seafood dining places near shores where fish abound and freshness is guaranteed.

Bouillabaisse Marseillaise

It is impossible to duplicate cioppino in Marseille as it is to make a real bouillabaisse in San Francisco. The Mediterranean Sea produces such fish as vive (weever), Saint Pierre (John Dory), baudroie or lotte (monkfish), grondin (sea rbin), rascasse (scorpion fish), and rouget, (goatfish), all necessary for the genuine bouillabaisse. In the United States, it would be hard to find all these species. They are available, but many fishermen consider some of them "junk fish," unwanted by consumers and many professionals. Nevertheless, everyone should be able to improvise a good bouillabaisse, provided the right variety of fish are combined for the stew.

In the northeastern and Middle Atlantic states, the following fish and shellfish are good substitutes: croaker, whiting, ocean perch, flounder, cod or cusk, striped bass, hake, tilefish, lobster, mussels, clams, and conger eel. In the southern and Gulf states, use pompano, redfish, red snapper, grouper, Spanish mackerel, seatrout, sheepshead, stone crab, and spiny lobster. On the West Coast, use white seabass, salmon, sole, halibut, Pacific cod, rockfish, goeducks, and razor clams. Freshwater fish species are not suitable for bouillabaisse. Whatever the varieties of seafood used, they must be *fresh*. In general, combine 75 percent lean fish with 25 percent fatty fish.

176

Cod and Potato Chowder

3	oz. ground salt pork
8	oz. chopped onion
1	clove minced garlic
1	bay leaf
¼	tsp. thyme
2	parsley stems
½	tsp. saffron
1	lb. diced potatoes
1	qt. fish stock
½	tsp. salt
¼	tsp. ground white pepper
1	cup milk
1½	lb. boneless cod
1	tbsp. chopped parsley

In a suitable soup pot, cook the salt pork until lightly brown. Stir in the onion, garlic, bay leaf, thyme, parsley stems, and saffron. Cook over low heat for 5 minutes.

Add the potatoes and fish stock. Season with salt and pepper. Bring to a boil and simmer for 30 minutes.

A few minutes before serving, cut the cod into cubes and add to the soup. Simmer for 5 minutes. Add the milk and parsley. Heat before serving.

Serves: 6
Calories per serving: 302

Codfish Chowder

2	lb. cod fillets
2	cups water
2	cups fish fumet
1	lb. diced potatoes
2	oz. cubed salt pork
4	oz. diced onion
2	cups milk
½	tsp. salt

¼	tsp. ground white pepper
1	oz. butter

Poach the fish in water and fumet until flaky but firm.

Remove the fish from the liquid and add the potatoes. Cook until the potatoes are done.

Brown the salt pork in a soup pot. Add the onion and cook over low heat until transparent. Stir in the stock and potatoes.

Add the fish and milk. Bring to a boil. Season to taste. Mix in the butter. Serve hot.

Serves: 6
Calories per serving: 332

Conch Chowder

16	oz. conch
4	oz. chopped salt pork
4	oz. chopped onion
1	tbsp. flour
8	oz. chopped tomatoes
3	oz. tomato paste
1	tsp. poultry seasoning
2	bay leaves
2	tsp. dry oregano
1	tsp. salt
2	qt. water

Pound the conch. Sprinkle with salt. Let stand for 15 minutes. Wash the conch and boil in salted water for 30 minutes. Drain the conch and put through a meat grinder.

In a medium saucepan, fry the salt pork with onion. Blend in the flour. Add the conch and the remaining ingredients. Simmer for about 2 hours.

Remove the bay leaves before serving.

Serves: 8
Calories per serving: 194

Manhattan Clam Chowder

4	oz. diced bacon
4	oz. diced carrots

1	oz. diced leek whites
4	oz. chopped onion
2	oz. chopped celery
½	tsp. minced garlic
4	oz. chopped tomatoes
4	oz. diced potatoes
6	oz. chopped clams
2½	cups water
½	tsp. salt
¼	tsp. ground pepper
¼	tsp. thyme
1	bay leaf

In a heavy soup pot, render the bacon. Add the carrots, leek, onion, and celery. Simmer over low heat for 5 to 10 minutes. Add the garlic and tomatoes and cook for a few minutes. Cook the potatoes separately with enough water to cover.

Bring the clams, clam juice, and water to a boil. Strain into the vegetables. Save the clams. Add the salt, pepper, thyme, and bay leaf. Simmer the soup for 30 minutes. Add the potatoes and clams. Serve hot.

Note: The above recipe is also called Philadelphia Chowder. Use the same recipe for Abalone Chowder, and Conch Chowder, substituting abalone and conch for clams.

Serves: 6
Calories per serving: 103

New England Clam Chowder

2	cups water
6	oz. shucked clams
6	oz. diced potatoes
2	oz. ground salt pork
4	oz. diced onion
1	oz. flour
1	cup milk
½	cup light cream
½	tsp. salt

| ½ | tsp. worcestershire |
| ¼ | tsp. ground white pepper |

Combine the water and clams. Bring to a boil. Remove the clams from stock. Strain the stock through a cheese cloth.

Melt the salt pork in a heavy soup pot. Add the onions and cook over low heat for 10 minutes. Stir in the flour to make a roux. Cook for 5 minutes.

Pour in the clam stock. Mix well until smooth. Add the chopped clams, milk, cream, and potatoes. Simmer until the potatoes are done. Season to taste with salt, worcestershire, and pepper. Serve hot.

Serves: 6
Calories per serving: 142

Bili-Bi Soup

2	oz. butter
½	cup flour
2	large chopped shallots
1	cup dry white wine
½	cup chopped parsley
2	oz. butter
⅛	tsp. ground white pepper
2½	lb. cleaned mussels
4	cups heavy cream

Melt the butter in a saucepan. Remove from heat and whisk in the flour. Cook until the roux is light brown.

Combine the shallots, wine, parsley, butter, and pepper in a separate saucepan. Bring to a boil. Add the mussels. Cover the pan and steam mussels until opened.

Strain cooking liquid and add to the roux. Whisk over medium heat until thickened. Simmer for a few minutes. Add the cream and simmer for 10 to 15 minutes. Season to taste with salt and pepper.

Remove the mussels from shells. Add to soup. Serve hot.

Serves: 12
Calories per serving: 229

Bouillabaisse

| 3 | lb. dressed fish |
| 12 | mussels |

12	clams
2	lb. live lobster
¼	cup olive oil
1	large chopped onion
1	medium chopped leek
2	cloves minced garlic
2	tbsp. chopped parsley
1	lb. peeled tomatoes
1	bouquet garni
4	oz. julienne fennel
1	tsp. salt
1	tsp. crushed saffron
12	slices garlic bread

Use a variety of fish like bass, cod, flounder, whiting, orange roughy, tilefish, or other. Cut into small portions. Scrub and wash the mussels and clams. Cut the lobster across into pieces, and crack the claws.

Heat the oil in a heavy pot. Add the onion and leek. Cook over low heat for 5 minutes. Add the garlic, parsley, chopped tomatoes, bouquet garni, salt, and saffron. Layer the fish on top of the vegetables. Cover with boiling water. Simmer 15 to 20 minutes.

Arrange the fish in a serving earthenware dish. Reduce cooking liquid by one third.

Cut bread into round slices. Toast lightly. Rub with a garlic clove.

Pour liquid over fish. Heat, and serve in soup plates with bread.

Serves: 12
Calories per serving: 144

Boula Boula

4	oz. green peas
1	qt. chicken stock
1	cup clear turtle soup
6	oz. turtle meat
¼	cup sherry wine
½	cup whipped cream

Thaw the peas if frozen. Puree in a blender.

Combine the peas, stock, and turtle soup in a soup pot. Simmer for 20 minutes. Strain the soup. Add the wine and turtle meat.

Pour the soup into individual earthenware soup tureens. Spoon whipped cream on top of soup. Brown under the broiler and serve hot.

Note: Any leftover pea soup and turtle soup can be used to prepare this recipe.

Serves: 6
Calories per serving: 109

Cod Bouillabaisse

1½	lb. salted cod
¼	cup oil
1	medium chopped onion
2	oz. white leek
3	cloves minced garlic
1½	qt. water
½	tsp. thyme
2	bay leaf
1	tsp. saffron
8	oz. diced potatoes
1	tbsp. chopped parsley
12	thin slices French bread
1	clove garlic

Soak the cod for 12 hours.

Heat the oil in a heavy wide pot. Add the onions, chopped leek, and garlic, and cook over low heat for 10 minutes.

Pour in the water. Add the thyme, bay leaves, and saffron. Bring to a boil. Add the potatoes and cook for 10 to 15 minutes.

Cut the cod into small pieces. Add to the soup. Simmer until the cod is flaky and the potatoes are done. Mix in the parsley.

Toast the thin slices of bread. Rub with garlic. Serve with the soup.

Serves: 6
Calories per serving: 203

Consommé Belle Vue

4	lb. soft-shell clams
3	stalks celery
1½	qt. chicken stock
½	tsp. salt
¼	tsp. ground white pepper
½	cup whipped cream

Wash the soft-shell clams thoroughly in cold water.

In a soup pot, combine the clams, celery, chicken stock, salt, and pepper. Bring to a boil and simmer for 5 minutes. Remove from the fire. Let stand for 10 minutes. Strain the broth through a fine china cap or cheese cloth. Top each serving with whipped cream. Serve the clams separately.

Serves: 6
Calories per serving: 112

Curried Clam Soup

2	cups chopped clams
2	cups clam juice
1	tsp. chopped shallots
2	sprigs parsley
1	cup dry white wine
2	tsp. powder curry
2	cups heavy cream
3	egg yolks
½	tsp. salt
¼	tsp. ground white pepper

Combine the clams, clam juice, shallots, parsley, white wine, and curry. Simmer for 10 minutes.

Make a liaison with the cream and egg yolks. Stir into the soup. Season. Heat the soup without boiling. Hold over a water-bath.

Serves: 6
Calories per serving: 266

Golden Caviar Consommé

6	whole spinach leaves
1	cup golden caviar★
1	cup lobster meat chunks
6	truffle slices
4	cups chicken consommé

Blanch the spinach leaves in boiling water. Drain, pat dry, and lay flat.

Spoon a tablespoon of the caviar at one end of each spinach leaf. Fold the edges over the caviar to form a small package. Place in the center of each soup bowl.

Arrange the lobster meat and truffle slices into each bowl. Pour the chilled consommé into each bowl. Serve immediately.

★American golden caviar is available in specialty gourmet food stores.

Serves: 6
Calories per serving: 88

Key West Fish Stew

2	medium chopped onions
1	clove minced garlic
2	medium chopped leeks
¼	cup olive oil
1	lb. kingfish★ fillets
2	large tomatoes
1	bay leaf
2	cups fish stock
12	chopped oysters
1	cup cooked shrimp
½	cup chopped pimento
1	tsp. saffron
1	cup white wine
½	tsp. salt
¼	tsp. ground white pepper

Sauté the onions, garlic, and leeks in olive oil. Add the diced fish, peeled, seeded, and diced tomatoes, bay leaf, and fish stock. Simmer for 20 minutes.

Add the remaining ingredients and simmer for 5 to 10 minutes.

Serve hot with slices of toasted garlic bread.

*Kingfish may be substituted with grouper, snapper, redfish, or sheepshead.

Serves: 8
Calories per serving: 200

Key West Turtle Soup

1	qt. beef consommé
⅛	tsp. thyme
¼	tsp, basil
⅛	tsp. rosemary
⅛	tsp. fennel seeds
6	oz. turtle meat
1	tbsp. cornstarch
2	oz. dry sherry wine
½	tsp. salt
¼	tsp. ground white pepper

Combine the consommé and herbs in a soup pot. Simmer for 10 minutes. Strain consommé.

Dice the turtle meat. Add to consommé and simmer for 20 minutes.

Dissolve the cornstarch in wine. Stir into the hot soup to thicken. Simmer for 2 to 3 minutes. Season and serve hot.

Serves: 6
Calories per serving: 80

Lobster Bisque

1½	lb. live lobster
3	oz. butter
1	cup mirepoix
2	oz. cognac
½	cup dry white wine

1	tbsp. tomato paste
½	tsp. thyme
1	bay leaf
¼	cup rice
1½	qt. fish stock
½	cup heavy cream
½	tsp. salt
¼	tsp. ground white pepper
¼	tsp. cayenne pepper

Cut the live lobster across into sections. Remove the claws and crack. Split the head in half lengthwise. Remove the stomach, then cut crosswise into quarters. Separate the legs.

In a heavy pot, melt the butter. Add the mirepoix and cook over low heat without browning. Add the lobster pieces and cook until they turn red.

Pour in cognac. Ignite. Add the wine, tomato paste, thyme, bay leaf, and half the stock. Cook for 15 minutes.

In a separate pot, cook the rice with the remaining stock.

Remove the lobster pieces from soup. Dice the lobster meat. Blend the rice and stock. Combine with the soup. Strain through a fine strainer. Add the cream and seasonings. Stir in the lobster pieces. Heat and serve hot.

Serves: 6
Calories per serving: 244

Mussel Soup

2	lb. fresh mussels
2	tbsp. butter
2	tbsp. chopped shallots
¼	cup chopped onions
½	tsp. saffron
2	parsley sprigs
1	bay leaf
½	tsp. dry thyme
1	cup dry white wine
2	cups heavy cream
½	tsp. salt

¼	tsp. ground white pepper
½	cup stewed tomatoes

Scrub the mussels under cold running water, remove the beards, and drain.

Heat the butter in a saucepan. Add the shallots and onions. Cook briefly, stirring, but do not brown.

Add the mussels, saffron, parsley, bay leaf, thyme, white wine, and bring to boil.

Cover and cook over high heat for 4 to 5 minutes. Add cream, salt, and pepper to taste. Bring to a boil and simmer for 2 minutes.

Strain the mixture through a fine mesh strainer. Reserve the broth.

Remove the mussels from the shells. Transfer the reserved broth to the saucepan and add the mussels and tomatoes. Bring to a boil. Serve at once.

Serves: 5
Calories per serving: 460

Mussel Soup Trois Gros

4½	lb. fresh mussels
3	oz. dry white wine
1	tbsp. chopped shallots
¼	cup olive oil
5	oz. diced carrots
5	oz. chopped onion
2	chopped leek whites
2	cloves minced garlic
4	oz. chopped tomatoes
½	tsp. saffron threads
1	qt. fish fumet
3	oz. heavy cream
½	tsp. dry thyme
½	tsp. salt
¼	tsp. ground white pepper

Wash and scrub the mussels, remove the beards, and discard any dead open mussels.

In a heavy, deep pot, combine the wine and shallots. Bring to a boil. Add the mussels, cover the pot, and steam until all mussels are open, tossing occasionally. Strain the cooking liquid. Take the mussels out of the shells.

In the same pot, heat the oil. Add the mirepoix (carrots, onion, leeks) and simmer for 5 minutes. Add the garlic, chopped tomatoes, and saffron. Pour in the fish fumet and mussel cooking liquid. Bring to a boil and simmer for 30 to 40 minutes.

Before serving, stir the cream, mussels, and thyme into the soup. Season to taste with salt and pepper.

Serves: 6
Calories per serving: 173

Oyster Bisque Florentine

1	pt. shucked oysters
3	oz. butter
2	oz. chopped onion
¼	cup flour
2	cups fish stock
1	cup dry white wine
4	oz. spinach
½	cup heavy cream
½	tsp. salt
¼	tsp. ground white pepper

Remove any shells from the oysters. Save the oyster liquid.

In a saucepan, melt the butter. Stir in the onion until transparent. Add the flour and cook over low heat for 5 minutes. Add the stock and wine. Mix well. Bring to a boil and simmer for 15 minutes.

Cook the spinach in boiling water. Drain, squeeze to remove any excess water, and chop the spinach. Add to the soup, together with the oyster juice and the cream. Simmer for 5 minutes. Season to taste.

Serves: 6
Calories per serving: 197

Oyster Stew

1	cup shucked oysters
4	oz. butter
1	tsp. worcestershire

1	qt. hot milk
1	oz. butter
1	oz. flour
¼	tsp. salt
⅛	tsp. ground white pepper
1	tbsp. chopped chives
¼	tsp. paprika
1	cup oyster crackers

Gently heat the cleaned oysters in their own juice until the edges start to curl. Heat the butter, worcestershire, and milk. Mix the flour and butter, and add to the milk mixture to thicken.

Just before serving, add the oysters. Season to taste with salt, pepper chives, and paprika. Serve hot with oyster crackers.

Serves: 6
Calories per serving: 226

Provençale Fish Soup

1	lb. grouper★ fillet
2	tsp. saffron
2	tbsp. olive oil
½	tsp. aromat
2	medium chopped shallots
1	small diced white leek
1	large minced garlic clove
1	14-oz. can tomatoes
½	cup dry white wine
1½	qt. fish stock
½	tsp. seafood seasoning
4	oz. roux
1	tsp. salt
¼	tsp. tabasco
16	garlic croutons

★Other white firm fish besides grouper may be used for this recipe.

Dice the grouper fillet. Season with half the saffron, half the olive oil, and aromat seasoning.

Pour the remaining olive oil in a heavy bottom soup pot.

Sauté the shallots, leek, and garlic over low heat. Stir in the remaining saffron and the chopped tomatoes.

Add the wine, fish stock, and seafood seasoning. Whip in the roux to slightly thicken the soup. Allow to simmer for 20 minutes. Season with salt, pepper, and tabasco.

A few minutes before serving, add the diced grouper. Simmer the soup for 5 minutes. Serve in soup plates or cups with croutons.

Serves: 8
Calories per serving: 180

San Francisco Cioppino

½	cup oil
1	medium chopped onion
1	tsp. chopped garlic
1	tbsp. chopped parsley
1½	lb. chopped tomatoes
1	tbsp. tomato paste
1½	cups dry white wine
1	tsp. salt
¼	tsp. ground white pepper
1	lb. live bluecrab
1	lb. live lobster
1	lb. rockfish fillet
12	medium shelled shrimp
12	small cherrystone clams
12	mussels

In a heavy pot, heat the oil. Add the onion, garlic, and parsley. Stir over moderate heat. Do not brown. Add the chopped, seeded tomatoes, tomato paste, wine, salt, and pepper. Simmer for 10 minutes. Cut the lobster across into sections. Crack the legs. Split the head lengthwise. Remove the stomach and cut the head into quarters. Cut the crab into serving pieces. Add the lobster and crab to soup. Simmer for 10 minutes. Cut the rockfish into portions. Add to the pot together with the clean shrimp. Cook for 5 minutes. Steam the clean cherrystone clams and mussels in a pot with a little water. Add to the stew with the strained juice. Heat before serving.

Serves: 6
Calories per serving: 404

Shrimp Bisque

2	oz. butter
1	oz. chopped onion
1	oz. chopped carrots
1	oz. chopped celery
1¼	lb. shrimp
2	oz. cognac
3	oz. dry white wine
¼	tsp. thyme
1	bay leaf
6	parsley stems
1	qt. fish stock
2	oz. rice
¾	cup cream
2	oz. shrimp butter
½	tsp. salt

In a large saucepan, melt the butter. Add the onion, carrots, celery, and cook over low heat for 5 minutes stirring occasionally. Rinse the shrimp and add to the vegetables. Sauté over high heat until the shells turn pink. Flambé with cognac. Deglaze with wine. Add parsley stems, bay leaf, and thyme. Reduce by half. Add the rice and cook for 20 minutes. Shell and devein the cooked shrimp saving some for garnish. Puree the bisque in a food processor or blender and strain through a fine china cap. Press to extract all juices. Add the cream and heat. Season to taste with salt. Stir in the shrimp butter. Garnish the bisque with the reserved shrimp. Serve hot.

Serves: 6
Calories per serving: 327

Spanish Fish Stew

1	lb. cod fillet
1	lb. haddock fillet
2	lobster tails
½	lb. squid rings
6	cleaned mussels

6	medium deveined shrimp
¼	cup olive oil
8	oz. chopped onion
1	lb. chopped tomatoes
3	cloves minced garlic
1	tsp. saffron
3	cups fish stock

Use cusk, halibut, or other lean white fish. Cut fish into portions.

In a heavy casserole or a large pot, heat the oil. Add onion and cook over low heat. Add the tomatoes, garlic, saffron, and fish stock. Simmer for 15 minutes.

Arrange all the fish over the bottom of an ovenproof serving dish. Pour the soup over the fish. Bake at 375°F (190°C) for 5 minutes, basting the fish occasionally. Serve hot.

Serves: 6
Calories per serving: 310

Fish Matelote

2	lb. conger eel steak
1	lb. perch steak
2	oz. butter
2	oz. chopped shallots
1	cup dry white wine
1	qt. fish stock
½	tsp. salt
¼	tsp. ground white pepper
¼	tsp. leaves thyme
2	oz. butter
2	oz. flour
1	tbsp. lemon juice
1	cup diced mushrooms
2	egg yolks
½	cup heavy cream

Use eel, perch, bass, pickerel, or trout.

In a heavy bottom pot, melt the butter. Add the shallots and cook over low heat for 5 minutes. Add the wine, fish stock, salt, pepper, and thyme.

Cut the fish steaks into small sections. Add to stock and simmer for 10 minutes or until fish is tender.

Mix the butter and flour in a small saucepan. Cook for 5 minutes over low heat. Transfer the fish to a shallow serving dish.

Stir the roux (butter and flour) into the fish stock and simmer until thick. Add the lemon juice and mushrooms and cook for 5 minutes. Combine the egg yolks and cream and stir into the hot soup. Pour over the fish. Serve hot.

Serves: 6
Calories per serving: 380

Matelote Illhaeusern

3½	lb. cleaned fish
2	oz. butter
2	oz. chopped shallots
1	cup Rhine wine
1	qt. fish fumet
½	tsp. salt
¼	tsp. ground black pepper
¼	tsp. thyme leaves
⅛	tsp. ground nutmeg
2	oz. butter
2	oz. flour
2	tbsp. lemon juice
1	cup diced mushrooms
2	egg yolks
½	cup heavy cream

Use eel, perch, pickerel, or other white firm fish. Cut the fish into steaks. In a heavy bottom pot, melt the butter. Add the shallots and simmer for 5 minutes. Add the wine, fish fumet, salt, pepper, thyme, and nutmeg. Place the pieces of eel into the stock and simmer for 15 to 20 minutes. Add other pieces of fish, ending with the most tender.

Prepare a roux with butter and flour. Transfer the fish to a serving dish. Pour the cooking stock over the roux and stir until smooth. Simmer for 10 minutes. Add the lemon juice and mushrooms. At serving time, add the liaison of egg yolks and heavy cream. Pour the sauce over the fish and serve hot.

Serves: 6
Calories per serving: 354

Matelote of Salmon

2	oz. oil
1½	lb. steak salmon
½	tsp. salt
¼	tsp. ground white pepper
4	oz. chopped onion
1	tbsp. chopped shallots
1	cup dry red wine
2	cups fish stock
1	clove chopped garlic
1	tbsp. soft butter
1	tbsp. flour
12	small peeled pearl onions
12	small cleaned mushroom caps

Heat the oil in a frying pan. Brown the salmon steaks on both sides. Remove any excess oil. Season the steaks with salt and pepper. Add the onion and shallots to salmon and cook over low heat for 2 minutes. Pour in the wine and fish stock. Add the garlic. Bring to a boil and simmer for about 10 minutes.

Transfer the salmon to a serving dish. Remove the bones and skin. Reduce the cooking liquid to half.

Mix the butter and flour and whip into the liquid to thicken. Add the pearl onions and mushrooms. Simmer for 10 minutes. Pour the soup over fish and serve hot.

Serves: 6
Calories per serving: 227

11

Fish Sauces

Classical sauces are the foundation of culinary art. Although international cooking has been altered and adapted to meet new tastes, the preparation of sauces remains, by professional standards, the same as at the beginning of this century. One fact is clear: no one dares weaken the very foundation of one of the oldest arts.

Fish sauces must be prepared with great care and seasoned to perfection. These criteria apply to any sauce, but particularly to fish and shellfish hot sauces. Of course, the use of herb mixes, flavor enhancers, numerous aromats, and seafood seasoning mixes available commercially can instantly improve the taste of a dull sauce. The reduction of a weak sauce, or one without character, will invariably improve its taste and flavor. One often hears that the sauce makes the dish; undoubtedly, hot and cold sauces contribute immensely to the success of any fish dish. A large number of cooking techniques applied to fish and shellfish require the complement of a quality sauce. Fish stocks and fumets are often the base of these sauces.

COLD SAUCES
Aioli Sauce

1	large boiled potato
4	cloves minced garlic
2	egg yolks
½	tsp. salt
1	cup olive oil
1	tsp. lemon juice

Rice the boiled potato.

Prepare the sauce like a mayonnaise, mixing the first four ingredients and beating the oil in very slowly. Add the lemon juice.

Serves: 6
Calories per serving: 355

195

Chantilly Sauce

| 1½ | cups lemon mayonnaise |
| ¼ | cup whipped heavy cream |

Prepare the mayonnaise with lemon juice. Fold in the whipped cream. Serve with cold fish or seafood.

Serves: 6
Calories per serving: 218

Cocktail Sauce

1½	cups mayonnaise
½	cup chili sauce
2	oz. catsup
2	tsp. worcestershire
1	tbsp. lemon juice
1	tbsp. brandy
¼	tsp. seasoned salt
¼	tsp. paprika
½	cup whipped heavy cream

Blend all ingredients until smooth. Serve with cold seafood.

Serves: 6
Calories per serving: 276

Frozen Horseradish Sauce

1	cup whipped heavy cream
1½	tbsp. grated horseradish
2	tsp. white vinegar
¼	tsp. salt
¼	tsp. sugar
¼	tsp. ground white pepper

Combine the whipped cream with the horseradish and vinegar. Gently mix in the salt, sugar, and white pepper. Roll the sauce in greased parchment paper and freeze until set.
At serving time, cut into ¼-inch (½-cm) thick slices.

Serves: 6
Calories per serving: 76

Green Goddess Dressing

1	clove garlic
1	anchovy fillet
5	oz. mayonnaise
2	oz. sour cream
1	tbsp. tarragon vinegar
1	tsp. lemon juice
1/8	tsp. ground white pepper
2	tbsp. water
1	tbsp. minced parsley
2	tsp. chopped chives

Mince the garlic with the anchovy. Combine with the mayonnaise, sour cream, vinegar, lemon juice, white pepper, water, parsley, and chives. Chill the sauce before serving.

Serves: 6
Calories per serving: 80

Mayonnaise

2	egg yolks
1/2	tsp. salt
1/8	tsp. cayenne pepper
1	tsp. Dijon mustard
1 1/2	cups oil
3/4	tsp. lemon juice

To ensure perfect emulsification, all ingredients should be at room temperature.

In a mixing bowl, mix the egg yolks, salt, pepper, and mustard. Whip continuously while pouring in the oil in a small stream.

When the sauce thickens, alternate the oil and lemon juice until used. If the sauce is too thick after the ingredients have been combined, stir in a small amount of lukewarm water.

Note: Mayonnaise can also be prepared in a food processor.

Serves: 15
Calories per serving: 108

Picadilly Sauce

1½	cups mayonnaise
¼	cup sour cream
¼	tsp. worcestershire
1	tsp. lemon juice
1	oz. chopped fennel

Blend all the ingredients to make a smooth sauce. Serve with cold fish.

Serves: 15
Calories per serving: 210

Pittsburgh Sauce

1	cup mayonnaise
¼	cup catsup
2	tbsp. white wine
1	tbsp. chopped chervil

Combine all the ingredients in a mixing bowl. Chill the sauce. Use for Galantine of Scallops.

Serves: 10
Calories per serving: 89

Remoulade Sauce

1½	cups mayonnaise
1	tbsp. capers
1	tbsp. chopped pickles
1	chopped anchovy fillet
1	tsp. chopped tarragon
1	tsp. chopped shallots
2	tsp. chopped parsley
1	tsp. prepared mustard

Combine all ingredients together. Serve cold with cold fish or fried seafood.

Serves: 15
Calories per serving: 84

Russian Sauce

1½	cups mayonnaise
2	oz. pressed caviar
½	tsp. worcestershire

Combine all ingredients. Serve cold with cold fish or fried seafood.

Serves: 15
Calories per serving: 92

Sauce Albigeoise

2	tsp. capers
1	tbsp. chopped dill pickles
2	hard-cooked eggs
2	tsp. chopped parsley
1	clove garlic
1½	cups salad oil
½	cup wine vinegar
¼	tsp. salt
⅛	tsp. ground black pepper
3	minced anchovy fillets

Puree the capers, pickles, hard-cooked eggs, parsley, and garlic together. Mix in the oil and vinegar as for a mayonnaise. Season with salt and pepper. Stir in the anchovy paste.

Serves: 15
Calories per serving: 114

Sauce Andalouse

1½	cups mayonnaise
2	tsp. tomato paste
1	tbsp. diced pimentos

¾   tsp. lemon juice

¼   tsp. worcestershire

Combine all ingredients.

Serves: 15
Calories per serving: 81

Sauce Antiboise

1½   cups mayonnaise

1   tsp. anchovy paste

2   tsp. tomato paste

¾   tsp. chopped fresh tarragon

Combine all ingredients.

Serves: 15
Calories per serving: 82

Sauce Cypriote

1½   cups mayonnaise

3   hard-cooked egg yolks

1   tbsp. tomato puree

½   tsp. anchovy paste

2   tsp. chopped fennel

Chop the egg yolks finely. Combine all ingredients to make a smooth sauce. Serve with cold poached fish.

Serves: 15
Calories per serving: 93

Sauce Gribiche

3   hard-cooked egg yolks

1½   tsp. dijon mustard

¼   tsp. salt

⅛   tsp. ground white pepper

2   oz. tarragon vinegar

¾	cup oil
2	tbsp. chopped pickles
1	tbsp. chopped capers
1	hard-cooked egg white
1	tbsp. chopped parsley

In a food processor or a blender, make a paste with the hard-cooked egg yolks. Add the mustard, salt, pepper, and vinegar. Continue mixing, adding the oil gradually as for a mayonnaise.

Transfer to a mixing bowl. Blend in the chopped pickles, capers, and the egg whites cut into julienne. Stir in the parsley.

Serves: 10
Calories per serving: 114

Sauce Ravigotte

½	cup vinaigrette sauce
1	tsp. chopped parsley
1	tsp. chopped chervil
1	tsp. chopped tarragon
1	tsp. chopped chives
1	tbsp. chopped onion
1	tbsp. capers

Combine all the ingredients. Serve with cold fish, or use to marinate seafood.

Serves: 6
Calories per serving: 83

Sauce Verte

½	oz. fresh spinach
½	oz. fresh watercress
½	oz. parsley
½	oz. fresh tarragon
⅛	tsp. garlic powder
2	tsp. lemon juice
1½	cups mayonnaise

Blanch and drain the spinach, watercress, parsley, and tarragon. Squeeze out excess water. Puree in a blender with the garlic powder.

Stir the herb puree and lemon juice in the mayonnaise. Serve cold with cold salmon or other cold fish.

Serves: 15
Calories per serving: 81

Tartar Sauce

2	hard-cooked eggs
1½	cups mayonnaise
2	tsp. chopped chives
1	tsp. chopped shallots
1	tsp. chopped tarragon
1	tsp. chopped chervil
1	tsp. chopped parsley

Chop the eggs in a food processor. Combine with the remaining ingredients. Adjust seasoning to taste. Serve with fried fish or fried seafood.

Serves: 6
Calories per serving: 91

Tuna–Anchovy Sauce

½	cup olive oil
6	hard-cooked egg yolks
1	tbsp. flaked tuna
1	tbsp. chopped parsley
1	tbsp. anchovy paste
6	chopped dill pickles
3	oz. wine vinegar
½	tsp. salt
⅛	tsp. ground white pepper

Whip the oil with the crushed egg yolks until smooth. Add the tuna, chopped parsley, anchovy paste, and pickles. Pour in the vinegar. Season with salt and pepper. Stir the sauce well. Serve with cold seafood.

Serves: 6
Calories per serving: 154

Vinaigrette

¼	tsp. salt
1	tbsp. dijon mustard
2	oz. wine vinegar
¾	cup oil
⅛	tsp. onion powder
⅛	tsp. ground black pepper

Dissolve the salt and the mustard in the vinegar.
Add the oil and remaining ingredients and blend well.

Serves: 6
Calories per serving: 159

Vincent Sauce

1½	tsp. chopped tarragon
1½	tsp. chopped parsley
1½	tsp. chopped chives
1½	tsp. chopped chervil
½	oz. chopped spinach
½	oz. chopped watercress
2	hard-cooked eggs
1½	cups mayonnaise
¼	tsp. worcestershire

Chop the eggs finely. Combine all ingredients. Serve cold with cold fish or fried seafoods.

Serves: 15
Calories per serving: 91

HOT SAUCES

Anchovy Sauce

1½	cups sauce Normande
1¼	oz. anchovy butter
½	oz. anchovy paste

Bring the sauce Normande to a boil. Remove from the fire and stir in the anchovy butter and anchovy paste. Keep the sauce in a double boiler until ready to use.

Serves: 6
Calories per serving: 32

Béarnaise

10	oz. butter
2	tsp. chopped shallot
1	tsp. cracked peppercorns
¼	cup tarragon vinegar
1½	tbsp. chopped tarragon
4	egg yolks
1½	tsp. chopped parsley
¼	tsp. ground white pepper

Clarify the butter and keep warm. Place the shallots, peppercorns, vinegar, and half of the chopped tarragon in a saucepan. Reduce by three quarters and cool. Add the egg yolks with 1 tsp. of water. Transfer to a stainless steel bowl. Place the bowl over boiling water but do not allow the bowl to touch the water as it would overcook the egg yolks. Slow, progressive heating is best when making béarnaise. Whip the egg yolk mixture until it reaches a creamy consistency. Remove from heat. Add the warm clarified butter and strain through a fine china cap. Garnish with remaining chopped tarragon and parsley. Season with cayenne pepper.

Serves: 15
Calories per serving: 148

Sauces Derived From Béarnaise

Sauce Choron: add 1½ tsp. tomato paste to béarnaise

Sauce Arlésienne: add 1½ tsp. tomato paste and ¾ tsp. anchovy paste to béarnaise

Sauce Véron: add 1½ oz. (40 g) cooked pureed spinach and ¾ tsp. anchovy paste

Béchamel

2	tbsp. butter
1	oz. flour
2	cups milk
½	tsp. salt
¼	tsp. ground white pepper
⅛	tsp. ground nutmeg

Melt the butter in a sauce pot. Stir in the flour and cook over low heat for 10 minutes, stirring occasionally to create a roux. Do not brown. Cool the roux. Heat the milk and pour over the roux. Mix with a wire whip until smooth. Simmer for 5 minutes. Season with salt, pepper, and nutmeg. Béchamel can be stored in a bowl for future use. Lightly coat the top of the sauce with melted butter to prevent skin formation.

Serves: 6
Calories per serving: 100

Beurre Blanc

2	oz. chopped shallots
2	oz. wine vinegar
3	oz. dry white wine
8	oz. butter

In a saucepan, combine the shallots, vinegar, and wine. Reduce to two thirds. Cool and stir in small pieces of butter with a whisk, making sure the butter does not get too hot. Season with salt and pepper to taste.

Serves: 12
Calories per serving: 140

Bordeaux Wine Sauce

1	tbsp. chopped shallots
¾	cup red wine
¼	tsp. thyme
½	tsp. crushed peppercorns
1½	cups velouté sauce
1	tsp. chopped tarragon

In a saucepan, combine the chopped shallots, red wine, thyme, and peppercorns. Reduce by half.

Mix in the velouté sauce. Simmer for 10 minutes. Strain through a fine china cap. Stir in the chopped tarragon.

Serves: 6
Calories per serving: 105

Bretonne Sauce

1	oz. leek whites
1	oz. celery
1	oz. onion
1	oz. mushroom
1	oz. butter
1½	cups velouté sauce
¼	cup heavy cream

Cut the vegetables into julienne.

Melt the butter in a heavy pan. Add the vegetables and simmer over low heat without coloring. Stir frequently, adding a small amount of water to steam the vegetables.

Mix in the velouté sauce. Bring to a boil. Stir in the heavy cream. Simmer for 5 to 6 minutes.

Serves: 6
Calories per serving: 120

Caper Sauce

1½   cups velouté sauce

1½   tbsp. capers

At serving time, stir the capers into the hot velouté sauce.

Serves: 6
Calories per serving: 111

Cardinal Sauce

1½   cups cream sauce

½   cup fish fumet

½   cup heavy cream

1½   oz. lobster butter

Combine the cream sauce with the fish fumet and the heavy cream. Reduce by one quarter. Remove from the fire and gradually add the lobster butter while stirring.

Serves: 6
Calories per serving: 135

Clam Sauce for Noodles

1   lb. chopped clams

½   cup clam liquor

4   oz. butter

2   oz. flour

1   tsp. worcestershire

¼   tsp. paprika

¼   tsp. ground white pepper

2   egg yolks

Drain and save the liquor from the clams. Melt the butter, stir in the flour, then add the clam liquor and seasonings.

Stir a little of the hot liquid into the beaten egg yolks, then add the remaining liquid, stirring constantly. Add the clams. Heat again and serve with pasta.

Serves: 6
Calories per serving: 179

Cream Sauce

1	tbsp. butter
1	tbsp. flour
1	cup milk
½	tsp. salt
¼	tsp. ground white pepper

Melt the butter in a saucepan. Stir in the flour to make a roux. Add the milk and stir until sauce is thick and smooth. Season with salt and pepper. Pour the sauce in a stainless steel container. Cover with buttered wax paper and save for future uses.

Serves: 4
Calories per serving: 71

Creole Sauce

1	oz. butter
1	tbsp. oil
1	tbsp. flour
1	cup tomato puree
½	cup ½" chopped onions
1	stick sliced celery
½	cup ½" chopped green pepper
1	tsp. minced garlic
½	tsp. thyme
2	bay leaves
1	tsp. chili powder
¼	tsp. cayenne pepper
⅛	tsp. ground black pepper
½	tsp. worcestershire
1	cup chicken stock

Combine the butter, oil, and flour in a saucepan. Cook over low heat until light brown. Add the onions, celery, and green pepper. Cook until the vegetables are tender. Add the remaining ingredients. Simmer for 15 to 20 minutes. Adjust the seasoning if necessary. Use for shrimp creole and other creole dishes.

Serves: 6
Calories per serving: 84

Curry Sauce

2	oz. butter
2	oz. chopped onion
1	tsp. curry powder
⅛	tsp. ground mace
½	diced apple
¼	diced banana
1½	cups velouté sauce
¼	cup heavy cream

Melt the butter. Add the onion and cook over low heat for 10 minutes.

Mix in the curry powder, mace, diced apple, and banana. Cook for 5 more minutes. Stir in the velouté sauce and heavy cream. Simmer for 20 minutes. Strain the sauce through a china cap. Adjust seasoning if necessary.

Serves: 6
Calories per serving: 146

Demi Glace Sauce

3	lbs. veal bones
1	large onion
2	ribs celery
2	medium carrots
¼	tsp. dried thyme
1	bay leaf
1	tsp. crushed peppercorns
1	clove crushed garlic
1	tsp. salt
¼	cup flour
2	qts. water
½	cup tomato puree
1	medium chopped leek
2	sprigs parsley

In a roasting pan, combine the veal bones with the coarsely chopped onion, celery, and carrots. Add the thyme, bay leaf, peppercorns, garlic, and salt. Bake at 475°F (240°C) for 30 to 40 minutes, or until bones are brown.

Sprinkle bones with flour. Stir the bones to distribute the flour. Bake for 10 more minutes.

Transfer the bones to a large kettle. Add some water to the roasting pan. Heat to dissolve the brown particles in the bottom of the pan. Pour the liquid in the kettle, together with the remaining water, tomato puree, leeks, and parsley. Simmer for 2 hours.

Strain the liquid, and reduce to half to obtain a rich brown glaze.

Dill Sauce

1½	cups velouté sauce
3	oz. heavy cream
1	tbsp. chopped dill

Combine the velouté sauce with the heavy cream. Bring to a boil and simmer to reduce by one quarter. Strain through a china cap and mix in the fresh dill.

Serves: 6
Calories per serving: 105

Diplomate Sauce

1½	cups sauce Normande
1	oz. lobster butter
1	oz. diced lobster meat
1	tsp. diced truffles

Heat the sauce Normande. Whip in the lobster butter. Add the lobster meat and truffles. Adjust the seasoning if necessary.

Serves: 6
Calories per serving: 89

Fine Herb Sauce

1½	cups veloute sauce
1	oz. shallot butter
1	tbsp. chopped parsley
1	tsp. chopped tarragon
½	tsp. chopped basil

If using dry herbs, use half the amount.
Combine all ingredients. Simmer the sauce for 5 minutes.

Serves: 6
Calories per serving: 84

Hollandaise*

4	egg yolks
1½	tbsp. cold water
pinch	cayenne pepper
⅛	tsp. salt
10	oz. butter
1	tbsp. lemon juice

Clarify the butter to measure 10 ounces. Whip egg yolks and water together in a stainless steel bowl over boiling water. Do not allow the bowl to touch the water as it will overcook the egg yolks. Slow, progressive heating is best when making hollandaise sauce. Whip the yolks until they reach a creamy consistency. Add the seasonings. Remove from heat. Slowly pour warm butter into yolks, whipping continuously to blend.

Note: Add the lemon juice at serving time to prevent fermentation of the sauce.

*See additional recipes for sauces derived from hollandaise

Serves: 6
Calories per serving: 373

Sauces Derived From Hollandaise

Sauce Mousseline: Fold 2 oz. whipped cream into hollandaise
Sauce Maltaise: Add 2 oz. orange juice and ½ tsp. grated orange zest to
    hollandaise
Sauce Moutarde: Add 1 tsp. imported mustard to hollandaise
Hazelnut Sauce: Mix 4 tbsp. ground hazelnuts into hollandaise
Macadamia Sauce: Mix 4 tbsp. chopped macadamia nuts into hollandaise
Maximilian Sauce: Add ¾ tsp. anchovy paste to hollandaise

Lobster Sauce

1½	cups fish velouté sauce
¼	cup heavy cream
1	oz. lobster butter

Bring the velouté sauce to a boil. Add the cream and simmer for
10 minutes. Remove from the fire and stir in the lobster butter.

Serves: 6
Calories per serving: 146

Mornay Sauce

1½	cups cream sauce
3	oz. fish fumet
1	oz. grated parmesan
1	egg yolk

Combine the cream sauce and fish fumet. Reduce by one quarter.
Mix the parmesan cheese with the egg yolk. Stir the mixture into
the sauce and bring to the boiling point.

Serves: 6
Calories per serving: 75

Mussel Sauce

2	tbsp. mussel stock
1½	sauce bercy
2	egg yolks

Mix the mussel stock with the egg yolks. Stir in the boiling bercy
sauce. Keep the sauce hot over a waterbath until serving time.

Serves: 6
Calories per serving: 132

Mustard Sauce

1½	tsp. butter
1½	tsp. chopped shallots
3	oz. white wine
1½	cups velouté sauce
1	tbsp. dijon mustard

Brown the shallots in butter. Deglaze with white wine. Reduce by half. Add the velouté sauce and bring to a boil. Simmer for 10 to 15 minutes. Before serving, stir in the mustard.

Serves: 6
Calories per serving: 88

Newburg Sauce

1½	cups cream sauce
1¼	oz. lobster butter
2	oz. sherry wine
2	oz. paprika
½	tsp. salt
¼	tsp. ground white pepper

Bring the cream sauce to a boil. Stir in the remaining ingredients. Adjust the seasoning.

Serves: 6
Calories per serving: 102

Oyster Sauce

1½	cups sauce Normande
1	oz. oyster stock
6	small cooked oysters

Combine the sauce Normande with the oyster stock. Simmer for 5 minutes or to desired consistency. At serving time, mix in the cooked oysters.

Serves: 6
Calories per serving: 128

Sauce Allemande

1	egg yolk
2	oz. heavy cream
1½	cups hot velouté sauce
1	tbsp. lemon juice
⅛	tsp. ground nutmeg
¼	tsp. ground white pepper

Prepare a liaison by mixing the egg yolk and cream. Stir in the hot velouté sauce and bring to a boil quickly. Add the lemon juice. Season with nutmeg and pepper. Strain through a fine china cap.

Note: to make mushroom sauce, add sliced cooked mushrooms to the sauce Allemande.

Serves: 12
Calories per serving: 53

Sauce Américaine

1	1½ lb. lobster
2½	oz. butter
2	oz. olive oil
2	oz. cognac
4	oz. white wine
½	cup fish stock
1	clove crushed garlic
1	medium chopped shallot
2	tsp. tomato paste
½	cup velouté sauce
1	tsp. chopped parsley
1	tsp. chopped tarragon
⅛	tsp. cayenne pepper

Cut the tail of a live lobster into sections at the joints. Break off the claws and crack for easy extraction of the meat. Split the head in half lengthwise. Remove the stomach. Take out the coral (if female) and other creamy parts. Mix with about ⅔ of the butter and set aside. In a heavy pan, heat the oil and remaining butter.

Add the lobster pieces and sauté over a brisk fire until the shells turn red. Pour in the cognac and ignite. Add the lobster, fish stock, garlic, shallots, and tomato paste. Simmer for 15 minutes. Remove the lobster pieces. Extract all the meat. Reduce the sauce to half. Add the velouté. Simmer for 10 minutes. Whip in the coral-butter mixture. Add the lobster, herbs and cayenne pepper.

Serves: 6
Calories per serving: 202

Sauce Aurora

2	tbsp. butter
2½	tbsp. flour
2	cups fish stock
½	cup dry white wine
1	minced shallot
¼	cup tomato puree
½	tsp. salt
¼	tsp. ground white pepper

To make the velouté, heat butter in a saucepan. Add flour and cook over low heat for 3 minutes. Stir in the fish stock. Whip over medium heat until the sauce thickens. Simmer for 15 minutes. In a separate saucepan, reduce the white wine and shallots to a syrup. Combine the velouté sauce with wine–shallot concentrate and tomato puree. Adjust the seasoning.

Serves: 8
Calories per serving: 66

Sauce Bercy

1	oz. butter
1	tsp. chopped shallots
½	cup white wine
½	cup fish stock
1½	cups velouté sauce
1	tsp. chopped parsley

In a heavy skillet, melt half the butter, stir in the shallots, and cook over low heat for 5 minutes. Add the wine and the fish stock. Reduce by one half, then add the velouté. Simmer the sauce for 30 minutes or until it reaches a medium thick consistency.

Away from heat, drop pieces of the remaining butter into the sauce, stirring until melted. Adjust the seasoning and add the chopped parsley.

Serves: 12
Calories per serving: 56

Sauce Genevoise

2	oz. butter
1	small chopped carrot
1	small chopped onion
¼	tsp. thyme
1	bay leaf
4	parsley stems
8	oz. fish bones
1½	tsp. crushed peppercorns
¾	cup red wine
1	cup fish fumet
2	oz. sauce demi glace
½	tsp. anchovy paste

Melt the butter in a saucepan. Add the carrot and onion and cook over low heat for 5 minutes. Add the thyme, bay leaf, parsley stems, fish bones, and peppercorns. Cover and steam for 10 minutes. Pour off the excess butter. Add the wine and fish fumet. Reduce over medium heat for 10 minutes. Add the demi glace sauce. Bring the sauce to a boil and simmer for 5 minutes. Strain, pressing the bones to extract all the sauce. Stir in the anchovy paste.

Serves: 6
Calories per serving: 77

Sauce Joinville

1½	cups sauce Normande
1	oz. shrimp butter
1	tsp. chopped truffles

Bring the sauce Normande to a boil. Whip in the shrimp butter. Add the truffles.

Serves: 6
Calories per serving: 136

Sauce Nantua

¼	cup soft butter
¼	cup cooked crayfish meat
½	tbsp. chopped shallots
½	tsp. salt
¼	tsp. ground white pepper
1	tsp. lemon juice
2	tbsp. clarified butter
1	small chopped onion
2½	tbsp. flour
2	cups hot milk
1	bay leaf
2	tbsp. tomato sauce
⅓	cup heavy cream
¼	cup brandy

Combine the first six ingredients thoroughly. Set aside. Heat butter over medium heat. Add the onion and cook until translucent. Stir in the flour. Cook over low heat for 3 to 5 minutes, stirring occasionally. Add the milk and bay leaf. Whip until thickened. Reduce the heat and simmer for 10 minutes. Strain the sauce. Adjust the seasoning. Stir in the tomato sauce, heavy cream, and crayfish butter. Simmer the sauce. Stir in the brandy.

Serves: 8
Calories per serving: 182

Sauce Normande

1½	cups velouté sauce
¼	cup oyster liquid
¼	cup mushroom stock
½	cup heavy cream

3	egg yolks
1	tsp. lemon juice
1¼	oz. butter

Combine the first three ingredients and reduce by one quarter. Make a liaison with the egg yolks and the heavy cream. Slowly stir in the velouté sauce. Bring the sauce to a boil quickly. Strain. Season to taste, add the lemon juice, and stir in the butter pieces.

Serves: 12
Calories per serving: 83

Sauce Orientale

1½	cups sauce Américaine
2	tsp. curry powder
¼	cup heavy cream

Combine all the ingredients and reduce by one quarter. Serve with poached fish.

Serves: 15
Calories per serving: 109

Sauce Poulette

1½	cups velouté sauce
¼	cup mushroom stock
2	egg yolks
¼	cup heavy cream
1	tbsp. lemon juice
1	oz. sweet butter
1	tbsp. chopped parsley

Combine the velouté and the mushroom stock. Simmer for 5 minutes. Slowly add the liaison of egg yolks and heavy cream. Bring to a boil quickly and strain. Season to taste. Add the lemon juice, sweet butter, and chopped parsley.

Serves: 15
Calories per serving: 23

Sauce Rouille

1	red pepper
4	medium cloves garlic
½	cup boiled potatoes
½	cup olive oil

Broil the red sweet peppers until the skin is blackened. Rub off the skin. Trim the bottoms and remove the seeds. In a food processor or a blender, puree the garlic and pepper. Add the potatoes and oil to make a thick paste. Add one cup of the strained liquid from the bouillabaisse.★

★Serve with bouillabaisse.

Serves: 10
Calories per serving: 64

Sauce St. Malo

2	cups velouté sauce
¼	cup white wine
1½	tsp. dijon mustard
¾	oz. anchovy butter
1½	tsp. anchovy paste

Combine the velouté sauce and white wine. Reduce to a medium thick consistency. Remove from the heat and stir in the mustard, the anchovy butter, and the anchovy paste.

Serves: 15
Calories per serving: 50

Sauce Soubise

7	oz. chopped onion
2	oz. butter
1½	cups medium béchamel
2	oz. heavy cream

Blanch the onion in boiling water. Drain. Melt the butter. Add the onions and cook over low heat for 10 minutes. Mix in the béchamel and heavy cream. Simmer for 10 minutes. Strain through a fine china cap.

Serves: 15
Calories per serving: 54

Sauce Souchet

1¼	oz. butter
2	oz. julienne celery
2	oz. julienne carrot
½	cups white wine
½	cup fish fumet
1½	cups velouté sauce

Melt the butter in a saucepan. Stew the vegetables in the butter. Add the wine and fish fumet. Reduce by one half. Mix in the velouté sauce. Bring to a boil. Adjust the seasoning if necessary.

Serves: 12
Calories per serving: 60

Sauce Vénitienne

½	cup tarragon vinegar
1	tsp. chopped shallots
1	tbsp. chopped parsley
1½	cups veloute sauce
1	oz. green butter
1	tsp. chopped tarragon
2	tsp. chopped parsley

Combine the vinegar and shallots in a medium saucepan. Reduce by two thirds. Add the parsley and white wine sauce. Bring to a boil and simmer for 10 minutes. Strain through a fine china cap. Remove from the heat and stir in the green butter, chopped tarragon, and parsley.

Serves: 15
Calories per serving: 45

Shrimp Sauce

1½	cups velouté sauce
3	oz. fish fumet
3	oz. heavy cream
1	tsp. tomato paste
2	oz. cooked shrimp

Dice the shrimp. Combine the fish velouté, fish fumet, and heavy cream. Reduce by one quarter. Strain through a china cap. Adjust seasoning. Hold the sauce in a waterbath. At serving time, stir in the tomato paste and diced shrimp.

Serves: 6
Calories per serving: 120

Stir Fry Oyster Sauce

2	tsp. cornstarch
1	tbsp. dry sherry
1	tbsp. peanut oil
2	tsp. minced ginger
2	chopped scallions
1	tsp. minced garlic
1	tbsp. oyster sauce
1	tbsp. dark soy sauce
⅓	cup chicken stock

Combine the cornstarch and sherry.
Pour the oil into a wok and heat until oil is hot. Add the ginger, scallions, garlic, and stir fry for a minute. Add the oyster sauce, soy sauce, and chicken stock. Bring to a boil. Stir the cornstarch and sherry. Then add to the sauce, stirring until it thickens. Use the finished sauce the same day with stir fried vegetables, meat, or fish.

Serves: 2
Calories per serving: 95

Sushi Sauce

2   oz. soy sauce

2   oz. dry sherry*

1   cup chicken stock

Combine all ingredients. Use for shrimp tempura.

*Sake may be substituted for sherry.

Serves: 6
Calories per serving: 22

Sweet and Sour Sauce

¾   cup water

½   cup sugar

½   cup cider vinegar

1   tbsp. cornstarch

1   tbsp. soy sauce

¼   cup water

Bring the water to a boil. Add the sugar and stir until dissolved. Stir in the vinegar.

Blend the cornstarch, soy sauce, and remaining water. Stir the blend into the boiling liquid to thicken.

Note: The addition of one or several of the following ingredients is common: cooked green pepper, pineapple chunks, grated ginger root, tomatoes, pickles, bamboo shoots, or crab apples.

Serves: 6
Calories per serving: 63

Tarragon Sauce

2   tbsp. chopped tarragon*

1½   cups fish veloute sauce

1   tsp. minced tarragon*

Combine the coarsely chopped tarragon with a small amount of hot fish veloute sauce. Puree in blender. Combine with the remaining hot sauce. Strain through a fine china cap. Garnish with minced tarragon.

*Use fresh tarragon for this recipe.

Serves: 12
Calories per serving: 40

Tomato Sauce

1½	cups fish velouté sauce
2	oz. tomato puree
7	oz. fresh tomatoes
1	clove minced garlic
1	oz. butter

Blanch, peel, and quarter the fresh tomatoes. Combine fish velouté sauce with tomato puree, fresh tomatoes, and garlic. Bring to a boil and simmer for 10 minutes. Strain through a china cap and adjust the seasoning to taste. At serving time, stir in the butter in pieces.

Serves: 6
Calories per serving: 29

Velouté Sauce

1½	oz. butter
1½	oz. flour
1	pt. fish fumet
¼	tsp. salt
1	pinch ground white pepper

Melt the butter, stir in the flour to make a roux, and cook over low heat until slightly brown. Gradually pour in the fish fumet, whipping until smooth. Bring to a boil, stirring occasionally, until the sauce thickens. Simmer for 10 minutes and season to taste.

Serves: 6
Calories per serving: 78

White Wine Sauce

1½	cups velouté sauce
½	cup fish fumet
2	oz. white wine
1	egg yolk
1¼	oz. fresh butter

Combine the velouté sauce, fumet, and white wine. Simmer to reduce by one quarter. Cream the egg yolk. Slowly pour the sauce over the creamed egg yolk and bring to a boil quickly. Strain and stir in the butter.

Serves: 6
Calories per serving: 120

CHAPTER 12

Saltwater Fish Recipes

This chapter contains recipes for the following:

Anchovy	Porgy
Bluefish	Redfish
Butterfish	Red snapper
Cod	Rockfish
Croaker	Sablefish
Cusk	Salmon
Dolphin	Sardine
Eel	Seabass
Flounder	Sea trout
Grouper	Shad
Haddock	Shark
Hake	Skate
Halibut	Sheepshead
Herring	Smelt
Lingcod	Sole
Mackerel	Spot
Miscellaneous	Striped bass
fish recipes	Swordfish
Monkfish	Tilefish
Mullet	Tuna
Ocean perch	Turbot
Pollock	Turtle
Pompano	Whiting

═══ Anchovy

Anchovy Stuffed Eggs

6	hard-cooked eggs
2	oz. butter
2	oz. cream cheese
¼	tsp. salt

1	tbsp. mayonnaise
1	dash hot pepper sauce
2	tsp. paste anchovy
6	anchovy fillets

Peel the hard-cooked eggs and cut in halves lengthwise. Remove the yolks. Mix the yolks, butter, cream cheese, salt, mayonnaise, hot pepper sauce, and anchovy paste in a food processor. Pipe the mixture into egg whites and top with strips of anchovy fillets. Serve with seafood salads.

Serves: 6
Calories per serving: 178

Bagna Cauda

3	oz. butter
2	oz. olive oil
3	crushed garlic cloves
12	anchovy fillets
1	cup celery sticks
1	cup carrot sticks
1	cup pepper sticks

Bagna cauda is a specialty of Piemont, Italy. It is used as a dip with raw vegetables, such as fennel, celery, carrots, and green or red sweet peppers.

In a fondue pot, place the butter, oil, garlic, and anchovies. Heat until the garlic is slightly brown. The sauce must be kept hot.

Serve with pieces of celery, carrots, and peppers. Fondue forks are often used to dip the vegetable pieces.

Note: Stir in some heavy cream if the mixture becomes too thick.

Serves: 6
Calories per serving: 134

Pissaladière

1	recipe pizza dough
½	cup olive oil
2	tbsp. chopped onion
2	lb. seedless tomatoes
2	cloves crushed garlic

½	tsp. salt
¼	tsp. ground black pepper
12	anchovy fillets
2	oz. niçoise olives

Line a 9-inch (22.5 cm) pie dish with the pizza dough. Heat the oil in a skillet. Add the onions and cook until tender over low heat.

In a separate skillet, combine the tomatoes and crushed garlic and reduce over medium heat. Season with salt and pepper.

Spread the onion over the pizza dough and add the chopped tomatoes. Crisscross the anchovy fillets on top and decorate with olives.

Bake at 375°F (190°C) for 30 to 40 minutes. Serve hot.

Serves: 6
Calories per serving: 410

For additional anchovy recipes, see

Anchovy Butter in Chapter 15.
Anchovy Canapés in Chapter 15.
Anchovy Sauce in Chapter 11.
Salade Nicoise in this chapter.
Sauce Algigeoise in Chapter 11.
Sauce Antiboise in Chapter 11.
Sauce Cypriote in Chapter 11.
Sauce Maximilian (see hollandaise in Chapter 11).
Sauce St. Malo in Chapter 11.
Sauce Veron (see béarnaise in Chapter 11).
Tartelettes Arkangel in Chapter 15.
Tuna-Anchovy Sauce in Chapter 11.

The following are additional suggestions for anchovies, some of which appear in other chapters of this book.

Potato Salad and Anchovies

Dress potato salad on a bed of lettuce. Sprinkle with chopped egg yolk and egg white. Arrange stuffed anchovies on the salad.

Anchovy Allumettes

Roll out puff pastry dough (see Chapter 7). Cut into small rectangles. Spread half of the rectangles with anchovy butter and top with remaining rectangles. Arrange a anchovy fillet on top of each pastry. Bake at 375°F (190°C).

Scallopine of Veal Holstein

Pan fry veal scallopines garnished with fried eggs and anchovy fillets.

Bluefish *(Blue Runner)*

Bluefish Espagnole

2	oz. oil
4	oz. sliced onion
2	lb. seedless tomatoes
2	cloves chopped garlic
½	tsp. salt
¼	tsp. ground black pepper
2	lb. bluefish fillets
1	tbsp. lemon juice
1	tbsp. chopped parsley

Heat the oil in a skillet. Add the onion and cook over low heat for 10 minutes. Stir in the chopped tomatoes, garlic, salt, and pepper. Cook over low heat for 10 to 15 minutes.

Arrange bluefish portions in a buttered baking dish. Sprinkle with lemon juice. Spoon the sauce over fish. Bake at 400°F (205°C) for 15 minutes. Transfer to a heated serving platter. Sprinkle with chopped parsley.

Serves: 6
Calories per serving: 273

Grilled Bluefish Fillets

2	lb bluefish fillets
½	tsp. salt
¼	tsp. ground white pepper
½	cup oil
2	oz. lemon juice

| 1 | tbsp. capers |
| 1 | tbsp. chopped parsley |

Cut the fillets into 5-oz. (140 g) portions. Season with salt and pepper and brush with oil. Cook the fish on a hot grill or charcoal broiler. Turn the fillets a quarter turn to obtain a grilled checkered effect. Turn the fish over and repeat the process until fully cooked. Arrange the pieces on preheated platter. Sprinkle with lemon juice, capers, and parsley.

Note: This dish can also be served with anchovy butter.

Serves: 6
Calories per serving: 257

Stuffed Bluefish

1	4-lb. whole bluefish
½	tsp. salt
¼	tsp. white ground pepper
1	lb. crabmeat
½	cup cream sauce
2	oz. olive oil
1	oz. lemon juice

Scale and clean the fish. Place on a large baking pan. Season the cavity with salt and pepper.

Combine the crabmeat with cream sauce and stuff the cavity of the fish. Secure the stuffing by inserting small skewers into the belly flaps.

Rub the fish with olive oil, sprinkle with lemon juice. Bake at 400°F (200°C) for 40 to 45 minutes. Serve on a preheated serving platter.

Serves: 6
Calories per serving: 298

For an additional bluefish recipe, see

Smoked Fish Dip in Chapter 15.

Butterfish *(Dollar Fish, Harvest Fish)*

Butterfish Provençale

6	whole butterfish
½	tsp. salt
¼	tsp. ground white pepper
2	oz. flour
½	cup olive oil
2	cloves chopped garlic
6	grilled tomatoes
6	anchovy fillets
12	ripe olives

Clean and wash the dressed fish. Season with salt and pepper. Coat with flour. Fry in olive oil, turning the fish once. Add the garlic to flavor the fish.

Arrange the cooked butterfish on a warm serving platter. Garnish with the grilled tomatoes, anchovy fillets, and ripe olives.

Serves: 6
Calories per serving: 424

Butterfish en Papillotte*

6	oz. anchovy butter
6	whole butterfish
6	slices Canadian bacon
½	tsp. salt
¼	tsp. ground black pepper
6	oz. tomato sauce
1	tbsp. chopped parsley

Cut heart-shaped pieces of parchment paper large enough to hold the whole dressed fish. Spread anchovy butter on one half of each paper. Top with the butterfish and Canadian bacon. Season with salt and pepper. Spoon 1 oz. (25 g) of tomato sauce on top of each fish and sprinkle with chopped parsley. Fold the other side of parchment paper over the fish and seal the edges of paper. Bake at 425°F (220°C) for 15 to 20 minutes.

*For more details, see the cooking technique, en papillotte, in Chapter 6.

Serves: 6
Calories per serving: 361

Steamed Butterfish

6	large whole butterfish
¼	cup dry sherry
6	small scallions
1	tbsp. grated ginger
2	tbsp. peanut oil
2	tbsp. soy sauce
½	tsp. sugar

If desired, substitute butterfish with snapper, pike, sea bass, or spot.

Clean and scale the fish. Remove the head. Arrange on a rack that will fit in a steamer. Sprinkle the sherry over the fish. Bring water to a boil in a steamer. Place the fish over steam. Cover tightly and steam the fish for 10 minutes per inch of thickness.

Cut the scallions into 2-inch (5 cm) pieces. Mix with the ginger. In a wok or large skillet, heat the oil. Add the ginger and scallions and stir fry for a few seconds over high heat. Add the soy sauce and sugar. Remove from the heat. Arrange the fish on a serving platter. Pour the sauce over. Serve hot.

Serves: 6
Calories per serving: 329

Broiled Butterfish, Sauce Bercy

See Grilled Fillets of Bluefish. Serve with Sauce Bercy.

Butterfish Meunière with Almonds

See Dover Sole Meunière.

Smoked Butterfish

Smoked butterfish are available commercially and have a delicate flavor. Bone them and serve with frozen horseradish, lemon wedges, and capers.

══ Cod

Batter-Fried Pacific Cod

3	lb. Pacific cod fillets
½	tsp. salt
4	oz. flour
2	beaten eggs
6	oz. beer
½	tsp. salt
¼	tsp. ground ginger
6	lemon wedges
1	bunch parsley

Bone and skin the fillets. Cut into portions. Season with salt and pepper. Combine the flour, eggs, beer, salt, and ginger into a batter. Mix until smooth and refrigerate for 30 minutes.

Dip the fish into the batter. Deep fry at 375°F (190°C) for 3 to 5 minutes. Serve on a warm platter. Garnish with parsley and lemon wedges.

Serves: 6
Calories per serving: 295

Billingsgate Fish and Chips

2	lb. skinless cod
½	tsp. salt
1	recipe beer batter
2	lb. baking potatoes
6	lemon wedges

Cod can be substituted with dogfish or other white, firm, skinless and boneless fish.

Cut the fish into 5-oz. (140 g) pieces. Wash under cold water and dry. Season with salt. Coat in the cold beer batter. Deep fry at 360°F (190°C) for 4 to 5 minutes.

Arrange on a warm dish lined with a napkin. Serve with chips and lemon pieces, or the traditional malt vinegar. (The chips are actually large French-fried potatoes, made with the baking potatoes, and deep fried.)

Serves: 6
Calories per serving: 460

Cod Basque

3	lb. cod fillets
4	oz. flour
1	tsp. salt
¼	tsp. ground white pepper
5	oz. olive oil
7	oz. sliced mushrooms
10	oz. seedless tomatoes
1	clove minced garlic
5	oz. dry white wine

Cut the cod into portions. Use cod steaks if desired.

Mix the flour with salt and pepper. Flour the cod and sear on both sides in the hot oil. Transfer the fish to an ovenproof serving dish.

Sauté the mushrooms in the oil. Add the tomatoes and garlic. Stir together and pour in the wine.

Spoon the sauce over the fish and bake at 350°F (180°C) for 10 to 15 minutes.

Serves: 6
Calories per serving: 394

Cod Boulangère

6	oz. butter
1	lb. sliced potatoes
4	oz. sliced onions
½	tsp. salt
2	lb. cod steaks
1	clove minced garlic
2	tbsp. chopped parsley
1	oz. fresh bread crumbs

Butter ovenproof serving dish(es).

Blanch the thinly sliced potatoes in boiling water and drain. Arrange in the bottom of the dish with the onion slices and season with salt.

Place the cod on top of onions. Dot with remaining butter. Bake at 360°F (185°C) until potatoes are done and the fish is flaky.

Baste occasionally. Combine the garlic, parsley, and bread crumbs. Sprinkle over the fish and bake until brown.

Serves: 6
Calories per serving: 391

Cod Fillets Florentine

3	lb. cod fillets
1	tsp. salt
¼	tsp. ground white pepper
½	cup dry white wine
1½	lb. clean spinach
2	cups mornay sauce
3	oz. grated swiss cheese

Bone and skin the fillets. Cut into equal portions. Arrange in a buttered baking pan. Season with salt and pepper. Pour the wine over. Cover with foil and bake at 350°F (180°C) until flaky.

Blanch the spinach in salted boiling water. Drain and squeeze out excess water. Chop spinach. Mix a small amount of mornay sauce into spinach. Spread the bottom of an ovenproof serving dish with chopped spinach.

Arrange the fish on top and pour the remaining sauce over. Sprinkle with cheese and brown under a broiler.

Serves: 6
Calories per serving: 296

Cod Mornay with Noodles

3	lb. cod fillets
1	gal. No. 3 court bouillon
4	oz. egg noodles
1½	cups mornay sauce
2	oz. grated swiss cheese

Poach the cod in court bouillon. Cook the noodles in salted boiling water. Flake the cod fish. Arrange the noodles in the bottom of a buttered, ovenproof serving dish. Spread the cod over the noodles and coat with mornay sauce. Sprinkle with cheese and bake at 350°F (130°C) for 15 to 20 minutes or until brown.

Serves: 6
Calories per serving: 260

Codfish Cakes

2½	lb. codfish
7	large cubed potatoes
1	cup chopped onions
½	tsp. salt
¼	tsp. ground white pepper
2	eggs
1	tsp. dijon mustard
1	tsp. worcestershire
3	tbsp. chopped parsley
½	cup flour
½	cup oil

Put codfish in a rack of a steamer. Place rack over boiling water and cover. Let steam for 7 minutes.

Cover potatoes with water. Add onions, salt, and pepper. Bring to a boil and cook for 12 to 15 minutes or until the potatoes are tender.

Drain and put through a food mill. Remove and discard the skin and bones from cod. Flake the flesh. Combine the potatoes with eggs, mustard, worcestershire, and parsley. Add the fish and blend well. Spoon the mixture onto a baking sheet and smooth it over. Chill.

Shape the mixture into round cakes. Dredge the cakes lightly in flour. Heat oil in a skillet, and brown the cakes on both sides.

Serves: 6
Calories per serving: 386

Codfish Steaks Dantin

1	tbsp. softened butter
1	oz. chopped shallots
4	oz. seedless tomatoes
3	oz. sliced mushrooms
1	tbsp. chopped parsley
6	8-oz. codfish steaks
½	tsp. salt
¼	tsp. ground white pepper

¼	cup dry white wine
¼	cup fumet
2	oz. butter
1	oz. flour

Butter a baking sheet pan. Sprinkle the shallots, chopped tomatoes, mushrooms, and half the parsley over the whole surface of the pan. Arrange the fish steaks over the vegetables. Season with salt and pepper and moisten with the wine and fish fumet. Bake at 400°F (205°C) for 15 minutes.

Skin and bone the steaks. Arrange on a serving platter. Garnish the fish with the vegetables. Strain the cooking liquid. Reduce for 5 to 10 minutes. Thicken with beurre manié (mixture of butter and flour). Bring to a boil and simmer for 5 minutes or until the sauce reaches a medium consistency. Pour over the fish. Sprinkle with remaining chopped parsley and serve hot.

Serves: 6
Calories per serving: 270

Deep-Fried Cod Patties

1	lb. salted cod
1	lb. mashed potatoes
1	tbsp. chopped parsley
1	tsp. dry mustard
¼	tsp. ground white pepper
2	beaten eggs

Soak the cod in cold water for 12 hours. Drain and poach, starting with fresh cold water. Simmer for 15 minutes or until fish becomes flaky. Drain and flake the fish.

Combine with the remaining ingredients. Shape into patties, allowing two per person. Deep fry at 375°F (190°C) until brown.

Arrange on a serving platter and serve hot. Serve with a sauce.

Note: Use any leftover fresh or salted codfish for this recipe.

Serves: 6
Calories per serving: 145

Fillets of Cod Orientale

½	cup oil
8	oz. fresh fennel
10	oz. tomatoes
2	cloves crushed garlic
1	tsp. saffron
¼	tsp. cumin
¼	tsp. ground coriander
6	7-oz. cod fillets
1	tsp. salt
¼	tsp. ground white pepper
1	cup dry white wine
1	tbsp. chopped parsley
6	lemon wedges

Heat the oil in a sauté pan. Stir in the fennel and cook over low heat for 10 minutes. Peel the tomatoes, remove seeds, and chop. Add the tomatoes, garlic, and saffron to the fennel. Season with cumin and coriander. Simmer for 20 minutes.

Arrange the fish fillets on buttered sheet pans. Season with salt and pepper. Pour the wine over and cover with the sauce. Bake for 10 minutes at 400°F (205°C). Transfer the fillets onto a serving platter. Coat with the sauce. Sprinkle with parsley and garnish with lemon wedges.

Serves: 6
Calories per serving: 371

Fillets of Cod Polonaise

3	hard-cooked eggs
4	oz. sandwich bread
½	cup oil
6	7-oz. cod fillets
1	tsp. salt
¼	tsp. ground white pepper
1½	oz. flour

6	oz. butter
2	tbsp. chopped parsley
6	lemon wedges

Shell the hard-cooked eggs. Separate the egg yolks from the whites and chop each finely. Dice the bread into small pieces and fry in a small amount of oil to make croutons.

Season the cod fillets with salt and pepper. Coat in flour and fry in oil on both sides. Arrange the fish on a heated platter. Melt the butter to brown and pour over the fish. Sprinkle with chopped egg, parsley, and croutons. Serve with lemon wedges.

Serves: 6
Calories per serving: 531

Fried Fillets of Cod

2½	lb. cod fillets
1	tsp. salt
¼	tsp. ground white pepper
4	oz. flour
2	beaten eggs
3	cups bread crumbs
1	bunch parsley
1½	cup tartar sauce

Cut the fillets into 7-oz. (200 g) portions. Season with salt and pepper. Coat with flour. Dip in eggs and roll in bread crumbs. Deep fry at 360°F (180°C) for 3 to 4 minutes. Drain.

Arrange on a serving platter. Garnish with fresh parsley. Serve with tartar sauce (see Chapter 11 for recipe).

Serves: 6
Calories per serving: 528

Poached Cod Hollandaise

1	5-lb. dressed cod
2	gallon No. 3 court bouillon
1	bunch parsley
6	oz. hollandaise

Poach the whole fish, following directions described for the poaching technique in Chapter 6.

Transfer the cooked fish to a serving platter. Garnish with parsley. Serve the hollandaise separately.

This recipe can also be served cold with a cold sauce.

Serves: 6
Calories per serving: 281

Salted Cod Aioli

2½	lb. salted cod
1½	lb. small potatoes
3	hard-cooked eggs
½	cup aioli sauce

Soak the cod in cold water for 12 hours. Cut into equal portions. Poach starting in cold fresh water.

Peel and shape the potatoes into olive shape. Cook in salted water. Peel and cut the hard-cooked eggs in halves. Drain the cooked cod and arrange on a warm serving platter. Garnish with the warm eggs and potatoes. Serve the sauce separately.

Serves: 6
Calories per serving: 397

Salted Cod Pie

2½	lb. salted cod
3	egg yolks
2	cups béchamel
1	lb. dough puff pastry
1	egg yolk

Soak the cod in cold water for 12 hours. Poach, starting with cold fresh water, until flaky. Mix the egg yolks with the béchamel. Combine the sauce with the flaked fish.

Line a pie dish with the rolled out puff pastry dough. Spoon in the fish. Cover with more puff pastry dough. Brush pastry with egg yolk. Bake at 350°F (180°C) for 20 minutes.

Serves: 10
Calories per serving: 333

Salted Codfish Salad

1	lb. salted cod
2	lb. potatoes
1	sliced green pepper
1	large sliced onion
¼	cup olive oil
¼	cup wine vinegar
½	tsp. paprika
6	large lettuce leaves
6	tomato slices
3	hard-cooked eggs

Soak the cod in cold water for 12 hours, changing the water several times. Place the fish in a suitable pot. Cover with fresh water. Bring to a boil. Reduce. Heat and simmer until the fish is tender and flaky. Drain off water. Flake the codfish.

Boil potatoes in their skin. Cool, peel, and slice.

Arrange fish, potatoes, green pepper, and onion on a platter.

Mix together the oil, vinegar, and paprika. Season with salt and pepper to taste. Blend well and pour over the salad. Serve cold on lettuce leaves. Garnish with tomato slices and sliced hard-cooked eggs.

Serves: 6
Calories per serving: 270

Tomato-Crowned Cod

2	lb. cod fillets
2	tbsp. lemon juice
⅛	tsp. ground pepper
2	large sliced tomatoes
½	medium chopped green pepper
2	tbsp. chopped onion
¼	cup dry bread crumbs
½	tsp. crumbled basil
1	tbsp. oil

Place the fish in an oiled baking dish and season with lemon juice and pepper. Place ¼-inch thick tomato slices on the fish, then sprinkle with the finely chopped green pepper and onion. In a small bowl, combine the bread crumbs, basil, and oil. Spread the crumb mixture over the tomatoes. Bake, uncovered, in a preheated 350°F (180°C) oven for 25 minutes.

Serves: 6
Calories per serving: 184

For additional cod recipes, see

Cod and Potato Chowder in Chapter 10.
Cod Bouillabaisse in Chapter 10.
Codfish Chowder in Chapter 10.
Spanish Fish Stew in Chapter 10.

Croaker (Crocus, Hard Head, King Billy)

Croaker Meunière

See Dover Sole Meunière in Chapter 12.

Broiled Croaker

See broiling cooking technique in Chapter 6.

Pan-Fried Croaker

See pan-fried cooking technique in Chapter 6.

Golden Fried Croaker

See deep-frying cooking technique in Chapter 6.

Cusk (Tusk, Torsk)

See Cod and Haddock recipes in this chapter.

Dolphin *(Dorado, Mahimahi)*

Broiled Mahimahi, Dill Sauce

Follow the cooking technique for broiling in Chapter 6. Serve with dill sauce.

Deep-Fried Mahimahi Steaks

Follow the deep-frying technique in Chapter 6.

Pan-Fried Hawaiian Dolphin

Follow the pan-frying technique in Chapter 6.

Dorado Espagnole

See Bluefish Fillets Espagnole in this chapter.

Poached Dorado

Poach fillets of dorado in milk and coconut milk. Serve with mousseline sauce.

Poached Mahimahi, Fine Herb Sauce

Follow the cooking technique for poaching in Chapter 6. Serve with a fine herb sauce.

Ceviche of Dorado

See Scallop Ceviche in Chapter 13.

Eel

Eel in Green Herbs

3	lb. skinned eel
2	oz. butter
2	oz. chopped onion

1	cup white wine
2	cups fish fumet
2	oz. chopped sorrel
½	cup mint leaves
1	tsp. cornstarch
1	tbsp. cold water
4	egg yolks
½	cup heavy cream

Cut the eel into 3-inch pieces. Brown in butter. Add the onion and cook until brown. Add the white wine and fish fumet. Bring to a boil. Mix in the sorrel and mint leaves and cook for 10 to 12 minutes. Remove eel pieces. Keep warm.

Mix cornstarch into the cold water. Pour into cooking liquid to thicken. Mix egg yolks and heavy cream. Stir into the sauce. Do not boil. Pour the sauce over the eel pieces. Serve hot.

Serves: 6
Calories per serving: 473

Eel Matelote

2	lb. 3-inch eel
2	oz. flour
1	tsp. salt
¼	tsp. ground white pepper
2	oz. butter
2	cloves crushed garlic
4	oz. sliced onion
2	oz. cognac
6	oz. red wine
2	cups fish stock
¼	tsp. crushed thyme
1	bay leaf
1	oz. beurre manié
6	crouton triangles

Roll eel pieces in flour. Season with salt and pepper. Brown in butter. Add the garlic and onion. Stir until lightly colored. Remove eel pieces.

Deglaze with cognac and ignite. Add the red wine, fish stock, thyme, and bay leaf. Simmer for 30 minutes. Strain the cooking liquid and thicken with beurre manié. Return the eel pieces to the sauce. Simmer for 5 minutes. Serve and surround with croutons cut into triangles.

Serves: 6
Calories per serving: 377

Eel with Tarragon Sauce

2	oz. chopped onion
4	oz. butter
2	lb. skinned eel
8	oz. mushroom caps
1½	cups tarragon sauce

Brown the onion in half the butter. Add the eel pieces to color lightly. Sauté the mushroom caps in the remaining butter. Add to the eel pieces. Pour in the sauce and simmer for 10 to 15 minutes. Serve hot.

Serves: 6
Calories per serving: 371

Pan-Fried Eel Provençale

3	lb. skinned eel
2	oz. flour
1	tsp. salt
¼	tsp. ground white pepper
½	cup olive oil
3	cloves minced garlic

Cut the eel into 3-inch (7.5 cm) pieces. Dredge in flour, season with salt and pepper. Sauté in oil until brown. Add the chopped garlic and parsley. Continue cooking until eel pieces are done. Season to taste and serve on a warm platter.

Serves: 6
Calories per serving: 429

Smoked Eel Hors d'Oeuvres

2	lb. smoked eel
1½	cup frozen horseradish
12	slices pumpernickel bread

Remove skin and bones from smoked eel. Carve into thin slices. Arrange on a serving platter. Garnish with frozen horseradish slices and pumpernickel bread.

Serves: 6
Calories per serving: 330

For additional eel recipes, see

Fish Matelote in Chapter 10.
Matelote Illhaeusern in Chapter 10.

Flounder *(Blackback, Dab, Fluke, Plaice)*

Flounder with Tart Apple

3	lb. flounder fillets
½	tsp. salt
¼	tsp. ground white pepper
3½	oz. flour
6	oz. butter
3	oz. oil
1	lb. tart apples

Season the fillets with salt and pepper. Dredge in flour. Heat half the butter and the oil in a large skillet. Brown the fish fillets on both sides until crisp.

Peel and slice the apples. Sauté in remaining butter.

Arrange the flounder fillets on a preheated serving platter. Top with the apples. Serve hot.

Note: Most sole recipes can be adapted for flounder as the quality of the fish is very similar.

Serves: 6
Calories per serving: 456

Korean Flounder Fillets

8	small flounder fillets
½	tsp. ground black pepper
3	tbsp. light soy sauce
1	tbsp. grated onion
1	tsp. grated ginger
½	grated lemon rind
1	tsp. sugar
⅓	cup oil

Season fillets with pepper. Combine the remaining ingredients except oil and coat fish with the mixture. Allow to stand for 15 to 20 minutes.

In a skillet, heat the oil. Sauté the fish fillets over high heat to brown quickly on both sides. Serve hot.

Serves: 4
Calories per serving: 423

Summer Flounder Nicolas

1	4-lb. whole flounder
½	tsp. salt
¼	tsp. ground white pepper
1	lb. crabmeat
1	cup dry white wine
1	cup white wine sauce★
6	fleurons

Bone the flounder according to the directions in Chapter 5. Prepare a fumet with the bones; use additional fish bones if necessary.

Season the cavity of the fish with salt and pepper. Fill with crabmeat. Turn fish over onto a buttered baking pan. Pour the white wine and fish fumet over the fish. Cover with foil and bake at 400°F (205°C) for 35 to 40 minutes.

Combine the cooking liquid with the white wine sauce. Reduce to a medium consistency. Transfer fish to a serving platter. Cover with some of the sauce. Garnish with fleurons. Serve the remaining sauce on the side.

★See recipe for White Wine Sauce in Chapter 11.

Serves: 6
Calories per serving: 300

For an additional flounder recipe, see Fish Canapés in Chapter 15.

═ Grouper

Cajun Baked Fish

4	oz. melted butter
3	lb. grouper★ fillets
½	tsp. salt
¼	tsp. ground white pepper
½	tsp. fish seasoning★★
1	tsp. lemon juice
2	tsp. wine worcestershire
½	tsp. paprika
½	cup white wine

Brush half the butter over the bottom of a baking dish. Lay clean fish fillets in dish. Brush with remaining butter and sprinkle with remaining ingredients. Bake at 400°F (205°C) for 30 to 40 minutes.

★Other fish that can be used for this recipe are cod, halibut, tilefish, and snapper.

★★See recipe for fish seasoning in this chapter.

Serves: 8
Calories per serving: 220

Kedgeree

1	cup rice
2	lb. grouper fillet
1	qt. No. 1 court bouillon
3	hard-cooked eggs
1	tbsp. chopped parsley
2	oz. butter
½	tsp. curry powder
1	cup velouté sauce

Cook the rice according to standard directions. Poach the fillets in court bouillon No. 1. Chop the eggs and mix with the parsley. Flake the fish and combine with the rice, melted butter, curry powder, and half the egg mixture. Heat and toss together.

Sprinkle the remaining egg blend over the fish mixture. Heat in the oven before serving.

Serve the velouté sauce separately.

Serves: 6
Calories per serving: 305

Gougeonnettes of Grouper

See Gougeonnettes of Sea Trout in this chapter.

Batter-Fried Grouper Fillet

See Billinsgate Fish and Chips in this chapter.

Note: Grouper fillets can also be poached, and served with hollandaise or other hot sauce.

For additional grouper recipe, see
Provençale Fish Soup in Chapter 10.

Haddock

Finnan Haddie Basquaise

2	lb. smoked haddock
1	qt. water
2	cups milk
8	oz. sliced onion
2	oz. butter
1½	lb. chopped tomatoes
½	tsp. basil
8	oz. egg noodles
2	cups velouté sauce

Simmer the smoked haddock in water and milk.

Sauté the onion in butter and cook over low heat for 5 to 10 minutes. Add the seedless tomatoes and basil. Simmer into a medium thick sauce. Cook noodles in salted boiling water. Drain and stir in the velouté sauce. Transfer into a casserole serving dish. Flake the haddock and arrange over noodles. Pour the tomato sauce over. Serve hot.

Serves: 6
Calories per serving: 580

Finnan Haddie Macaroni

1½	lb. smoked haddock	
6	oz. macaroni	
2	cup light cream sauce	
1	tbsp. grated parmesan	
1	tbsp. melted butter	

Poach the smoked haddock in half milk and half water. Cook macaroni in salted boiling water. Drain.

Combine macaroni, flaked haddock, and cream sauce. Arrange in an oven-proof serving dish. Sprinkle with cheese and melted butter. Bake at 350°F (180°C) for 15 to 20 minutes, or until brown.

Serves: 6
Calories per serving: 305

Haddock Breval

2	oz. chopped shallots
2	oz. butter
3	lb. haddock fillets
½	tsp. salt
¼	tsp. ground white pepper
8	oz. sliced mushrooms
½	cup dry white wine
1	tbsp. chopped parsley
1½	cup fish velouté sauce
½	cup hollandaise
2	tbsp. whipped heavy cream
3	oz. seedless tomatoes

Spread the shallots in a buttered pan. Cut the haddock fillets into equal portions. Line up fillets side by side in the pan. Season with salt and pepper. Add the mushrooms, white wine, and parsley. Cover with buttered parchment paper. Bring to a boil on top of the stove, then bake at 350°F (180°C) until fish are done. Transfer the fish to a serving platter.

Reduce the cooking liquid to syrup consistency. Add the fish velouté and hollandaise. Fold in the whipped cream. Add the peeled, chopped tomatoes and correct seasoning.

Pour sauce over the fish, and glaze under a broiler.

Serves: 6
Calories per serving: 297

Haddock Soufflé

5	eggs
1	pt. milk
2	oz. butter
2	oz. flour
1	tsp. salt
¼	tsp. ground white pepper
⅛	tsp. ground nutmeg
1	lb. poached haddock
1	cup grated swiss cheese
1½	cups tomato sauce

Separate the eggs and set aside. Boil the milk. In a separate pan, melt the butter and stir in the flour. Cook over low heat for 5 minutes. Add the milk and mix with a whip until sauce thickens and comes to a boil. Season with salt, pepper, and nutmeg. Simmer for 8 to 10 minutes. Strain the sauce into a mixing bowl.

Stir in the flaked haddock, egg yolks, and cheese. Whip the egg whites to a medium peak. Fold into the haddock mixture. Butter and flour a medium soufflé dish. Fill with the mixture to three quarters. Bake at 350°F (180°C) for 35 to 40 minutes. Serve as soon as the soufflé is ready. Serve the tomato sauce separately.

Serves: 6
Calories per serving: 370

Haddock with Broccoli

3	lb. haddock fillets
½	cup dry white wine
2	chopped scallions
1	tbsp. lemon juice
10	oz. cooked broccoli
½	tsp. salt
¼	tsp. ground white pepper
1	cup heavy cream sauce
½	cup grated chedder cheese

Cut the fish fillets into equal portions. Combine the white wine, lemon juice, and scallions. Poach the fish in the simmering liquid.

Arrange trimmed broccoli in a buttered baking dish. Place the fillets on top. Season with salt and pepper.

Reduce the cooking liquid to half. Stir in the cream sauce. Simmer until the sauce reaches a medium-thick consistency. Pour the sauce over the fish. Sprinkle with cheese and bake at 400°F (205°C) until brown.

Serves: 6
Calories per serving: 350

Broiled Haddock Fillet, Sauce Choron

Follow the broiling cooking technique in Chapter 6. Serve fish with sauce Choron.

For an additional haddock recipe, see

Spanish Fish Stew in Chapter 10.

Hake *(Ling)*

Hake can be prepared like haddock or cod. This fish is best when served poached, hot or cold, with a variety of sauces.

═ Halibut

Singapore Fish Curry

4	tbsp. butter
4	tbsp. flour
2	cups milk
2	tsp. powder curry
1	tbsp. mango chutney
½	cup pineapple strips
1	tsp. lime juice
½	cup cooked rice
1	lb. poached halibut★
2	boiled eggs

In a saucepan, melt the butter. Add the flour and stir over low heat until blended and smooth. Add the milk and stir with a whip until thickened. Add the curry, chutney, pineapple, and lime. Blend well and cover. Simmer for 10 minutes. Add the rice, flaked fish, and quartered eggs. Mix gently, cover, and heat through.

★Other lean fish can be used for this recipe.

Serves: 4
Calories per serving: 445

═ Herring

Fried Herring Bercy

2	lb. herring fillets
2	tbsp. lemon juice
½	tsp. salt
¼	tsp. white pepper
4	oz. butter
1	tbsp. capers
1	tbsp. chopped parsley
1½	cup Sauce Bercy

Remove dorsal fin. Sprinkle the herring fillets with lemon juice and season with salt and pepper. Roll the fillets in flour. Fry in butter until brown on both sides.

Transfer the fillets to a preheated serving platter. Garnish with capers. Add parsley and serve with sauce bercy (see recipe in Chapter 11).

Serves: 6
Calories per serving: 424

Herring Cocktail

2	large cucumbers
1	lb. smoked herring
2	hard-cooked eggs
2	tsp. grated horseradish
6	ripe olives

Peel cucumbers and cut in half lengthwise. Slice and blanch in boiling salted water. Bone the herring. Blend into a paste in a food processor, adding the eggs and horseradish. Alternate layers of smoked herring puree and cucumber slices in cocktail glasses. Top with a ripe olive.

Serves: 6
Calories per serving: 174

Pickled Herring

1	lb. schmaltz herring fillets
1	cup white vinegar
½	cup water
2	tsp. sugar
2	medium sliced carrots
4	oz. sliced red onion
2	tsp. pickling spices
2	bay leaf
1	cup sour cream

Soak the herring in cold water for 2 days, changing water twice.

Combine the vinegar, water, and sugar and boil for 2 minutes. Set aside. Slice the drained herring into 2-inch (5 cm) pieces.

Arrange the herring, sliced carrots, sliced onion, pickling spices, and bay leaves in a glass or earthenware bowl. Cover and refrigerate for at least 2 days before using.

Stir in the sour cream before serving.

Serves: 6
Calories per serving: 196

For additional herring recipes, see

Herring Butter in Chapter 15.
Herring Roe Butter in Chapter 15.
Herring in Mustard Sauce in Chapter 15.

Lingcod (Bluecod, Buffalo Cod, Cultus Cod)

Lingcod fillets and steaks can be broiled, sauteed in butter, or poached. Whole fish can be baked or poached. A popular method of preparation is to pan fry or deep fry for fish and chips (see Billingsgate Fish and Chips in this chapter).

Mackerel

Fish Teriyaki

6	tbsp. soy sauce
6	tbsp. mirin
6	tbsp. sake
1	tbsp. sugar
1½	lbs. mackerel fillets

In a saucepan, combine the soy sauce, mirin, and sake with the sugar. Bring to a boil and simmer for 2 to 3 minutes. Remove from heat and cool.

Place the fish fillets in a shallow pan. Pour the sauce over them and allow to stand for 15 minutes turning once. Broil 5 minutes on each side while brushing with the remaining sauce. When done, fish should have a dark brown color.

Note: Mirin is a sweet cooking wine and is available in oriental groceries or can be substituted with sweet sherry wine.

Serves: 4
Calories per serving: 414

Mackerel Ravigotte

2	lb. mackerel fillets
½	tsp. salt
¼	tsp. ground white pepper
3	oz. flour
3	oz. oil
3	oz. butter
1½	cups ravigotte sauce

Cut mackerel fillets into 5-oz. (140 g) portions. Season with salt and pepper. Coat with flour. Fry in oil and butter until crisp.

Arrange on a preheated serving platter. Garnish with parsley. Serve the sauce separately.

Serves: 6
Calories per serving: 567

Marinated Mackerel

3	fresh mackerel
4	oz. sliced onion
1	tbsp. chopped parsley
1	tsp. peppercorns
½	tsp. salt
1	bay leaf
2	cups dry white wine
1	tbsp. lemon juice
1	small bunch parsley

Clean the fish and discard heads. Wash the fish thoroughly and dry. Place in a baking pan. Sprinkle with salt, onion, parsley, and peppercorns. Add the bay leaf. Pour the wine and lemon juice over. Bring to a boil on top of the stove then bake at 350°F (180°C) for 15 minutes. Cool at room temperature. Refrigerate for several hours. Debone mackerel and arrange on serving platter. Strain cooking liquid and pour over fillets. Garnish with sprigs of parsley.

Note: This recipe can be prepared using half white wine and half vinegar.

Serves: 6
Calories per serving: 241

Mustard-Broiled Mackerel

2	lb. whole mackerel
2	tbsp. melted butter
1	tbsp. chopped parsley
1	tsp. salt
1	pinch pepper
1	tsp. prepared mustard
⅛	tsp. dried dill weed
1	tbsp. lemon juice
4	slices lemon

Clean and fillet the mackerel. Rinse under cold water and pat dry. Place the fillets, skin side down, on a greased broiler pan.

Combine half the butter with the parsley, salt, and pepper, and brush the fish well. Broil 2 to 3 inches from the heat, about 5 minutes. Do not turn.

Mix remaining butter with the mustard, dill weed, and lemon juice. Pour over the fillets and broil 5 minutes longer or until fish flakes easily with a fork. Serve garnished with lemon slices.

Serves: 4
Calories per serving: 289

Grilled Mackerel

Serve with curry sauce, sauce verte, or maître d'hôtel. (See grilled Dover Sole in this chapter.)

Mackerel Baked with Shallots

Follow the baking cooking technique in Chapter 6.

Mackerel Meunière

Follow the meunière cooking technique in Chapter 6.

Poached Spanish Mackerel

Serve with sauce bercy. Follow the poaching technique in Chapter 6.

Miscellaneous Seafood Recipes

Aspic Jelly*

8	oz. ground beef
½	cup diced leeks
½	cup diced onion
½	cup diced celery
4	egg whites
1	gal. cold fish stock
1	cup dry white wine

In a large pot, combine the lean beef, vegetables, and egg whites, then add one gallon of cold stock. Bring to a boil, stirring occasionally with a wooden spoon. Simmer for 30 minutes to an hour and strain through a cheesecloth. Add the white wine. Refrigerate a sample of the jelly. If it sets firmly, the aspic is ready. Otherwise reduce to concentrate the jelly.

*Aspic jelly is available commercially and can be prepared instantly.

Avocado Seafood Salad

· 1½	doz. small clams
½	lb. bay scallops
½	lb. medium shrimp
1	large avocado
1½	tsp. fresh lime juice
2	tbsp. sour cream
⅛	tsp. cayenne pepper
2	tbsp. minced chives

Scrub the clams well. Simmer the scallops in salted water about 1 minute. Remove with a slotted spoon and cook the shrimp in same liquid for 1½ minutes. Remove and cook the clams in same liquid until the shells are open. Discard any clams that do not open. Cool enough to handle. Peel and devein the shrimp, remove the clams from the shells. Cut the scallops in half. Cut the clams and shrimp into small pieces. Cut the avocado in half lengthwise, peel, chop, and sprinkle with lime juice. Toss the avocado with the sour cream, shellfish, cayenne, and chives. Season to taste with salt and pepper. If storing in refrigerator, bring to room temperature before serving.

Serves: 4
Calories per serving: 435

Fish Brochettes

2½	lb. fish fillets
1	green pepper
¼	cup oil
¼	cup lemon juice
1	tbsp. chopped parsley
¼	cup soy sauce
½	tsp. salt
¼	tsp. ground white pepper
8	oz. mushroom buttons
8	oz. cherry tomatoes

For this recipe, use firm fish such as tilefish, monkfish, grouper, or snapper.

Cut the fish fillets into chunks. Cut the green pepper into 1-inch (2.5 cm) squares and blanch for 1 minute. Combine the oil, lemon juice, parsley, soy sauce, salt, and pepper. Pour over the fish and vegetables and let stand for 30 minutes, stirring occasionally.

Using long skewers, alternate fish, mushrooms, green peppers, and cherry tomatoes, until skewers are filled. Broil about 4 inches (10 cm) from source of heat. Baste with the marinade while cooking. Turn after 5 minutes. Cook for 5 to 7 more minutes or until the fish flakes. Serve hot on a warm serving platter.

Serves: 6
Calories per serving: 238

Fish Seasoning

1	tbsp. sweet paprika
1	tsp. salt
1	tsp. onion powder
1	tsp. cayenne pepper
1	tsp. garlic powder

½	tsp. ground white pepper
½	tsp. ground black pepper
½	tsp. thyme leaves
½	tsp. oregano

Blend all ingredients together. Seal in an air-tight container and store in a dry place away from heat.

Use with any cajun fish or seafood recipe.

Fruits de Mer Cervelas

2	tsp. minced shallots
1	tbsp. butter
1	lb. diced lobster
1	lb. diced shrimp
1	lb. diced sea scallops
10	oz. cleaned crabmeat
5	egg whites
2	cups heavy cream
1	tsp. salt
½	tsp. ground white pepper
⅓	tsp. cayenne pepper
¼	cup cognac
5	feet rinsed lamb's casing
3	cups nantua sauce

Sauté shallots in clarified butter until tender. Let cool. Reserve half the lobster, shrimp, scallops, and crabmeat. Puree the remainder of the seafood and shallots in a food processor to a fine paste. Add the egg whites and blend until smooth. Add the heavy cream and pulse machine on and off to combine. Transfer to a bowl. Fold in the reserved seafood and seasonings. Blend well. Stuff the cleaned, rinsed casings with the mixture. Twist or tie into 4-inch (10 cm) links and tie ends securely. Poach the sausages in barely simmering water for 10 minutes or until fully cooked. Serve three links with sauce.

Serves: 12
Calories per serving: 357

Lemon Seafood Pasta

1	lb. fettucini
8	oz. snow peas
1	sweet red pepper
1	large lemon
12	oz. cleaned shrimp
12	oz. cleaned scallops
1/3	cup butter
2	cloves chopped garlic
1	cup heavy cream
1/2	tsp. salt
1/4	tsp. ground white pepper

Cook the pasta in boiling water until al dente and drain.

Clean the snow peas and cut into 1-inch pieces.

Seed and chop the pepper. Grate the lemon peel and set aside. Squeeze the juice from the lemon and store.

Sauté the seafood in butter for 2 to 3 minutes over high heat. Remove seafood with slotted spoon and set aside.

Add vegetables to the pan. Stir for 1 minute then remove vegetables from the pan. Add garlic to the pan containing cooking liquid and reduce by half. Add cream. Boil vigorously to reduce sauce until slightly thickened.

Stir in lemon peel and juice. Add the seafood and vegetables to the sauce. Season and toss with pasta until hot. Serve immediately.

Serves: 6
Calories per serving: 544

Paella Valenciana

1	lb. cooked lobster
1	lb. cooked shrimp
6	mussels
1/2	lb. chorizo
1	2-lb. quartered chicken
1	tsp. salt
1/4	cup olive oil
2	oz. chopped onion
1	tsp. minced garlic

1	medium sliced sweet pepper
2	medium peeled tomatoes
1	cup rice
1	tsp. saffron
1	qt. chicken stock
½	cup frozen peas

Cut the lobster meat and shrimp into chunks. Wash and scrub the live mussels and remove beards.

Cover sausage (kielbassa or other garlic-smoked pork sausage) with water and simmer for 10 minutes.

Season the chicken pieces with salt and pepper. Brown both sides in half the oil.

In a heavy cast iron pot, heat the remaining oil. Stir in the onion, garlic, peppers (red and green, if desired), and cook over low heat for 10 minutes. Add the chopped, seeded tomatoes, rice, saffron, and stock. Bring to a boil. Simmer for 10 minutes. Stir in chicken, all seafoods, and sliced sausage. Bake 25 minutes at 375°F (190°C). Cook the peas and sprinkle on top. Serve hot in a serving dish.

Serves: 6
Calories per serving: 449

Quick Blinis

1	cup buckwheat flour★
1	tsp. baking powder
1	tsp. sugar
1	large beaten egg
2	tbsp. sour cream
1	tbsp. melted butter
¾	cup warm milk

In a mixing bowl, combine the flour, baking powder, and sugar. Stir the remaining ingredients into the dry ingredients until the batter is smooth.

Drop the batter by the teaspoonful on a hot, greased griddle to make 2-inch (5 cm) cakes. Turn the blinis over when the bottoms are lightly browned. Cook about a minute on the other side. Serve hot.

★Use buckwheat pancake mix with eggs and milk to make a quick light batter.

Serves: 6
Calories per serving: 136

Salade Niçoise

1	lb. potatoes
1	small sliced onion
1	lb. beans
4	eggs
2	medium tomatoes
1	small head lettuce
8	oz. canned tuna
2	tbsp. capers
12	small black olives
3	tbsp. parsley
4	flat anchovy fillets
½	cup vinaigrette

Use new potatoes if possible. Boil potatoes in their jacket. Cool, peel, and slice while warm. Mix half the vinaigrette in potatoes with onions.

Snap small string beans if available and cook in boiling water until al dente. Cool under cold water and drain well. Boil eggs for 10 minutes, then shell.

Arrange clean lettuce leaves in the bottom of a bowl. Place a ring of potatoes on the lettuce. Top with string beans, egg slices, tomato slices, tuna chunks, capers, chives, parsley and anchovy fillets.

Pour remaining dressing over or serve separately.

Serves: 4
Calories per serving: 444

Seafood à la King

3	hard-cooked eggs
3	oz. cooked lobster
3	oz. cooked shrimps
6	oz. crabmeat
4	oz. diced mushrooms
2	oz. butter
2	tsp. lemon juice
2	diced red peppers

¼	cup dry white wine
2	cups medium cream sauce
1	tsp. worcestershire
½	tsp. salt
¼	tsp. ground white pepper

Dice the hard-cooked eggs and set aside. Combine the first four ingredients.

Sauté the mushrooms in the butter and lemon juice over a brisk fire. Add the peppers and white wine. Reduce the liquid to two thirds. Combine all the above ingredients with the cream sauce. Simmer for 10 minutes. Season with worcestershire, salt, and pepper.

Serves: 6
Calories per serving: 180

Seafood Brochettes

6	medium shelled shrimps
¾	lb. sea scallops
12	cherry tomatoes
1	large green pepper
8	oz. fresh pineapple
1	medium onion
½	cup dry sherry
2	tbsp. sesame oil
1	tbsp. sesame seeds
1	medium chopped garlic clove
¼	tsp. salt
2	tbsp. grated ginger

Combine the sherry, oil, sesame seeds, garlic, salt, and ginger in a shallow pan.

Coat the shrimp and scallops with the marinade and let stand at room temperature for 30 minutes.

Thread the shellfish on skewers alternating with vegetables and pineapple. Reserve the marinade.

Broil or grill the brochettes for 8 to 10 minutes or until seafood is cooked. Turn several times and brush with reserved marinade.

Serves: 6
Calories per serving: 255

Seafood Crêpes

5	oz. crabmeat
5	oz. cooked lobster
5	oz. cooked shrimp
2	cups medium béchamel
½	cup hollandaise
¼	cup sherry wine
½	cup heavy cream
3	oz. butter
12	crêpes

Dice the lobster and shrimp. Combine the crabmeat, lobster, and shrimp with a small amount of béchamel sauce and hollandaise to bind. Stir in the wine. Fill the crepes with the seafood mixture.

Arrange in a buttered, ovenproof serving dish. Combine the remaining béchamel and hollandaise with the heavy cream. Coat the crepes with this mixture. Brown in oven at 350°F (180°C).

Use left over seafood for this recipe.

Note: Veloute Sauce, Sauce Cardinal, or other sauces can be used to prepare seafood crepes.

See recipe for Crêpe Batter in Chapter 7.

Serves: 6
Calories per serving: 446

Seafood Fondue

1	lb. sole fillets
½	tsp. salt
1	oz. flour
1	beaten egg
1	cup bread crumbs
8	oz. breaded sea scallops
8	oz. breaded shrimp
8	oz. breaded oysters
½	cup rémoulade sauce
½	cup vincent sauce
½	cup tartar sauce

½   gal. oil for frying

6   lemon wedges

Cut fillets of sole into strips. Season with salt and roll in flour. Dip in egg and cover with bread crumbs.

Arrange a fondue set (pot, plates, forks) on a table with the uncooked seafood. Let the guests cook their own servings. Place the sauces on the table as dips.

Serve with lemon.

Serves: 8
Calories per serving: 442

Seafood Newburg

4   oz. butter

5   oz. cooked lobster

5   oz. cooked shrimp

5   oz. cooked crabmeat

1   oz. flour

½   tsp. paprika

¼   tsp. ground nutmeg

¼   cup cognac

½   cup sherry wine

4   egg yolks

1½   cup light cream

½   tsp. salt

¼   tsp. ground white pepper

2   cups cooked rice

Melt the butter in a shallow sauté pan. Dice the lobster, shrimp, and crabmeat. Add to the pan. Add the flour, mix well, and simmer for 5 minutes. Season with paprika and nutmeg. Pour in the cognac and sherry.

Make a liaison with the egg yolks and cream and, just before serving, stir into the seafood until thickened. The sauce must not boil. Season to taste with salt and pepper. Serve hot with rice.

Serves: 6
Calories per serving: 367

Seafood Pizza

1	lb. pizza dough
1	lb. Italian tomato sauce
1	clove minced garlic
1	tsp. oregano
8	oz. grated mozzarella
4	oz. sliced mushrooms
4	oz. crabmeat
4	oz. diced shrimp
4	oz. diced clams

See the recipe for pizza dough in Chapter 7.

Roll out the dough to fit a 14 × 17-inch (35 × 42.5-cm) baking sheet pan. Mix the tomato sauce, garlic, and oregano. Spread over the dough. Sprinkle the cheese and mushrooms over and bake for 15 minutes at 425°F (220°C). Sprinkle the seafood over and bake 5 more minutes or until the crust is golden brown.

Serves: 6
Calories per serving: 217

Seafood Sausages

12	oz. sole fillets
1	egg white
¾	cup heavy cream
½	tsp. salt
¼	tsp. ground pepper
1	tbsp. chopped parsley
2	oz. cooked mushrooms
2	oz. diced salmon
2	oz. diced shrimp
2	oz. diced scallops
2	feet sausage casing
¼	cup oil
1	cup velouté sauce

Use fillet of sole or other lean fish.

Cut fish fillets into strips. Puree in a food processor while gradually adding the egg white, heavy cream, salt, and pepper. Transfer to a mixing bowl. Fold in the cooked mushrooms, and diced salmon, shrimp, and scallops.

Using a sausage stuffer or funnel, stuff mixture into casings to make sausage links. Poach the sausages in salted boiling water, and simmer for 15 to 20 minutes. Brown in oil.

Arrange on a serving platter and coat with the boiling velouté sauce. Serve hot.

Serves: 6
Calories per serving: 255

Fish Soufflé

Fish soufflé can be prepared using, in volume, ⅓ quenelle force-meat and ⅓ velouté sauce or béchamel. Use 1 egg per serving. Mix in the egg yolks. Season with season salt, onion powder, and Knorr Swiss Aromat. Beat the egg whites until stiff. Fold into the soufflé mix. Bake in 350°F (180°C) oven. Spoon into buttered and floured soufflé mold(s). Serve with a sauce.

Monkfish *(Anglerfish, Goosefish)*

Ginger Lobster–Monkfish

1	2-lb. lobster
1	lb. monkfish fillets
1½	cup heavy cream
1	oz. grated ginger
½	tsp. grated salt
¼	tsp. ground white pepper
1	oz. flour
1	egg
1	tbsp. olive oil
2	oz. butter
2	oz. cognac
2	beaten egg yolks

Boil lobster in salted boiling water for 20 minutes. Remove from pot and let cool. Take the meat out of the tail and claws. Save the shell and head. Chop the shell into small pieces. Put in a saucepan with cream and ginger. Reduce for 10 minutes. Strain well to extract all juices.

Cut monkfish into small thin slices. Season with salt and pepper, dredge in flour, and then in the beaten egg and half of the olive oil. Sauté in the remaining oil for 2 minutes on each side. Keep warm.

Cut the lobster into thick slices. Sauté briefly in butter and cognac.

Place the lobster in center of a platter. Arrange the monkfish around the lobster.

Whip the egg yolks in the hot sauce. Pour over the fish. Brown under a broiler.

Serves: 4
Calories per serving: 564

Honey Vinegar Monkfish

4	lb. monkfish fillets
4	oz. butter
3	medium chopped shallots
2	tbsp. red wine vinegar
2	tsp. honey
½	cup heavy cream
6	egg yolks
½	tsp. salt
¼	tsp. ground white pepper
1	cup cooked cranberries

Cut fish fillets into ½-inch thick slices. Sauté the fish in hot butter about 3 minutes on each side. Keep fish warm on platter. Discard the butter then add shallots and vinegar. Reduce to evaporate three quarters of the vinegar. Add honey and cream. Bring to a boil.

Whip the egg yolks to double in volume. Stir in hot sauce without boiling. Season to taste with salt and pepper. Pour the sauce over the hot fish. Serve with freshly cooked cranberries.

Serves: 8
Calories per serving: 312

Mock Lobster Newburg

3	lb. cooked monkfish
3	oz. butter

1	cup madeira wine
1	cup heavy cream
3	beaten egg yolks
½	tsp. salt
⅛	tsp. cayenne pepper
3	cups cooked rice

Cut the monkfish into small pieces and heat slowly in the butter for about 5 minutes. Add wine and simmer until the wine is almost evaporated. Beat cream into the egg yolks and add to the fish. Season with salt and cayenne pepper. Heat stirring constantly until thickened. Do not boil. Serve with rice.

Serves: 6
Calories per serving: 492

Monkfish Américaine

2	lb. monkfish fillets
2	oz. oil
2	oz. butter
4	oz. chopped onion
1	clove minced garlic
4	oz. chopped carrot
2	oz. cognac
1	cup dry white wine
2	tbsp. tomato paste
1	bay leaf
½	tsp. salt
¼	tsp. ground white pepper
1	tbsp. beurre manié
1	tbsp. chopped parsley
1	tbsp. chopped tarragon

Heat the butter and oil in a sauté pan. Brown the monkfish fillets.
    Add the onion, garlic, and carrots, and cook for 5 minutes. Add the cognac and ignite. Moisten with wine and stir in the tomato paste and bay leaf. Season with salt and pepper.
    Cover sauté pan and bake at 350°F (180°C) for 25 minutes. Remove the fish from the pan. Slice thinly. Transfer to a serving

platter and keep hot. Thicken the cooking stock with beurre manié. Bring to a boil. Strain the sauce over the fish. Sprinkle with chopped parsley and tarragon. Serve hot.

Serves: 6
Calories per serving: 275

Monkfish Niçoise

2¼	lb. monkfish fillets
2	oz. flour
4	oz. butter
4	oz. chopped onion
1	cup tomato sauce
1	cup dry white wine
½	tsp. salt
¼	tsp. ground white pepper
¼	tsp. thyme
1	bay leaf
1	tbsp. beurre manié
2	cups cooked rice

Roll the monkfish fillets in flour. Sauté in half the butter until brown. Remove the fish from the pan. Add the onion and cook until light brown. Stir in the tomato sauce, wine, salt, pepper, and herbs.

Place monkfish fillets in the sauce and simmer for 30 to 40 minutes. Cook the rice according to standard directions. Remove the cooked fish from sauce, and thicken sauce with beurre manié. Remove the bay leaf from sauce.

Arrange the fish on a serving platter. Cover with sauce. Serve the rice separately.

Serves: 6
Calories per serving: 375

Mullet

Key Lime Florida Mullet

2	lb. mullet fillets
½	tsp. salt

¼	tsp. white pepper
3	oz. lime juice
4	oz. butter
6	lime wedges

Skin the mullet fillets and cut into serving portions. Place the fish on a buttered sheet pan. Season with salt and pepper. Pour the lime juice over and let stand for 30 minutes, turning the fish once. Melt the butter, combine with lime juice, and brush the fillets with this mixture. Place under a broiler about 4 inches (10 cm) from the source of heat, for 8 to 10 minutes, or until done. Serve at once.

Serves: 6
Calories per serving: 315

Mullets Grenobloise

3	lb. mullet fillets
½	tsp. salt
¼	tsp. ground white pepper
3	oz. oil
5	oz. butter
2	oz. capers
3	oz. flour
4	oz. croutons
2	lemons
1	tbsp. chopped parsley

Skin the mullet fillets and cut into portions. Season with salt and pepper. Sauté in oil and half the butter, browning the fish on both sides.

Arrange on a serving platter. Sprinkle with capers, croutons, and peeled lemon slices.

Brown the remaining butter, pour over the fish, and sprinkle with chopped parsley before serving.

Serves: 6
Calories per serving: 470

Stuffed Baked Mullet

6	1-lb. dressed mullet
8	oz. diced bacon
2	oz. chopped onion
4	oz. chopped celery
2	oz. fresh breadcrumbs
1	tsp. oregano
½	tsp. salt
¼	tsp. ground white pepper
8	oz. cooked shrimp
2	beaten eggs
1½	cups tomato sauce

Scale, clean, and wash the fish. Fry the bacon over low heat. Add the onions and celery. Cook until tender. Stir in the bread crumbs and seasonings. Mix the shrimp and eggs, and combine with the stuffing ingredients. Stuff the cavity of each fish with some of the mixture. Close the cavity with small skewers. Place the fish on a greased baking pan. Bake at 450°F (230°C) for 30 to 40 minutes, or until the fish is tender and flaky. Transfer onto a serving platter.

Serve the tomato sauce separately.

Serves: 6
Calories per serving: 394

Grilled Mullet Béarnaise

See Grilled Dover Sole Béarnaise in this chapter.

Smoked Mullet

This is a delicacy used in salads or diced for appetizer.

Ocean Perch (Rosefish)

Ocean Perch en Cocotte

6	dressed perch
½	tsp. salt

3	oz. butter
1	oz. chopped shallots
1	tbsp. chopped parsley
¾	cup dry white wine
2	oz. lemon juice
12	small Parisienne potatoes

Clean, scale, wash, and dry the perch. Season with salt. Butter an ovenproof serving dish. Sprinkle shallots and parsley over bottom of dish. Arrange the perch on top. Pour the wine and lemon juice over. Bake at 350°F (180°C) for 15 to 20 minutes. Serve hot with Parisienne potatoes.

Serves: 6
Calories per serving: 335

Perch des Gourmets

2	lb. perch fillets
½	tsp. salt
¼	tsp. ground white pepper
1	oz. lemon juice
2	eggs
2	oz. flour
4	oz. butter
1	lb. boiled potatoes
6	oz. béarnaise
2	diced tomatoes

Marinate the fillets in lemon juice, salt, and pepper. Dip the fillets in flour, coat with beaten egg, and fry in butter until brown on both sides.

Arrange the cooked fish on a preheated serving platter. Garnish with boiled potatoes. Serve with the béarnaise sauce combined with the cooked tomatoes.

Serves: 6
Calories per serving: 487

Perch Fillets Béarnaise

2	lb. perch fillets
½	tsp. salt
¼	tsp. pepper
3	oz. flour
4	oz. butter
6	grilled tomatoes
1	small bunch parsley
6	oz. béarnaise

Season the fillets with salt and pepper. Coat with flour. Fry in butter until crisp. Arrange on a preheated platter. Garnish with tomatoes and parsley. Serve the béarnaise separately.

Serves: 6
Calories per serving: 374

Perch Fish Fry

6	dressed perch
2	oz. cornmeal
2	oz. flour
1	tsp. salt
½	cup oil
1	tbsp. lemon juice
1	bunch parsley

Dip the perch in water. Coat with a mixture of cornmeal, flour, and salt. Fry in hot oil, browning both sides, until the fish flakes easily when tested with a fork. Arrange on a serving platter. Sprinkle with lemon juice and garnish with parsley.

Serves: 6
Calories per serving: 300

Pollock *(Boston Bluefish)*

Pollock can be prepared like cod and haddock.

Pompano *(Cobblerfish, Butterfish, Palmento)*

Scallopine of Pompano

8	oz. sliced onion
½	cup oil
1½	lb. chopped tomatoes
2	cloves minced garlic
1	cup tomato juice
½	tsp. salt
¼	tsp. ground white pepper
2	lb. pompano fillets
8	oz. egg noodles
1	cup velouté sauce
1	tbsp. chopped parsley

Sauté the onion in half the oil until tender. Add the chopped tomatoes, garlic, tomato juice, salt, and pepper. Cook over low heat for 15 minutes.

Skin and slice the pompano into scallopines. Flatten with a mallet. Season with salt, pepper, and lemon juice. Dredge the pompano in flour and sauté briskly in the remaining oil.

Cook the noodles in salted boiling water. Drain and combine with velouté sauce. Arrange the noodles on a preheated serving platter. Top with pompano slices. Spoon hot tomato and onion sauce over the fish. Sprinkle with parsley. Serve hot.

Serves: 10
Calories per serving: 339

Pompano Captiva

2	lb. pompano fillets
½	tsp. salt
¼	tsp. ground white pepper
4	oz. shelled shrimp
1	tbsp. chopped shallots
5	oz. dry white wine
5	oz. fish fumet

7	oz. sliced mushrooms
1	oz. beurre manié
3	oz. heavy cream
1	oz. lemon juice
1	lb. chopped tomatoes
1	oz. butter

Flatten the pompano fillets with a mallet. Season with salt and pepper.

Prepare a quenelle forcemeat with the shrimp (see recipe for Quenelles and Mousse in Chapter 9). Spread quenelle forcemeat over half of each pompano fillet and fold other half over.

Butter a baking pan. Sprinkle with shallots. Arrange the fillets on top in one layer. Add wine and fumet. Arrange the mushrooms on top of the fish. Bake at 400°F (204°C) for 20 to 25 minutes. Transfer fillets onto a serving platter. Reduce the cooking liquid by one third. Stir in beurre manié and cream. Reduce to a medium consistency. Add lemon juice. Season to taste and pour over the fish. Sauté tomatoes in butter and arrange around the pompano. Brown the fish under a broiler.

Serves: 6
Calories per serving: 382

Pompano Papillottes

2	lb. pompano fillets
4	oz. butter
2	tbsp. chopped scallions
5	oz. white wine
½	tsp. salt
¼	tsp. pepper
2	oz. sherry wine
6	oz. cooked shrimp
6	oz. crabmeat
2	cups cream sauce
1	dash tabasco

Melt half the butter in a sauté pan. Add the scallions. Place the pompano fillets on top, cover, and steam for 3 to 5 minutes. Add the white wine, sherry, salt, and pepper. Cook until the pompano is firm. Transfer the fish to a pan and keep warm. To the same pan, add the cooked sliced shrimp and crabmeat. Stir in the sauce. Bring to a boil. Adjust seasonings to taste.

Follow the procedure "en papillotte" described in Chapter 6. Cut the parchment paper into heart shapes, about 14 inches (35 cm) wide. Oil one side of the paper. Place two tablespoons of seafood on the right side of each heart. Top with pompano and sauce and fold left half of heart. Roll edges to seal. Bake in a hot oven until bags puff. Serve hot.

Serves: 6
Calories per serving: 380

Porgy *(Scup)*

Porgies are best sautéed meunière or pan fried. See cooking techniques in Chapter 6.

Redfish *(Channel Bass, Red Drum, Red Bass)*

Blackened Redfish

6	oz. butter
2	tbsp. fish seasoning★
30	oz. redfish★★ fillets
6	lemon wedges

Heat a large cast iron skillet over very high heat until it is very hot. Melt the butter in a saucepan. Clarify and save half the butter for serving with the fish.

Dip the fish fillets in butter to coat both sides. Sprinkle with fish seasoning. Place the fish fillets in the hot skillet. Cook over high heat until the fish is very brown. Turn the fish over. Lower the heat and cook fish until it is done.

Serve hot with melted butter and lemon wedges.

★See recipe for Fish Seasoning in this chapter.

★★You may substitute salmon, red snapper, tilefish, pompano, or other white firm fish for redfish.

Serves: 6
Calories per serving: 330

Redfish Polonaise

See Cod Polonaise in this chapter.

Gougeonnettes of Redfish

See Sole recipes in this chapter.

Red Snapper

Poached Red Snapper

5	lb. dressed red snapper
2	gal. No. 1 court bouillon
1	lb. peeled potatoes
6	lemon wedges
6	oz. hollandaise
1	lemon basket
1	bunch parsley

Poach the fish in court bouillon according to the poaching technique described in Chapter 6. Transfer the cooked fish onto a serving platter and garnish with boiled potatoes, lemon wedges, lemon basket, and parsley.

Serve the hollandaise separately.

Serves: 6
Calories per serving: 358

Baked Red Snapper

1	5-lb. whole red snapper
½	tsp. salt
¼	tsp. white pepper
1	cup white wine
4	oz. butter
2	cups fish fumet
1	cup heavy cream
2	oz. beurre manié
1	small bunch parsley

Wash and scale the red snapper. Season with salt and pepper. Place on a greased baking pan. Pour the wine over, along with melted butter. Bake at 350°F (180°C), timing 15 minutes per inch of thickness as measured at the thickest point. Baste frequently with the pan juices. Transfer baked fish to a platter.

Combine pan juices with the fumet. Boil for 10 minutes. Add cream and reduce by half. Thicken with beurre manié to a medium consistency. Serve the fish whole, garnish with parsley.

Serve the sauce separately.

Serves: 6
Calories per serving: 516

Fillet of Red Snapper Louisianne

Sauté meunière (see cooking technique in Chapter 6). Garnish with chopped cooked tomatoes, sliced green peppers cooked in butter, sliced cooked bananas, and top with lemon butter.

Grilled Red Snapper Maître d'Hôtel

See Sole recipes in this chapter.

Mousseline of Red Snapper Royale

See Salmon recipes in this chapter.

Rockfish *(Bocaccio)*

Rockfish and Pizza Sauce

1	cup sliced mushrooms
½	cup chopped onion
1	clove minced garlic
½	cup water
½	cup tomato paste
1	tsp. crushed basil
1	tsp. crushed oregano
½	tsp. sugar
½	tsp. fennel seeds
¼	tsp. crushed red pepper
4	4-oz. rockfish fillets

| 4 | green pepper rings |
| 3/4 | cup shredded mozzarella |

Combine the first ten ingredients in a saucepan. Simmer for 10 minutes uncovered, stirring occasionally.

Place the fish fillets in a baking dish. Pour the sauce over. Top with rings of green peppers and the mozzarella.

Bake at 450°F (230°C) for 8 to 10 minutes or till the fish flakes easily when tested.

Serves: 4
Calories per serving: 224

Prepare rockfish in the same manner as red snapper. For an additional rockfish recipe, see

San Francisco Cioppino in chapter 10.

Sablefish *(Black Cod)*

Broiled Sablefish

3	lb. sablefish fillets
1/2	cup oil
1	tsp. oregano
1/2	tsp. garlic salt
2	oz. lemon juice
1	tsp. chopped dill
6	lemon wedges
1	bunch parsley

Cut the sablefish fillets into equal portions. Marinate the fish in oil, oregano, garlic salt, lemon juice, and dill. Broil the fish on both sides.

Arrange on a serving platter. Serve with lemon wedges and decorate with parsley.

Serves: 6
Calories per serving: 534

Salmon

Braised Blueback

| 6 | lb. dressed blueback |
| 3 | tbsp. chopped shallots |

1	tbsp. butter
2	cups fish stock
2	cups champagne
2	oz. butter
2	oz. flour
1	tsp. salt
¼	tsp. ground white pepper
6	mushroom caps
1	oz. butter

Clean, scale, and place the whole fish on one side in a buttered baking dish. Sprinkle the shallots around the fish. Pour the champagne and the stock over the fish. Cover with a sheet of foil. Bake in 350°F (180°C) oven, allowing 10 to 12 minutes per pound for cooking time. Baste the fish occasionally. Transfer the fish to a serving platter. Skin both sides and cover with the foil. Strain the cooking liquid and reduce to 2 cups. Combine the butter and flour. Whip the beurre manie in the stock to make a creamy sauce. Season with salt and pepper.

Cover the fish with sauce, and garnish with mushroom caps sautéed in butter.

Serves: 8
Calories per serving: 435

Cajun Salmon Grenobloise

2	oz. butter
2	lb. salmon fillets
1	tbsp. wine worcestershire
½	tsp. onion salt
1	tsp. fish seasoning
1	tsp. dry oregano
1	tbsp. capers
8	oz. angel hair
2	oz. butter

Butter a baking dish. Lay the boneless salmon fillet in dish. Season with wine worcestershire, onion salt, fish seasoning, and oregano.

Bake at 450°F (230°C) for 10 minutes. Brown under a broiler for 2 to 3 minutes. Sprinkle capers over fish.

Cook the angel hair pasta in boiling water for 1 minute. Drain. Toss in the butter. Serve with the salmon.

Serves: 6
Calories per serving: 492

Chinook Bellevue

10	lb. dressed salmon
2	gal. No. 1 court bouillon
1	large cucumber
12	slices tomatoes
6	oz. smoked salmon mousse
6	radish
2	cups mayonnaise

Clean, scale, and wash the chinook fresh salmon. Cut the fish in half crosswise. Keep the tail piece whole and fillet the other piece. Remove all bones. Poach the tail piece and the fillet in court bouillon, following the directions described for the poaching technique in Chapter 6. Allow the fish to cool in court bouillon.

Remove the salmon from court bouillon. Slice the fillets into serving portions. Skin the tail piece and decorate with cucumber slices.

Arrange the tail piece and slices on a large platter or mirror. Decorate each slice with radish slivers.

Pipe the salmon mousse on top of the tomato slices. Arrange around the salmon. Serve cold with mayonnaise.

Serves: 12
Calories per serving: 462

Coulibiac

1½	lb. sliced salmon fillets
1	tbsp. lemon juice
½	tsp. salt
⅛	tsp. ground white pepper
1	chopped onion
1	tbsp. oil
1	oz. chopped mushrooms

1	tbsp. chopped parsley
6	oz. cooked rice
2	chopped hard-cooked eggs
½	cup velouté sauce
1	tbsp. melted butter
1	recipe brioche dough
1	beaten egg

Slice the salmon thin and season with salt, pepper, and lemon juice. Sauté onion in oil. Add the mushrooms and parsley. Cook over medium heat for 5 minutes. Roll out brioche dough into a rectangle ¼-inch thick. Place on a baking sheet. Arrange a layer of onion mix, rice, and eggs over the whole length of dough to within one inch from edges. Top with salmon slices. Place remaining onion mix, rice, and eggs over salmon. Top with remaining salmon. Pour velouté over filling. Brush edges of dough with water. Fold over mix. Seal all edges and roll pastry so that seam is underneath. Brush dough with the beaten egg. Decorate with pieces of dough. Let rise at room temperature for 30 minutes. Bake at 375°F (190°C) for 30 minutes.

Serves: 6
Calories per serving: 510

Creamed Salmon

1½	lb. cooked salmon
2	oz. butter
1	oz. chopped onion
1	tbsp. chopped shallots
8	oz. sliced mushrooms
½	cup dry white wine
1	oz. flour
½	cup milk
½	cup heavy cream
½	tsp. salt
¼	tsp. ground white pepper
1	tbsp. chopped parsley
2	cups cooked rice

Break up the canned or fresh salmon and set aside. Sauté the onion, shallots, and mushrooms in butter until tender. Add the wine and cook to reduce by half. Cool mixture and add the flour. Stir in the milk and cream to make a cream sauce. Season to taste and simmer for 5 minutes. Mix in the salmon and heat through. Sprinkle with parsley and serve in a casserole dish with rice.

Serves: 6
Calories per serving: 385

Fettucine with Salmon

8	oz. fresh fettucine★
2	tbsp. olive oil
1	cup fresh peas
¼	lb. sliced smoked salmon
1	pint heavy cream
1	tbsp. minced shallots
2	tbsp. dry white wine
¼	tsp. salt
⅛	tsp. ground white pepper

Slice the smoked salmon very thin.

Cook the pasta in salted water. Drain and toss lightly with olive oil. Set aside in a warm place.

Blanch the peas in lightly salted boiling water. Drain and plunge into ice water. Drain and set aside.

Puree half the salmon and a small amount of cream and shallots in a blender until smooth. Bring the wine to a boil. Add the remaining cream. Cook, stirring constantly, until mixture coats the back of a wooden spoon.

Add the salmon puree and blend thoroughly. Stir over low heat until mixture is hot. Season with salt and pepper.

Cut remaining salmon in strips. Toss the pasta with salmon and peas. Pour the hot sauce over. Toss well.

★Use spinach fettucine.

Serves: 4
Calories per serving: 625

Fried Salmon Steaks

6	salmon steaks
½	tsp. salt
¼	tsp. white pepper
2	tsp. olive oil
2	tsp. butter
2	tbsp. chopped shallots
1½	cups white wine
¾	cup heavy cream
1½	tbsp. butter
2	tsp. flour

Season the salmon steaks with salt and pepper. Heat the butter and oil in a frying pan. Brown the salmon steaks on both sides. Carefully remove bones and skin and transfer to a serving platter. Keep warm.

Sprinkle the shallots in the frying pan and cook over low heat for 2 minutes. Add the white wine and simmer for 10 minutes. Pour in the heavy cream and boil for 5 minutes. Drop pieces of the butter and flour mixture into the boiling liquid. Whip until the sauce is smooth and medium thick. Season with salt and pepper to taste. Cook the sauce for about 10 minutes. Pour over the salmon steaks and serve at once.

Serves: 6
Calories per serving: 431

Gravlax

5	lb. salmon fillets
2½	oz. salt
5½	oz. sugar
6	stems fresh dill
1	sliced onion
1	tsp. ground black pepper
1	crushed juniper berry
2	lemons
20	slices rye bread

Scale, wash, and dry the salmon thoroughly. Extract all bones. Mix the salt and sugar and rub the mixture into the salmon fillets. Place dill and thinly sliced onion on the botton of a rectangular pan. Lay the salmon fillets on top, skin side up. Sprinkle pepper and juniper berry over the fish. Place a board on top of the fish with a weight on it. Marinate in the refrigerator for 2 to 3 days, basting the fish each day with marinade. Slice thinly and serve with rye bread.

Serves: 20
Calories per serving: 280

Poached Salmon Steaks

6	7-oz. salmon steaks
1	gal. No. 1 court bouillon
1	cup grated cucumber
1	cup sour cream
1	tsp. minced scallion
1½	tsp. lemon juice
¾	tsp. salt
¼	tsp. ground pepper
½	tsp. dill weed

If frozen, thaw the salmon steaks.

Poach the salmon in court bouillon following the procedure described for the poaching technique in Chapter 6.

Chill the salmon. Remove the skin and bones. Arrange the salmon on plates or a serving platter.

To make the sauce, combine the remaining ingredients, except dill. Spoon over the salmon. Sprinkle with chopped dill.

Serves: 6
Calories per serving: 258

Salmon au Gratin

1½	lb. cooked salmon
4	oz. cooked duxelle
2	cups velouté sauce
½	cup hollandaise
2	cups cooked rice

Bone, skin, and flake the salmon. Arrange in a buttered casserole dish. Spread the duxelle over the fish. Heat in oven at 350°F (180°C).

Combine the velouté sauce with the hollandaise. Ladle over the salmon, blending the sauce with the fish. Brown under the boiler. Serve with rice.

Serves: 6
Calories per serving: 381

Salmon Brochettes

2½	lb. salmon fillets
1	tsp. salt
¼	tsp. ground pepper
4	oz. butter
12	mushroom caps
2	oz. fresh bread crumbs

Bone and skin the salmon into 1-inch (2.5 cm) cubes. Season with salt, pepper, and lemon juice.

Sauté the mushroom caps in a small amount of butter until cooked.

Alternate the salmon pieces and mushroom caps on skewers. Dip in melted butter and roll in the fresh bread crumbs. Sauté in the remaining butter for about 10 minutes or until golden brown on all sides.

Serve with a hot sauce.

Serves: 6
Calories per serving: 450

Salmon Cakes

1½	lb. fresh salmon steaks
2	beaten eggs
1¼	cups fresh cracker crumbs
½	tsp. paprika
¼	cup chopped chives
2	tbsp. chopped parsley
2	tbsp. oil

Steam the salmon steaks 7 minutes. Discard the skin and bones. Flake the fish in a bowl with the eggs and half the crumbs, chives, and parsley. Blend. Shape the mixture into cakes of equal size. Coat the cakes on all sides with remaining crumbs.

Heat the oil in a heavy skillet. Add a few cakes at a time and cook 2½ minutes on each side or until golden brown.

Drain on absorbent paper towels.

Serves: 6
Calories per serving: 280

Salmon Cutlet Pojarsky

1½	lb. fresh salmon
4	oz. white bread
1	cup milk
4	oz. soft butter
½	tsp. salt
¼	tsp. ground pepper
½	cup butter

Skin, bone, and cube the salmon. Chop the salmon finely in a food processor. Soak the bread in milk for 10 minutes. Squeeze out excess moisture and mix well into a salmon paste. Blend in the butter until the mixture is smooth. Season with salt and pepper to taste.

Shape the salmon into cutlets. Sauté in clarified butter. Serve with hot sauce.

Serves: 6
Calories per serving: 496

Salmon Florentine

1½	lb. fresh spinach
2	tsp. butter
2½	lb. cooked salmon
2	cups mornay sauce
2	oz. grated swiss cheese

Cook the spinach in salted boiling water. Cool and squeeze out excess moisture. Chop coarsely and sauté in butter. Spread spinach over bottom of a buttered baking dish.

Skin, bone, and flake the salmon. Cover the spinach with salmon and coat with the mornay sauce. Sprinkle with cheese and add a few dots of butter on top. Bake for 10 to 15 minutes at 375°F (190°C).

Brown under a broiler. Serve hot.

Serves: 6
Calories per serving: 477

Salmon Gratiné Nantua

6	oz. mushroom caps
1	oz. butter
2	tsp. lemon juice
2½	lb. poached salmon
2	cups nantua sauce
2	oz. grated swiss cheese

Wash and slice the mushroom caps. Melt the butter in a saucepan. Add the lemon juice and mushrooms. Cook over medium heat until the mushrooms are tender.

Remove the bones and skin from the poached salmon. Flake the salmon in a buttered baking dish. Spread the mushrooms over the salmon and cover with the nantua sauce. Sprinkle with cheese and bake at 375°F (190°C) for 15 minutes, or until golden brown.

Serves: 10
Calories per serving: 339

Salmon in Wine Sauce

6	8-oz. salmon steaks
½	tsp. salt
¼	tsp. ground white pepper
2	cups fish stock
¼	cup white wine
1½	cup veloute sauce
1	egg yolk
¼	cup heavy cream

Season the salmon steaks with salt and pepper and arrange side by side in a baking dish. Pour the fish stock and the white wine over. Bring to a simmer and poach for 5 to 10 minutes. Arrange the fish on a serving platter. Remove the bones and skin. Reduce the cooking liquid to a half cup. Stir in the veloute sauce. Bring to a boil. Simmer to reach a medium-thick consistency.

Mix the egg yolk with the cream. Whip into the sauce, but do not allow to boil.

Strain the sauce over the hot salmon steaks and serve at once.

Serves: 6
Calories per serving: 377

Salmon Medallions Aurora

2¼	lb. salmon fillets
¾	tsp. salt
¼	tsp. ground white pepper
1	tbsp. lemon juice
¼	cup oil
6	baby carrots
4	oz. snow peas
1	fennel bulb
2	oz. butter
1	cup sauce aurora

Cut the salmon fillets across into equal portions. Flatten the fish to the shape of medallions. Season with salt, pepper, lemon juice, and brush with oil.

Peel the carrots, wash the snow peas and snap the ends. Separate the fennel leaves and cut into sticks. Cook the vegetables in salted boiling water until done.

Grill the salmon fillets on a hot broiler or grill.

Drain the vegetables. Sauté in butter. Arrange salmon medallions on plates surrounded by the vegetables and the hot sauce aurora.

Serves: 6
Calories per serving: 431

Salmon Mousseline Royale

9	oz. fresh salmon
2	egg whites
10	oz. heavy cream

⅛	tsp. cayenne pepper
¾	tsp. salt
½	oz. minced truffle
10	oz. fresh spinach
2	oz. butter
10	oz. puff pastry dough
2	egg yolks
1	cup velouté sauce

If not already done, skin and bone salmon. In a food processor, mix the salmon and egg whites. Add the cream gradually. Season with salt and cayenne pepper. Stir in the truffles. Poach egg-shaped dumplings in salted boiling water, following the recipe for Pike Quenelles in Chapter 9.

Clean and cook the spinach with butter and a small amount of water. Season with salt and pepper. Chop.

Roll puff pastry out to a ⅛-inch, (2 mm) thickness. Cut into two large rectangles. Place 1 tbsp. spinach every 4 inches (10 cm) across and down the dough. Top the spinach with dumplings and spread other puff pastry sheet over, pressing down firmly. Cut into oval shapes. Brush with egg yolks. Bake for 10 minutes at 425°F (220°C). Serve with hot sauce.

Serves: 6
Calories per serving: 407

Salmon Provençale

½	cup sliced onion
2	tsp. olive oil
1	clove minced garlic
12	nicoise olives
2	cups tomato sauce
2½	lb. cooked salmon
1	oz. fresh bread crumbs

Heat the oil in a frying pan and sauté the onion over low heat until tender. Add the garlic and sliced olives. Simmer over medium heat for 5 minutes. Mix in the tomato sauce and simmer for 10 minutes.

Flake the boneless and skinless salmon in a buttered baking dish. Pour the sauce over. Sprinkle with the bread crumbs and bake at 350°F (180°C) for 15 minutes.

Serves: 6
Calories per serving: 448

Salmon Rillettes

8	oz. fresh salmon
8	oz. smoked salmon
1	tbsp. minced shallots
½	cup unsalted butter
¼	cup chopped parsley
1	tbsp. lemon juice
1	tsp. dijon mustard
1	tsp. capers
1	tsp. cognac
1	tsp. lemon zest
¼	tsp. ground white pepper
8	slices pumpernickel

Poach the fresh salmon. Cool and remove the bones and skin. Put in a mixing bowl. Mix to a smooth paste. Dice the smoked salmon and add to the paste. Add the remaining ingredients. Season to taste with salt and mix thoroughly.

Spoon the salmon mixture into small crock or serving bowl. Refrigerate for an hour. Serve with thin slices of pumpernickel.

Serves: 8
Calories per serving: 220

Salmon Salad

2½	lb. cooked salmon
1	cup mayonnaise
½	cup sauce vinaigrette
½	tsp. salt
¼	tsp. ground white pepper
12	wedges tomatoes
1	small cucumber

Bone and skin the cooked salmon. Combine the mayonnaise, vinaigrette, salt, and pepper. Fold the mayonnaise mixture with the flaked salmon. Arrange on a serving platter with tomato wedges and peeled sliced cucumber.

Serves: 10
Calories per serving: 343

Salmon Steak Papillotte

6	7-oz. salmon steaks
½	tsp. salt
⅛	tsp. ground white pepper
1	tbsp. lemon juice
6	slices bacon
18	juniper berries
6	parchment sheets
1	tbsp. melted butter
6	oz. hollandaise

Season the salmon steaks with salt, pepper, and lemon juice. Wrap a slice of bacon around each steak. Place three juniper berries on top of each steak.

Cut the parchment paper into heart shapes.

Place each steak on one side of a sheet of parchment paper. Fold the other side of the parchment paper over and seal well. Brush the paper with melted butter to prevent burning. Arrange the salmon steaks on a baking sheet and bake at 400°F (200°C) for 15 to 20 minutes. The bags will then be puffed. Unwrap and transfer the steaks to a serving platter.

Serve the hollandaise separately.

Serves: 6
Calories per serving: 451

Salmon Steak St. Laurent

1½	oz. butter
1	small chopped onion
1	tbsp. chopped shallots
2	tsp. chopped chives
1	tsp. chopped tarragon
2	tbsp. chopped mushrooms
2	small tomatoes
½	cup white wine
1½	cups fish fumet
2	tsp. brandy
6	7-oz. salmon steaks

½	cup heavy cream
1	tbsp. lobster butter
1	tbsp. hollandaise
6	cooked mushroom caps

Melt the butter in a saucepan. Add the onion, shallots, chives, tarragon, and mushrooms. Cook over low heat for 5 minutes. Add the peeled chopped seedless tomatoes. Simmer for a few minutes. Pour in the white wine, fish fumet, and brandy. Place the salmon steaks in a buttered baking pan. Pour the cooking liquid over and bake for 20 minutes at 350°F (180°C). Bone and skin the salmon. Transfer to a serving platter. Keep the fish warm.

Reduce the cooking liquid by half. Add the heavy cream and lobster butter and boil sauce to a medium thick consistency. Mix in the hollandaise sauce. Pour over the salmon steaks. Top with mushroom caps. Serve hot.

Serves: 6
Calories per serving: 364

Salmon Steaks Italienne

1½	tbsp. chopped shallots
6	oz. sliced mushrooms
6	salmon steaks
1½	cups dry white wine
¾	cups fish stock
1	diced green pepper
12	oz. canned tomatoes
2	tsp. flour
2	tbsp. butter

Butter a large baking pan. Sprinkle shallots and mushrooms on bottom. Place salmon steaks over them side by side.

Pour the wine and fish stock over, and add the chopped tomatoes and green pepper. Cover with a sheet of foil. Bring to a boil over medium heat. Then bake at 350°F (180°C) for 10 to 12 minutes. Skin and bone the steaks and transfer to a serving platter.

Strain the cooking liquid and boil for 10 minutes. Thicken with the mixture of flour and soft butter, and whip until the sauce is smooth and medium thick. Cover the salmon with the sauce and serve at once.

Serves: 6
Calories per serving: 320

Salmon–Shrimp Terrine

2	oz. butter
2	oz. chopped shallots
8	oz. cleaned shrimp
1	cup dry white wine
1	tbsp. tomato paste
10	oz. fresh salmon
2	oz. soft butter
1	cup heavy cream
2	eggs
½	tsp. salt
¼	tsp. ground white pepper
1	tbsp. chopped parsley
1	tbsp. chopped dill
1	recipe beurre blanc

Melt the butter in a sauté pan. Add shallots and cook over low heat for 5 minutes. Add peeled and deveined shrimp. Pour in the wine. Bring to a boil. Stir in the tomato paste.

Cube the boneless and skinless salmon. Puree in a food processor, adding the butter, cream, eggs, salt, pepper, and herbs. Transfer to a bowl. Fold in the shrimp mixture.

Spoon mixture in a greased terrine, smoothing the top with a spatula. Cover the terrine and bake in a waterbath at 300°F (155°C) for 45 to 60 minutes. Remove the terrine from the waterbath. Slice and serve with beurre blanc.

Serves: 10
Calories per serving: 279

Smoked Salmon Mousse

1	lb. smoked salmon
½	cup mayonnaise
¾	cup aspic jelly★
1	tbsp. lemon juice
¼	tsp. ground white pepper
1	cup heavy cream

Remove the bones and skin from salmon. Cut in pieces and mix in a food processor. Transfer to a mixing bowl and stir in the mayonnaise. Run the mixture through a food mill. Mix in the cold liquid aspic jelly, lemon juice. wine, and pepper.

Whip the cream until firm. Fold in the salmon mixture.

Spoon the mousse into decorative molds. Refrigerate until mousse is well set and firm.

Unmold on serving dish or plate and surround with lettuce leaves.

★See recipe for aspic jelly.

Serves: 6
Calories per serving: 425

Smoked Salmon Salad

10	oz. cleaned spinach★
8	slices smoked salmon
8	slices swiss cheese★
½	cup olive oil
¼	cup wine vinegar
1	tsp. honey
½	oz. cognac
¼	tsp. salt
⅛	tsp. ground white pepper

Trim the stalks from the spinach and shred leaves finely. Place in a large bowl. Cut the smoked salmon and cheese into matchstick strips.

Heat the dressing ingredients in a pot. Bring to boil. Pour hot dressing over spinach and toss well.

Divide the spinach among salad plates. Top with salmon and cheese.

★Vary the amount of spinach and cheese as desired.

This recipe was provided by Canada's Olympic Chefs.

Serves: 4
Calories per serving: 310

Steelhead Napa Valley

4	lb. dressed steelhead
1½	cups chablis wine
1½	cups fumet
1	cup heavy cream
2	oz. beurre manié
8	oz. button mushrooms
8	oz. peeled pearl onion
1	tbsp. butter
1	tbsp. chopped parsley
1	tbsp. chopped dill
1	tbsp. chopped sage
10	oz. cooked asparagus

Clean the trout. Place in a fish poacher. Add the fish fumet and the wine. Cover and bring the fumet to 180°F (83°C). Time 10 minutes per inch of thickness of the fish. When cooked, remove the fish from the cooking liquid, skin, and arrange on a serving platter. Reduce the strained liquid to half. Add the cream. Reduce again for 5 minutes. Stir in the beurre manié and simmer the sauce for 10 minutes. Season with salt and pepper to taste. Sauté the mushrooms in butter until done. Cook the onions in salted boiling water. Combine the mushrooms and onions in sauce. Pour the sauce over the trout. Sprinkle the parsley, dill, and sage over the fish and garnish with asparagus. Serve hot.

Serves: 6
Calories per serving: 460

Smoked Salmon Soufflé

5	eggs
2	oz. butter
2	oz. flour
1½	cups scalded milk
¼	tsp. ground white pepper
⅛	tsp. ground nutmeg
10	oz. chopped smoked salmon
4	oz. diced mushrooms
1	oz. butter

2	oz. butter
1	oz. flour

Separate the eggs and set aside.

Melt the butter in a saucepan. Add the flour and cook over medium heat for 5 minutes. Cool the roux. Pour the milk in the roux. Whip and return to heat until the sauce thickens and comes to a boil. Season with pepper and nutmeg.

Sauté the mushrooms in butter. Mix the chopped salmon and the mushrooms into the sauce. Stir in the egg yolks. Whip the egg whites until medium stiff. Fold into the salmon mixture. Butter and flour a 7-inch (17.5 cm) round soufflé mold. Spoon the soufflé mix into mold. Bake 30 minutes at 350°F (180°C). Serve immediately.

Note: A velouté sauce made with salmon bones is the ideal accompaniment for this soufflé.

Serves: 6
Calories per serving: 339

Sole and Salmon Mousse

1	lb. boneless salmon
2	egg whites
1	cup heavy cream
½	tsp. salt
¼	tsp. ground white pepper
¼	tsp. ground nutmeg
1	tsp. chopped dill
1½	lb. sole fillets
2	cups white wine
6	fleurons

Prepare a mousse with the salmon, egg whites, cream, salt, pepper, nutmeg, and dill (see recipes for Quenelles and Mousses in Chapter 9).

Line the bottom and sides of a buttered ring mold with the fillets of sole. Season with salt and pepper. Fill the mold with the salmon mousse. Cover with parchment paper or foil. Bake in a waterbath at 400°F (200°C) for 40 to 45 minutes.

Invert mold onto a serving platter. Coat with sauce, garnish with fleurons, and serve immediately.

Serves: 6
Calories per serving: 399

Terrine of Salmon

2	oz. butter
1	medium diced onion
2½	lb. boneless salmon fillets
1	tsp. unflavored gelatin
4	oz. white bread
1	egg
1	tsp. salt
½	tsp. ground white pepper
⅓	tsp. ground nutmeg
2	cups heavy cream
½	bunch chopped dill
2	tbsp. chopped chervil
2	tbsp. chopped parsley
½	cup whipped cream
2	tbsp. salmon caviar

Sauté the onion in butter until transparent. Trim the salmon fillets to fit the terrine. Dust with gelatin and set aside. Cube the resulting salmon trimmings and season with salt and pepper. Cube the crustless bread and soak with eggs and some cream. Place the salmon trimmings in food processor. Add the onion, bread, salt, and seasoning. Emulsify while adding heavy cream slowly. Line the terrine with plastic wrap. Fill a third full with forcemeat. Press salmon fillet in the center. Top with forcemeat, pressing to avoid air pockets. Enclose with plastic wrap. Cover with a lid. Bake in a waterbath at 170°F (77°C) for 40 to 50 minutes. Chill, unmold, roll in herbs. Serve with cream and caviar.

Serves: 10
Calories per serving: 359

▬ Sardine *(Atlantic Herring)*

Pita Sardine Sandwiches

8	oz. canned sardines
1	tbsp. lemon juice

6	pita bread pockets
½	cup mayonnaise
1	cup shredded lettuce
4	thin slices red onion
12	cucumber slices

Drain the sardines. Sprinkle with lemon juice. Cut the pita bread in half across and open pocket. Spread inside with mayonnaise.

Crush the sardines and lemon juice until blended. Divide between pita halves alternating with layers of lettuce, red onion, and cucumber slices. Serve at once.

Serves: 6
Calories per serving: 450

Sardine Summer Salad

3	cups shredded lettuce
2	cups sliced mushrooms
1½	cups cubed tomatoes
2	cans drained sardines
1	cup diced cheddar cheese
1	cup sliced red onion
1½	cups cooked peas
½	cup plain yogurt
½	cup vinaigrette
2	tsp. prepared mustard
2	tbsp. lemon juice

Cut sardines into bite-sized pieces.

In a suitable salad bowl, layer lettuce, mushrooms, tomatoes, sardines, cheese, onion, and peas.

In a small bowl mix yogurt, vinaigrette, mustard, and lemon juice. Spread over top of salad. Cover. Chill overnight. To serve, garnish as desired.

Serves: 6
Calories per serving: 263

For additional sardine recipes, see

Sardine Canapés in Chapter 15.
Sardine Dip in Chapter 15.
Sardine Tapenade in Chapter 15.
Toasted Grilled Sardines in Chapter 15.

Sea Bass

Sea Bass Royale

See Mousseline of Salmon Royale in this chapter. Sea bass can also be prepared following trout recipes.

Braised Soy Bass

2½	lb. whole bass
1	tsp. salt
¼	cup flour
1½	tsp. grated ginger
2	minced scallions
1	small minced garlic clove
1	cup chicken broth
2	tbsp. soy sauce
2	tbsp. oyster sauce (optional)
3	tbsp. sherry
1	pinch cayenne pepper
¼	cup salad oil

The fish should be cleaned and scaled but left whole. Score both sides of the fish with 2 diagonal cuts. Wipe dry. Season with salt and dust with flour.

In a saucepan, combine remaining ingredients except oil. Heat to a simmer then keep warm.

In a heavy skillet, heat oil over high heat. Fry the fish for 1 minute on one side then turn carefully and fry 2 more minutes.

Pour the broth mixture over fish. Cover and simmer for 15 minutes. Baste the fish twice while cooking. Serve hot.

Serves: 4
Calories per serving: 294

White Sea Bass Marinière

8	oz. sliced onion
2	medium sliced carrots
2	medium sliced leeks
2	sticks sliced celery
2	bay leaves
2	oz. olive oil
2	oz. butter
5	lb. dressed white sea bass
2	cups white wine
1	tsp. salt
¼	tsp. ground white pepper

Brown the onion, carrots, leeks, and celery in oil and butter. Add bay leaves and wine. Simmer for 10 minutes.

Clean and scale the white sea bass. Place in a buttered baking pan. Add the cooking liquid and the vegetables. Season with salt and pepper. Bake at 350°F (180°C) for 25 to 30 minutes.

Transfer the fish to a serving platter. Pour the cooking liquid over fish. Garnish with vegetables.

Serves: 6
Calories per serving: 328

Sea Trout *(Weakfish, Gray Sea Trout, Squeteaques, Summer Trout)*

Fillet of Trout Key West

12	4-oz. trout fillets
6	medium stone crab claws
6	small shrimp quenelles
2	cups fumet
1½	cup white wine sauce

Poach the trout fillets and the shrimp quenelles in fumet. Arrange the trout fillets on a warm serving platter. Garnish with shrimp quenelles and warm crab claws. Pour the hot sauce over the fish. Serve hot.

Serves: 6
Calories per serving: 280

Gougeonnettes of Trout

2¼	lb. sea trout fillets
½	tsp. salt
¼	tsp. ground white pepper
2	oz. lemon juice
3	oz. flour
3	eggs
8	oz. fresh bread crumbs
8	oz. ground almonds
½	tsp. seasoned salt
1	cup fried parsley
6	cups lemon wedges
1½	cup mustard sauce

Wash and skin fillets of sea trout. Cut into strips 3 inches (7.5 cm) long. Season with salt, pepper, and lemon juice. Toss the fish and marinate for 3 to 4 hours in the refrigerator.

Roll the fish in seasoned flour, dip in beaten eggs, and cover with the mixture of bread crumbs, ground almonds, and seasoned salt.

Deep fry at 350°F (180°C) for 3 to 5 minutes. Serve on a warm platter covered with a napkin or doilies.

Top gougeonnettes with fried parsley. Surround with lemon wedges. Serve sauce separately.

Serves: 6
Calories per serving: 293

Sea trout can also be prepared following rainbow trout and salmon recipes.

═ Shad

Broiled Fillets of Shad

2	lb. shad fillets
½	cup oil
1	oz. lemon juice
1	tsp. salt
1	tbsp. chopped parsley
1	tsp. rosemary
1	bay leaf
¼	cup mayonnaise
1	chopped scallion
¼	cup vinaigrette

Place the fillets of shad, skin side down, in a shallow dish. Combine all the ingredients for the marinade. Pour over the fillets. Refrigerate overnight. Before broiling, allow the fillets to come to room temperature. Place fillets, skin side down, on a preheated broiler pan, about 3 inches (7.5 cm) from the source of heat. Baste liberally with the marinade after 2 minutes of broiling. Continue broiling about 6 to 8 minutes or until the fish is flaky.

The juice at the bottom of the pan can be used to prepare a sauce to accompany the fish. The shad roe can be marinated at the same time and broiled on both sides.

Serves: 6
Calories per serving: 460

Shad Fillets Provencale

2	lb. shad fillets
½	tsp. salt
1	tsp. worcestershire
¾	cup dry white wine
4	oz. chopped onion
2	cloves minced garlic
2	medium diced green peppers

| 1 | lb. chopped tomatoes |
| 1 | tbsp. chopped parsley |

Arrange the boned shad on a greased sheet pan. Sprinkle with worcestershire sauce and salt. Pour the wine over.

Sauté the onion in hot oil, add the garlic, green peppers, and seedless tomatoes, and cook over medium heat for 15 minutes. Spoon the sauce over the shad fillets and bake at 350°F (180°C) for 15 to 20 minutes. Test for doneness. Transfer to a warm serving platter. Sprinkle with chopped parsley before serving.

Serves: 6
Calories per serving: 352

Shad Roe Soufflé

2	oz. butter
2	oz. flour
2	cups fish stock
1	pair shad roe
1	tbsp. lemon juice
5	egg yolks
1	tbsp. chopped parsley
½	tsp. salt
¼	tsp. ground white pepper
2	tsp. soft butter
1	tbsp. flour

Melt the butter in a saucepan. Stir in flour and cook over low heat for 5 minutes. Add the hot fish stock to make a velouté. Cook until thickened, stirring continuously. Transfer to a mixing bowl. Cook the shad roe in salted boiling water. Remove the membrane. Stir into the velouté. Mix in the egg yolks and parsley. Season to taste with salt and pepper. Beat the egg whites until stiff. Fold into the sauce. Butter and flour a 2-qt. (2 l) soufflé dish. Pour in the soufflé mixture. Bake at 350°F (180°C) for 30 to 40 minutes. Serve immediately.

Serves: 6
Calories per serving: 182

Stuffed Fillets of Shad

2	lb. shad fillets
1	shad roe
2	oz. melted butter
4	oz. bread crumbs
½	tsp. salt
1	beaten egg
¼	tsp. ground sage
3	oz. butter
1	tbsp. lemon juice

Parboil the shad roe in salt water for 5 to 6 minutes. Drain and allow to cool. Remove the tissues and break the small eggs apart. Add the melted butter, bread crumbs, salt, egg, and sage. Spread the stuffing over the two fillets. Lift one fillet and place on top of second so that the stuffing is in the middle and the skin on the outside. Tie the pair with a string. Place the trussed fillets on a greased sheet pan. Bake at 400°F (204°C) for 25 to 30 minutes, basting with the mixture of melted butter and lemon juice while cooking. Transfer to a warm serving dish when done.

Serves: 6
Calories per serving: 482

▬ Shark

Shark Marseillaise

2	lb. mako shark fillets
4	oz. oil
1	medium chopped onion
1	lb. stewed tomatoes
1	clove minced garlic
1	tbsp. chopped parsley
½	tsp. salt
¼	tsp. ground white pepper
½	dry white wine

Cut mako shark into serving portions. Heat the oil in a skillet. Add onions and cook over low heat for 5 minutes. Stir in the tomatoes, garlic, and parsley. Arrange the fish portions over the vegetables. Season with salt and pepper. Pour the wine over. Bake at 350°F (180°C) for 15 minutes. Transfer the fish onto a preheated platter. Pour the sauce over and serve hot.

Serves: 6
Calories per serving: 238

Jaw's Burger

1½	lb. dogfish fillets
1	beaten egg
1	tsp. salt
¼	tsp. ground white pepper
6	hamburger buns
6	slices american cheese
1	lb. crisp french fries
½	cup tartar sauce
½	cup catsup

Skin the fillets. Wash in cold water and drain. Cut into cubes and grind coarsely. Combine with the egg. Season with salt and pepper.

Shape the ground fish into 4-oz. (110 g) patties. Fry on a hot griddle about 3 minutes on each side. Place on toasted bun half and top with a cheese slice. Melt the cheese under a broiler. Cover with the other bun half. Serve with french fries, tartar sauce, and catsup.

Serves: 6
Calories per serving: 536

Curried Shark

2¼	lb. mako shark fillets
4	oz. butter
1½	cups curry sauce
¾	cup sour cream
1½	tsp. curry powder
1	tbsp. chopped parsley

Cut the shark fillets into 1-inch (2.5 cm) cubes. Sauté in butter for 3 to 5 minutes. Stir in the remaining ingredients and simmer for 5 minutes. Serve over rice.

Serves: 6
Calories per serving: 413

Barbecued Shark Steaks

2	lb. shark steaks
¼	cup oil
2	oz. chopped onion
2	oz. chopped green pepper
1	clove minced garlic
1	cup tomato sauce
1	tbsp. lemon juice
1	tbsp. worcestershire
1	tsp. salt
¼	tsp. pepper

If frozen, thaw the steaks. Heat oil in a frying pan. Add the onion, green pepper, and garlic, and cook until tender. Add the remaining ingredients except for steaks. Simmer for 10 minutes and cool. Arrange the steaks in baking pans. Pour cold sauce over and marinate for 30 minutes. Broil the steaks on a grill until the fish is flaky and tender. Arrange on a warm serving platter. Pour the heated marinade over.

Serves: 6
Calories per serving: 335

Mako Poivre

6	8-oz. mako steaks
½	tsp. salt
¼	tsp. ground white pepper
¼	cup oil
1	tsp. white wine worcestershire
1	tbsp. green peppercorns
1	tbsp. chopped shallots

¼	cup cognac
¾	cup heavy cream
⅓	cup veal stock

Season the mako steaks with salt and pepper. Brush with oil. Broil on a hot broiler for 2 minutes on each side. Set the fish aside and season with the white wine worcestershire. Sprinkle the green peppercorns on both sides of fish steaks, and press to adhere to the fish.

Finish cooking the steaks in a frying pan. Transfer to a warm plate. Add shallots to pan. Cook over low heat for 2 to 3 minutes. Add the cognac. Ignite, then add the cream and the veal stock. Reduce sauce for 5 minutes. Arrange the mako steaks on a platter. Pour the sauce over or around fish. Serve hot.

Serves: 6
Calories per serving: 366

Sheepshead

Sheepshead can be prepared following Fillet of Sole recipes in this chapter.

Skate

Skate wings are most often sautéed meunière, and served with capers and lemon butter.

Smelt *(Icefish, Frostfish, Candlelight Fish)*

Fried Smelts

3	lb. whole smelt
4	oz. flour
1	tsp. seasoned salt
1	bunch fresh parsley
¼	tsp. ground white pepper
6	lemon wedges

Select small to medium smelts.

Clean and toss in the seasoned flour. Deep fry at 375°F (190°C) until golden brown and crisp. Fry the dried parsley for 3 to 5 seconds.

Arrange the smelts in a round serving platter. Garnish with lemon wedges and fried parsley. Serve hot.

Serves: 6
Calories per serving: 189

Sole

Broiled Fillets of Sole*

12	medium sole fillets
½	tsp. salt
¼	tsp. ground white pepper
2	oz. flour
2	oz. oil
6	lemon wedges
1	small bunch parsley

Trim the fillets of sole. Season with salt and pepper. Dredge in flour, dip in oil, and broil on a hot grill, making a quarter turn to mark the fillets with a checkered pattern. Turn the fillets over and cook until flaky. Arrange the fillets on a heated platter. Garnish with lemon wedges and sprigs of parsley.

★This recipe can be served with sweet and sour sauce, or other hot sauce.

Serves: 6
Calories per serving: 378

Dover Sole Béarnaise

6	7-oz. dover soles
½	tsp. salt
¼	tsp. ground white pepper
¼	tsp. crushed thyme
1	sliced lemon
½	cup oil
2	oz. melted butter

1	lemon basket
1	small bunch parsley
1½	cup béarnaise

Skin and dress the dover soles. Wash under cold water and dry well.

Arrange the soles on a sheet pan. Season with salt, pepper, thyme, and lemon slices. Sprinkle with oil and refrigerate while preparing the béarnaise sauce. Cook the soles on a hot grill, or broiler. Give the fish a quarter turn to obtain a checkered pattern. Turn the fish over and repeat the same process until fully cooked.

Arrange the fish on a warm serving platter. Garnish with a lemon basket filled with parsley. Brush melted butter over the fish before serving. Serve the béarnaise separately.

Serves: 6
Calories per serving: 250

Dover Sole Meunière

6	whole dover soles
½	tsp. salt
¼	tsp. ground pepper
3	oz. flour
6	oz. butter
3	oz. oil
6	lemon slices
1	tbsp. chopped parsley

Skin the soles. Cut off the fins and remove the intestines. Wash under cold running water. Season with salt and pepper on both sides. Dredge in flour. Heat a small amount of butter and oil in a large skillet and brown the soles with the white skin side down. Turn the fish and cook until the flesh can be separated easily from the bones. Remove the bones. Arrange the whole soles on a serving platter. Melt the butter in a clean frying pan until brown. Pour the lemon juice over the soles. Decorate with lemon slices and serve immediately.

Serves: 6
Calories per serving: 400

Fillet of Sole Dieppoise

4	oz. butter
1	tbsp. chopped shallots
12	2-oz. sole fillets
5	oz. white wine
2	cups fish fumet
4	oz. cooked mussels
4	oz. cooked shrimp
6	medium fluted mushrooms
12	fleurons

Butter a baking dish. Sprinkle with chopped shallots. Fold the fillets in half and arrange in the pan. Pour the wine, fish fumet, and the mussel cooking juice over the shallots and fillets. Cover with parchment paper and bring to a boil on top of the stove. Bake at 350°F (180°C) for about 5 to 8 minutes.

Arrange the fish fillets on a serving platter. Garnish with the mussels, shrimp, and fluted mushrooms. Prepare the white wine sauce★ with the fish fumet. Pour over the fish. Garnish with fleurons and serve hot.

★For more details, see the recipe for White Wine Sauce in Chapter 11.

Serves: 6
Calories per serving: 279

Fillets of Sole Domino

12	medium sole fillets
½	tsp. salt
¼	tsp. ground white pepper
2	cups fish fumet
1	cup dry white wine
1	recipe truffle aspic sheet
1	cup mayonnaise
1	cup aspic jelly★

Trim and flatten the fillets. Season with salt and pepper. Fold the fillets in thirds with a maximum length of 3 inches (7.5 cm). Place the fillets in a buttered baking dish. Cover with fumet and wine.

Bake for 15 minutes at 400°F (205°C). Cool the fish. Trim each fillet into a rectangle, 3 by 1¼ inches (7.5 by 3 cm).

Combine mayonnaise with liquid aspic and coat the fish. Decorate the rectangles like dominos using the truffle aspic sheet (see Orange Aspic Sheet recipe in Chapter 16). Arrange on a platter and garnish with aspic jelly made with fish fumet and white wine.

*For more details, see the recipes for aspic jelly.

Serves: 6
Calories per serving: 498

Fillets of Sole Rosette

12	medium sole fillets
½	tsp. salt
¼	tsp. ground white pepper
3	eggs
8	oz. bread crumbs
4	oz. butter
1	medium eggplant
3	oz. flour
4	oz. lemon butter

Season the clean fillets with salt and pepper. Mix the eggs with the oil. Dip the fillets in the egg mixture and coat in bread crumbs. Sauté the fillets in butter until golden brown on both sides. Peel and slice the eggplant into rings. Season with salt and dip in flour. Deep fry in oil. Drain on absorbent paper. Arrange the fillets on a serving platter. Garnish with eggplant rings. Sprinkle with lemon butter and serve hot.

Serves: 6
Calories per serving: 663

Gougeonnettes of Sole

2	lb. sole fillets
½	tsp. salt
¼	tsp. ground pepper
3	oz. flour
4	beaten eggs

12	oz. fresh bread crumbs
6	lemon wedges
1	cup tartar sauce

Cut the fillets. Season with salt and pepper. Roll the strips in flour, dip in beaten eggs, and coat in bread crumbs. Deep fry for 2 to 3 minutes.

Arrange the fillets on a warm serving platter covered with a napkin. Garnish with lemon wedges. Serve the tartar sauce separately.

Serves: 6
Calories per serving: 621

Lemon Sole Tart

2	medium whiting fillets
2	cups fumet
1	cup white wine
7	oz. chopped mushrooms
1	tbsp. chopped shallots
1	oz. butter
6	medium sole fillets
2	oz. butter
2	oz. flour
¼	oz. heavy cream
½	tsp. salt
¼	tsp. ground white pepper
1	8-inch cooked pie crust
6	small artichoke bottoms
5	oz. cooked shrimp

Poach the whiting fillets in fumet and white wine. Drain and flake the fillets. Sauté the shallots in butter. Add the mushrooms. Mix in the flaked whiting.

Flatten and roll the fillets of sole, holding them with toothpicks. Poach in the fumet. Drain and reserve in a warm place. Prepare a roux with the butter and flour. Add the fumet. Bring to a boil. Stir in the cream. Season to taste with salt and pepper.

Spread the bottom of the pie shell with the whiting mixture. Arrange the artichoke bottoms on top. Place the cooked sole on the artichoke bottoms, removing the toothpicks. Strain the sauce. Add the shrimp, and coat the fish with sauce. Heat and serve.

Serves: 6
Calories per serving: 454

Pâté of Fillet of Sole

1	lb. sole fillets
¾	tsp. salt
¼	tsp. ground white pepper
12	oz. salmon quenelle
1	oz. diced truffles
2	oz. pistachio nuts

Flatten the fillets of sole. Season with salt and pepper.

Prepare the salmon quenelle forcemeat according to the recipe for Quenelles and Mousses in Chapter 9. Spread each fillet of sole with some of the prepared salmon quenelle forcemeat. Set into a suitable pâté mold, alternating with leftover salmon forcemeat, truffle, and pistachios. Cover the mold. Bake in a waterbath at 350°F (180°C) for 45 minutes. Cool, then refrigerate until well chilled. Slice onto a serving platter, and serve with a cold sauce.

Serves: 6
Calories per serving: 181

Sesame Seed Sole Fillets

2	peeled tomatoes
¼	cup oil
1	tsp. minced garlic
2	tbsp. fresh basil
½	tsp. salt
¼	tsp. ground black pepper
2	tbsp. sesame seeds
4	6-oz. sole fillets
4	lemon wedges

Peel, seed, and cube the tomatoes. Heat half the oil in a pan. Add garlic and cook briefly. Stir in the tomatoes, basil, salt, and pepper. Cook for 5 minutes. Coat the fillets with the sesame seeds to cover fish lightly on both sides. Heat the remaining oil in a frying pan. Cook fish on both sides until golden brown.

Transfer the cooked fish to warm plates. Cover with sauce. Serve hot with lemon.

Serves: 4
Calories per serving: 260

Sole Bonne Femme

2	oz. butter
2	oz. chopped shallots
1	tbsp. chopped parsley
6	oz. sliced mushroom
12	4-oz. sole fillets
½	tsp. salt
¼	tsp. ground white pepper
¾	cup dry white wine
2	cups fish fumet
1	cup heavy cream
1	cup velouté sauce
3	oz. hollandaise

Butter a baking sheet. Sprinkle with shallots, chopped parsley, and sliced mushrooms. Flatten and fold the fillets in half. Arrange on top of the mushrooms. Season with salt and pepper. Moisten with the white wine and the fish fumet. Cover fish with parchment paper and bake at 350°F (180°C) for 10 to 15 minutes.

Pour the cooking liquid into a saucepan. Reduce to two thirds. Add the heavy cream and velouté sauce.★ Bring to a boil and stir in the hollandaise.★

Transfer the fillets to a warm serving platter. Cover with sauce and glaze under a hot broiler.

Serve immediately.

★See recipes for Velouté Sauce and Hollandaise in Chapter 11.

Serves: 6
Calories per serving: 332

Sole Colbert

6	medium dover soles
3	eggs
1	tbsp. oil
½	tsp. salt
¼	tsp. ground white pepper
3	oz. flour
10	oz. fresh bread crumbs
3	lemon wedges
6	oz. Maître d'Hôtel Butter

Wash the soles. Cut off the fins and skin both sides. Clean and butterfly the fish. Mix the eggs and oil, and season with salt and pepper. Dip the dry fish lightly in the flour, egg mixture, and bread crumbs.

Fry in a deep fryer at 360°F (185°C) for 6 to 8 minutes. Drain the soles and remove the center bones. Serve with lemon wedges and Maître d'Hôtel butter.

Serves: 6
Calories per serving: 442

Sole Quiche

1	lb. sole fillets
1	8-inch pie crust shell
¼	cup sliced stuffed olives
½	cup chopped red pepper
¼	cup chopped scallions
4	large eggs
¼	cup light cream
¾	cup ricotta cheese
¼	tsp. paprika
½	tsp. salt
¼	tsp. ground white pepper

Cut sole fillets in half lengthwise, then cut across into pieces about 1½ inches long.

In bottom of pie shell, layer olives, red pepper, and scallions in the order given. Spread sole evenly over all.

In a bowl, combine eggs, cream, cheese, paprika, salt, and white pepper. Blend well and pour mixture over sole.

Bake at 350°F (180°C) for 35 to 40 minutes. Serve hot.

Serves: 4
Calories per serving: 256

Sole Tour d'Argent

12	medium sole fillets
½	tsp. salt
¼	tsp. ground white pepper
2	cups strong fumet
1	cup dry vermouth
1	lb. peeled tomatoes
4	oz. hollandaise

Trim and flatten the fillets. Season with salt and pepper. Poach in the fumet, vermouth, and the chopped seeded tomatoes.

Drain the fillets and keep warm on a serving platter.

Reduce the cooking liquid until thickened. Stir in the hollandaise. Adjust seasoning. Strain over the fillets and serve at once.

Serves: 6
Calories per serving: 197

Sole Vénitienne

1	lb. cooked spinach
2	oz. butter
1	clove crushed garlic
½	tsp. salt
¼	tsp. ground white pepper
12	medium sole fillets
1	tbsp. chopped parsley
2	oz. fresh bread crumbs
2	oz. melted butter
6	lemon wedges
1	small bunch parsley

Chop the spinach and sauté in butter. Add garlic and season with half the salt and pepper.

Flatten the fillets. Season with the remaining salt and pepper. Spread the spinach over each fillet.

Starting with the thickest end, roll the fillets and hold them with toothpicks. Arrange in a buttered baking dish. Sprinkle with the bread crumbs and melted butter. Bake at 350°F (180°C) for 20 to 25 minutes. Serve hot. Garnish with parsley and lemon wedges.

Serves: 6
Calories per serving: 158

Stuffed Fillets of Sole

12	medium sole fillets
12	small fish quenelles
2	cups fumet
½	cup dry white wine
3	oz. sliced mushrooms
2	oz. butter
1	oz. flour
½	tsp. salt
¼	tsp. ground white pepper
½	cup heavy cream
2	oz. diced shrimp

Flatten the fillets of sole. Roll each fillet around a quenelle. Secure with a toothpick. Poach in the fumet and wine.

Sauté the sliced mushrooms in half the butter. Prepare a roux with the remaining butter and flour. Stir in the fumet to make a veloute.

Arrange the stuffed fillets on a serving platter. Season the sauce to taste. Add the cream and reduce for 5 to 10 minutes. Strain the sauce. Garnish the fish with the mushrooms and shrimp. Coat the fish with the hot sauce before serving.

Serves: 6
Calories per serving: 206

Tuna–Sole Carpino

| 4 | oz. sole fillets |
| 4 | oz. fresh tuna |

2	medium chopped shallots
½	cup white wine
½	cup stewed tomatoes
½	cup chicken stock
1	tsp. roux
½	cup sliced mushrooms
1	tbsp. clarified butter
½	tsp. salt
⅛	tsp. ground white pepper
⅛	tsp. aromat

Cut the fillets of sole into 3-inch (7.5 cm) pieces. Slice the tuna into thin slices.

Flatten the fish into thin scallopines. Put the tuna slices on top of the sole. Flatten the two fillets together so that the sole and tuna stick together.

In a saucepan, combine shallots and wine. Reduce to ¾. Add tomatoes and chicken stock. Thicken with the roux then mix in mushrooms. Cook the sauce until thick.

Sauté the tuna–sole scallopines in butter. Season with salt, pepper, and aromat. Add to the sauce. Heat and serve.

Serves: 2
Calories per serving: 276

Turban of Sole

1	oz. butter
1	lb. sole fillets
1	recipe snapper quenelle
2	cups cardinal sauce

Butter a ring mold and line with the boneless, trimmed fillets of sole. Fill the mold with the red snapper quenelle forcemeat. Cover with foil. Bake in a waterbath at 350°F (180°C) for 30 to 35 minutes.

Unmold on a round serving platter. Coat with the hot sauce. Serve immediately.

Serves: 6
Calories per serving: 250

Mousse of Sole Pavillon

Prepare a mousse of sole (see Chapter 9). Cover with a champagne sauce made with fish veloute and champagne. Garnish with truffle slices.

Mousse of Sole Joinville

Prepare a mousse of sole. Coat with sauce Americaine. Garnish with cooked, diced bay scallops, shrimp, crabmeat, mushrooms, and truffle slices.

Délices of Sole Laperouse

Poach fillets of sole in fumet, white wine, and shallots. Poach scallops in same fumet. Reduce the cooking liquid. Whip in fresh butter. Garnish fillets of sole with scallops. Pour the light sauce over the fish.

Fillets of Sole with Cucumbers

Simmer fillets of sole in lemon butter. Shape peeled cucumbers into large olive shapes and cook in fish fumet. Sauté in lemon butter. Garnish the fillets of sole with the cucumbers.

Fried Fillets of Sole with Tartar and Cocktail Sauces

Bread the fillets of sole according to the standard technique. Deep fry, and serve with tartar and cocktail sauces.

For additional sole recipes, see

Shrimp Quenelles in Chapter 9.
Fish Canapés in Chapter 15.

Spot (Lafayette, Goody)

For preparation of Spot, refer to Croaker recipes in this chapter.

═══ Striped Bass *(Rockfish, Striper)*

Poached Striped Bass

4½	lb. dressed striped bass
2	gal. No. 1 court bouillon
1	lb. potatoes
1	small bunch parsley
6	oz. sauce bercy

Wash and clean the whole fish. Cut off the head and save to prepare the fumet for sauce bercy.

Cut the striped bass at 1½-inch (4 cm) intervals until the knife
meets the back bone. Do not cut through the bones. Poach the
fish in the court bouillon, following the technique described for
poaching in Chapter 6. Lift the fish out of the court bouillon.
Transfer to a serving platter and skin the fish.

Garnish with boiled Parisienne potatoes and parsley. Serve
with sauce bercy.

Serves: 6
Calories per serving: 262

Striped Bass and Seaweed

4	lb. dressed striped bass
3	lb. fresh seaweed
¼	cup fumet
1	oz. lemon juice
4	oz. chopped tomatoes
1	tsp. dried tarragon
1	tbsp. chopped parsley

Clean, scale, and wash the striped bass.

Arrange half of the seaweed over the bottom of a fish steamer
or poacher. Place the fish on top. Add the remaining seaweed.
Pour 1 inch (2.5 cm) of water into the steamer or poacher. Steam
the fish until flaky. Arrange on a serving platter. Remove the
skin. Combine the remaining ingredients. Spoon over the fish.
Serve at room temperature.

Serves: 6
Calories per serving: 153

Striped Bass in Brioche

1	4-lb. striped bass
4	oz. butter
4	oz. chopped shallots
½	cup vermouth
2	oz. chopped onion
4	oz. fresh mushrooms
4	oz. fresh bread crumbs
½	tsp. salt
¼	tsp. ground white pepper
1	boiled egg
1	tbsp. chopped parsley
1	recipe brioche dough★
1	beaten egg
½	cup beurre blanc★

Fillet the fish. Sauté in butter and half the shallots to stiffen the flesh. Deglaze with vermouth. Cool the fillets. Sauté the remaining shallots with onion in butter. Add chopped mushrooms. Cook until the onion is tender. Stir in the bread crumbs and the liquid from the fillets. Season to taste with salt and pepper. Add the chopped egg and parsley. Spread this stuffing over the middle of each fillet. Assemble the fillets by twos. Wrap each fillet in rolled out brioche dough. Seal the edges. Brush with egg. Allow to rise for 30 minutes. Brush again. Bake at 350°F (180°C) for 35 to 40 minutes. Arrange on a platter. Serve with beurre blanc.

★See recipes for Brioche Dough in Chapter 7 and Beurre Blanc in Chapter 11.

Serves: 6
Calories per serving: 735

Striped Bass Italienne

2	lb. striped bass fillets
½	tsp. salt
¼	tsp. ground white pepper
2	oz. flour
12	small clams

12	cleaned mussels
1	lb. chopped tomatoes
2	cloves minced garlic
1	tbsp. chopped parsley
1	tbsp. chopped basil
¾	cup clam juice

Cut the fillets into equal portions. Season with salt and pepper. Dredge in flour. Deep fry at 360°F (185°C) for 5 minutes, or until half cooked. Drain well. Arrange the fish on a sheet pan. Surround with cherrystone clams and mussels. Spoon the chopped, seeded tomatoes and garlic over fish. Sprinkle with herbs and pour the clam juice over. Bake at 350°F (180°C) for 10 to 15 minutes, or until the shellfish open.

Arrange the fish and shellfish on a serving platter. Pour the cooking liquid over. Serve hot.

Serves: 6
Calories per serving: 218

Striped Bass Jacals

2	lb. striped bass fillets
6	oz. crabmeat
6	anchovy fillets
½	cup heavy cream
½	cup mayonnaise
½	tsp. salt
¼	tsp. ground white pepper
1	tbsp. lemon juice

Skin and bone the stripped bass fillets. Arrange on a buttered baking pan. Top with the crabmeat.

Chop the anchovy fillets. Combine with the heavy cream, mayonnaise, salt, pepper, and lemon juice. Pour the sauce over the fillets.

Bake at 350°F (180°C) for 15 to 20 minutes, or until the fish flakes when tested.

Serves: 6
Calories per serving: 284

Striped Bass Mayonnaise

4½	lb. dressed striped bass
2	gal. No. 1 court bouillon
2	cups aspic jelly
6	radishes
6	deviled eggs
6	oz. mayonnaise
1	bunch parsley

Fillet the striped bass. Remove the backbones. Poach in court bouillon. Allow the fish to cool in court bouillon. Lift the cold fillets out. Slice crosswise into portions. Glaze each piece of fish with aspic jelly. Decorate with radish slices. Arrange the fish slices on a platter. Garnish with stuffed deviled eggs, chopped aspic jelly, and parsley. Serve with mayonnaise.

Serves: 6
Calories per serving: 381

Striped Bass with Fennel

4	lb. dressed striped bass
¼	cup pernod
6	oz. chopped fennel
1	oz. butter
1	cup sauce allemande
4	oz. duxelle
2	egg yolks
1	tbsp. chopped parsley
2	tbsp. pernod
1	cup dry white wine
1	tbsp. chopped shallots

Bone the whole fish, leaving the head and tail attached to the fillets. Sprinkle fillets with pernod. Prepare a fumet with the bones. Make the sauce Allemande (see recipe in Chapter 11) with the fumet.

Sauté the fennel in butter until tender. Add the duxelle, egg yolks, parsley, and remaining pernod. Stuff the fish with this mixture and place on a baking pan. Cover with foil and bake at 350°F (180°C) for 35 to 40 minutes. Skin the fish and place on a serving platter. Reduce the cooking liquid to a glaze and add to the allemande sauce. Coat the fish with the sauce and serve at once.

Serves: 6
Calories per serving: 316

Fillet of Striped Bass Amandine

Sauté meunière. Top with toasted sliced almonds.

Fillet of Striped Bass Bonne Femme

See recipe for Fillet of Sole Bonne Femme in this chapter.

Striped Bass Royale

See recipe for Mousseline of Salmon Royale in this chapter.

Striped Bass en Croûte

Skin striped bass fillets. Spread with a quenelle forcemeat. Wrap in puff pastry dough (see recipe in Chapter 7). Bake at 450°F (230°C) allowing 10 minutes per inch thickness. Serve with a hot sauce.

Swordfish

Broiled Swordfish

3	lb. swordfish steak
2	tbsp. olive oil
1	tbsp. melted butter
½	tsp. salt
¼	tsp. ground black pepper
½	cup beurre blanc

Preheat the broiler.
Brush the fish with oil and butter. Season with salt and pepper.

Place the fish on baking pan and broil about 4 inches (10 cm) from the source of heat for about 5 minutes. Turn the steaks over and continue broiling until done.

Serve with beurre blanc.

Serves: 8
Calories per serving: 230

Swordfish is best when broiled. Serve with a hot sauce. It can also be used for Seafood Fondue or Seafood Brochettes (see Miscellaneous Seafood Recipes in this chapter).

Other recent innovative recipes created with swordfish include Scallopine of Swordfish with lemon butter and capers.

Also, see recipe for Mako Poivre in this chapter, substituting swordfish for mako.

Tilefish

Fish Kebabs Teriyaki

2	lb. fillets tilefish
¼	cup juice pineapple
½	cup soy sauce
¼	cup sherry wine
4	oz. brown sugar
1	tbsp. grated ginger root
1	tsp. dry mustard
1	minced garlic clove
1	lb. chunked pineapple
1	blanched green pepper
2	cups cooked rice

Cut the blanched green pepper into 1-inch squares.

Cut the fish into 1-inch cubes. Combine the pineapple juice, soy sauce, wine, sugar, ginger, mustard, and garlic. Pour over fish and marinate for 1 hour, then refrigerate. Drain the fish. Thread on skewers, alternating with pineapple chunks and green peppers.

Broil for 5 minutes or until the fish flakes. Brush with a little oil and marinade. Serve with rice.

Serves: 6
Calories per serving: 354

Tilefish is a firm fish and is excellent in soups, chowders, salads (see recipe for Mock Lobster Newburg, and substitute monkfish with tilefish.)

Tilefish can also be prepared following recipes for cod and haddock.

══ Tuna

Braised Fresh Tuna

4	oz. butter
2	lb. fresh tuna
4	oz. chopped onion
1	oz. flour
1	cup white wine
½	cup tomato puree
3	oz. fresh mushrooms

Melt the butter in a braising pan. Brown the tuna on all sides. Remove from pan and set aside. Add the onions to color lightly. Stir in the flour to make roux. Add the wine and tomato puree. Season with salt and pepper to taste.

Place tuna in the sauce. Cover and braise at 350°F (180°C) for 45 to 60 minutes. Slice the mushrooms and add to the dish. Cook for 5 more minutes. Trim and slice the tuna.

Arrange on a serving platter and add the sauce.

Serves: 6
Calories per serving: 426

Curried Tuna Indienne

2	cups curry sauce
1	lb. canned tuna
1	cup cooked rice

Bring the curry sauce to a boil. Flake the tuna. Mix in the sauce. Cook the rice according to the standard directions. Heat the tuna mixture. Serve the rice separately.

Serves: 6
Calories per serving: 219

Fresh Tuna Italienne

2	lb. fresh tuna
2	oz. butter
4	oz. chopped onion
1	oz. flour
6	oz. dry white wine
6	oz. tomato puree
2	cups water
8	oz. button mushrooms
1	tbsp. chopped parsley

Wash the tuna in cold water. Slice into equal portions. Brown in butter on both sides. Transfer to a hot plate and reserve. Add onion to the butter and brown lightly. Stir in the flour to make a roux. Add the white wine, tomato puree, and water. Bring to a boil while mixing.

Place the tuna in the sauce and bake at 325°F (165°C) for 10 minutes or until the tuna is firm and fully cooked. Transfer the tuna to a serving platter.

Reduce the sauce until medium thick. Add mushrooms and cook for 5 minutes. Pour the sauce over the fish. Sprinkle with parsley. Serve hot.

Serves: 6
Calories per serving: 322

Mousseline of Tuna

6	large lemons
10	oz. white tuna
2	oz. butter
½	cup mayonnaise
½	tsp. worcestershire
½	tsp. salt
1	tbsp. lemon juice
⅛	tsp. ground white pepper
1	tbsp. unflavored gelatin
2	hard-cooked eggs

1	tbsp. chopped parsley
¼	tsp. paprika

Cut off the tops of the lemons. Remove the pulp without damaging the skin. Save the pulp and juice for later use.

Drain the tuna. Puree the tuna in a food processor with the butter, mayonnaise, spices, and lemon juice.

Dissolve the gelatin in a quarter cup of water. Melt over low heat, and mix into the tuna.

Surround each lemon shell with a piece of foil to make a 1-inch (2.5 cm) collar. Fill the shells with the tuna mix to the top of the foil. Refrigerate for an hour or until set, then remove foil. Chop half of the eggs and mix with parsley. Sprinkle over the tuna shells. Shake paprika over. Arrange the tuna on a platter with wedges of the remaining hard-cooked eggs.

Serves: 6
Calories per serving: 194

Neptune's Burger

1	lb. light tuna
½	cup mayonnaise
1	tbsp. chopped scallions
1	tsp. dijon mustard
¼	tsp. garlic salt
4	oz. cream cheese
6	toasted buns
6	tomato slices
2	oz. grated swiss cheese

Drain the tuna. Blend the mayonnaise, scallions, mustard, and garlic salt together. Fold in the tuna.

Spread cream cheese over bottom halves of the buns. Top with equal amounts of the tuna mixture, a tomato slice, and cheese. Brown under a broiler, 3 inches (8 cm) from the source of heat. Top with remaining bun halves before serving.

Serves: 6
Calories per serving: 383

Raw Tuna and Hot Pepper

1	lb. fresh tuna
3	tbsp. lemon juice
1	tbsp. olive oil
½	tsp. ground black pepper
½	tsp. salt
1	chopped jalapeño
2	lemons

Trim the tuna and remove all dark meat. Slice very thinly and place on cold plates. Season with salt and pepper and jalapeño. Spoon over a small amount of oil.

Garnish with very thin slices of lemon. Serve very cold.

Serves: 4
Calories per serving: 220

Tuna Antiboise

6	large tomatoes
½	cup vinaigrette
1	lb. white tuna
2	hard-cooked eggs
1	oz. capers
½	cup mayonnaise
1	tsp. anchovy paste

Slice off the bottoms of the tomatoes and scoop out the pulp. Season the insides of the tomatoes with the vinaigrette. Drain and flake the tuna. Combine the tuna, eggs, capers, mayonnaise, and anchovy paste. Pour excess dressing out of the tomatoes and fill with the tuna mixture. Arrange on plates or on a round serving platter. Serve chilled.

Serves: 6
Calories per serving: 226

Spaghetti with Tuna

12	oz. thin spaghetti
2	oz. olive oil

1	medium chopped onion
1	clove minced garlic
1	lb. chopped tomatoes
8	oz. flaked tuna
2	oz. butter
½	tsp. chopped basil

Cook the spaghetti according to the standard directions.

Heat the oil. Add the onion and garlic. Cook over medium heat for 10 minutes. Add the tomatoes and simmer for 10 to 15 minutes. Heat the tuna in its own juice.

Drain the spaghetti and toss in the butter. Serve on a warm platter.

Top with the tuna and spoon the sauce over. Sprinkle with basil and serve immediately.

Serves: 6
Calories per serving: 367

Tuna Antipasto

1	lb. asparagus
2	cucumbers
8	oz. fresh mushrooms
1	cup vinaigrette
1	lb. white tuna
6	lettuce leaves
8	oz. cherry tomatoes
6	hard-cooked eggs

Cook the asparagus in salted boiling water. Cool and drain. Peel the cucumbers, slice lengthwise, remove seeds, and slice across. Slice the mushrooms.

Dividing the vinaigrette between them, marinate the cucumber, mushrooms, and asparagus in separate containers and refrigerate for an hour. Place the tuna in the center of a round platter lined with lettuce leaves. Garnish the platter with the marinated vegetables, tomatoes, and slices of hard-cooked eggs. Pour the remaining dressing over the tuna.

Serves: 6
Calories per serving: 214

Tuna Casserole

12	oz. medium egg noodles
8	oz. cooked broccoli
12	oz. flaked light tuna
1½	cups medium cream sauce
2	oz. dry bread crumbs
1	oz. butter

Cook the noodles in salted boiling water. Drain and arrange in a buttered ovenproof serving dish. Top the noodles with broccoli and tuna, and cover with the cream sauce. Sprinkle with bread crumbs and drizzle with melted butter. Bake at 400°F (205°C) for 20 to 30 minutes or until bubbly and brown.

Serves: 6
Calories per serving: 406

Tuna Niçoise

4	medium tomatoes
½	tsp. salt
½	tsp. ground pepper
1	cucumber
2	green peppers
2	hard-cooked eggs
1	lb. light tuna
2	chopped scallions
1	tbsp. olive oil
1	tbsp. chopped parsley
6	anchovy fillets
3	oz. ripe olives
6	cherry tomatoes

Wash and cut the tomatoes into wedges. Season with half the salt and pepper.

Cut the cucumber lengthwise, removing seeds, then slice crosswise. Cut the peppers in halves, removing seeds, then cut into strips. Cut the eggs into wedges.

Flake the tuna in its juices. Combine the tuna with the cucumber, green pepper, tomatoes, and scallions. Season with salt, pepper, and olive oil. Serve in a salad bowl. Sprinkle with parsley and garnish with anchovy fillets, olives, egg wedges, and cherry tomatoes.

Serves: 6
Calories per serving: 156

Tuna Pâté

1	oz. dill pickles
1	tbsp. capers
½	cup pitted ripe olives
1	lb. solid white tuna
1	tbsp. chopped parsley
½	tbsp. chopped dill
½	cup mayonnaise
½	tsp. salt
¼	tsp. ground white pepper
2	hard-cooked eggs

Coarsely chop the pickles, capers, and olives. Drain and flake the tuna, and combine with the chopped condiments. Add the parsley and dill and mix in the mayonnaise. Season with salt and pepper. Spoon the tuna into a spring mold. Chill for 2 hours. Unmold onto a serving platter, and garnish with sliced hard-cooked eggs.

Serves: 6
Calories per serving: 206

Tuna Stuffed Zucchini

5	oz. cubed white bread
¾	cup milk
6	medium zucchini
1	lb. light tuna
2	eggs
½	tsp. salt
¼	tsp. ground nutmeg
1	cup chicken stock
1	cup tomato sauce
2	oz. grated swiss cheese

Remove the crust from the bread, then soak the bread in milk.
Cut the zucchini length-wise. Scoop out the pulp and cook in
salted boiling water. Drain well.

Blanch the zucchini halves for 5 to 6 minutes. Squeeze the excess milk out of the bread and mix with the cooked zucchini pulp.
Flake the tuna. Combine with the bread mixture and beat in the
eggs, salt, and nutmeg.

Arrange the zucchini halves in a buttered baking dish or sheet
pan, and fill with the tuna mixture. Pour the chicken bouillon
around the zucchini. Cover the zucchini with tomato sauce.
Sprinkle the cheese over and bake at 400°F (205°C) for 30 to 40
minutes.

Serves: 6
Calories per serving: 290

For additional tuna recipes, see

Barquettes of Tuna in Chapter 15.
Canapés cancalaise in Chapter 15.
Hot Tuna Canapés in Chapter 15.
Salade Niçoise in this chapter.
Stuffed Tomato Surprise in Chapter 15.
Tuna Bites in Chapter 15.
Tuna Fritters in Chapter 15.
Tuna Puffs in Chapter 15.
Tunafish Butter in Chapter 15.
Tunafish Cheese in Chapter 15.

Turbot

Turbot Sauce Champagne

8	lb. dressed turbot
1	oz. parsley stems
4	oz. mushroom stems
6	peppercorns
1	tbsp. chopped shallots
2	cups dry champagne
4	cups fumet
¾	tsp. salt
¼	tsp. ground white pepper
4	oz. melted butter

4	oz. flour
1	cup heavy cream
12	small cooked mushroom caps
12	fleurons
12	sliced truffle

Wash and clean the fish. Place on a wire rack. Combine the parsley stems, mushroom stems, peppercorns, shallots, champagne, and fumet in a suitable fish poacher. Immerse the fish in poaching liquid. Season with salt and pepper. Cover and braise in an oven at 350°F (180°C) for 40 minutes, basting frequently. When the fish is cooked, transfer to a serving platter. Skin the fish and keep warm.

Make a roux with the butter and flour. Add the cooking liquid and boil to a medium-thick consistency. Add the heavy cream. Reduce to a medium-thick consistency. Strain the sauce and pour over the fish. Garnish with mushroom caps, fleurons, and truffle slices. Serve immediately.

Serves: 12
Calories per serving: 400

Poached Turbot Hollandaise

Cut turbot into steaks or fillets. Poach and serve with hollandaise.

Turtle

Maryland Terrapin Soup*

4	oz. butter
2	tbsp. flour
1	qt. milk
½	tsp. salt
¼	tsp. ground white pepper
6	hard-cooked eggs
6	oz. turtle meat
2	cups heavy cream
½	cup sherry

Melt the butter in a saucepan. Blend in the flour. Add the milk, salt, and pepper. Stir in the finely chopped egg whites. Add the terrapin turtle meat to the soup.

Chop egg yolks finely and add to the soup. Heat the cream and add to the soup.

Stir in the sherry at serving time.

*This recipe was supplied by the Maryland Department of Community and Economic Development.

Serves: 6
Calories per serving: 479

Turtle is used mostly in soups. See Boula Boula and Key West Turtle Soup in Chapter 10.

Whiting (Silver Hake, Silver Perch)

Paupiettes of Whiting

6	whole whitings
½	tsp. salt
¼	tsp. pepper
2	eggs
6	oz. fresh bread crumbs
1	small bunch parsley
1½	cups tomato sauce

Fillet the whitings leaving the fillets attached to the fish heads. Cut off the bone at base of head. Dredge the fish fillets in flour, dip in beaten egg, and roll in bread crumbs. Roll up each fillet and secure with a small skewer or toothpicks. Deep fry at 360°F (185°C) for 3 to 4 minutes. Arrange on a preheated serving platter. Garnish with fried parsley. Serve the tomato sauce separately.

Serves: 6
Calories per serving: 251

Deep-Fried Whiting

6	9-oz. dressed whitings
3	oz. milk
½	tsp. salt

¼	tsp. ground white pepper
3	oz. flour
1	small bunch parsley
2	lemon baskets
6	lemon wedges
2	cups light tomato sauce

Cut off the fins of the whitings and remove the gills. Wash under cold water and drain well. Curl the fish and insert the caudal tails into the mouths. Secure the heads and tails with strings. Season the milk with salt and pepper. Dip the fish in milk, then roll in flour. Shake off excess flour.

Deep fry at 350°F (180°C) for 5 to 8 minutes. When cooked, the fish will rise to the surface. Drain the fish and remove strings. Arrange on a warm platter.

Serves: 6
Calories per serving: 244

Fried Fillets of Whiting

2	eggs
½	tsp. salt
¼	tsp. ground white pepper
1	oz. oil
2	lb. whiting fillets
3	oz. flour
7	oz. fresh bread crumbs
3	oz. oil
2	oz. butter
6	wedges lemon
6	oz. Maître d'Hôtel Butter

Beat the eggs, salt, pepper, and oil. Dredge the boneless fillets in flour, dip in eggs, and roll in bread crumbs. Fry in oil and butter until golden brown on both sides.

Arrange on a serving platter. Garnish with lemon wedges. Serve Maître d'Hôtel Butter separately.

Serves: 6
Calories per serving: 557

Whiting Lyonaise

6	whole whitings
2	lb. small potatoes
3	medium onions
2	oz. butter
1	cup white wine
2	sprigs thyme
2	tbsp. chopped parsley

Clean and dry the whitings. Boil the potatoes in their skins. Cool, peel, and slice thinly. Peel and slice the onions. Sauté in butter until tender. Butter an ovenproof serving dish. Line with potatoes and onions. Arrange the whiting over the bed of potatoes and onions, and pour the wine over. Season with salt, pepper, and thyme. Dot with butter and bake at 350°F (180°C) for 15 to 20 minutes.

Sprinkle with parsley and serve.

Serves: 6
Calories per serving: 395

Quenelles of Whiting au Gratin

Prepare a quenelle forcemeat with boneless fillets of whiting. Shape into quenelles (see Chapter 9). Cover with mornay sauce (see Chapter 11) and bake at 350°F (180°C) until brown.

13

Shellfish Recipes

This chapter contains recipes for the following:

1. Saltwater Crustaceans
   American Lobster
   Crab
   Norway (Icelandic) Lobster
   Shrimp
   Sea Urchin
   Spiny Lobster

2. Freshwater Crustaceans
   Crayfish

3. Mollusks
   Abalone
   Clams
   Mussels
   Octopus
   Oysters
   Scallops
   Snails
   Squid

SALTWATER CRUSTACEANS

American Lobster

Avocado Mexicaine

8	oz. cooked lobster meat
8	oz. diced king crab
3	oz. shredded lettuce
1	tbsp. capers

1	cup mayonnaise
1	tsp. lemon juice
¼	tsp. ground white pepper
3	ripe avocados
1	tbsp. chopped parsley

Dice the cooked lobster meat. Combine the lobster meat, king crab, lettuce, and capers. Mix in the mayonnaise, lemon juice, and pepper. Adjust seasoning if necessary. Cut the avocados in half lengthwise and remove stones. Fill with seafood. Sprinkle with chopped parsley. Arrange on a platter and serve chilled.

Serves: 6
Calories per serving: 535

Broiled Lobster Windsor

6	1½ lb. live lobsters
4	oz. melted butter
2	oz. cognac
½	tsp. salt
¼	tsp. ground white pepper
1	tbsp. chopped shallots
1	cup dry white wine
4	oz. chopped tomatoes
1	tsp. chopped basil
1	tsp. chopped tarragon
¾	cup béarnaise

Cook the lobsters in boiling water for 5 minutes. Split in half and remove the veins and stomach. Clarify the butter, and pour over lobsters. Broil under a hot broiler for 5 minutes.

Pour cognac over each lobster and ignite. Season with salt and pepper.

Cook the shallots in wine. Add the tomatoes and reduce liquid to half. Stir in the herbs and béarnaise.

Pour the sauce over the lobsters and heat 5 minutes. Serve hot on preheated serving plates.

Serves: 6
Calories per serving: 465

Creamed Lobster and Leek

2	large leeks
3	tbsp. butter
2	minced garlic cloves
4	1¼-lb. cut up lobsters
2	cups dry white wine
2	cups heavy cream
2	tbsp. minced chives
⅛	tsp. cayenne pepper
½	tsp. salt
1	tbsp. lemon juice

Wash the leeks well, trim, and chop. Heat butter in a large skillet. Add the leeks and sauté over low heat until very tender but not brown. Add the garlic and sauté a moment longer. Add the lobster pieces and toss until the shells begin to turn red. Pour in the wine, bring to a simmer, cover, and cook 15 minutes. Remove the lobsters to serving dish, cover and keep warm. Boil down the cooking liquid until it has reduced to three fourths of a cup. Add the cream and cook over medium-high heat until the sauce has reduced and thickened. Add the chives, cayenne pepper, salt, and lemon juice.

Return the lobster pieces to pan, toss, and heat before serving.

Serves: 4
Calories per serving: 550

Lobster Américaine

½	cup chopped parsley
1	cup chopped watercress
¼	cup chopped dill
4	oz. soft butter
½	cup mayonnaise
½	cup aspic jelly
8	oz. sliced smoked salmon
2	lb. lobster chunks
½	tsp. salt

¼	tsp. ground white pepper
1	tbsp. lemon juice
¼	tsp. seafood seasoning

Combine the parsley, watercress, and dill.

In a bowl, mix the mayonnaise with liquid aspic jelly and butter.

Place a sheet of wax paper or film wrap on a flat surface. Lay the smoked salmon over the surface of the paper or wrap.

Combine the herbs with the mayonnaise and aspic. Fold in the lobster chunks. Season to taste with the remaining ingredients.

Spoon the lobster mix over the center of the salmon. Shape into a log. Lift the paper or film so that the smoked salmon seals the lobster mix. Twist both ends of lobster roll and refrigerate for 2 to 3 hours.

Slice the chilled lobster roll and serve with mayonnaise or other cold sauce.

Serves: 10
Calories per serving: 295

Lobster Fra Diavolo

6	whole boiled lobsters
½	tsp. salt
¼	tsp. ground white pepper
2	cloves minced garlic
1	tbsp. chopped parsley
1	oz. olive oil
1	oz. butter
1	lb. chopped tomatoes

Cut the lobsters in half lengthwise and crack the claws. Season with salt and pepper. Arrange in baking pans.

Sauté the garlic and parsley in olive oil and butter. Add the tomatoes and cook over medium heat for 5 to 10 minutes. Spoon the tomato mixture over the lobster. Heat in oven. Arrange on a serving platter and serve hot.

Serves: 6
Calories per serving: 306

Lobster Newburg

2	lb. cooked lobster
2	oz. butter
¾	cup dry sherry wine
1	cup heavy cream
3	egg yolks
¼	tsp. salt

Cut the lobster meat into large chunks. Cook slowly in butter about 5 minutes. Deglaze with wine. Simmer to reduce wine. Beat cream into the egg yolks, add to the lobster, and season. Heat to the boiling point, stirring continuously until thickened. Serve immediately in timbales.

Serves: 6
Calories per serving: 392

Lobster Soufflé

2	oz. butter
1	oz. lobster butter
2	oz. flour
1	oz. cornstarch
½	tsp. paprika
2	cups milk
7	eggs
1	lb. cooked lobster meat
1	oz. fresh bread crumbs
1	tsp. salt
¼	tsp. ground pepper
⅛	tsp. ground nutmeg
2	oz. dry sherry
1	tbsp. butter
1	tbsp. flour

Mince the lobster meat. Melt the butter and lobster butter. Add the flour, cornstarch, and paprika. Cook for 5 minutes over low flame. Boil milk and stir in, whipping until smooth. Cook 10 minutes, stirring occasionally.

Separate the eggs. Mix egg yolks into the sauce, one by one. Add the lobster meat, bread crumbs, seasonings, and sherry. Beat the egg whites to medium-stiff peaks and fold into mixture. Grease and flour 10-inch (25 cm) soufflé dish(es). Pour the lobster soufflé mix into dish(es). Bake at 350°F (180°C) for 40 to 45 minutes. Serve immediately.

Serves: 6
Calories per serving: 298

Lobster Thermidor

2	oz. butter
1	oz. chopped shallots
6	oz. diced mushrooms
½	cup white wine
2	lb. diced lobster meat
½	tsp. salt
¼	tsp. ground white pepper
1½	cups cream sauce
¾	cup heavy cream
½	tsp. dry mustard
1	tbsp. chopped chives
1	tbsp. chopped parsley
6	lobster shells

Sauté the shallots and mushrooms in butter. Deglaze with wine. Simmer for 5 minutes. Add the lobster and seasonings. Stir in the cream sauce, cream, mustard, chives, and parsley. Bring to a boil and season to taste.

Fill the lobster shells with the mixture. Top with glazing sauce,★ and brown under the broiler.

★For glazing sauce, combine ⅓ cream sauce, ⅓ whipping cream, and ⅓ hollandaise.

Serves: 6
Calories per serving: 336

Lobster with Pernod

6	1½ lb. live lobsters
½	cup olive oil
4	oz. butter
1	tbsp. chopped shallots
1	clove minced garlic
2	oz. cognac
4	oz. chopped tomatoes
2	oz. tomato puree
¼	tsp. thyme leaves
1	bay leaf
¾	cup dry white wine
5	oz. heavy cream
1	tbsp. lemon juice
1	oz. pernod
2	cups cooked rice

Split live lobsters in half. Remove the coral and creamy parts from the head and save. Crack the claws. Sauté the lobster halves in hot oil until the shells turn red. Remove the oil from the pan. Add half the butter, the shallots, and garlic to pan. Brown lightly. Deglaze with cognac and ignite. Add the tomatoes, tomato puree, and seasonings. Bring to a boil. Remove the lobster pieces. Extract the meat from the tails and claws. Cut into chunks and save the shells. Strain the cooking liquid and reduce by half. Combine the remaining butter with the coral and creamy parts. Stir in reduction. Add the cream, lemon juice, and pernod. Mix in the lobster pieces. Fill the shells with the mixture and brown under a broiler. Serve hot with rice.

Serves: 6
Calories per serving: 557

Mousseline of Lobster

1	lb. raw lobster meat
1	cup heavy cream
3	egg whites
½	tsp. salt
¼	tsp. ground white pepper
⅛	tsp. ground nutmeg

2	cups lobster sauce
6	slices truffles
6	fleurons

Keep the raw lobster meat well chilled. Place in a food processor and mix to a paste. Gradually add the cream, egg whites, salt, white pepper, and nutmeg. Butter a 7-inch ring mold and fill with the mousseline. Cover with wax paper and bake in a waterbath for 30 to 40 minutes in a 325°F (165°C) oven. Unmold on a suitable platter. Pour the hot sauce over the platter. Garnish with truffle slices and fleurons.

Serves: 6
Calories per serving: 316

Roasted Lobster

6	1¼ lb. lobsters
3	oz. sweet butter
6	small chopped shallots
2	cups champagne
½	tsp. salt
¼	tsp. ground white pepper
1	cup heavy cream
½	tsp. ground saffron
2	tbsp. olive oil
2	cups cooked rice

Combine the butter and shallots in a saucepan and cook slowly until shallots are translucent. Add champagne and reduce by half. Add the cream and salt and pepper to taste. Bring to a boil and reduce for about 5 minutes. Add the saffron. Whip in the butter. Strain the sauce through a fine strainer. Lay the live lobsters on their backs. Fill a large syringe with the sauce and inject the lobster tails. Put the lobsters on a baking sheet. Brush the shells with oil. Bake at 450° F (190°C) for 15 to 20 minutes.

When lobsters are done, split in half. Serve with rice, with the remaining sauce on the side.

Serves: 6
Calories per serving: 496

Homard à la Nage

Cook live lobsters in salted boiling water. Split warm lobster in half lengthwise. Crack claws. Serve with lemon butter.

Curried Lobster

Sauté cooked lobster meat in butter. Combine with curry sauce. Serve with saffron rice.

Lobster Hollandaise

Cook live lobsters in salted boiling water. Split warm lobsters in half lengthwise. Crack claws. Serve lobster warm with Parisienne potatoes and hollandaise.

Lobster Savannah

Follow the recipe for Lobster Thermidor. Use minted béarnaise for glaze. Garnish with strips of green pepper, red pimentos, and anchovy fillets.

For additional lobster recipes, see

═ **Crab**

Aspic of Crab

1	cup liquid aspic jelly
1	lb. crabmeat
1	cup cocktail sauce
3	oz. black olives
8	oz. Russian salad

Pour the jelly into a decorative ring mold. Allow to set in the refrigerator. Arrange the olives on the top of the jelly. Combine crabmeat and sauce. Pack the mold with the crabmeat. Cool in the refrigerator for 1 to 2 hours. Dip in hot water to unmold. Serve with Russian salad.

Serves: 6
Calories per serving: 147

Boiled Blue Crab

6	qt. boiling water
2	cups vinegar
1	tbsp. cayenne pepper
2	tsp. celery salt
1	tbsp. mace
1	tbsp. ground ginger
2	dozen blue crab

Add the vinegar and all the seasonings to the boiling water. Simmer for 5 minutes. Add the crabs. Boil and simmer for 15 minutes. Drain. Serve hot or cold.

Serves: 6
Calories per serving: 108

Boiled Dungeness Crab

3	live dungeness crabs
10	qt. boiling water
½	cup salt

| 12 | oz. melted butter |
| 1 | cup mayonnaise |

Dress the crabs by prying off the top shell. Remove the spongy parts underneath the shells (gills, stomach, intestines), and wash the body cavities. Place in salted boiling water. Return to boiling and simmer for 15 minutes. Drain. Crack the claws and legs. Serve hot with butter, or chill and serve with mayonnaise.

Serves: 6
Calories per serving: 264

Crab Cakes

3	oz. melted butter
2	oz. chopped onion
6	oz. chopped mushrooms
2	oz. flour
1	tsp. dry mustard
½	tsp. paprika
½	tsp. cayenne pepper
½	cup heavy cream
1	lb. crabmeat
1	cup fresh bread crumbs
2	oz. white wine
1	tbsp. chopped parsley
½	tsp. worcestershire
1	egg
½	tsp. salt

Sauté the onion and mushrooms in butter. Add the flour, mustard, paprika, and pepper. Mix in the cream. Flake the crabmeat and add to the sauce. Mix in the remaining ingredients. Allow the mixture to cool. Portion into two cakes per person. Shape into patties and dredge in flour. Fry in butter until golden brown.

Serves: 6
Calories per serving: 309

Crabmeat Crunch

2	lb. crabmeat
4	oz. butter
4	oz. diced celery
1	oz. cornstarch
2	cups chicken stock
4	oz. sliced almonds
1	tbsp. lemon juice
5	oz. chinese noodles

If frozen, thaw the crabmeat. Drain and remove any shell or cartilage. Melt the butter in a skillet or sauté pan. Add the celery and crabmeat. Cook over low flame for 5 to 10 minutes, stirring frequently. Dissolve the cornstarch in the chicken stock. Add the crabmeat, stirring constantly until thick. Add the toasted almonds and lemon juice. Adjust seasonings and serve with the noodles.

Serves: 6
Calories per serving: 323

Crabmeat Imperial

1	lb. crabmeat
2	oz. butter
4	oz. chopped green pepper
½	cup heavy cream
1½	cups fresh mayonnaise
½	tsp. salt
¼	tsp. ground white pepper

Remove any pieces of the shell or cartilage from crabmeat. Sauté the green pepper in butter until wilted, then set aside. Beat the cream until stiff and fold in the mayonnaise. Add the crabmeat, salt, pepper, and green pepper. Stir until well blended.

Arrange the crab mixture in individual small casserole dishes. Bake at 425°F (220°C) until bubbly and lightly browned.

Serves: 6
Calories per serving: 619

Crabmeat Omelette

12	eggs
½	tsp. salt
¼	tsp. ground white pepper
3	oz. butter
7	oz. flaked crabmeat
1	cup cream sauce
1	tsp. curry

Beat the eggs. Season with salt and pepper. Melt the butter in an omelette pan. Pour in the eggs. Cook over a brisk flame. Combine the crabmeat, cream sauce, and curry powder, and spoon into the middle of the omelette. Fold the omelette and arrange on a warm serving platter.

Serves: 6
Calories per serving: 287

Crabmeat Orientale

½	cup olive oil
2	tbsp. soy sauce
3	tbsp. vinegar
¼	tsp. tabasco
1	tsp. dijon mustard
3	cups cooked rice
8	oz. sliced mushrooms
4	oz. sliced water chestnut
4	oz. diced green pepper
3	chopped pimentos
1	lb. flaked crabmeat
1	tbsp. chopped parsley
1	tbsp. chopped chives

Prepare a dressing with the oil, soy sauce, vinegar, tabasco, and mustard.

Combine the remaining ingredients except parsley and chives. Mix in the dressing. Arrange in a salad bowl. Sprinkle with parsley and chives. Serve cold.

Serves: 6
Calories per serving: 312

Crabmeat Ravigotte

1	lb. crabmeat
2	tbsp. chopped pickles
2	tbsp. lemon juice
¼	tsp. salt
1	hard-cooked egg
1	tbsp. chopped parsley
¼	cup mayonnaise
2	tbsp. stuffed green olives
¼	tsp. paprika

Remove any shell or cartilage from the crabmeat. Combine the pickles, lemon juice, salt, chopped hard-cooked egg, parsley, and crabmeat.

Arrange on a serving platter. Combine mayonnaise, chopped olives, and paprika. Spread over the top of the crabmeat. Serve cold.

Serves: 6
Calories per serving: 121

Deviled Soft-Shell Crabs

¼	cup flour
¼	cup cornmeal
1	tsp. chili powder
¼	tsp. cayenne pepper
¼	tsp. ground cumin
¼	tsp. ground coriander
¼	tsp. salt
12	large softshell crab
1	cup mustard sauce

Combine the flour, cornmeal, chili powder, cayenne pepper, cumin, coriander, and salt in a shallow pan.

Clean the crabs thoroughly. Coat the crabs in the seasoned flour mixture and deep fry at 350°F (180°C) about 5 minutes until golden brown. Drain and serve hot with mustard sauce.

Serves: 6
Calories per serving: 350

Fried Soft-Shell Crabs

1½	doz. live soft-shell crabs
¾	tsp. salt
¼	tsp. ground pepper
2	oz. lemon juice
1	oz. soy sauce
3	oz. flour
3	beaten eggs
2	cups fresh bread crumbs
2	cups sauce verte★
2	oz. fried parsley
1	lemon basket

Clean the crabs. Rinse under cold water. Arrange the crabs on a sheet pan. Season with salt, pepper, lemon juice, and soy sauce. Refrigerate for 2 hours. Roll the crabs in flour, dip in eggs, and coat in bread crumbs. Deep fry at 375°F (190°C) for 2 minutes. Arrange on a heated platter lined with napkins. Garnish with fried parsley and the lemon basket. Serve hot with the sauce verte.

★See recipe for Sauce Verte in Chapter 11.

Serves: 6
Calories per serving: 540

Key Lime Stone Crab

4	oz. butter
2	oz. flour
1	cup milk
½	tsp. salt
1	grated lime rind
2	tbsp. lime juice
1	lb. stone crab
2	tbsp. cognac
2	cups cooked rice

Melt half the butter in a saucepan. Blend in the flour to make a roux. Stir in the milk until the sauce is smooth. Season with salt. Add the grated rind and lime juice.

Heat the remaining butter and add crabmeat. Pour in the cognac and ignite. Fold in the cream sauce. Serve with hot rice.

Serves: 6
Calories per serving: 267

King Crab Salad

½	cup sour cream
1	tbsp. grated horseradish
1	cup cocktail sauce
1	lb. king crabmeat
6	oz. seedless grapes

Combine the sour cream, horseradish, and cocktail sauce. Flake the crabmeat and fold in the sauce.

Arrange on a shallow serving dish. Decorate with cleaned grapes. Chill before serving.

Serves: 6
Calories per serving: 174

Snow Crab Casserole

12	oz. snow crab
4	oz. butter
½	sliced green pepper
¼	cup chopped onion
2	cups cooked rice
1	cup grated cheese
2	hard-cooked eggs
1½	tbsp. flour
1½	cups milk
1½	tbsp. mayonnaise
¾	tsp. salt
⅛	tsp. pepper
½	cup dry bread crumbs
1	oz. butter

Thaw and drain the snow crab.

In a heavy saucepan, melt half the butter and sauté the green pepper and onion until soft. Place the rice in a suitable casserole. Layer half the crab, cheese, sliced eggs, remaining crab, green pepper, and onion.

To prepare the sauce, melt the rest of the butter and blend in the flour to make a roux. Stir in the milk. Cook over low heat until the sauce thickens and is smooth. Stir in the mayonnaise, salt, and pepper. Pour the sauce over the casserole ingredients. Sprinkle with bread crumbs and dot with butter. Bake at 350°F (180°C) for 30 to 40 minutes.

Serves: 6
Calories per serving: 310

Stone Crab au Gratin

2	lb. stone crab claws
2	oz. butter
2	oz. chopped shallots
1	cup dry white wine
2	cups cream sauce★
½	cup hollandaise★
½	tsp. salt
¼	tsp. ground white pepper
6	fleurons★★

Crack the crab claws to remove the meat. Save one claw per serving as garnish. Sauté the shallots in butter over low heat. Add the flaked crabmeat and deglaze with the wine.

Combine an equal volume of cream sauce with the hollandaise. Stir the remaining cream sauce into crab. Season with salt and pepper. Transfer the crab into an ovenproof serving dish. Cover with the hollandaise cream sauce and glaze under a broiler. Garnish with warm crab claws and fleurons. Serve hot.

★See recipes for hollandaise and Cream Sauce in Chapter 11.

★★Fleurons are small crescent shapes made with puff pastry.

Serves: 6
Calories per serving: 278

For additional crab recipes, see

Avocado Mexicaine in Chapter 13.
Crab Appetizer in Chapter 15.
Crab Canapés in Chapter 15.
Crab Cheese in Chapter 15.
Crab Puffs in Chapter 15.
Crabmeat Balls in Chapter 15.
Fillet of Trout Key West in Chapter 14.
Fruits de Mer Cervelas in Chapter 12.
Lake Trout Mexicaine in Chapter 14.
San Francisco Cioppino in Chapter 10.
Seafood a la King in Chapter 12.
Seafood Newburg in Chapter 12.
Seafood Crêpes in Chapter 12.
Seafood Pizza in Chapter 12.

Norway (Icelandic) Lobster (Langostino, Lobsterette, Langoustine)

Langostino Omelette

12	eggs
½	tsp. salt
¼	tsp. ground white pepper
6	oz. butter
8	oz. cooked langostinos
1	cup sauce Américaine

Beat the eggs. Season with salt and pepper.

Dice the cooked langostino tails, and combine with the sauce Américaine. Simmer the sauce for 5 to 10 minutes.

Melt butter in an omelette pan. Pour in the eggs. Cook over medium heat while stirring the eggs until medium soft. Spoon the langostino mixture into the middle of the omelette. Fold the omelette and arrange on a preheated plate or platter. Repeat with the remaining eggs and filling. Serve hot.

Note: For this recipe, make individual omelettes or one large omelette.

Serves: 6
Calories per serving: 557

Langostinos au Gratin

3	lb. langostino tails
2	oz. butter
8	oz. mushrooms
3	oz. cognac
1½	cups cardinal sauce
2	cups boiled rice

Cook the langostino tails in salted boiling water. Drain, cool, shell, and devein the langostino tails.

Sauté the langostino tails in butter. Cut the mushrooms into quarters, add to the langostino tails, and cook for a moment. Deglaze with cognac. Stir in the cardinal sauce. Simmer for 5 minutes. Brown under a broiler. Serve hot with rice.

Serves: 6
Calories per serving: 436

Langostinos Cocktail

12	large langostino tails
12	orange sections
1	tbsp. chopped chutney
1	tbsp. lemon juice
1	tsp. chopped dill
1	tsp. grated horseradish
1	cup whipped cream
1	head boston lettuce
6	lemon wedges

Cook the langostino tails in salted boiling water. Remove the shells and devein. Combine the langostino tails with orange sections. Add the chutney, lemon juice, dill, and horseradish. Marinate for half an hour. Fold in the whipped cream. Shred the cleaned lettuce leaves in cocktail glasses. Arrange a layer of lettuce and two langostino tails in each glass. Spoon over the sauce. Garnish with lemon wedges. Serve cold.

Serves: 6
Calories per serving: 153

Deep-Fried Langostinos Sauce Remoulade

See recipes for Deep-Fried Shrimp in this chapter with Sauce Rémoulade in Chapter 11.

Langoustines Meunière

See the cooking technique for sauté meunière in Chapter 6.

═ Shrimp

Aspic of Shrimp

10	oz. recipe shrimp mousse
12	large whole shrimp
1	tsp. fish seasoning
1	tbsp. lemon juice
4	oz. tiny shrimp
3	cups liquid aspic jelly
1½	cups sauce antiboise

Prepare the shrimp mousse according to the recipe in Chapter 9, omitting the truffles. Cook the shrimp in boiling water containing fish seasoning. Simmer for 5 minutes. Drain and cool the shrimp. Shell, devein, and marinate in lemon juice.

Pour some of the aspic jelly in a cold decorative mold. Refrigerate to set. Arrange the large shrimp over the set jelly. Pour a small amount of aspic over the shrimp to seal them. Combine the tiny shrimp with the mousse and spoon in to fill the mold. Pour a small amount of aspic to cover mousse. Refrigerate for 2 hours or more.

Dip the mold in lukewarm water to unmold. Invert on a chilled serving platter. Serve with sauce antiboise.

Serves: 6
Calories per serving: 318

Bouquet of Shrimp

2½	lb. fresh shrimp
1	tbsp. fish seasoning
1	large grapefruit
3	avocados
6	lime wedges
6	oz. cocktail sauce

Use fresh whole shrimp with the heads on.

Boil enough water to cook the shrimp. Add the fish seasoning, then add the shrimp. Bring to a quick boil, simmer for 5 minutes, and drain the shrimp. Save a few whole shrimp and arrange in a bouquet, inserting the pointed ends of the heads into the grapefruit.

Cut the avocados in half lengthwise. Remove the stones, peel, and slice. Arrange the avocado slices on a serving platter, alternating with small bunches of shrimp. Place the bouquet of shrimp in the center of the platter. Garnish with lime wedges. Serve the cocktail sauce separately.

Serves: 6
Calories per serving: 430

Brochettes of Shrimp

2½	lb. medium shrimp
1	tbsp. lemon juice
½	cup chili sauce
2	oz. soy sauce
½	tsp. salt
1½	cups curry sauce
2	oz. flour
2	oz. butter
2	cups steamed rice

Shell and devein the shrimp. Wash and drain and marinate in mixture of lemon juice, chili sauce, soy sauce, and salt for half an hour. Prepare the curry sauce (see recipe in Chapter 11).

Thread shrimp through the head and tail on skewers. Roll in flour. Sauté in butter until shrimp turn pink and are slightly brown. Serve on a bed of steamed rice and top with curry sauce.

Serves: 6
Calories per serving: 385

Broiled Spanish Shrimp

2	doz. jumbo Spanish shrimp
1	tsp. salt
¼	tsp. white pepper
1	tbsp. lemon juice
4	oz. melted butter
6	lemon wedges
1	small bunch parsley

Peel and fantail the shrimp. Devein and butterfly. Arrange the shrimp on a baking dish. Season with salt, pepper, and lemon juice. Pour the melted butter over and broil about 4 inches (10 cm) from the source of heat for 10 minutes.

Transfer to a serving platter. Garnish with lemon wedges and parsley.

Serves: 6
Calories per serving: 310

Crevettes en Coquille

6	scallop shells
10	oz. duchess potatoes
2½	cups velouté★ sauce
5	oz. mushroom buttons
1	oz. butter
1	tbsp. lemon juice
1¾	lb. cooked shrimp
6	truffle slices

Select scallop shells of the same size. Spoon the duchess potatoes into a pastry bag fitted in a star tube. Pipe the potatoes using an up and down motion around the edges of the shells. Spoon a tablespoon of the velouté sauce into each shell. Wash the mushrooms, drain, and sauté over a brisk fire in butter and lemon juice. Season with salt.

Combine the shrimp with the remaining sauce and mushrooms. Garnish the shells. Glaze under the broiler.

Place a slice of truffle in the center of each shell. Serve hot.

★Mornay sauce can be substituted for the velouté sauce.

Serves: 6
Calories per serving: 354

Deep-Fried Shrimp

2¼	lb. raw shrimp
1	tbsp. lemon juice
½	tsp. salt
⅛	tsp. white pepper
3	beaten eggs
3	oz. flour
2	cups fresh bread crumbs
1	gal. oil
1	bunch fried parsley
6	oz. rémoulade sauce

Shell and devein the shrimp. Rinse under cold water and drain.

Butterfly the shrimp and arrange on a tray. Season with salt, pepper, and lemon juice. Marinate for half an hour or more. Dip each shrimp in flour and egg, then in bread crumbs. Deep fry for 2 to 4 minutes, according to size. Arrange on a platter covered with a napkin. Surround with the fried parsley. Serve the rémoulade sauce separately.

Serves: 6
Calories per serving: 551

Dilled Shrimp

2	lb. peeled shrimp
3	tbsp. butter
2	tbsp. chopped shallots
1	clove minced garlic
2	tbsp. cognac
1	cup white wine
½	cup fish stock
1	cup tomato sauce
½	tsp. salt
¼	tsp. ground white pepper
1	tbsp. chopped dill

Devein the shrimp. Sauté in butter over high heat until they turn pink-white and transfer immediately to a serving dish.

Add the shallots and garlic to the pan and sauté for about a minute. Pour cognac and white wine over and boil until reduced to three quarters. Add the fish stock and tomato sauce, then boil for 15 minutes or until the sauce reduces to half. Season to taste. Pour the juices from the shrimp into the boiling sauce. Add the dill. Spoon the sauce over the warm shrimp. Serve hot.

Serves: 4
Calories per serving: 405

Flambéed Shrimp Suédoise

6	oz. wild rice
2	lb. shrimp
2	tbsp. butter
1	tbsp. chopped shallots
2	oz. brandy
½	cup velouté sauce
3	oz. sour cream
3	oz. heavy cream
1	tsp. dill weed
½	tsp. salt
¼	tsp. ground white pepper

Cook the wild rice according to directions on the package.

Shell and devein the shrimp. Rinse under cold water and drain. Melt butter in a sauté pan. Add the shallots and cook over low heat for 5 minutes. Add the shrimp and cook over high heat for 2 more minutes. Pour in the brandy and ignite. Add the velouté sauce, sour cream, heavy cream, dill, salt, and pepper.

Stir to combine and bring to a boil. Do not overcook. Pack hot rice in a buttered ring mold. Invert onto a serving platter. Spoon the shrimp suédoise in the middle. Serve hot.

Serves: 6
Calories per serving: 385

Jumbo Shrimp Louisiana

2¼	lb. jumbo shrimp
½	cup olive oil
2	oz. whiskey
¾	cup dry sherry

2½	cups fumet
3	oz. chopped onion
1	oz. flour
1	lb. canned tomatoes
½	tsp. salt
¼	tsp. ground white pepper
1	pinch cayenne pepper
1	tbsp. lemon juice

Shell and devein the shrimp. Rinse under cold water and drain. In a sauté pan, heat the oil to a smoking point. Add the shrimp and stir well to color lightly. Pour off the oil and save for later use. Pour the whiskey over the shrimp, ignite, then deglaze with the wine. Add half of the fish fumet, bring to a boil, and simmer for a minute.

Heat up the oil in a frying pan. Add the onion and stir until golden brown. Sprinkle with the flour and stir to mix. Cook over low heat for 2 minutes. Add the chopped, diced, seedless tomatoes, moisten with remaining fumet, and bring to a boil. Combine the sauce with the shrimp. Season with salt, peppers, and lemon juice. Serve hot.

Serves: 6
Calories per serving: 375

Modern Shrimp Salad

12	shelled shrimp
½	tsp. salt
¼	tsp. ground white pepper
4	tbsp. oil
3	oz. julienne green pepper
1	tsp. curry powder
3	oz. chopped tomatoes
6	peeled lichee fruit
½	clove minced garlic
4	tbsp. fish stock
2	tbsp. lemon juice
1	tbsp. mango chutney
4	leaves lettuce

Devein the shrimp. Season with salt and pepper. Heat the oil and sauté the shrimp and green pepper. Dust with curry and add the tomatoes. Halve the lichees and add along with the garlic, fish stock, and lemon. Simmer, covered, for 5 minutes. Chill and add the chutney.

Arrange on lettuce leaves.

Serves: 4
Calories per serving: 244

Red Shrimp Cap Ferrat

18	jumbo Spanish shrimp
1	tsp. salt
2	tbsp. butter
2	tbsp. chopped shallots
2	oz. roux
1	cup white wine
1	lb. chopped tomatoes
1	cup heavy cream
6	sprigs parsley
2	cups cooked rice

Butterfly the unshelled Spanish jumbo red shrimp. Remove the sand veins. Rinse under cold water and drain. Sprinkle with salt.

Melt the butter in a skillet. Stir in the shallots and cook over low heat for 5 minutes. Add the roux and wine. Whip until smooth. Add the tomatoes and cream. Simmer until the sauce is medium thick.

Place the shrimp in a baking dish. Spoon a small amount of the sauce over each shrimp. Bake at 400°F (200°C) for 10 to 15 minutes. Transfer to a serving platter. Garnish with parsley. Serve with rice.

Serves: 6
Calories per serving: 413

Salad Mignon

4	oz. cooked shrimp
3	medium artichoke bottoms
½	cup mayonnaise

1	tbsp. heavy cream
1/8	tsp. cayenne pepper
4	large lettuce leaves

Dice the shrimp and artichoke bottoms.
  Mix the mayonnaise, heavy cream, and cayenne pepper.
  Combine with the shrimp and artichoke. Serve on lettuce leaves.

Serves: 4
Calories per serving: 282

Scampi Style Shrimp

4	oz. butter
1	large chopped shallot
2	tsp. minced garlic
1	lb. cleaned shrimp
1/2	cup white wine
2	tbsp. chopped parsley
1	tsp. wine worcestershire
2	tbsp. lemon juice
1/2	tsp. salt
1/4	tsp. ground white pepper
2	cups cooked rice

Melt the butter in a sauté pan. Add the shallot and garlic. Sauté over low heat for 5 minutes.
  Stir in the shelled, deveined, cleaned shrimp and cook until they start turning pink. Add the remaining ingredients. Reduce the sauce over medium heat.
  Serve hot with rice.

Serves: 4
Calories per serving: 363

Shrimp Américaine

| 2 | lb. shrimp |
| 3 | oz. butter |

½	tsp. salt
¼	tsp. paprika
2	cups cooked rice
1	cup sauce Américaine

Shell and devein the shrimp. Rinse under cold water and drain. Melt half the butter in a sauté pan. Add the shrimp and sauté until pink and tender. Season with paprika. Add the sauce Americaine (see recipe in Chapter 11.) and simmer for 5 minutes. Butter a ring mold. Pack in the hot rice. Invert onto a serving platter.

Spoon the shrimp in the center and serve hot.

Serves: 6
Calories per serving: 418

Shrimp and Avocados

1	tbsp. fish seasoning*
2	tsp. salt
2	qt. water
1½	lb. shelled shrimp
3	ripe avocados
3	oz. vinaigrette
6	cleaned lettuce leaves
6	lemon wedges
6	oz. sauce verte*

Add the salt and fish seasoning to water and boil. Add the cleaned and deveined shrimp. Bring to a boil again, then simmer for 2 minutes. Drain and cool. Split the avocados in half lengthwise and remove the stones. Marinate the avocado halves in oil and vinaigrette for 15 minutes or more.

Cover a round serving platter with lettuce leaves. Fill the avocado halves with shrimp and arrange on a platter. Garnish with lemon wedges. Serve cold with sauce verte.

*See recipes for Fish Seasoning in Chapter 12 and Sauce Verte in Chapter 11.

Serves: 6
Calories per serving: 431

Shrimp au Gratin

2	lb. shrimp
1	oz. butter
2	oz. chopped onion
1½	cups sauce Allemande
2	oz. grated swiss cheese
1	oz. dry bread crumbs
1	tbsp. melted butter

Peel and devein the shrimp. Sauté in butter until pink. Do not overcook. Remove the shrimp and set aside.

Add the onion to pan and cook over low heat for 10 minutes. Add the sauce Allemande and heat to boiling point. Mix in the shrimp.

Transfer to an ovenproof serving dish. Combine the cheese, bread crumbs, and melted butter, and sprinkle over the shrimp. Bake at 400°F (200°C) for 10 to 15 minutes, or until golden brown.

Serves: 6
Calories per serving: 300

Shrimp Cocktail

6	lettuce leaves
1	grapefruit
6	oz. cocktail sauce
6	large whole shrimp
2	lb. cooked shrimp
6	lemon wedges

Cover a round serving platter with lettuce leaves. Make a four-petal tulip flower with the grapefruit. Hollow the inside of the grapefruit. Pour the cocktail sauce into the grapefruit (for individual servings, use lemons).

Place the filled grapefruit in the center of platter. Decorate with the whole, unshelled shrimp. Surround with the cooked, shelled, and deveined shrimp. Garnish with lemon wedges.

Serves: 6
Calories per serving: 142

Shrimp Egg Foo Yung

4	oz. bean sprouts
8	oz. diced shrimp
¼	cup peanut oil
3	eggs
2	oz. diced mushrooms
1	tbsp. cornstarch
¾	cup chicken stock
1	tbsp. soy sauce
½	tsp. salt

Rinse and strain the bean sprouts.

Clean and devein the shrimp. In a skillet or wok, heat half the oil. Stir fry shrimp for 1 minute, then set aside. Beat the eggs lightly. Add the shrimp, bean sprouts, and mushrooms to the eggs. Heat a little oil in a skillet. Pour in one quarter cup of mixture. Cook until light brown. Turn the pancake over and cook another minute. Transfer to a platter. Make more pancakes using the remaining mixture. Stack two by two and pour hot sauce over. Serve hot.

For the sauce, dissolve cornstarch in half the stock. Boil the remaining stock, add soy sauce and salt, and mix in the cornstarch. Stir until thick. Pour over the shrimp egg foo yung.

Serves: 6
Calories per serving: 178

Shrimp Fritters

8	oz. cooked shrimp
½	cup chopped parsley
½	tbsp. chopped dill
½	cup flour
¼	tsp. salt
2	tsp. baking powder
1	egg
¼	cup milk
⅛	tsp. tabasco
1	cup tuna–anchovy sauce

Chop the shrimp and mix with the parsley and dill. With the flour, salt, baking powder, egg, milk, and tabasco, prepare a batter. Mix in the shrimp. Drop the shrimp mixture by small teaspoonfuls into deep fryer at 375°F (190°C). Fry for 2 minutes or until crisp and golden brown. Drain on absorbent paper. Serve hot with tuna–anchovy sauce.

Serves: 12
Calories per serving: 123

Shrimp in Patty Shells

2	lb. whole shrimp
2	oz. lobster butter
1	oz. cognac
1	cup dry white wine
¾	cup fumet
1	cup heavy cream
1	oz. beurre manie
½	cup hollandaise
½	tsp. salt
¼	tsp. ground white pepper
6	baked patty shells

Peel and devein the shrimp. Rinse under cold water and drain. Heat the lobster butter in a sauté pan. Toss in the shrimp and cook over medium heat for 5 minutes. Pour in the cognac and ignite. Deglaze with white wine and cook 5 more minutes. Remove the shrimp and keep warm.

Pour the fumet and heavy cream into the sauté pan. Reduce by one quarter over high heat. Whip in the beurre manie. Bring the sauce to a quick boil and add the hollandaise. Combine the shrimp with the sauce and heat thoroughly. Season with salt and pepper. Heat the patty shells and fill with the shrimp mixture. Serve at once.

Serves: 6
Calories per serving: 438

Shrimp Omelette Soufflé

| 12 | eggs |
| ½ | tsp. salt |

¼	tsp. ground white pepper
9	oz. cooked shrimp
6	oz. shrimp sauce

Separate half the eggs. Mix the yolks with the remaining whole eggs. Salt and pepper the mixture and beat lightly.

Beat the egg whites to a medium-soft peak. Fold into the whole egg mixture. Prepare individual or large omelettes melting some of the butter in an omelette pan. Pour in omelette mixture. Stir with a fork over medium heat. Before the eggs set, spoon some shelled and deveined shrimp in the middle of the omelette. Fold omelete over, transfer to a serving platter, and keep warm.

Using the remaining egg mixture, make more omelettes. Coat each omelette with shrimp sauce.

Serves: 6
Calories per serving: 265

Shrimp Orientale

1	cup tomatoes
4	oz. chopped onion
4	oz. butter
1	cup rice
½	tsp. saffron
2½	cups water
2	lb. raw shrimp
½	tsp. salt
½	tsp. white pepper
1½	cups velouté sauce★

Peel, seed, and chop the tomatoes. Sauté the onion in half the butter until transparent. Stir in the tomatoes. Cook for 5 minutes.

Add the rice, saffron and water. Stir well, cover, and bake for 20 minutes at 350°F (180°C). Pack the rice in a buttered ring mold and keep warm.

Shell and devein the shrimp. Rinse in cold water. Melt the remaining butter in a skillet. Add the shrimp and cook over high heat until pink. Season with salt and pepper. Add the velouté sauce and simmer for 5 minutes. Unmold the rice on a round serving platter. Spoon the shrimp and sauce in the middle. Serve hot.

★See recipe for Velouté Sauce in Chapter 11.

Serves: 6
Calories per serving: 335

Shrimp Quiche

8	oz. pie crust
2	oz. butter
1	tbsp. chopped shallots
3	oz. dry white wine
8	oz. diced raw shrimp
4	whole eggs
1½	cups half and half
½	tsp. salt
¼	tsp. white pepper
⅛	tsp. nutmeg

Roll out the dough and line a 9-inch pie plate. Cover the bottom and sides with foil so that the dough keeps its original shape while baking. Bake at 350°F (180°C) for 15 to 20 minutes or until brown. Remove the foil. Melt the butter, add the shallots, and cook over low heat for 5 minutes. Deglaze with the wine. Stir in the shrimp and cook for 5 minutes, or until the shrimp turn pink.

Beat the remaining ingredients together. Mix in the slightly cooled shrimp, and fill the crust. Bake at 350°F (180°C) for 25 to 30 minutes, or until set and golden brown.

Serves: 6
Calories per serving: 240

Shrimp Salad Roscoff

1	cup mayonnaise
2	tbsp. catsup
1	tbsp. cognac
1	drop tabasco
8	oz. cooked shrimp
6	lettuce leaves
2	fresh tomatoes
2	hard-cooked eggs
6	artichoke hearts
1	oz. small capers
6	black olives

Combine the mayonnaise, catsup, cognac, and tabasco. Fold in the shrimp. Arrange lettuce leaves on a serving platter. Spoon on the shrimp mixture. Blanch and peel the tomatoes, and cut into wedges. Arrange around the shrimp, alternating with slices of hard-cooked eggs and artichoke hearts. Sprinkle capers over the shrimp and decorate with olives.

Serves: 6
Calories per serving: 262

Shrimp Tempura

1	gal. oil
3	lb. shelled shrimp
1	recipe tempura batter★

Heat the oil in deep fryer to 365°F (185°C). Shell and devein the shrimp, leaving the tails attached. Dip shrimp into the tempura batter, then drop in oil and cook for 3 to 4 minutes. Drain on absorbent paper.

Arrange on a warm serving platter. Serve with sushi sauce.★

★See recipe for Tempura Batter in Chapter 7 and Sushi Sauce in Chapter 11.

Serves: 6
Calories per serving: 424

Shrimp with Tarragon

8	oz. fettucine
2	tbsp. butter
2	tbsp. chopped shallots
½	cup dry white wine
1	cup heavy cream
2	tbsp. fresh tarragon
¼	tsp. salt
¼	tsp. saffron
¼	tsp. ground white pepper
8	oz. peeled shrimp
1	egg yolk

Cook the pasta according to package directions.

Melt the butter in a frying pan. Add the shallots. Stir for a minute. Pour in the wine and boil vigorously until most of the liquid evaporates. Add the cream, chopped tarragon, salt, saffron, and white pepper. Boil and reduce for 5 minutes. Add the shrimp to the sauce. Simmer until done. Whisk a little sauce into the egg yolk in a bowl. Stir into the shrimp dish.

Drain the pasta but do not rinse. Toss the pasta with the shrimp sauce. Serve hot.

Serves: 4
Calories per serving: 560

Shrimp-Stuffed Eggplant

2	large eggplant
4	oz. chopped onion
2	oz. chopped celery
2	oz. butter
1	tsp. minced garlic
1	lb. canned tomatoes
1	tsp. salt
¼	tsp. ground white pepper
1¼	lb. cleaned shrimp
1	cup dry bread crumbs
1	oz. melted butter

Trim off ends of the eggplants and cut in halves lengthwise. Scoop out the pulp and set aside, leaving the shells about ½-inch (1.25 cm) thick. Place the shells on baking pans, open side down. Add a little water to pan and bake at 400°F (200°C) for 20 minutes or until the shells are cooked. Chop the pulp. Sauté the onion and celery in butter until transparent. Add the garlic, eggplant pulp, and chopped tomatoes, and simmer for 10 to 15 minutes. Season with salt and pepper.

Mix in the shelled and deveined shrimp and half the bread crumbs. Fill the eggplant shells. Sprinkle with remaining crumbs and butter. Bake at 350°F (180°C) for 15 to 20 minutes. Serve hot.

Serves: 6
Calories per serving: 257

Stir-Fried Shrimp and Peas

2	small cleaned scallions
1½	lb. shelled shrimp
12	oz. small peas
2	tsp. cornstarch
1	beaten egg white
2	oz. dry sherry
½	tsp. salt
2	oz. oil
3	slices ginger

Cut the scallions into 2 inch (5 cm) pieces. Devein the shrimp. Split shrimp in half lengthwise, then cut each half in two crosswise. Defrost the peas and blanch for 5 minutes. Toss the shrimp in cornstarch until slightly coated, then dip into a mixture of egg whites, sherry, and salt. Heat the oil in a large skillet to the smoking point. Add the scallions and ginger and stir for 30 seconds to flavor. Remove the scallions and ginger with a slotted spoon and discard. Add the shrimp to the oil and stir fry for about 2 minutes. Stir in the peas and heat for a few more seconds. Transfer to a warm platter and serve at once.

Serves: 6
Calories per serving: 235

For additional shrimp recipes, see

Avocado Seafood Salad in Chapter 12.
Barquettes Marivaux in Chapter 15.
Barquettes of Shrimp in Chapter 15.
Canapés Paulette in Chapter 15.
Fillet of Trout Key West in Chapter 14.
Fruits de Mer Cervelas in Chapter 12.
Lemon Seafood Pasta in Chapter 12.
Marinated Shrimp in Chapter 15.
Paella Valenciana in Chapter 12.
Salmon–Shrimp Terrine in Chapter 12.
San Francisco Cioppino in Chapter 10.
Seafood a la King in Chapter 12.
Seafood Brochettes in Chapter 12.
Seafood Crêpes in Chapter 12.
Seafood Fondue in Chapter 12.

Seafood Newburg in Chapter 12.
Seafood Pizza in Chapter 12.
Seafood Sausages in Chapter 12.
Shrimp Bisque in Chapter 10.
Shrimp Bouchées in Chapter 15.
Shrimp Butter in Chapter 15.
Shrimp Canapés in Chapter 15.
Shrimp Fritters in Chapter 13.
Shrimp Mousse in Chapter 9.
Shrimp Pastries in Chapter 7.
Shrimp Puffs in Chapter 7.
Shrimp Quenelles in Chapter 9.
Shrimp Ravioli Pastries in Chapter 15.
Shrimp Tartlets Russe in Chapter 15.
Spanish Fish Stew in Chapter 10.

Sea Urchin

See Chapter 4 for details on Sea Urchins.

Spiny Lobster

All recipes for lobster are applicable to Spiny Lobster. See lobster recipes, substituting spiny lobster for lobster.

FRESHWATER CRUSTACEANS
Crayfish (Crawfish)

Boiled Crawfish

4	lb. whole crawfish
1	tbsp. salt
¼	tsp. cayenne pepper
1	lemon
1	sliced onion
1	clove garlic
1	tbsp. fish seasoning
6	oz. melted butter
1	oz. lemon juice

Wash the crawfish in cold water until clean. Purge the crawfish by placing them in salted cold water for 5 minutes. Wash once more in plain water.

Fill a large pot with enough water to cover the crawfish. Add the salt, cayenne pepper, garlic, and fish seasoning to water. Bring to a boil and add the crawfish. Bring to a boil again for 3 to 5 minutes. Turn off the heat. Let the crawfish soak for 20 to 30 minutes.

Strain the crawfish and serve warm with lemon butter.

Serves: 6
Calories per serving: 363

Crawfish au Gratin

3	doz. large crawfish
2	oz. butter
1	cup dry white wine
½	tsp. salt
¼	tsp. thyme leaves
1	bay leaf
1	cup velouté sauce
6	oz. duxelle mushrooms
1	tbsp. chopped parsley
2	oz. bread crumbs

Sauté the whole crawfish in butter until shells turn red. Deglaze with white wine. Add salt, thyme leaves, and bay leaf. Cook covered for 10 minutes. Remove the crawfish and shell them. Reduce the cooking liquid to half. Add the velouté sauce and mushroom duxelle. Combine with the crawfish and parsley. Arrange in a casserole baking dish. Sprinkle with bread crumbs. Brown under a broiler and serve hot.

Serves: 6
Calories per serving: 294

Crawfish Tails Nantua

3	doz. shelled crawfish tails
2	oz. butter
8	oz. fresh mushrooms
¾	cup nantua sauce
6	truffle slices

Sauté the crawfish tails in butter. Cut the mushrooms into quarters and add to fish. Stir in the sauce nantua. Simmer for 5 to 10 minutes.

Spoon into a casserole serving dish. Top with truffle slices. Serve hot.

Serves: 6
Calories per serving: 323

Mousselines of Crawfish

3	oz. butter
6	truffle slices
12	large shelled crawfish
1	lb. crawfish mousse
1½	cups mornay sauce
8	oz. asparagus tips

Prepare the crawfish mousse according to the recipe for mousse in Chapter 9.

Butter individual molds. Garnish with a truffle slice and two crawfish tails in each mold. Fill the molds with crawfish mousse.

Place molds in a waterbath and bake at 350°F (180°C) for 20 to 30 minutes. Turn the molds out onto warm plates or platter. Coat the mousselines with hot mornay sauce. Garnish with asparagus tips.

Serves: 6
Calories per serving: 286

For additional crawfish recipe, see

Crawfish Cheese in Chapter 15.

MOLLUSKS
Abalone

Abalone Meunière

6	abalone steaks
½	tsp. salt

¼	tsp. ground white pepper
2	oz. flour
3	oz. olive oil
4	oz. sweet butter
1	tbsp. lemon juice
2	tbsp. chopped parsley
6	lemon wedges

Pound the abalone steaks to tenderize them. Flatten them to ¼-inch (½ cm) thickness. Cut into halves and season with salt and pepper. Dredge the abalone steaks with flour and shake off the excess. Heat the oil and half the butter in a heavy skillet or a sauté pan. Brown the abalone steaks about 30 seconds on each side. Remove steaks to a serving platter. Pour off fat from the skillet. Add the remaining butter and brown. Add the lemon juice and chopped parsley. Pour this sauce over the abalone steaks and serve at once. Garnish with lemon wedges.

Serves: 6
Calories per serving: 341

Marinated Abalone

1½	lb. abalone steaks
1	lb. tomatoes
2	oz. diced onion
½	cup lemon juice
2	oz. olive oil
2	oz. diced cucumber
1	tbsp. minced chili peppers
2	oz. diced sweet pepper

Pound the abalone steaks to tenderize them and cut into small cubes. Combine the remaining ingredients in a mixing bowl.
Add the abalone cubes to the mixture and marinate in the refrigerator for 2 hours.

Serves: 6
Calories per serving: 193

Stir-Fried Abalone

2	lb. canned abalone★
2	tbsp. cornstarch
2	tbsp. soy sauce
4	oz. oyster sauce
3	oz. oil
2	oz. minced ham

Drain the abalone, reserving the juice, and cut into 1-inch (2.5 cm) cubes.

Blend the cornstarch into the reserved liquid. Stir in the soy sauce and oyster sauce.

Stir fry the abalone in oil to heat. Blend in the cornstarch mixture to thicken. Add the ham. Heat and serve hot.

★Prolonged heating will toughen the abalone.

Serves: 6
Calories per serving: 278

Abalone Chowder

See recipe for New England Clam Chowder in Chapter 10 and substitute clams with chopped abalone.

Clams

Clam Loaf

1	lb. bread loaf
2	oz. melted butter
2	oz. chopped onion
1	clove minced garlic
4	oz. chopped celery
2	oz. butter
1	oz. flour
½	tsp. salt
¼	tsp. ground white pepper
¼	tsp. thyme leaves

1	tbsp. chili sauce
1	qt. chopped clams
2	eggs
8	oz. bread crumbs
1	tbsp. chopped parsley

Slice a 1-inch (2½ cm) thick crust horizontally off the bread loaf. Hollow out the loaf, leaving a 1-inch (2½ cm) edge. Brush the inside with melted butter. Toast the loaf and top crust in a 350°F (180°C) oven for 10 minutes. Cook the onion, garlic, and celery in butter until tender. Stir in the flour, salt, white pepper, thyme leaves, and chili sauce. Add the clams and cook while stirring until thick. Beat in the eggs. Add the bread crumbs and parsley. Spoon the mixture into the toasted loaf. Cover with the top crust. Bake at 350°F (180°C) for about 30 minutes. Serve hot.

Serves: 10
Calories per serving: 284

Clam Soufflé

2	cups shucked clams
1	cup clam juice
2	oz. butter
2	oz. flour
½	tsp. salt
¼	tsp. ground white pepper
⅛	tsp. ground nutmeg
3	eggs

Simmer the clams in their own juice until the edges curl. Drain and save the liquid. Chop the clams.

Make a roux with the butter and flour. Add the clam juice and seasonings. Stir until the sauce thickens and becomes smooth. Separate the eggs. Stir the egg yolks into the hot sauce. Add the clams. Beat the egg whites to a medium-firm peak. Fold into the clam mixture.

Butter and flour a soufflé dish. Pour the soufflé mix into mold until three quarters full. Bake at 350°F (180°C) for 30 to 40 minutes, or until the center of the soufflé is firm. Serve immediately.

Serves: 6
Calories per serving: 166

Clams with Pasta

18	cherrystone clams
5	qts. water
1½	cups fresh clam juice
¾	lb. spaghetti
6	tbsp. olive oil
½	cup heavy cream
1	tbsp. minced garlic
⅓	cup chopped parsley

Shuck the clams and reserve the clams and juice. Chop the clams finely.

Cook the spaghetti in boiling water until al dente. Drain the spaghetti, then add the clam juice.

Heat the oil in a frying pan. Add the clams, garlic, and parsley to the oil and cook over high heat for 3 to 5 minutes.

Spoon over the spaghetti and serve immediately.

Serves: 6
Calories per serving: 537

For additional recipes with clams, see

Avocado Seafood Salad in Chapter 12.
Boston Dip in Chapter 15.
Bouillabaisse in Chapter 10.
Clam Fritters in Chapter 15.
Consommé Belle Vue in Chapter 10.
Curried Clam Soup in Chapter 10.
Manhattan Clam Chowder in Chapter 10.
New England Clam Chowder in Chapter 10.
San Francisco Cioppino in Chapter 10.
Seafood Pizza in Chapter 12.
Squid and Clam Appetizer in Chapter 15.
Stuffed Clams Oregonati in Chapter 15.

Mussels

Marinated Mussels

48	mussels in shell
2	garlic cloves
2	oz. olive oil
10	chopped anchovy fillets

1½	cups dry white wine
1½	cups wine vinegar
2	tbsp. chopped parsley

Scrub and debeard the mussels. Brown the garlic cloves in oil. Discard the garlic. Add the mussels in shells, anchovy fillets, white wine, and vinegar. Cover the pot and steam until mussels open. Discard the shells and arrange the mussel meat in an earthenware dish. Sprinkle with parsley. Reduce cooking liquid by half. Pour over mussels and marinate for 2 to 3 days. Serve chilled as appetizers.

Serves: 6
Calories per serving: 108

Mussel Pasta Salad

3	lb. mussels
½	cup dry white wine
½	lb. cooked fettuccine
6	large diced celery stalks
2	tbsp. chopped parsley
1	tbsp. chopped basil
½	tsp. fresh chives
½	cup aioli sauce★
½	tsp. salt
¼	tsp. ground white pepper
2	large diced tomatoes

Scrub and debeard the mussels under cold running water, then drain. Combine the mussels and wine in a heavy medium sauce-pan. Cover and cook over high heat, shaking pan occasionally, until the mussels open. Remove the mussels using a slotted spoon (discard any that do not open).

Let the cooking liquid stand 15 minutes. Shell the mussels. Strain the cooking liquid through a fine sieve lined with dampened cheese-cloth. Gradually whisk the cooking liquid into aioli sauce.

Combine the fettuccine, celery, herbs, and aioli sauce in a bowl. Toss until blended. Season with salt and pepper. Gently stir in the mussels and tomatoes. Serve the salad at room temperature.

★See recipe for Aioli Sauce in Chapter 11.

Serves: 4
Calories per serving: 425

Mussels and Spaghetti

3	lb. mussels
1	bay leaf
6	peppercorns
2	whole cloves
¼	cup dry white wine
3	qt. water
½	tsp. salt
1	lb. spaghetti
4	tbsp. olive oil
1	tbsp. minced garlic
1	cup stewed tomatoes
1	tbsp. chopped basil
¼	tsp. salt
⅛	tsp. ground white pepper

Scrub and debeard the mussels under cold running water, then drain.

In a large saucepan or kettle add the mussels, bay leaf, peppercorns, cloves, and wine. Cover and bring to a boil. Cook over high heat 4 to 6 minutes until the mussels open. Strain the mussels and remove from shells. Save the broth.

Cook the spaghetti in boiling water for 6 minutes. Drain.

Heat the oil in a large skillet. Add the garlic and cook briefly, stirring, but do not brown. Add the tomatoes, broth, and spaghetti. Cook, stirring often, until the spaghetti is done. Add the mussels. Stir and heat for a moment. Add the basil and season with salt and pepper to taste. Toss and serve hot.

Serves: 6
Calories per serving: 359

Mussels in White Wine

3	qt. mussels
1	tbsp. chopped parsley
¾	cup dry white wine
2	oz. chopped shallots
2	oz. chopped onion

3	egg yolks
½	tbsp. lemon juice
½	tsp. salt
¼	tsp. ground white pepper

Scrub and debeard the mussels under cold running water, then drain. Combine the parsley, white wine, shallots, and onions. Bring to a boil. Steam the mussels in the boiling liquid until opened. Drain and save the cooking stock. Remove only the top shells of the mussels. Then arrange mussels in an ovenproof serving casserole. Strain the cooking liquid and reduce by half. Pour a little cooking liquid into the egg yolks, mix well, and stir into the remaining stock. Season to taste with salt, pepper, and lemon juice. Pour the sauce over the hot mussels. Serve immediately.

Serves: 6
Calories per serving: 108

Mussels Marinière

5	lb. mussels in shell
2	oz. butter
2	oz. chopped shallots
2	tbsp. chopped parsley
¼	tsp. ground white pepper
1½	cup dry white wine

Scrub and debeard the mussels under cold running water, then drain. Heat the butter in a kettle. Add the shallots and cook for 5 minutes. Add half of the parsley, pepper, wine, and mussels. Cover and steam until the mussels open. Serve in soup bowls with the strained cooking liquid. Sprinkle with the remaining chopped parsley.

Serves: 6
Calories per serving: 183

Paella of Mussels

3	qt. in shell mussels
2	oz. chopped onion
1	clove minced garlic
½	cup olive oil

1	cup rice
½	tsp. saffron
1	medium sliced red pepper

Scrub and debeard the mussels under cold running water, then drain. In a kettle containing a small amount of water, steam the mussels until they open. Drain them and retain the cooking liquid. Remove only the top shells of the mussels.

Brown the onion and garlic in oil. Stir in the rice and saffron.

Pour the strained cooking liquid (2½ cups, 6 dl) over the rice. Add the mussels in their half shells. Stir in the red pepper. Bake covered at 350°F (180°C) for 20 minutes.

Serve the paella in a preheated casserole dish.

Serves: 6
Calories per serving: 183

Tomatoes with Mussels

6	medium ripe tomatoes
¼	tsp. salt
⅛	tsp. ground white pepper
1½	lb. poached mussels
¾	cup mayonnaise
1	tsp. chopped dill
6	lemon wedges

Wash the tomatoes, cut off the tops, scoop out insides, and sprinkle cavities with salt and pepper.

Combine the mussels with mayonnaise and fill the tomatoes. Sprinkle with dill. Arrange the tomatoes on a serving platter. Garnish with lemon wedges.

Serves: 6
Calories per serving: 197

For additional mussel recipes, see

Bili-bi Soup in Chapter 10.
Bouillabaisse in Chapter 10.
Canapés cancalaise in Chapter 15.
Mussel Soup in Chapter 10.
Mussel Soup Trois Gros in Chapter 10.
Mussels in Mustard Sauce in Chapter 15.

Paella Valenciana in Chapter 12.
San Francisco Cioppino in Chapter 10.
Spanish Fish Stew in Chapter 10.

▬ Octopus

Octopus Salad

2	lb. dressed octopus★
3	cloves minced garlic
4	oz. diced celery
4	oz. pitted ripe olives
½	cup olive oil
½	cup lemon juice
¼	cup chopped parsley
1	tbsp. chopped basil

Blanch the octopus in salted boiling water. Drain and cook in boiling water for 20 to 30 minutes, or until tender. Drain and cool the octopus. Cut into bite-sized pieces, discarding any nonfleshy parts. Combine the remaining ingredients in a bowl. Mix in the octopus.

Refrigerate for an hour or more before serving.

★Select small octopus for best results.

Serves: 6
Calories per serving: 163

▬ Oysters

Fried Oysters

2	cups shucked oysters
2	eggs
1	tbsp. milk
2	cups fresh bread crumbs
½	tsp. dried tarragon
1	tsp. chopped chives
1	tsp. chopped parsley

¼	tsp. salt
⅛	tsp. ground white pepper
6	lemon wedges

Pat the oysters dry. Beat the eggs and milk. Combine the bread crumbs, tarragon, chives, and parsley.

Dip the oysters into the beaten egg mixture. Coat with bread crumbs and deep fry for 3 to 4 minutes until golden brown and crisp.

Drain and serve hot with lemon wedges and a cold sauce.

Serves: 6
Calories per serving: 213

Oysters Florentine

2	cups shucked oysters
10	oz. blanched spinach leaves
2	oz. butter
½	tsp. salt
1½	cups mornay sauce★
2	oz. grated swiss cheese
¼	tsp. ground white pepper

Poach the oysters in their own juice.

Sauté chopped spinach in butter. Season to taste with salt and pepper.

Put a small amount of the spinach in the oyster shells. Top with the oysters, one on each shell. Coat with mornay sauce. Sprinkle with cheese and brown in a hot oven.

Note: If oyster shells are not available, the dish can be prepared in individual casseroles.

★See recipe for mornay sauce in Chapter 11.

Serves: 6
Calories per serving: 180

Oysters Rockefeller

1	tbsp. chopped shallots
1	oz. chopped celery
1	oz. chopped fennel

1	tbsp. chopped parsley
6	oz. melted butter
2	cups watercress leaves
⅓	cup dry bread crumbs
2	oz. pernod
¼	tsp. salt
⅛	tsp. cayenne pepper
2	doz. on shell oysters
1	lb. rock salt

Sauté the shallots, celery, fennel, and parsley in half the butter. Add the watercress to wilt. Combine the mixture with the remaining butter, bread crumbs, and pernod, and blend in a food processor. Season to taste with salt and cayenne pepper.

Loosen the oysters in their half shells. Spoon a teaspoon of the mixture on top of each oyster.

Place the oysters on a bed of rock salt. Bake at 450°F (230°C) for 4 to 5 minutes. Serve hot.

Serves: 6
Calories per serving: 173

Oyster Omelette

Prepare the omelette in the usual fashion. Fold in oysters and velouté sauce, or use fried oysters.

Oysters on the Half Shell

See Chapter 5 for instructions on how to open oysters. Connoisseurs prefer to eat oysters raw on the half shell. They are usually served with brown bread, wine vinegar with chopped shallots, and lemon wedges.

Mushrooms Stuffed with Oysters

Cook medium mushroom caps in lemon juice and white wine. Poach shucked oysters in their own juice and a small amount of port wine. Drain mushrooms and oysters, reserving the liquids. Stuff mushrooms with oysters. Reduce both cooking liquids together. Add heavy cream and boil to a syrupy consistency. Spoon the sauce over the oysters. Sprinkle with parmesan cheese. Brown under a broiler and serve hot.

For additional oyster recipes, see

Angels on Horseback in Chapter 15.
Key West Fish Stew in Chapter 10.
Oyster Bisque Florentine in Chapter 10.
Oyster Stew in Chapter 10.
Oysters and Caviar in Chapter 14.
Oysters and Mustard Sauce in Chapter 15.
Seafood Fondue in Chapter 12.

══ Scallops

Grilled Scallops

24	sea scallops
½	tsp. salt
¼	tsp. ground black pepper
¼	cup olive oil
¼	tsp. red pepper flakes
1	tsp. dijon mustard
½	tsp. chopped thyme leaves
8	oz. zucchini

Preheat grill to high.

Clean the scallops and season with salt, pepper, half of the oil, pepper flakes, mustard, and thyme.

Trim off ends of the zucchini and cut crosswise into medium pieces. Add to the scallops and mix together.

Thread a piece of the zucchini on a skewer. Insert two scallops, and repeat the same process twice more. Continue with the remaining zucchini and scallops.

Place the skewers on the grill and broil on both sides until done. Brush with the remaining olive oil and serve hot.

Serves: 4
Calories per serving: 222

Scallop Ceviche

3	limes
1	lemon
1	lb. bay scallops

½	med. diced red pepper
½	med. diced yellow pepper
1	med. diced red onion
¼	tsp. crushed chili peppers
1	garlic clove
¼	cup chopped coriander
2	tbsp. olive oil

Cut the zest of one lime and the lemon in long strips. Squeeze the juice from the limes and lemon.

Combine all ingredients in a mixing bowl. Marinate at room temperature for an hour while stirring occasionally.

Remove the zest from the ceviche and season to taste with salt, if needed.

To serve, line a dish with lettuce leaves and spoon the ceviche onto leaves.

Serves: 8
Calories per serving: 105

Scallop and Oyster Ragoût

3	tbsp. butter
1	tsp. chopped shallots
12	large shelled scallops
12	shucked oysters
1	tbsp. whiskey
½	cup white wine
½	cup light cream
½	cup corn
½	tsp. salt
¼	tsp. ground white pepper
½	cup peeled tomatoes

Melt half the butter in a sauté pan. Stir in the shallots and scallops for a minute without browning. Add the oysters and sauté for 30 seconds.

Add the whiskey to the sauté pan and set alight. Allow flames to subside. Set the scallops and oysters aside. Save cooking liquid.

Add the white wine and reduce to half. Stir in the cream and reduce to half. Whisk the remaining butter into the sauce. Add the corn and heat through without boiling.

Arrange the scallops and oysters on warm plates. Pour the sauce over and garnish with chopped, seedless tomatoes.

★This recipe was created by the Canadian Culinary Olympic Team.

Serves: 4
Calories per serving: 237

Scallops Américaine

1½	lb. sea scallops
2	tbsp. olive oil
2	tbsp. chopped shallots
½	tsp. minced garlic
½	cup dry white wine
1	tsp. dry tarragon
½	cup bottled clam juice
2	cups crushed tomatoes
⅛	tsp. cayenne pepper
2	tbsp. butter
2	tbsp. cognac
½	salt
¼	tsp. white pepper

Clean the scallops. Heat half the oil in a saucepan and add the shallots and garlic. Cook over medium heat until wilted. Add the wine and tarragon. Cook until the wine is reduced by half. Add the clam juice, tomatoes, cayenne, salt, and pepper. Bring to a boil and allow to simmer for 5 minutes. Strain the sauce through a fine strainer. Discard the solids.

Heat the remaining oil and butter in a saucepan. Add the scallops and cook over brisk heat. Add the cognac. Cook for 30 seconds, then add the chopped tomatoes. Bring to a boil. Serve with sauce.

Serves: 4
Calories per serving: 339

Scallops au Gratin

1	cup dry white wine
1	tbsp. chopped shallots
2	lb. sea scallops
10	oz. duchesse potatoes
6	scallop shells
8	oz. button mushrooms
1	oz. butter
1½	cups velouté sauce
2	oz. grated parmesan

Combine the wine and shallots in a medium pan. Poach the cleaned scallops in the simmering liquid for a short time, 3 to 4 minutes. If the scallops are overcooked, they become rubbery and tough. Remove the scallops from the wine. Cut in halves and reserve.

Pipe the duchesse potato mix (mashed potato and egg yolk mixture) around the edges of scallop shells using a pastry bag fitted with a star tube. Sauté the cleaned mushrooms in butter until firm. Combine the scallops and mushrooms and divide among the shells. Reduce the wine and shallots to half and add the velouté sauce. Simmer to a medium consistency. Pour the sauce over the scallops. Sprinkle with cheese.

Brown the scallops under a hot broiler and serve hot.

Serves: 6
Calories per serving: 349

Scallops in Caviar Cream

1	cup dry white vermouth
2	tsp. dry tarragon
1½	lb. sea scallops
2	cups heavy cream
6	oz. black caviar
6	lemon wedges

Simmer the vermouth and tarragon in a saucepan. Add the cleaned scallops and poach until just opaque. Remove the scallops and set aside.

Boil the cooking liquid and reduce by half. At the same time, reduce cream to half in another pan. Combine the two liquids. Cool slightly. Add the caviar to the sauce.

Arrange the scallops in a serving dish or in scallop shells. Pour the sauce over scallops and serve warm or chilled. Garnish with lemon.

Serves: 6
Calories per serving: 347

Scallops Oriental

2	lb. scallops
¼	cup honey
¼	cup prepared mustard
1	tsp. curry powder
1	tsp. lemon juice

Rinse the scallops under cold water and place in a baking pan.
Combine the remaining ingredients. Brush the scallops with the sauce.
Broil until brown but do not overcook.

Serves: 8
Calories per serving: 155

Scallops Parisienne*

1	lb. duchesse potatoes
6	scallop shells
2	lb. cleaned scallops
½	cup fumet
½	cup dry white wine
1½	cups wine sauce

Using a pastry bag fitted with a star tube, pipe the duchesse potatoes (mashed potato and egg yolk mixture) around the edges of the scallop shells.
Poach the cleaned scallops in the fumet and white wine. Do not overcook. Cut the scallops in half if too large, and arrange in the shells.
Reduce the wine and fumet to a glaze, then combine with the white wine sauce (see recipe in Chapter 11). Mask the scallops with the sauce. Brown under a broiler. Serve hot.

*Add mushrooms to the recipe if desired. Poached fish can also be a good substitute for scallops. If substituting poached fish for scallops, name the recipe after the fish that is used.

Serves: 6
Calories per serving: 334

Szechuan Scallops

4	tsp. cornstarch
2	tbsp. soy sauce
2	tbsp. chicken broth
2	tbsp. sherry
2	tbsp. oil
¾	lb. sea scallops
1	clove minced garlic
1	tbsp. minced ginger
¼	lb. snow peas
¼	lb. sliced mushrooms
2	sliced scallions
2	cups chopped bok choy
4	dried hot peppers

Dissolve the cornstarch with the soy sauce. Mix with the chicken broth and sherry. Set aside. Preheat the oil in a wok. Add the scallops, garlic, and ginger. Stir for 2 minutes. Remove the scallops from the wok, leaving the cooking stock.

Add the snow peas, mushrooms, scallions, bok choy, and hot peppers to the cooking stock. Stir fry for 2 to 3 minutes. Add the scallops and soy mix. Cook and stir until thick. Serve at once.

Serves: 4
Calories per serving: 145

Broiled Scallops en Brochette

See Seafood Brochettes in Chapter 12.

Scallops Florentine

Prepare like Scallops au Gratin. Cover the bottom of scallop shells with creamed spinach.

Fried Scallops

Bread fresh scallops following procedure in Chapter 6 or purchase scallops frozen and breaded. Deep fry at 360°F (185°C) for 3 to 5 minutes. Serve with a cold sauce.

For additional scallop recipes, see

Snails

How to Cook Fresh Snails

With fresh snails, it is first necessary to deprive them of food for about a week. After this period of time, put them in small cages or baskets in a well aerated place, out of drafts. In a large container, mix 1 pound (450 g) of coarse salt with a small amount of flour. Stir the snails in this mixture and leave them for 2 hours. Then wash them thoroughly in cold running water to eliminate sliminess. Plunge them into boiling water for 5 minutes. Drain and cool. Remove the snail from its shell using a needle or toothpick.

Cooking: Boil the snails in half dry white wine and half water. Season with salt and crushed peppercorns. Add thyme, bay leaves, parsley stems, and 1 to 2 cloves. Simmer the snails for 2 to 3 hours or until tender. Allow to cool in the cooking liquid. Wash and boil the shells for a half hour in boiling water containing a small amount of baking soda. Carefully rinse the shells in running water. Drain and dry them. To save time and guarantee cleanliness, tiny round crocks, big enough to hold a large snail, are replacing real shells. They are favored in establishments serving a high volume of Escargots Bourguignonne or similar recipes. As a rule, snails are at their best when eaten with a special butter called escargot butter.

The following is an authentic recipe widely used in first class restaurants.

Escargots Bourguignonne

3	oz. butter
2	cloves garlic
1	peeled shallot
1	tbsp. sliced almonds
1	tbsp. pernod★
1	cup parsley sprigs
½	tsp. salt
¼	tsp. ground pepper
1	doz. snails
6	slices French bread

Peel and crush the garlic. Combine the butter, garlic, shallot, almonds, parsley, salt, and pepper in a food processor. Mix well for about 1 minute. Drain the snails. Place a small amount of butter mixture in the bottom of each shell. Insert a snail in each shell, then fill the shell with the butter mixture. Lay the shells, butter side up, on a snail pan. Heat in an oven at 375°F (190°C) until the butter is bubbling. Serve at once with French bread.

*Pernod is an aniseed-flavored aperitif.

Serves: 2
Calories per serving: 480

☰ Squid

Sautéed Squid Meunière

12	medium squid
4	oz. flour
1	tsp. salt
¼	tsp. ground white pepper
2	oz. oil
1	tbsp. chopped chives
4	oz. butter
1	tbsp. lemon juice
6	lemon slices

Clean the squid. Cut the mantle into medium pieces. Chop the tentacles into small pieces. Combine the flour, salt, and pepper. Roll the squid pieces in flour.

Heat the oil in a skillet and fry the squid pieces for 3 to 5 minutes. Turn and fry until done. Drain on paper. Sprinkle with chives.

Serve with lemon butter and garnish with lemon slices.

Serves: 6
Calories per serving: 281

Sautéed Squid

3	lb. squid
3	oz. butter
2	cloves minced garlic

2	tbsp. chopped parsley
1	tbsp. lemon juice
½	tsp. salt
¼	tsp. ground white pepper
2	cups cooked rice
1	cup tomato sauce

Clean the squid and cut into pieces.

Melt the butter in a sauté pan. Add the garlic and cook for a minute. Stir in the squid and the remaining ingredients and sauté for 1 to 2 minutes over a brisk fire. As soon as the squid is white and curls up, it is cooked. Do not overcook, as the squid will become tough. Serve hot with rice and tomato sauce.

Serves: 6
Calories per serving: 246

Squid Tempura

2	lb. squid
4	oz. flour
1	tbsp. cornstarch
1	tsp. baking powder
3	egg whites
½	cup water
2	oz. soy sauce
2	oz. sweet sherry
1	cup chicken broth
1	tsp. sugar

Clean the squid. Spread the squid mantles open and tenderize with a mallet. Cut in half across, then cut lengthwise into ¾-inch (2 cm) strips. Dredge in flour.

To make the batter, combine the flour, cornstarch, baking powder, slightly beaten egg whites, and water. Beat until smooth. Dip the pieces of squid into the batter and fry in a deep fryer at 375°F (190°C) for 3 to 5 minutes. To make the sauce, combine the soy sauce, sherry, chicken broth and sugar and heat over low fire.

Arrange the fried squid on a warm platter. Serve the sauce separately.

Serves: 6
Calories per serving: 246

Squid Siciliano

2	lb. squid
½	cup fresh bread crumbs
1	cup cooked rice
8	oz. ground beef
2	oz. butter
½	tsp. salt
¼	tsp. ground white pepper
1	clove minced garlic
2	oz. grated romano cheese
2	tbsp. chopped parsley
1	tsp. oregano
1½	cups tomato sauce

Clean the squid, leaving the mantle in one piece, and set aside. Sauté the bread crumbs, cooked rice, and ground beef in butter. Season with salt, pepper, and garlic. Cool the mixture. Add the cheese, parsley, and oregano.

Stuff the squid mantle with the filling. Place in a shallow baking dish and top with the tomato sauce. Bake at 350°F (180°C) for 20 to 30 minutes. Serve hot.

Serves: 6
Calories per serving: 362

Stuffed Squid Niçoise

2	lb. whole squid
3	oz. olive oil
1	large chopped onion
2	cloves minced garlic
1	lb. chopped tomatoes
1	cup white wine
1	bay leaf
½	tsp. salt
¼	tsp. ground white pepper

¾	tsp. saffron
1	cup cooked rice
2	oz. pitted black olives
1	tsp. chopped parsley

For this recipe, select small squid, clean, and prepare for stuffing. Cut the tentacles into small pieces and sauté in hot oil. Add the onion, cook until transparent, stirring frequently. Add the garlic, tomatoes, white wine, bay leaf, salt, pepper, and saffron. Cook over medium heat for 10 minutes. Combine the cooked rice with one quarter of the sauce. Stuff the squid mantles. Arrange in a baking dish. Pour the remaining sauce over the stuffed squid and bake at 400°F (200°C) for 10 to 15 minutes.

Transfer onto a serving platter. Sprinkle olives and parsley over the squid. Serve hot.

Serves: 6
Calories per serving: 247

Stuffed Squid Italienne

12	medium squid
¼	cup olive oil
2	oz. grated parmesan cheese
1	cup ricotta cheese
2	small anchovy fillets
2	beaten eggs
2	cups bread crumbs
¼	tsp. ground black pepper
2	cups tomato sauce

Clean the squid. Chop the tentacles finely. Heat the oil in a skillet, add the tentacles, and cook over low heat for 5 minutes. Transfer to a mixing bowl. Add the parmesan and ricotta cheese, anchovy fillets, eggs, and bread crumbs. Season with pepper. Stuff the squid cones with the stuffing. Arrange on a baking pan. Cover with the tomato sauce. Bake at 350°F (180°C) for 10 to 15 minutes. Serve on a preheated serving dish.

Serves: 6
Calories per serving: 360

Stuffed Squid Florentine

6	medium squid
½	cup olive oil
2	medium chopped onions
1	tsp. savory
¼	tsp. grated nutmeg
½	tsp. salt
3	egg yolks
½	cup grated parmesan
10	oz. cooked spinach
2	cups stewed tomatoes
1	cup dry white wine
½	tsp. saffron
½	tsp. salt
¼	tsp. ground white pepper
2	tbsp. chopped parsley

Clean the squid. Chop the tentacles finely. Heat half the oil in a skillet. Add the tentacles, half the onion, the savory, nutmeg, salt, and pepper. Cook over low heat for 10 minutes. Beat the egg yolks in a large bowl. Add the cheese, drained chopped spinach, and fried tentacles with seasonings. Stuff each squid cone with the filling.

For the sauce, heat the remaining oil in a large skillet. Add the remaining onions and cook over low heat for 5 minutes. Arrange the stuffed squid over the onions. Add the tomatoes, wine, saffron, salt and pepper. Cover and simmer for 20 to 25 minutes. Transfer the squid onto a serving platter. Reduce sauce to medium-thick consistency. Pour the sauce over squid. Sprinkle with parsley.

Serves: 6
Calories per serving: 266

For additional squid recipes, see

Spanish Fish Stew in Chapter 10.
Squid and Clam Appetizer in Chapter 15.

14

Freshwater Fish Recipes

This chapter contains recipes for the following:

Buffalofish
Carp
Catfish
Caviar
Chub
Freshwater Sheepshead
Frogs' Legs
Lake Herring
Lake Trout
Pike
Sturgeon
Trout
Whitefish
Yellow Perch

Buffalofish

All the preparations for Carp are applicable to Buffalofish.

Carp

Chinese Fried Fish

4	lb. dressed carp
¼	cup soy sauce
¼	cup rice wine
½	tsp. salt
4	slices ginger
1	medium chopped scallion
¼	cup chicken stock

| 1 | oz. dark brown sugar |
| 1 | qt. peanut oil |

If desired, substitute carp with snapper or sea bass.

Fillet, bone, and skin the fish. Cut crosswise into ½-inch (1.5 cm) slices. Combine the soy sauce, rice wine, salt, ginger root, and scallions, and marinate the fish for 3 to 4 hours. Drain the fish.

Simmer the marinade with the stock and sugar. Fry the fish in hot oil at 375°F (190°C) for 5 minutes, or until crisp. Serve hot. Serve the sauce separately.

Serves: 6
Calories per serving: 181

Deviled Carp

2	lb. skinned carp fillets
3	oz. chili sauce
3	oz. catsup
1	tbsp. lemon juice
2	tsp. horseradish
1	tsp. worcestershire

Place the fish in a shallow greased baking dish. Mix the remaining ingredients together. Spread over the fish. Bake 20 to 25 minutes at 350°F (180°C).

Serve on a preheated platter.

Serves: 6
Calories per serving: 149

Poached Carp

1	4 lb. dressed carp
	No. 2 court bouillon
1	small bunch parsley
1	pound boiled potatoes
¾	cup heavy cream
2	oz. horseradish
2	lemon wedges

Poach the carp in No. 2 court bouillon. Drain and skin the fish. Arrange on a serving platter. Garnish with parsley, potatoes, and lemon wedges.

Whip the heavy cream. Fold in the horseradish. Season with salt and pepper to taste. Serve the sauce separately.

Serves: 6
Calories per serving: 259

Hungarian Carp

2	lb. carp fillets
4	oz. chopped onions
2	oz. oil
1	tsp. paprika
1	cup fish fumet
3	oz. diced green peppers
8	oz. chopped tomatoes

Cut the fillets into 5-oz. portions. Season with salt and pepper. Brown the onions in oil. Sprinkle with paprika. Stir in the fumet, green peppers, and tomatoes. Arrange the fish in shallow baking pan. Pour the fumet and vegetables over. Bake at 350°F (180°C) for 20 minutes. Baste occasionally. Serve hot on a warm platter.

Serves: 6
Calories per serving: 240

Carp Gefilte Fish

See Gefilte Fish in Chapter 14.

▬ Catfish

Arkansas Crispy Catfish

6	8-oz. catfish fillets
1	tsp. salt

¼	tsp. ground white pepper
4	oz. flour
2	oz. cornmeal
1	tsp. paprika
½	cup evaporated milk
12	bacon slices

If frozen, thaw the fillets. Clean, wash, and dry the fillets. Season with salt and pepper.

Combine the flour, cornmeal, and paprika. Dip the fish in milk and roll in the flour mixture. Fry the bacon in a heavy pan until crisp. Remove the bacon. Fry the fish in the hot bacon fat until the fish is crisp on both sides and flakes easily. Drain on absorbent paper.

Arrange on a preheated serving platter. Serve with the bacon.

Serves: 6
Calories per serving: 504

Broiled Sesame Catfish

6	8-oz. catfish fillets
½	cup oil
2	oz. sesame seeds
2	oz. lemon juice
1	tsp. salt
¼	tsp. ground pepper
1	small bunch parsley

If frozen, thaw the fillets. Clean, wash, and dry the fillets. Place on a hinged wire grill.

Combine the remaining ingredients and baste the fish with the sauce. Broil for 5 minutes on each side, or until the fish flakes easily when tested with a fork. Arrange on a serving platter and garnish with parsley.

Serves: 6
Calories per serving: 404

Cajun Catfish

6	8 oz. dressed catfish fillets
½	cup tomato sauce
¼	tsp. garlic salt
½	tsp. onion powder
1	tbsp. chopped parsley
2	oz. oil
2	oz. parmesan cheese

If frozen, thaw the fillets. Clean, wash, and dry the fillets. Combine the tomato sauce, garlic salt, onion powder, parsley, and oil. Brush the fish on both sides with the sauce. Place on a well-greased baking pan and brush with the remaining sauce. Sprinkle with cheese.

Bake at 350°F (130°C) for 20 to 25 minutes. Brown under broiler.

Arrange on a serving platter and serve hot.

Serves: 6
Calories per serving: 350

Kansas Fried Fish

6	8-oz. catfish fillets
1	egg
2	oz. milk
½	tsp. salt
¼	tsp. ground white pepper
1	oz. lemon juice
3	oz. flour
1	cup dry bread crumbs
1½	cup tartar sauce

If frozen, thaw the fillets. Clean, wash, and dry the fillets. Combine the eggs and milk. Mix well. Season the fillets with salt, pepper, and lemon juice. Roll the fillets in flour, dip in the egg mixture, and coat with bread crumbs.

Deep fry at 350°F (180°C) for 4 to 5 minutes. Drain well and serve with tartar sauce.

Serves: 6
Calories per serving: 628

Caviar

Fine caviar should be eaten au naturel, with nothing more than a few drops of lemon juice and a little ground black pepper. Members of the very exclusive Beluga Club consider it a sacrilege to sprinkle caviar with chopped onions, egg white, or egg yolks, a practice that is de rigueur in the most expensive restaurants in the United States. The ultimate arbiters of the Beluga Club suggest that if you must have an accompaniment with caviar, the only thing permissible is a baked potato. Indeed, a freshly baked red bliss potato split in half, seasoned with salt and freshly ground pepper, and topped with sour cream (only if you must have it) makes the precious caviar a delightful experience. Another method favored by creative gourmets is to serve a heaping teaspoon of Beluga over a soft boiled egg with the top portion of the shell removed. Gently blend the caviar with the egg and savor it with buttered toast.

The Revival of American Caviar

The American caviar industry is growing and its future looks bright.

Indeed, caviar is not a new industry in the United States. At one point, caviar production exceeded that of Russia. At the turn of the century, 100,000 pounds a year were gathered from Atlantic sturgeons spawning in the Hudson and Delaware rivers and Pacific sturgeons in the Sacramento and Columbia rivers. However most of this caviar was enjoyed in Europe, for the American palate had not yet developed a taste for such sophisticated treats (in New York, saloonkeepers put out bowls of free caviar for the same reason that they now give peanuts away—to make their customers thirsty). Eventually, however, dam-building, pollution, and overfishing took their toll, and the sturgeon went the way of so many other fish, practically becoming extinct in American waters. By the end of World War I, the Caspian Sea was the center of worldwide caviar production.

Politics and the high price of foreign caviar prompted a come back of American caviar, which is now becoming world-class again. The American variety, in most abundance, is a Sevruga grade. Today, American caviar has replaced the void of Iranian caviar caused by the Iranian revolution and the resulting United States boycott of Iranian goods. American sturgeon caviar is also exported to England, West Germany, and France.

Fresh Domestic Caviar

Sturgeon: Sturgeon no longer has to be imported to be good. The American roe is primarily of the Sevruga grade, a small sized egg produced by the fisheries of the Southern Atlantic Seaboard states. The catch runs November through May, offering a continuous supply of fresh caviar to the market. American sturgeon caviar cost about half the price of the equivalent imported grade.

Paddlefish: The roe of this large prehistoric fish with a snout like a spatula is competing directly with the Russian Sevruga. The less salty Tennessee caviar is also gaining acceptance on the American market and can easily pass for Sevruga. In the forseeable future, the paddlefish could be stocked in public lakes and raised commercially for sale of their meat as well as their roe.

Keta Salmon: Keta salmon caviar is the whole grain roe from the Alaskan Chum salmon, a medium to large orange egg of superior taste and quality.

This is the same species that is caught by the Russians in the Siberian Sea. The domestic Keta salmon caviar is prepared in the traditional Russian style.

Golden Whitefish: The natural golden color and small crisp grain of Whitefish caviar is favored for all recipes, garnishings, salads, etc. The Whitefish is native of the Great Lakes of North America. The original processing of this caviar came from Sweden.

Black Lumpfish caviar: The primary world source for Lumpfish caviar is from the cold clear waters surrounding Iceland in the North Atlantic. The roe of the Lumpfish is processed into caviar much in the same manner as Salmon and Whitefish caviar. Lumpfish caviar is the largest selling type of caviar in the world due to its availability and affordable price.

The roe is colored artificially black or red to resemble genuine caviar.

Although some of the best American caviar is prepared in the same exact way as the Iranian and the Russian, only a few standards exist. The largely unregulated caviar business in the United States is a shadowy world market of deceit, secrecy, and all manner of accusations among competitors. As more Americans develop a taste for domestic caviar, it is expected that the quality will rise to meet the highest standards.

Oysters and Caviar

30	scrubbed oysters
4	oz. butter
1	cup dry white wine
3	chopped shallots
½	tsp. salt
¼	tsp. ground white pepper
1	cup heavy cream
12	small clean leek whites
6	oz. beluga caviar

Use Belon or blue-point oysters. Open the oysters and reserve bottom shells. Melt the butter in a saucepan. Add the wine, oysters, oyster juice, shallots, salt, and pepper. Boil for 2 minutes. Strain. Reserve the oysters.

Reduce the cooking liquid by half. Add one half of the heavy cream, and continue cooking to thicken the liquid. Cut the leeks into julienne. Blanch and cook in the remaining cream.

Place an oyster in each shell. Spoon some of the leek mixture over each oyster. Top with the reduced sauce. Spoon caviar over each oyster just before serving.

Serves: 6
Calories per serving: 301

For additional caviar recipes, see

Caviar Butter in Chapter 15.
Caviar Canapés in Chapter 15.
Caviar Cigarettes in Chapter 15.
Golden Caviar Consommé in Chapter 10.
Mousse of Salmon & Trout in Chapter 9.
Moscovite Butter in Chapter 15.
Oysters and Caviar in Chapter 14.
Pate of Trout and Caviar in Chapter 14.
Scallops in Caviar Cream in Chapter 13.
Smoked Trout Moscovite in Chapter 14.
Tartelettes Árkangel in Chapter 15.

Chub *(Bluefin, Blackfin, Tullibee)*

Chub can be prepared meunière, grilled with maître d'hôtel butter, or fried with sauce rémoulade or tartar sauce.

Freshwater Sheepshead *(Fresh Water Drum, White Perch, Gasperou, Gray Bass)*

Sheepshead can be prepared following the recipes for Red Snapper in Chapter 12.

Frogs' Legs

Batter-Fried Frogs' Legs

2	doz. small frogs' legs
2	oz. lemon juice
1	tbsp. chopped parsley
½	tsp. salt
¼	tsp. pepper
½	tsp. minced garlic
1	recipe beer batter★
2	oz. flour
1½	cups tomato sauce

Trim and wash the frogs' legs, and marinate in the lemon juice, parsley, salt, pepper, and garlic. Mix batter ingredients. Fold in the egg whites at last minute. Flour the frogs' legs, dip into the batter, and deep fry at 350°F (180°C) until golden brown. Arrange on a preheated serving platter. Serve with tomato sauce.

*See recipe for Beer Batter in Chapter 7.

Serves: 6
Calories per serving: 480

Frogs' Legs Paprika

2	doz. small frogs' legs
2	oz. chopped onion
3	oz. butter
1	tsp. paprika
4	oz. canned tomatoes
½	tsp. salt
¼	tsp. ground white pepper
1	tbsp. flour
5	oz. heavy cream

Trim and clean the frogs' legs.

Saute the onion in butter until tender. Sprinkle with paprika, add the chopped, peeled tomatoes, and cook for 10 minutes. Season the frogs' legs with salt and pepper, and add to the tomato mixture. Cook for 5 minutes. Stir the flour into heavy cream to blend and then add to the sauce. Allow to simmer for 3 to 4 minutes.

Arrange the frogs' legs on a serving platter. Cover with sauce and serve immediately.

Serves: 6
Calories per serving: 285

Frogs' Legs Poulette

12	medium dressed frogs' legs
½	tsp. salt
¼	tsp. ground white pepper
3	oz. sliced mushrooms
1	tbsp. chopped shallots
¾	cup dry white wine
¾	cup heavy cream

2	oz. butter
1	oz. flour
1	tbsp. lemon juice
1	tbsp. chopped parsley

Trim and wash the frogs' legs. Season with salt and pepper. Sprinkle the mushrooms and shallots over a baking pan large enough to fit the frogs' legs. Arrange the frogs' legs on top of the mushrooms and shallots.

Add wine and heavy cream to cover. Cover the pan and poach for 10 minutes or until the frogs' legs are done. Transfer the frogs' legs to a serving platter.

Bring the sauce to a boil and reduce to half. Blend the butter and flour and drop small dots into boiling sauce while stirring with a whip to thicken. Season with lemon juice, stir in the parsley, and pour over frogs' legs.

Serves: 6
Calories per serving: 226

Frogs' Legs Sautéed with Pecans

Sauté frogs' legs meunière (see cooking technique in Chapter 6). Garnish with pecan nuts.

Lake Herring (Cisco, Blueback)

Lake Herring can be prepared in the same manner as Whitefish.

Lake Trout (Mackinaw, Toque, Lonque)

Lake Trout Mexicaine

5	lb. dressed lake trout
2	gal. No. 2 court bouillon
3	small ripe avocados
1	oz. lemon juice
6	oz. crabmeat
¾	cup cocktail sauce
6	cherry tomatoes

1	small bunch parsley
6	oz. sauce antiboise

Poach the lake trout in court bouillon following directions for the poaching technique in Chapter 6. Cut the avocados in half lengthwise and remove the stones. Peel and sprinkle with lemon juice. Combine the crabmeat with cocktail sauce, and garnish with avocado halves. Lift the cool poached fish from the court bouillon, drain, and partly skin.

Arrange on a serving platter. Garnish with the avocados, cherry tomatoes, and parsley sprigs. Serve the sauce antiboise separately.

Serves: 6
Calories per serving: 562

Lake Trout can be prepared following the methods described for salmon and trout.

Pike *(Lake Pickerel, Grass Pike)*

Baked Pike

2	oz. butter
½	tsp. salt
1	tbsp. minced shallots
2	oz. diced carrots
2	lb. pike fillets
1	tbsp. minced parsley
1	cup fish stock
½	cup dry white wine
½	cup sour cream
1	beaten egg
2	oz. grated swiss cheese

Butter a baking dish with half the butter. Sprinkle the salt, shallots, carrots, and parsley over bottom. Place the fish in one layer over the vegetables and dot with the remaining butter. Add stock and wine, cover with foil, and bake at 350°F (130°C) for 10 to 15 minutes. Beat the egg and sour cream together and spoon over the fish. Sprinkle with cheese. Brown under a broiler and serve with the cooking stock.

Serves: 6
Calories per serving: 312

Pike Quenelles

3	oz. butter
4	oz. flour
2	cups scalded milk
6	egg yolks
½	tsp. salt
¼	tsp. ground white pepper
⅛	tsp. ground nutmeg
1	lb. pike fillet
1	lb. beef suet
2	egg whites
1	cup nantua sauce

Melt the butter, add flour, and mix. Pour in the milk and stir well to make a paste. Remove from heat and add the egg yolks. Season with the salt, pepper, and nutmeg. Set aside to cool. Finely grind the boneless and skinless pike fillet with the suet. Add the flour panada, and gradually mix in the egg whites. The mixture should remain cold and thick.

Shape oval dumplings with two tablespoons and drop in boiling salted water. Simmer for 10 to 12 minutes. Drain the quenelles. Serve with nantua sauce or other appropriate fish sauce.

Serves: 8
Calories per serving: 505

Pickerel Meunière

Follow recipe for Dover Sole Meunière in Chapter 12.

Poached Pike with White Butter

Poach the whole clean pike in court bouillon No. 2, following the poaching cooking technique in Chapter 6. Serve with white butter (see Chapter 11).

Quenelles of Pike Nantua

Prepare a pike quenelle forcemeat with panada, following the recipe in Chapter 9. Poach the quenelles in water. Serve with nantua sauce (see Chapter 11).

Quenelles of Pike Sauce Normande

Prepare quenelles as in previous recipe. Serve with sauce Normande (see Chapter 11).

For additional pike recipes see

Matelote Illhaeusern in Chapter 10.
Fish Canapés in Chapter 15.

Sturgeon

Sturgeon in White Wine

2	lb. sturgeon fillets
½	tsp. salt
¼	tsp. ground white pepper
5	oz. diced bacon
1½	cup dry white wine
1	oz. butter
6	oz. white wine sauce
½	cup sour cream

Skin the sturgeon fillets and cut into equal portions. Season with salt and pepper. Arrange the fillets on a buttered baking pan. Sprinkle the bacon pieces over fillets. Pour the wine in bottom of pan. Bake at 360°F (185°C) for 10 to 15 minutes, or until the bacon is crisp and the fish is flaky. Arrange the fish on a preheated platter.

Reduce the cooking stock to a glaze. Add to the white wine sauce. Stir in the sour cream. Pour sauce over fish. Serve hot.

Serves: 6
Calories per serving: 330

Trout (Rainbow, Steelhead)

Rainbow Trout Escabeche

6	10-oz. dressed trouts
1	tsp. salt

½	tsp. ground black pepper
1	cup olive oil
2	oz. sliced pimentos
8	oz. sliced onion
1	cup wine vinegar
1	tsp. black peppercorns
2	bay leaves

Season the dressed whole trouts with salt and pepper. Heat the oil in a large skillet and fry the fish for 3 minutes on each side until brown. Arrange the fish in one layer in a shallow pan and allow to cool. Add the pimentos and onion to the oil, cook over low heat for 5 minutes and allow to cool. Combine the vinegar, peppercorns, and bay leaves. Mix into the cooled oil and vegetables.

Heat up the marinade and pour over the fish.

Cool and refrigerate 2 to 3 days before using. The fish will keep for a week and are usually served cold as an entree or hors d'oeuvres.

Serves: 6
Calories per serving: 215

Broiled Trout Tournedos

2	lb. trout fillets
1	tsp. salt
¼	tsp. pepper
2	oz. oil
1½	cups sauce choron★

Flatten the fillets. Season with salt and pepper. Cut lengthwise and roll each piece to resemble a fillet mignon. Secure with toothpicks. Brush with oil. Broil on a grill until fully cooked. Serve on a warm platter. Garnish with parsley. Coat the fish with hot sauce choron.

★Sauce choron is derived from béarnaise with 1½ tsp. of tomato paste added.

Serves: 6
Calories per serving: 632

Fillet of Trout Maltaise

3	medium tomatoes
1	tbsp. anchovy butter*
1	tbsp. chopped tarragon
1	tsp. chopped mint
1	tbsp. chopped parsley
1	tbsp. chopped basil
½	tsp. salt
¼	tsp. ground white pepper
1	tbsp. lemon juice
2	lb. trout fillets

Peel and slice tomatoes and set aside.

Mix the anchovy butter with the tarragon, mint, parsley, and basil. Season with salt, pepper, and lemon juice. Spread the anchovy mix over each boneless trout fillet.

Place sliced tomatoes on top of trout fillets. Arrange in a baking dish. Bake at 350°F (180°C) for 10 to 15 minutes. Serve hot on a platter.

*Anchovy butter: Blend 6 anchovy fillets with 2 oz. sweet butter and mix into a paste.

Serves: 6
Calories per serving: 205

Fried Trout Fillets

6	8-oz. boneless trout
½	tsp. salt
¼	tsp. ground white pepper
3	oz. flour
3	eggs
8	oz. bread crumbs
6	lemon wedges
1½	cups tartar sauce

Butterfly the trout.

Season the trout with salt and pepper. Cover with flour, dip in the beaten eggs, and coat with breadcrumbs. Deep fry at 360°F (185°C) until crisp.

Arrange on a serving platter. Garnish with fried parsley and lemon wedges. Serve with tartar sauce.

Serves: 6
Calories per serving: 677

Pâté of Trout and Caviar

1	lb. trout fillets
3½	oz. fresh bread crumbs
1	cup heavy cream
½	tsp. salt
¼	tsp. ground pepper
½	oz. chopped truffles
1	qt. aspic jelly
6	oz. salmon caviar
6	artichoke bottoms
8	oz. salmon mousse

Puree the boneless, skinless trout fillets in a food processor. Add the bread crumbs and heavy cream to obtain a thick paste. Season with salt and pepper. Fold in the truffles.

Butter a suitable pâté mold. Spoon the mixture into the mold. Cover with parchment paper. Bake in a waterbath at 350°F (180°C) for about 35 to 40 minutes. Cool in mold and turn onto a rack.

Glaze the trout fillets with the cold aspic jelly and spread salmon caviar on top. Slice the pâté leaving a piece for display. Arrange the slices on a cold serving platter. Garnish with the un-cut piece. Stuff the artichoke bottoms with the salmon mousse. Place around the platter. Decorate with chopped aspic jelly.

Serves: 6
Calories per serving: 400

Paupiettes of Trout

12	3 oz. trout fillets
½	tsp. salt
¼	tsp. pepper
1	tbsp. lemon juice
6	oz. Maître d'hôtel butter
4	oz. lemon butter

Flatten the boneless trout fillets. Season with salt and pepper and lemon juice. Spread a small amount of Maître d'hôtel Butter over each fillet and roll. Secure with toothpicks. Sauté in lemon butter until cooked.

Transfer to a warm serving platter and serve hot.

Serves: 6
Calories per serving: 340

Smoked Trout Moscovite

12	smoked trout fillets
6	stuffed deviled eggs
4	oz. caviar
8	oz. cucumber salad
1	cup aspic jelly
½	cup horseradish

Bone and skin the trout fillets. Arrange on a serving platter. Garnish with deviled eggs, topped with caviar, alternated with cucumber salad and chopped aspic jelly. Serve the horseradish separately.

Serves: 6
Calories per serving: 360

Stuffed Trout Bretonne

6	whole trouts
½	tsp. salt
¼	tsp. ground white pepper
10	oz. fish forcemeat★
4	oz. butter
1½	cups bretonne★ sauce

Clean and bone the trout. Season with salt and pepper. Stuff trout with fish forcemeat; secure stuffing by inserting skewers in the belly flaps. Brown trout in butter, then bake at 350°F (180°C) for 15 minutes or until forcemeat is done.

Skin both sides of the trout and remove skewers. Arrange trouts on serving platter. Pour hot sauce over.

★See recipes for bretonne sauce in Chapter 11 and quenelles and mousses (Chapter 9) for fish forcemeat.

Serves: 6
Calories per serving: 354

Trout au Bleu

6	8 oz. live trouts
1	gal. No. 2 court bouillon
1	bunch parsley
6	oz. sauce mousseline

Follow directions for the au bleu cooking technique in Chapter 6.

Arrange trout on a serving platter. Garnish with parsley. Serve with sauce mousseline.

Serves: 6
Calories per serving: 282

Trout Fernand Point*

2	oz. chopped carrots
2	oz. chopped celery
2	tbsp. chopped truffles
2	oz. chopped mushrooms
1	oz. flour
5	egg yolks
6	8-oz. dressed trout
2	oz. melted butter
2	oz. sliced carrots
2	oz. sliced onion
2	cups port wine
1½	cups heavy cream
2	oz. butter
2	oz. flour

Blanch the chopped carrots and celery. Drain.

Butter the bottom of a saucepan. Add the carrots, celery, truffles, and mushrooms. Cook until moisture disappears. Add flour. Stir for a minute. Blend in the egg yolks away from the heat. Season with salt and pepper. Allow to cool. Bone trout and stuff with the mixture. Pour butter in a baking pan. Add sliced carrots and onion. Place trout on top. Add wine. Bake covered at 350°F (155°C) for 30 minutes. Skin trout. Arrange on a serving platter. Strain fish fumet into a saucepan. Add cream. Bring to a boil.

Combine butter and flour, then whip into the fumet to make a medium-thick sauce. Pour sauce over trout. Serve hot.

*If desired, garnish with shrimp.

Serves: 6
Calories per serving: 480

Trout with Chablis Wine

6	8-oz. dressed trout
6	oz. butter
½	tsp. salt
¼	tsp. ground white pepper
1	oz. chopped shallots
5	oz. chablis wine
1½	cups heavy cream
5	oz. cream sauce
6	medium cooked mushroom caps
6	fleurons

Arrange the cleaned whole trout on a buttered baking pan. Season with salt and pepper. Sprinkle with shallots. Pour wine over the fish. Cover with foil. Bake at 375°F (190°C) for 15 to 20 minutes, until trout are cooked. Skin both sides of trout and arrange on a serving platter. Reduce the cooking liquid to half. Add the heavy cream and cream sauce. Bring to a boil. Reduce to medium consistency. Strain the sauce over the trout. Top with cooked mushrooms. Garnish with fleurons. Serve hot.

Serves: 6
Calories per serving: 391

Fillet of Trout Grenobloise

See recipe for Mullet Grenobloise in Chapter 12.

Fillet of Trout Meunière

See recipe for Dover Sole Meunière in Chapter 12.

Poached Fillets of Trout Hollandaise

Poach boneless fillets of trout in court bouillon No. 2. Serve with hollandaise and parsleyed potatoes.

Trout Amandine

Sauté Trout Meunière. Garnish with toasted sliced almonds.

Trout Doria

Sauté meunière and serve with olive-shaped stewed cucumbers.

Trout Coulibiac

See recipe for Salmon Coulibiac in Chapter 12.

Mousseline of Idaho Trout Royale

See recipe for Salmon Mousseline Royale in Chapter 12.

The following are cold trout recipes.

au Bleu

Cook according to the technique au bleu in Chapter 6. Serve cold with a cold sauce.

Mousse of Trout Ondine

Prepare a standard salmon mousse. Mix in a few tiny cooked shrimp. Spoon into a fish mold decorated with aspic. Chill and unmold on a platter. Decorate with shrimp and aspic jelly.

Stuffed Trout Mongolfier

Stuff whole trout with fish forcemeat (see recipe for Stuffed Trout Bretonne in this chapter). Poach in fish fumet. Cool and skin. Coat with mayonnaise mixed with cold liquid aspic jelly and tomato puree. Serve with tomato salad and Russian salad.

For additional trout recipes, see

Canapés of trout Anne-Lise in Chapter 15.
Mousse of Salmon and Trout in Chapter 9.

Whitefish

Cold Whitefish Andalouse

4	lb. dressed whitefish
	No. 2 court bouillon
2	cucumbers
1	cup liquid aspic
6	stuffed eggs
1½	cups sauce andalouse

Wash and drain the whole fish.

Tie fish on the rack of a fish poacher (poissonnière) in an upright position. Secure with cheesecloth to hold fish firmly. Poach in court bouillon, following directions for poaching technique in Chapter 6. When done, lift the fish from court bouillon and skin. To decorate, slice whole cucumbers lengthwise, then crosswise into paper-thin slices. Arrange slices on fish, starting from the tail, overlapping each slice to resemble fish scales. Glaze fish with cold liquid aspic. Place fish on a serving platter. Garnish with stuffed eggs and serve cold. Serve andalouse sauce separately.

Serves: 6
Calories per serving: 532

Gefilte Fish

2	lb. whitefish fillets
8	oz. chopped onion
2	eggs
1	tbsp. matzo meal
1	tsp. salt
¼	tsp. ground white pepper
1	qt. fish stock
1	cup grated carrot
1	tbsp. grated horseradish

Skin, bone, and grind the fish fillets. Add the chopped onions, eggs, matzo meal, salt, and pepper, and mix well. Shape the mixture into dumplings using about 3 oz. (85 g) of mixture for each dumpling.

Simmer in stock for 1 to 1½ hours. Chill dumplings in the stock. Serve with grated raw carrots and horseradish.

Serves: 6
Calories per serving: 271

Whitefish Amandine

6	8-oz. whitefish fillets
2	oz. melted butter
½	tsp. salt
¼	tsp. paprika
3	oz. butter
2	oz. sliced almonds
1	oz. lemon juice
1	tbsp. chopped parsley

Arrange the whitefish fillets on a buttered baking pan. Brush with melted butter and broil without turning, 3 to 4 inches (8 to 10 cm) from source of heat, until fillets are flaky. Transfer to a heated serving platter. Season with salt and paprika. Brown almonds in butter over low heat. Stir in the lemon juice. Spoon over the fish. Sprinkle with parsley.

Serves: 6
Calories per serving: 390

Poached Whitefish Mousseline

Poach whole whitefish in court bouillon No. 2, following poaching technique in Chapter 6. Serve with sauce mousseline.

Note: All methods of trout preparation are applicable to whitefish.

Yellow Perch

Fillets of Perch Amandine

See directions for Trout Amandine in this chapter.

Fillets of Perch Hollandaise

Poach in court bouillon No. 2. Serve with hollandaise.

For additional perch recipes, see

Matelote Illhaeusern in Chapter 10.
Ocean Perch in Chapter 12.

CHAPTER 15

Nibbling on Seafood

CANAPÉS

Canapés, also called zakuski, are very popular tidbits consumed as appetizers at cocktail parties or before meals. Their presentation is left to the imagination of the preparer. Essentially dinner hors d'oeuvres, their presentation and preparation form the basis for the guests' expectations of dinner.

Canapés do not have to be made from costly foods like caviar, foie gras, or smoked salmon, unless specifically requested. In that case, the overall cost of the meal obviously is expected to be higher. Excellent canapés can be created easily from a large variety of seafood that are canned, pickled, or smoked. Many leftover poached fish and shellfish can also be used. Spreads can be made from leftover tuna, salmon, sardines, etc. Individual small mousses also heighten the presentation of canapé trays.

The base of a canapé can range from a plain paper-thin toast to sophisticated rice or seaweed crackers. There are also various imported wafers and wheat crackers available in all sizes and shapes. Bread, plain or toasted, is also a popular base for canapés. A wide selection of breads is available commercially; white, whole wheat, rye, and pumpernickel are used most often. The recent emphasis on eating healthy and wholesome food has popularized such breads as wheat germ, cracked wheat, oatmeal, brown bread, and granola, just to name a few. These may be used for canapés.

Anchovy Canapés

Mask rectangular canapés with anchovy butter. Garnish with anchovy fillets and chopped egg mimosa.

Caviar Canapés

Spread canapés with caviar butter. Top with a layer of caviar and a squeeze of lemon juice.

425

Caviar Cigarettes

Roll out thin slices of bread. Mix caviar and sour cream and spread over bread. Roll in the shape of cigarettes and cut to desired size.

Shrimp Canapés

Mix canapés with shrimp butter. Garnish with whole, tiny cooked shrimp or diced leftover shrimp. Top with a touch of mayonnaise or cocktail sauce.

Canapés Danoise

Spread rye canapés with horseradish butter. Top with smoked salmon and marinated herring slices.

Lobster Canapés

Butter round canapés with lobster butter. Top with sliced lobster and sprinkle with egg mimosa.

Fish Canapés

Use any poached fish (bass, flounder, sole, pike, salmon, snapper, or grouper). Spread canapés with mayonnaise, and top with slices of fish or fish salad. Spoon some aspic jelly over and garnish with capers or small diced lemon pieces.

Canapés Cancalaise

Mask canapés with tunafish butter. Top with poached or smoked mussels.

Canapés of Smoked Salmon

Mask rectangular canapés with mayonnaise or horseradish butter. Top with rolled slices of smoked salmon. Or, spread cream cheese over salmon slices and roll and place on canapés.

Sardine Canapés

Spread triangular canapés with sardine butter. Top with bristling boneless sardines. Pipe anchovy butter over sardines to decorate.

Canapés of Lobster Coral

Spread canapés with lobster cheese. Top with lobster butter. Decorate with piped mayonnaise.

Canapés of Trout Anne-Lise

Mask round canapés with anchovy butter. Top with slices of poached paupiettes of trout. Top with a light mayonnaise and chopped parsley.

Canapés Paulette

Mask round canapés with anchovy butter. Sprinkle half with chopped egg whites and half with chopped egg yolks. Lay a row of tiny shrimp between whites and yolks.

Lobster or Shrimp Bouchées

Fill bouchées (see puff pastry in Chapter 7) with mousse of lobster, shrimp, or other seafood.

Shrimp Puffs

Prepare profiteroles with cream puff dough (see Chapter 7). Fill with creamed diced shrimp.

Tartelettes Arkangel

Cover the bottom of small cooked tartlet shells (see Chapter 7) with caviar and fill to level with puree of smoked salmon. Top with a piece of anchovy fillet.

Angels on Horseback

8	bacon slices
2	doz. shucked oysters
1	tbsp. chopped parsley
¼	tsp. paprika

Cut bacon slices in thirds. Drain oysters. Sprinkle with parsley and paprika. Wrap bacon slices around oysters and secure with a toothpick. Place oysters on a sheet pan. Broil about 4 inches from source of heat for 8 to 10 minutes, or until bacon is crisp. Turn carefully and broil 3 to 4 minutes longer.

Serves: 6
Calories per serving: 84

Barquettes Marivaux

7	oz. cooked shrimp
4	oz. canned mushrooms
1	cup mayonnaise
12	small barquettes
2	hard-cooked eggs

Dice the shrimp and mushrooms. Combine with the mayonnaise. Garnish the barquettes and sprinkle with the chopped hard-cooked eggs. Serve cold.

Serves: 6
Calories per serving: 300

Barquettes of Shrimp

2	lb. shelled shrimp
1	cup mornay sauce
12	small barquettes
2	oz. grated parmesan

Devein and clean shrimp. Rinse under cold water. In a medium saucepan, heat the mornay sauce and mix in the diced shrimp. Fill the barquettes with the shrimp mixture. Sprinkle with parmesan cheese and glaze under a broiler. Serve hot.

Serves: 6
Calories per serving: 324

Barquettes of Tuna

7	oz. canned tuna
½	cup mayonnaise
1	tsp. lemon juice
½	tsp. salt

¼	tsp. ground white pepper
24	cooked barquettes
12	tuna fillets
1	tbsp. chopped parsley
2	hard-cooked eggs

Drain the solid white tuna. Mix in the mayonnaise and lemon juice. Season with salt and pepper.

Fill the barquettes with the tuna mixture. Top with the canned tuna fillets. Sprinkle with the parsley and the chopped hard-cooked eggs.

Serves: 12
Calories per serving: 207

Boston Dip

8	oz. canned clams
8	oz. soft cream cheese
1	tbsp. lemon juice
1	tbsp. chopped parsley
¼	tsp. salt
⅛	tsp. hot sauce
	crackers

Drain clams and reserve liquid. Cream the cheese. Add lemon juice, parsley, salt, hot sauce, and clams. Mix thoroughly. Chill for an hour. Add clam juice to the dip if too thick.

Serve with crackers, chips, or vegetables.

Clam Fritters

2	cups chopped clams
1	cup clam juice
2	eggs
8	oz. flour
2	tsp. baking powder
1	tsp. salt
¼	tsp. ground white pepper
1	cup cocktail sauce

Combine the chopped clams with the juice. Beat in the eggs, flour, baking powder, salt, and pepper. Drop teaspoonfuls of batter on a hot griddle or into a deep fryer. If using a griddle, cook 2 minutes on each side; if deep frying, cook 3 to 4 minutes at 360°F (185°C).

Serve with cocktail sauce.

Serves: 12
Calories per serving: 120

Crab Appetizer

8	oz. crabmeat
1	tbsp. minced onion
2	oz. butter
2	oz. flour
½	cup milk
1	egg yolk
½	tsp. wine worcestershire
¼	tsp. salt
½	cup dry bread crumbs

Remove any shell or cartilage from the crabmeat. Cook the onion in butter and blend in the flour. Add the milk gradually to make a cream sauce, stirring constantly. Add the egg yolk, wine worcestershire, and salt. Stir in the crabmeat, and blend into a paste. Allow to cool.

Portion the crabmeat with a teaspoon. Shape into small balls and roll in bread crumbs. Deep fry at 375°F (190°C) for 2 minutes. Drain on absorbent paper. Serve with toothpicks.

Serves: 12
Calories per serving: 79

Crab Canapés

6	oz. chopped crabmeat
2	oz. shredded swiss cheese
2	tbsp. mayonnaise
1	tsp. chopped chives
2	drops tabasco
¼	tsp. salt

| 2 | egg whites |
| 12 | cooked biscuits |

Combine the crabmeat with swiss cheese, mayonnaise, chives, tabasco, and salt.

Beat the egg whites until stiff and fold into the crab mixture.

Split the biscuits in half. Top each half with a teaspoonful of the crabmeat mixture. Bake at 450°F (230°C) for 5 to 6 minutes until golden brown.

Serves: 12
Calories per serving: 110

Crab Puffs

2	tbsp. chopped scallions
2	tbsp. minced celery
1	tbsp. peanut oil
8	oz. softened cream cheese
8	oz. clean crabmeat
2	tbsp. fresh bread crumbs
2	drops red pepper sauce
9	egg roll wrappers

Cook the scallions and celery in a small amount of oil until tender. Cream the cheese and stir in the crabmeat, scallions, celery, bread crumbs, and red pepper sauce. Cut each egg roll wrapper into four squares. Divide the mixture between the wrappers. Moisten the edges and seal. Deep fry at 350°F (180°C) for 2 to 3 minutes.

Serves: 9
Calories per serving: 170

Crabmeat Balls

12	bacon slices
7	oz. crabmeat
1	cup fresh bread crumbs
2	oz. dry sherry wine
1	tbsp. lemon juice
½	tsp. onion salt

¼	tsp. white pepper
2	tsp. prepared mustard
24	lemon wedges

Cut the bacon slices in halves. Flake the crabmeat and combine with the bread crumbs, sherry wine, lemon juice, onion salt, pepper, and mustard. Mix well and shape into two dozen small balls. Wrap each ball with a bacon slice. Broil under medium heat until the bacon is crisp, turning to brown evenly. Serve with lemon wedges.

Serves: 6
Calories per serving: 169

Herring in Mustard Sauce

2	oz. fresh horseradish
2	qt. white vinegar
1	lb. sugar
1	oz. dill
8	oz. sliced carrots
8	oz. sliced onions
20	juniper berries
4	cloves
1	tbsp. peppercorns
2	tsp. mustard seeds
20	small fresh herring
2	cups cold mustard sauce
1	tsp. dill weed

Cut fresh horseradish into sticks. Combine the horseradish, white vinegar, sugar, dill, carrots, onions, juniper berries, cloves, peppercorns, and mustard seeds for a marinade. Bring to a boil, then cool. Fillet herring and soak overnight in cold water.

Place herring fillets in a crock and pour cold marinade over them. Marinate for 4 to 5 days.

Remove fillets from marinade. Cut into 2-inch (5 cm) pieces. Drain well and mix with mustard sauce. Arrange in a serving dish, sprinkle with dill weed, and serve as appetizer.

Serves: 20
Calories per serving: 204

Hot Tuna Canapés

7	oz. canned tuna
1	tbsp. capers
1	tbsp. mayonnaise
1	tsp. paprika
1	tsp. minced onion
1	tsp. lemon juice
3	egg whites
16	toast fingers

Flake the tuna. Combine with capers, mayonnaise, paprika, onion, and lemon juice. Beat the egg whites until stiff. Fold in the tuna mixture. Spread the tuna mix on the toast fingers. Place on a sheet pan and broil 3 inches (7.5 cm) from source of heat until brown. Serve hot.

Serves: 8
Calories per serving: 82

Marinated Salmon

2	lb. salmon fillets
5	tbsp. green peppercorns
1	tsp. salt
10	oz. oil
2	tbsp. lime juice
6	minced shallots
4	tbsp. chopped olives
10	slices toasted French bread

Clean the salmon fillets.

To make marinade, combine chopped green peppercorns, salt, and oil. Set salmon fillets skin-side down into a stainless steel or porcelain dish. Cover with pepper marinade and marinate for 2 to 3 hours. Remove from marinade and slice thinly.

Arrange slices on plates. Sprinkle with lime juice, top with some of the marinade, and sprinkle with shallots and olives.

Serve with toasted French bread.

Serves: 10
Calories per serving: 261

Marinated Shrimp

1½	lb. shelled shrimp
2	medium sliced onions
1½	cups salad oil
1	cup white vinegar
1	tsp. salt
½	tsp. dill weed
½	tsp. celery salt
1	tsp. capers
8	lemon wedges
1	small bunch parsley

Clean and devein the shrimps. Cook in salted boiling water for 3 to 5 minutes. Drain and rinse under cold water.

In a sealable container, alternate layers of onion slices and shrimp. Mix remaining ingredients and pour over the shrimp. Cover to seal. Marinate in refrigerator for 24 hours, basting shrimp 2 or 3 times.

Arrange on a serving platter and garnish with lemon wedges and parsley.

Serves: 8
Calories per serving: 197

Mussels in Mustard Sauce

2	lb. cooked mussels
5	oz. mayonnaise
1	tsp. dijon mustard
6	oz. diced celery
1	tsp. lemon juice
6	radish roses

Combine the cooked mussels, mayonnaise, mustard, celery, and lemon juice. Spoon into a shallow dish. Decorate with radish roses.

Serves: 6
Calories per serving: 198

Oysters and Mustard Sauce

12	oysters
¼	cup dry white wine
¼	cup water
1	small bunch watercress
¼	small head radicchio
2	tbsp. sour cream
1	tbsp. mayonnaise
1½	tsp. dijon mustard

Shuck oysters. Save bottom shells. Boil wine and water. Add oysters. Return to boiling for 1 minute. Drain. Reduce liquid to two thirds. Chill.

Shred watercress and radicchio. Place in oyster shells.

In a bowl, mix the sour cream, mayonnaise, mustard, and cooking liquid.

Arrange the oysters on greens in shells. Top with sauce.

Serves: 12
Calories per serving: 34

Sardine Dip

4	oz. canned sardines
8	oz. cream cheese
1	tbsp. milk
2	tbsp. chopped parsley
1	tbsp. lemon juice
1	tsp. worcestershire

Combine all ingredients. Mix well to a smooth paste.

Serve with assorted cheeses, crackers, or raw vegetables.

Sardine Tapenade

4½	oz. can drained sardines
1	oz. cured black olives
¼	cup olive oil

1	tbsp. lemon juice
1	tsp. minced garlic
1	hard-cooked egg
1	tbsp. chopped parsley

Remove the pits from the olives. Blend the sardines, olives, oil, lemon juice, and garlic in food processor.

Chop the hard-cooked egg until fine. Combine with the parsley.

Serve sardine mixture on thin slices of French bread. Top with chopped egg and parsley.

Serves: 6
Calories per serving: 75

Scallop Tartlets

1½	lb. bay scallops
½	tsp. salt
¼	tsp. pepper
1	cup white wine
½	cup dry vermouth
1	oz. fresh mushrooms
2	oz. butter
2	oz. flour
½	cup heavy cream
6	medium cooked tartlet shells

Season the scallops with salt and pepper. Poach in white wine and vermouth. Do not overcook. Sauté the small mushrooms in butter and lemon juice.

Set aside. Prepare a roux with butter and flour. Moisten with the poaching liquid, stirring continuously, until the sauce thickens. Add the cream. Reduce the sauce for 5 minutes.

Add the mushrooms and scallops. Heat and spoon the mixture into prepared tartlets. Serve hot.

Serves: 6
Calories per serving: 348

Shrimp Pastries

1	tbsp. oil
1	oz. chopped onion
2	oz. chopped tomatoes
4	oz. cooked shrimp
1	hard-cooked egg
½	tbsp. chopped parsley
½	tsp. salt
8	oz. puff pastry dough
1	egg yolk

Heat the oil in a skillet. Stir in the onion and cook over low heat for 5 minutes. Add the peeled and seeded tomatoes and simmer to remove all moisture. Stir in the shrimp, chopped hard-cooked egg, parsley, and salt.

Roll out the puff pastry to ⅛-inch (3 mm) thickness. Cut into circles, 2½ inch (7 cm) in diameter. Brush the edges with water. Place a heaping teaspoon of the shrimp mixture in center. Fold one half over and seal, pressing edges together. Brush with egg yolk.

Bake at 400°F (200°C) for 10 minutes or until golden brown. Serve hot.

Serves: 12
Calories per serving: 105

Shrimp Ravioli Pastries

2	oz. chopped onion
2	oz. butter
¼	cup dry white wine
8	oz. cooked diced shrimp
½	cup heavy cream sauce
½	tsp. salt
¼	tsp. ground white pepper
1	lb. puff pastry dough

Sauté the onion in butter until transparent. Add wine and the diced shrimp. Cook over high heat for 5 minutes. Stir in the cream sauce. Season with salt and pepper. Cool mixture.

Divide the puff pastry dough into two pieces and roll into two rectangles of the same size, ⅛-inch (3 mm) thick. Using a sheet, place a teaspoonful of the shrimp mixture every 2 inches (5 cm) across and down the dough. Brush the dough with water all around the fillings.

Carefully place the second rectangle of dough over the first and press down around the fillings to seal the dough. Cut into squares between fillings with a ravioli cutter. Deep fry until brown. Serve hot.

Serves: 24 (2 pastries per person)
Calories per serving: 102

Shrimp Tartlets Russe

1	lb. cooked shrimp
1	oz. horseradish
½	cup mayonnaise
½	tsp. salt
½	tsp. sugar
1	tsp. paprika
1	tbsp. lemon juice
12	small tartlets
1	oz. caviar

Select tiny shrimp for this recipe.

Combine the cooked shrimp with the horseradish, mayonnaise, salt, sugar, paprika, and lemon juice.

Spoon mixture into tartlets. Garnish with dots of caviar. Serve cold.

Serves: 6
Calories per serving: 204

Smoked Fish Dip

8	oz. smoked bluefish★
8	oz. cream cheese
½	cup mayonnaise
1	tbsp. lemon juice
1	tbsp. chopped chives
½	tsp. onion powder

½	tsp. salt
¼	tsp. dried rosemary
	crackers

Skin, bone, and flake the smoked bluefish. Combine with the cream cheese, mayonnaise, lemon juice, chives, onion powder, salt, and rosemary. Mix in a food processor to obtain a paste. Chill for at least an hour.

Serve with crackers or other toasted bread fingers.

★Use other smoked fish if desired.

Squid and Clam Appetizer

½	lb. cleaned squid
1	cup whole clams
¼	cup lemon juice
⅓	cup salad oil
1	tbsp. chopped parsley
1	tbsp. chopped pimiento
½	tsp. salt
¼	tsp. ground white pepper
1	small lettuce head

A few hours before serving, cut the squid lengthwise into ½ inch (1½ cm) strips, then cut strips in half. Simmer in boiling water for 1 hour. Drain.

Drain the clams and rinse. In a large bowl, combine the lemon juice, oil, parsley, pimento, salt, and pepper.

Add the squid and clams. Marinate in the refrigerator for at least an hour.

Before serving, allow to stand at room temperature for 15 minutes. Drain and arrange on shredded lettuce.

Serves: 6
Calories per serving: 92

Stuffed Clams Oregonati

24	small clams
1	tbsp. chopped shallots
1	tsp. minced garlic

1	tbsp. chopped basil
1	tbsp. chopped parsley
1	chopped tomato
4	medium sliced mushrooms
¾	cup grated parmesan
3	bacon slices
1	tbsp. chopped chives
¼	cup olive oil
½	cup dry white wine

Open the cherrystone clams. Discard the top shells and loosen clams on the bottom shells. Combine the shallots, garlic, basil, parsley, tomato, mushrooms, bacon, and half of the parmesan cheese. Mix well in a food processor. Add chives. Spoon the mixture over the clams and smooth the top. Arrange the clams on a baking dish. Sprinkle with the remaining cheese, olive oil, and wine. Bake until golden brown at 400°F (205°C).

Serves: 12
Calories per serving: 80

Stuffed Cucumbers

3	medium cucumbers
8	oz. boned smoked salmon
4	oz. softened cream cheese
4	oz. butter
1	tsp. dijon mustard
1	tbsp. lemon juice
4	slices pumpernickel

Wash the cucumbers and trim the ends. With a lemon peeler, cut V-shaped grooves lengthwise, spacing grooves equally. Cut in half crosswise. Extract all seeds.

Remove the skin from the smoked salmon. Combine with the remaining ingredients, and mix into a paste in a food processor.

Fill the cavities of the cucumber halves with the salmon mixture. Chill for an hour. Slice the filled cucumber halves into ¼-inch (½ cm) pinwheels. Serve on round slices of buttered pumpernickel bread.

Serves: 10
Calories per serving: 141

Stuffed Tomato Surprise

7	oz. canned tuna
3	oz. softened cream cheese
1	medium avocado
1	tbsp. lemon juice
½	tsp. salt
¼	tsp. hot pepper sauce
½	tsp. worcestershire
3	doz. cherry tomatoes

Drain and flake the tuna. Mix with the cream cheese and avocado pulp to a smooth paste. Season with the lemon juice, salt, pepper sauce, and worcestershire. Wash the tomatoes and hollow out the centers. Fill each tomato with a heaping teaspoon of the tuna mixture.

Serves: 12
Calories per serving: 109

Toasted Grilled Sardines

12	large canned sardines
1	tbsp. lemon juice
6	slices toasted French bread
1	tbsp. mayonnaise
2	tsp. dijon mustard
1	cup parsley
¼	tsp. salt

Brown the sardines under a broiler. Sprinkle with lemon juice.
Spread mayonnaise and mustard over slices of toasted French bread. Arrange two sardines on each slice of toast.
Clean and drain the parsley sprigs and deep fry at 350°F (180°C) for 5 seconds. Sprinkle with salt and place on top of the sardines.

Serves: 6
Calories per serving: 150

Tuna Bites

14	oz. solid white tuna
4	oz. softened cream cheese
2	oz. blue cheese
1	tbsp. chopped chives
½	tsp. lemon juice
¼	tsp. salt
½	cup chopped parsley

In a food processor, combine the tuna, cream cheese, blue cheese, and chives. Add the lemon juice and season to taste with salt. Form into small balls and roll in parsley. Chill for an hour or more before serving.

Serves: 8
Calories per serving: 130

Tuna Fritters

4	slices bread
7	oz. canned tuna
1	hard-cooked egg
1	tbsp. capers
½	recipe beer batter★

Cut the crust off the bread slices.
    Combine the flaked white tuna with the chopped hard-cooked egg and capers. Spread over the bread and cut into small portions.
    Dip the bread into the beer batter. Deep fry at 350°F (180°C) until golden brown. Drain on absorbent paper. Serve with a sauce.

★See recipe for Beer Batter in Chapter 7.

Serves: 8
Calories per serving: 165

Tuna Puffs

½	recipe cream puff dough
7	oz. canned tuna
¼	cup mayonnaise

2	oz. cream cheese
1	tsp. lemon juice
¼	tsp. ground ginger

Make bite size cream puffs with the dough. Flake the tuna and combine with the remaining ingredients.

Split the puffs, fill one half with the tuna mixture, and top with the other half.

Serves: 6
Calories per serving: 272

Seafood Butter and Cheese Mixtures

Butter and cheese can be combined with a variety of seafoods and other ingredients to make spreads used in a variety of canapés. These spreads enhance the flavor and taste of the canapés. The following list of butter and cheese mixtures is by no means complete. In fact, there is no limit to the variations that can be created.

Anchovy Butter

Blend 12 anchovy fillets with 4 oz. (110 g) of sweet butter and mix into a paste.

Caviar Butter

Blend 2 oz. (50 g) of fresh caviar with 4 oz. (110 g) of butter and mix into a paste.

Crayfish Butter

Blend 2 oz. (50 g) of cooked crayfish tails with 4 oz. (110 g) of butter and mix into a paste.

Herring Butter

Blend 2 desalted fillets of herring with 12 oz. (340 g) of butter and mix into a paste.

Herring Roe Butter

Blend 3 oz. (85 g) of herring roe, which has been poached in white wine, with 4 oz. (110 g of butter). Add a small amount of mustard and mix into a paste.

Lobster Butter

Blend 4 oz. (110 g) of lobster coral with 8 oz. (225 g) of butter and mix into a paste.

Moscovite Butter

Blend 8 oz. (225 g) of butter with 4 oz. (110 g) of caviar and six hard-cooked egg yolks. Mix all ingredients into a paste. Season with salt and cayenne pepper.

Smoked Salmon Butter

Blend 8 oz. (225 g) of smoked salmon with 1 lb. (450 g) of butter and mix into a paste.

Sardine Butter

Blend 12 boneless sardines with 12 oz. (340 g) of butter and mix into a paste.

Shrimp Butter

Blend 2 oz. (50 g) of cooked shrimp with 4 oz. (110 g) of butter. Add 2 oz. (50 g) of chopped parsley. Season with salt and pepper and mix into a paste.

Tunafish Butter

Blend 2 oz. (50 g) of tunafish with 4 oz. (110 g) of butter and mix into a paste.

Crab Cheese

Blend 4 oz. (110 g) of crab meat with 8 oz. (225 g) of cream cheese. Add 2 oz. (50 g) of butter. Mix into a paste and season with salt and pepper.

Lobster or Crawfish Cheese

Follow the procedure described for Crab Cheese in Chapter 13, substituting 4 oz. (110 g) of cooked lobster or crawfish.

Salmon Cheese

Blend 4 oz. (110 g) of cooked salmon with 4 oz. (110 g) of cream cheese and 1 oz. (25 g) butter. Mix into a paste. Finish with a small amount of heavy cream and a little port wine.

Tunafish Cheese

Blend 8 oz. (225 g) of tunafish with 8 oz. (225 g) of cream cheese. Mix into a paste. Add a small amount of heavy cream if desired.

16

The Decorative Power of Cold Fish and Shellfish

In addition to cooking seafoods with precision and care, the decorative aspect of cold fish and shellfish presents a challenge. Colorful fish and shellfish, in various sizes and shapes, are easily adapted to decorative work. The pink color of salmon, the pure white of bass, cod, tilefish, and the coral red of several crustaceans provide numerous color contrasts when used with other ingredients. However, regardless of the motif or the theme selected for a specific occasion, simplicity is the rule for seafood decorations. Moreover, these decorations should not be time consuming. Fish and shellfish are perishable, and elaborate ornaments will spoil any dish kept too long at room temperature.

The great challenge is to decorate seafood platters that reflect today's marketing conditions and economics. The methods described in this book fulfill both these requirements and still please the eyes and whet the appetite. One of the most revolutionary decorative methods ever developed is the aspic sheet. The possibilities of these colorful sheets are innumerable. The following is the basic recipe; the main ingredient determines the final color.

Orange Aspic Sheet

¾	cup cold water
1	oz. unflavored gelatin
3½	oz. canned pimentos
¼	tsp. salt

Dissolve the water with the gelatin, allow to gelatinize, and melt over low heat.

Puree the pimentoes in a blender. Add the liquid gelatin and salt. Blend briefly. Pour the blend onto a slightly oiled 14×17-inch (35×42.5 cm) pan, spreading the mixture evenly over the whole surface of the pan. Refrigerate until firm.

For other color sheets, use the above recipe, substituting one of the following for pimentos:

Yellow sheet—use hard boiled egg yolks.
White sheet—use hard boiled egg whites.
Black sheet—use truffle trimmings.

How to Use Aspic Sheets

The very thin, gelatinized colorful sheets are now ready for use. A set of small cutters, especially designed for minute decorations, is necessary. Some cutters are geometric shapes, others are alphabet, animal, or leaf shapes. Freehand decorations can also be very effective.

After pressing a selected cutter against an aspic sheet, the shape can be lifted with a toothpick and placed on the cold seafood. Cold mousses, whole fish, pâtés and galantines of fish, fish steaks, and many other preparations are much more appealing when decorated. A smoked salmon mousse becomes a conversation piece when decorated with orange cutouts depicting small fish. Strips of green scallions or leeks make the decor even more attractive. Floral arrangements and geometric ornamentations can be executed easily with a selection of aspic sheets and cutters. Any leftover aspic can be remelted, poured into smaller trays or plates, and frozen for future use.

Other Decorative Approaches

There are basically 11 ingredients that can be used efficiently and economically for seafood decorations. They are:

Fresh raw vegetables.
Fresh cooked vegetables.
Canned or marinated vegetables.
Fresh raw fruit.
Canned fruit.
Fresh herbs.
Aspic sheets.
Hard-boiled eggs.
Fish roe.
Baked goods.
Dairy products.

Fresh Vegetables

The following vegetables are used primarily in food decorations: carrots, celery, cucumbers, leeks, potatoes, radishes, tomatoes, and turnips. Depending on the imagination and experience of the decorator, other vegetables can also be used.

The decorations that can be created with these vegetables are numerous. They can be carved into flowers, sliced (raw or blanched), and cut into many different designs. Carrots can be used raw or cooked; cucumbers, cut lengthwise and sliced very thin, make perfect fish scales for decorating a whole fish. Leeks are usually blanched and cut into flower stems or leaves. Cooked firm potatoes are sliced and cut with various decorative cutters; when raw, they can be turned into roses or turnips, but their use as flowers for seafood decorations is not recommended. Paper-thin sliced radishes are beautiful when simply arranged into flowers.

The skin of tomatoes can be curled or rolled to resemble flowers. Whole round tomato slices or half slices, alternated with sliced cucumbers, are always attractive for a quick, colorful presentation. Red cabbage, marinated in vinegar, can be shredded or sliced around a variety of cold seafood dishes. And turnips, yellow or white, can yield simple unique arrangements, classified as decorations or the new cuisine. A vase of white turnip flowers, adorned with delicate pink carrot buttons, will turn a seafood centerpiece into a showpiece.

How to Make a Flower Vase With a Butternut Squash

Remove the top of a medium butternut squash.

Scoop out the inside. Decorate the outside of the squash using turnip or carrot balls.

To make the turnip daisies:

1. Peel the turnip and cut into ¼-inch (6-mm) thick slices.
2. Using star cookie cutters in graduated sizes, cut stars from turnip slices. Cut two stars for each flower.
3. Use a small Parisian scoop to form carrot center for daisies.
4. Put an 8-to-10-inch (20-to-25-cm) Chinese skewer through larger star, then the smaller. Top with carrot center.
5. Push a green scallion stem over the skewer.
6. Arrange stems and daisies in the butternut squash vase. Use skewers of varying length for the bouquet.
7. Cut leaves out of green leek stems. Arrange attractively in the vase, using as many as needed to accompany the flowers.

How to Carve a Fisherman's Net From a Turnip

A fisherman's net is an innovation in the art of seafood decoration. Although it is a time-consuming preparation, it is certainly worthwhile for the dedicated pro or amateur alike.

1. Select a large rhutabaga.
2. Trim and shape into a square.
3. Insert a ⅜-inch (1-cm) dowel into the center of the turnip square. (Sharpen one end for easy penetration.)
4. Soak turnip in a strong solution of salt and water to soften its texture. This will take 2 to 3 days.
5. Place the turnip flat on the working surface. Starting at one end of the turnip, carve a ¼-inch slice until the knife reaches the dowel. A meat slicer is the best carving implement. Keep the knife horizontal to the working surface. Give the rhutabaga a half turn and make a similar cut.
6. Give the turnip a quarter turn and carve a ¼-inch slice, in the same fashion as above. Give the vegatable a half turn and make a similar cut. Continue this procedure until the turnip is sliced from end to end.
7. Soak turnip for 12 hours in the salted water to soften the core.
8. Round the turnip as shown.
9. Holding the turnip with one hand, slice the turnip in a continuous piece about ¼-inch (6-mm) thick. Special care should be exercised not to break the continuous cut.

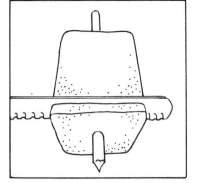

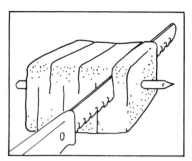

Step 5.

Step 6.

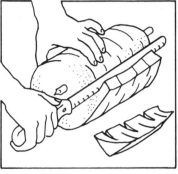

Step 8.

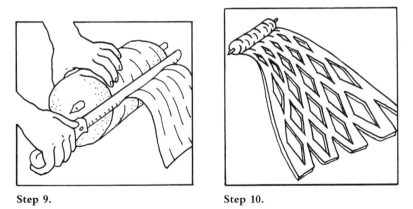

Step 9.

Step 10.

Figure 16-1. Carving a fisherman's net from a turnip, the final steps.

10. Stretch the net as shown. Use this original creation as a base on a platter. Arrange cold seafood on top. The turnip net can be kept in salted water for several days and reused many times.

Hard-Boiled Eggs

Hard-boiled eggs are often used as a focal point in seafood decoration. They can be sliced, whole, wedged, stuffed, or chopped. Chopped egg yolks and egg whites, mixed with chopped parsley (a colorful garnish called *mimosa*) are sprinkled over many seafood dishes to add color.

The Decorative Power of Cold Fish and Shellfish   **449**

To slice hard-boiled eggs, always use an egg slicer. For a simple decoration, alternate egg slices with tomato and cucumber slices around any cold seafood platter. To cut eggs into wedges, an egg wedger is recommended for a clean cut. Remove the yolks, stuff with a mousse, and use as appetizers. Hard-boiled eggs, cut in half lengthwise or crosswise, are usually stuffed, using the egg yolks in the stuffing.

The most eye-catching decorations can be made with whole eggs. Penguins, frogs, and other fancy decorations are easily done with a little imagination.

Baked Goods and Dairy Products

As described in Chapter 7, pie crust can be baked into barquettes (little boats) or tartelettes (little tarts); puff pastry is made into patty shells, bouchees, fleurons, etc. All of these can be decorative parts of seafood displays. Barquettes or tartelettes are usually filled with such colorful mixtures as mousses, Russian salad, and fish or shellfish salads, and arranged around seafood platters as accompaniments. Whole sandwich bread can be carved into a boat to contain appetizers or seafood salads.

The dairy product that is most adaptable to shaping and patterns is cream cheese. Cream cheese is usually applied with the help of a pastry bag, fitted with different sizes and shapes of metal tubes. Cream cheese roses are easily prepared with a rose tube. Softened cream cheese is also used to make mushroom clumps.

Fish Roe

Colorful fish roe especially that of salmon (red caviar), sturgeon, lumpfish, or other fish (black caviar), or lobster coral, are great favorites in food decoration. Fish roe is used mostly as garnish for a variety of seafood products. A smoked salmon mousse is best garnished with salmon caviar. Stuffed eggs, barquettes, and other individual garnishes can be topped with black or red caviar. Fish roe is also used in forming designs or patterns of all kinds.

Fresh Herbs

Generally, leeks are used to add to the design, color, or texture (relief) of the surface to be decorated. Whole leaves of various herbs can be used, but for seafood designs dill is the most suitable along with the blanched green part of leeks and parsley stems. Fresh herbs work well in the design of trees, flower stems, leaves, seaweed, and other floral motifs.

Carrot Spider Mum
1. Wash, trim, and peel a thick carrot about 5 to 6 inches (12.5 to 14 cm) long; slice lengthwise into ⅛ inch thick slices (an electric slicer or a manual potato slicer is necessary to achieve the best results).
2. To make one flower, use 5 carrot slices. Make cuts at ¼-inch intervals the length of the slices, leaving ½ inch uncut at both ends of carrot.
3. Note in the diagram for Step 2 that the two outside slices are cut free at the narrow end of the carrot. (See Step 4 in which the outside slices are free.)
4. Place one end of a carrot slice onto a toothpick. Fold the slice and place other end onto the same toothpick with a twist.

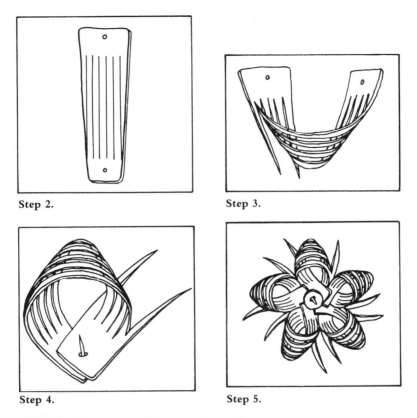

Step 2.

Step 3.

Step 4.

Step 5.

Figure 16-2. Creating a carrot spider mum, the carving steps.

5. Arrange remaining slices into an attractive five petal flower on the same pick. Conceal the tip of toothpick with a piece of ripe olive in the center of the flower to accent the color of the carrot spider mum.

COLD FISH DISPLAYS

Cold fish is best if poached whole or in one sizable piece (see poaching technique in Chapter 6). The fish will remain tender, flaky, and moist.

Such cold fish as salmon, whitefish, striped bass, and red snapper can be presented on a buffet table and attractively decorated using some of the ideas described in this section. A cold sauce should always be served with cold fish. Several garnishes may accompany cold fish to enhance their presentation. Some of these garnishes are:

Cherry tomatoes stuffed with egg salad.
Russian salad aspic mold.
Slices of eggs, tomatoes, and cucumbers overlapping around fish.
Stuffed deviled eggs.
Small boats (barquettes) filled with several types of foods.
Cucumber salad.
Marinated tomato salad.

The Decorative Power of Cold Fish and Shellfish **451**

Stuffed artichoke bottoms.
Mushroom caps stuffed with caviar.
Cooked shrimp.
Carrots and celery sticks.
Anchovy fillets.
Ripe and green olives.
Lettuce hearts.
Capers.
Green and white asparagus tips.
Smoked oysters.
Tomato wedges, quartered cooked eggs, and parsley sprigs.

Cucumber Salad

1	lb. cucumbers
1	tsp. salt
½	cup vinaigrette
1	tsp. chopped parsley

Peel the cucumbers. Cut lengthwise and remove the seeds. Slice thin and add salt. Allow to set for half an hour. Squeeze the cucumber slices in a clean towel to remove all water. Mix in the dressing. Sprinkle with chopped parsley. Serve cold.

Serves: 6
Calories per serving: 91

Russian Salad Aspic Mold

4	oz. diced potatoes
4	oz. diced carrots
4	oz. cooked peas
4	oz. diced green beans
½	cup mayonnaise
½	tsp. salt
¼	tsp. ground white pepper
½	cup liquid aspic jelly

Cook the potatoes, carrots, and green beans in salted boiling water. Drain the vegetables and cool.

Combine all the vegetables with the mayonnaise. Season with salt and pepper. Mix in the aspic jelly.

Spoon into small, individual molds. Allow to set in refrigerator for an hour. Dip the molds in cold water and unmold around cold fish.

Serves: 6
Calories per serving: 98

Marinated Tomato Salad

1	lb. fresh tomatoes
3	tbsp. oil
1	tbsp. wine vinegar
1	oz. chopped onion
1	tsp. chopped chives
½	tsp. salt
¼	tsp. ground white pepper
¼	tsp. chopped oregano

Blanch and peel the tomatoes. Slice thinly. Combine oil and vinegar. Add the onion, chives, salt, white pepper, and oregano.
Arrange tomatoes on a platter and pour dressing over. Allow to marinate for an hour before serving.

Serves: 6
Calories per serving: 83

Stuffed Artichoke Bottoms

3	medium anchovy fillets
1	large tomato
2	celery stalks
6	artichoke bottoms
½	cup green goddess dressing
1	green pepper

Cut the anchovy fillets into small pieces. Blanch, peel, and dice the tomato. Peel and dice the celery.
Mix the anchovy pieces, tomatoes, celery, and green goddess dressing. Stuff the artichokes with the mixture.
Decorate with rings or strips of green pepper.

Serves: 6
Calories per serving: 172

Stuffed Deviled Eggs

3	eggs
1	tbsp. mayonnaise
2	oz. softened cream cheese
¼	tsp. salt
⅛	tsp. ground white pepper
1	dash tabasco
1	tsp. chopped parsley

Boil the eggs for 10 minutes. Cool under cold water and shell. Cut the eggs in half and remove the yolks. Combine the yolks, mayonnaise, and cream cheese in a food processor. Mix to a smooth paste. Stir in the salt, white pepper, and tabasco.

Stuff the eggs with the mixture using a pastry bag fitted with a star tube. Sprinkle with parsley. Chill before serving.

Serves: 6
Calories per serving: 92

Cold Lobster Française

6	medium lobsters
6	deviled eggs
1	cup liquid aspic
6	lemon wedges
6	cherry tomatoes
1	cup mayonnaise

Boil the live lobsters in salted water for 10 minutes. Allow to cool. Remove the claws from the lobsters, break them and remove the meat in one piece. Wash under cold water. Split the lobsters in halves lengthwise and remove the sand track from the tails as well as any sandy parts from the head.

Display the lobster halves on a serving platter or large plate. Brush with cold liquid aspic. Garnish with stuffed deviled eggs, lemon wedges, and cherry tomatoes. Serve with mayonnaise.

Serves: 6
Calories per serving: 561

Cold Lobster Parisienne

3	5-lb. live lobsters
2	lb. prepared russian salad
2	cups liquid aspic
12	lemon wedges
12	cherry tomatoes
1	bunch parsley
1	cup mayonnaise

Insert a skewer through the whole length of each lobster tail to prevent tails from curling. Cook lobsters in salted boiling water for 20 minutes. Allow to cool at room temperature. To extract the tail meat, cut the carapace underneath with scissors and pull out. Remove tails. Extract the claw meat and dice and mix with the russian salad.

Blend half of the aspic with the russian salad. Pour in a mold. Chill for an hour.

Slice the lobster tail meat into medallions. Glaze with aspic jelly. Display the lobster slices on top of lobster shells, overlapping each slice. Display the lobster tails on a platter. Unmold the salad in the center of platter. Decorate with lemon, parsley, and tomatoes. Serve with mayonnaise.

Serves: 12
Calories per serving: 375

Lobster Armoricaine

½	cup chopped parsley
1	cup chopped watercress
¼	cup chopped dill
4	oz. soft butter
½	cup mayonnaise
½	cup aspic jelly
8	oz. sliced smoked salmon
2	lb. chunks lobster
½	tsp. salt
¼	tsp. ground white pepper

| 1 | tbsp. lemon juice |
| ¼ | tsp. seafood seasoning |

Combine the three green herbs. In a bowl, mix the mayonnaise with liquid aspic jelly and butter. Place a sheet of wax paper or film wrap on a flat surface. Lay the smoked salmon over the surface of the paper or wrap. Combine the herbs with the mayonnaise and aspic. Fold in the lobster chunks. Season to taste with the remaining ingredients.

Spoon the lobster mix over the center of salmon. Shape into a log. Lift the paper or wrap so that the smoked salmon seals the lobster mix. Twist both ends of lobster roll and refrigerate for 2 to 3 hours. Slice chilled lobster roll and serve with mayonnaise or other cold sauce.

Serves 10
Calories per serving: 295

Lobster Salad

8	oz. lobster meat
2	hard-cooked eggs
½	cup mayonnaise
1	tbsp. lemon juice
1	tbsp. mustard
⅓	tsp. salt
⅓	tsp. ground white pepper
5	lettuce leaves
1	tsp. chopped parsley
1	tsp. lobster coral

Dice the lobster meat and combine with the chopped eggs. Blend the mayonnaise with the lemon juice, mustard, salt, and pepper and combine with the lobster and egg mixture.

Place a serving of the salad on each lettuce leaf. Sprinkle with chopped parsley and coral if available.

Serves: 5
Calories per serving: 165

Galantine of Salmon

5	lb. fresh salmon
10	slices white bread
4	egg whites
2	tsp. salt
½	tsp. ground white pepper
¼	tsp. nutmeg
2	cups heavy cream
1½	oz. pistachio nuts
10	oz. diced pimentos
1	oz. white truffle paste
½	tsp. unflavored gelatin
1	cup aspic

Cut off the head and tail from the salmon. Starting with the backbone but without damaging skin, bone the salmon. Then remove salmon meat from the skin. Chill the skin and meat.

With the salmon bones, make a fish stock. In a food processor, emulsify half the salmon and the bread, egg whites, salt, pepper, and nutmeg. Slowly add the cream. Blanch and peel the pistachios. Fold the pistachios, pimentos, and truffle paste into the mixture. Cube remaining salmon. Season with salt and pepper. Dust with gelatin. Fold in the forcemeat. Place the salmon skin on a cheesecloth and spread the forcemeat over. Roll the cheesecloth and salmon. Tie at ends and across. Cover with stock. Poach at 170°F (77°C) to an internal temperature of 150°F (66°C). Chill and remove cloth. Slice, decorate, and brush with aspic before serving.

Serves: 20
Calories per serving: 186

Galantine of Scallops

20	oz. scallops
10	oz. sole fillets
½	tsp. salt
¼	tsp. ground white pepper
6	oz. bread panada

4	egg whites
1	pt. heavy cream
1	oz. gin
4	tbsp. chopped dill
1	gal. fish fumet
2	oz. unflavored gelatin
30	cantaloupe balls
1	sprig dill
2	cups sauce antiboise

Blend dry scallops and fish fillets in a food processor. Add the salt, pepper, panada, and blend well. Add the egg whites and blend well. Slowly add the heavy cream. Season with gin and chill for an hour.

Mix half of the forcemeat with the chopped dill. Spread the dill forcemeat on plastic wrap. Refrigerate for 10 minutes. Top with plain forcemeat and roll. Tie, pierce plastic with a needle, and poach in fish fumet with the unflavored gelatin for 30 minutes at 160°F (72°C). Cool in stock.

Unmold and slice. Brush with gelatinized stock, decorate with cantaloupe balls, and a sprig of dill. Serve with sauce antiboise. See recipe.

Serves: 15
Calories per serving: 222

Pâté of Salmon

2	oz. milk
3	oz. flour
3	egg yolks
1½	oz. butter
10	oz. cubed sole
1	egg white
1	oz. cold white wine
1	oz. brandy
21	oz. fresh salmon

1½	oz. pistachio nuts
1	oz. diced truffles
1	cup aspic jelly
1	cup whipped cream
2	tbsp. salmon caviar
1	small bunch dill

Prepare the panada by mixing milk, flour, egg yolks, salt, pepper, and nutmeg. Bring to a boil, stirring until thick. Mix in the butter and chill for 30 minutes.

Emulsify the sole in food processor. Add the panada, egg white, wine, and brandy. Cut the boneless salmon into cubes. Season with salt and pepper and chill.

Line a loaf mold with plastic wrap. Fill alternating the force-meat, salmon cubes, pistachio nuts, and truffles. Cover with plastic wrap and aluminum foil. Bake in a waterbath in a 350°F (175°C) oven to a 150°F (66°C) internal temperature. Press down, and cool 1 hour. Unmold and chill. Coat with aspic, decorate with whipped cream flavored with tomato catsup. Garnish with dill.

Serves: 14
Calories per serving: 180

Figure 16–10. Cold salmon displays for buffet, using the aspic sheet techniques for a unique visual impact.

APPENDIX A
CALORIE CONTENT OF RECIPES

The following chart lists in ascending order the number of calories per serving for all the recipes included in *The Complete Cookbook of American Fish and Shellfish*. Note that the majority of the recipes are relatively low in calories, ranging from 200 to 400 calories per serving.

Sushi Sauce **22**
Sauce Poulette **23**
Tomato Sauce **29**
Anchovy Sauce **32**
Oysters and Mustard Sauce **34**
Tarragon Sauce **40**
Sauce Ravigotte **42**
Sauce Venitienne **45**
Sauce St. Malo **50**
Sauce Allemande **53**
Sauce Soubise **54**
Sauce Bercy **56**
Sauce Souchet **60**
Sweet and Sour Sauce **63**
Sauce Rouille **64**
Sauce Aurora **66**
Cream Sauce **71**
Sardine Tapenade **75**
Mornay Sauce **75**
Frozen Horseradish Sauce **76**
Sauce Genevoise **77**
Velouté Sauce **78**
Crab Appetizer **79**
Stuffed Clams Oregonati **80**
Key West Turtle Soup **80**
Sauce Andalouse **81**
Sauce Verte **81**
Hot Tuna Canapés **82**
Sauce Antiboise **82**
Marinated Tomato Salad **83**
Sauce Normande **83**
Ravigotte Sauce **83**
Remoulade Sauce **84**
Angels on Horseback **84**
Creole Sauce **84**
Fine Herb Sauce **84**
Mustard Sauce **88**

Golden Caviar Consommé **88**
Pittsburgh Sauce **89**
Diplomate Sauce **89**
Green Goddess Dressing **89**
Cucumber Salad **91**
Tartar Sauce **91**
Vincent Sauce **91**
Russian Sauce **92**
Stuffed Deviled Eggs **92**
Squid and Clam Appetizer **92**
Sauce Cypriote **93**
Stir Fry Oyster Sauce **95**
Russian Salad Aspic Mold **98**
Béchamel **100**
Shrimp Ravioli Pastries **102**
Newburg Sauce **102**
Manhattan Clam Chowder **103**
Shrimp Pastries **105**
Scallop Ceviche **105**
Dill Sauce **105**
Bordeaux Wine Sauce **105**
Marinated Mussels **108**
Mussels in White Wine **108**
Mayonnaise **108**
Boiled Blue Crab **108**
Sauce Orientale **109**
Boula Boula **109**
Stuffed Tomato Surprise **109**
Crab Canapés **110**
Caper Sauce **111**
Consommé Belle Vue **112**
Panada for Quenelles **112**
Sauce Gribiche **114**
Sauce Albigeoise **114**
Bretonne Sauce **120**
Shrimp Sauce **120**
Clam Fritters **120**

464   Cookery

Saltwater Fish

Anglerfish, Monkfish	Baudroie or Lotte
Anchovy	Anchois
Cod (fresh)	Cabillaud
Cod (salted)	Morue
Conger eel	Congre
Dolphin	Dauphin
Eel	Anguille
Flounder	Plie
Frogs' Legs	Cuisses de grenouilles
Grouper	Merou
Haddock	Aiglefin
Hake	Merluche, Merlu
Halibut	Fletan
Herring	Hareng
Lingcod	Julienne, Lingue bleue
Mackerel	Maquereau
Mullet	Mulet
Ocean Perch	Perche d'ocean
Pollock	Colin
Pompano	Pompano
Salmon	Saumon
Sardine	Sardine
Shad	Alose
Sea Robin	Grondin
Sea Trout	Truite de mer
Skate	Raie
Shark	Requin
Smelt	Eperlan
Sole	Sole
Striped Bass	Bar, Loup de mer
Swordfish	Espadon
Tuna	Thon
Turtle	Tortue
Whiting	Merlan

Freshwater Fish

Carp	Carpe
Catfish	Poisson chat
Lake Herring	Hareng de lac

466

Lake Trout	Truite de lac
Pike	Brochet
Sturgeon	Esturgeon
Rainbow Trout	Truite Arc-en-ciel
Whitefish	Fera
Trout	Truite

Mollusks

Abalone	Ormeau
Octopus	Poulpe
Oysters	Huitre
Scallops	Coquille St. Jacques
Snails	Escargots
Squid	Calamare

Crustaceans

Crawfish	Ecrevisse
Crab	Crabe
Lobster	Homard
Lobsterette	Langoustine
Spiny Lobster	Langouste
Shrimp	Crevette

APPENDIX C
GOING METRIC

Our traditional system of weights and measures is slowly being replaced by the simpler metric system. Although the metric system is logical, and easy to learn and use, many people are perplexed by the new system. The following information on converting ounces into grams, quarts into liters, and degrees Fahrenheit into degrees Celsius or centigrade should help. As a basic guide, remember that: water freezes at 0 degrees C (Centigrade) and boils at 100 degrees C; that 1 meter equals 100 centimeters (cm); and 1 liter equals 100 centiliters (cl). We have to learn to live with C g, dl, l, etc. You can begin by thinking metric.

Weight Conversion

The metric system has the gram as its basic unit of weight, with decimal multiples. One-thousand grams equals 1 kilogram (kg). To convert avoir-

Table
C-1. Weight Conversions

Avoirdupois Ounces	Grams	Grams	Avoirdupois Ounces
1 oz.	28.35g	10g	0.35 oz.
2 oz.	56.70g	15g	0.53 oz.
3 oz.	85.05g	20g	0.70 oz.
4 oz.	113.39g	30g	1.05 oz.
5 oz.	141.74g	40g	1.41 oz.
6 oz.	170.09g	50g	1.76 oz.
7 oz.	198.44g	60g	2.11 oz.
8 oz.	226.79g	70g	2.47 oz.
9 oz.	255.14g	80g	2.82 oz.
10 oz.	283.49g	90g	3.17 oz.
11 oz.	311.48g	100g	3.52 oz.
12 oz.	340.19g	200g	7.04 oz.
13 oz.	368.54g	300g	10.56 oz.
14 oz.	396.89g	400g	14.08 oz.
15 oz.	425.25g	450g	15.87 oz.
16 oz.	453.59g	500g	17.64 oz.
2 lb.	907.18g	1000g 1 kg	35.27 oz.
3 lb.	1360.77g	2000g 2 kg	70.54 oz.
4 lb.	1814.36g	3000g 3 kg	105.82 oz.
5 lb.	2267.80g	4000g 4 kg	141.09 oz.
6 lb.	2721.54g	5000g 5 kg	176.36 oz.

NOTE: Most recipes do not follow the above chart precisely. For convenience, a close equivalent conversion is widely used. For example: 7 oz. equals 200 g; 16 oz. equals 450 g; 100 g equals 3½ oz.; 230 g equals 8 oz.

dupois ounces into grams, multiply the ounces by 28.35. For example: 6 oz. ×
28.35 = 170.1 g. Table C-1 lists some commonly used weight conversions.

TEMPERATURE CONVERSION

Table C-2 shows the conversion of degrees Farenheit to degrees Celsius or
centigrade, ranging from deep-freeze temperatures to deep-frying temperatures. To convert degrees F to degrees C quickly, refer to the following
example:

(F − 32) × 5 ÷ 9 = C

In reverse, (C × 9 ÷ 5) + 32 = F.

Table
C-2. Temperature Conversion

Farenheit	Celsius or Centigrades
− 0.4 F.	−20 C.
10.4 F.	−12 C.
21.2 F.	− 6 C.
26.6 F.	− 3 C.
32 F.	0 C. (freezing point of water)
37.4 F.	3 C.
42.8 F.	6 C.
48.2 F.	9 C.
53.6 F.	12 C.
59 F.	15 C.
64.4 F.	18 C.
69.8 F.	21 C.
75.2 F.	24 C.
80.6 F.	27 C.
86 F.	30 C.
91.4 F.	33 C.
98.6 F.	37 C.
212 F.	100 C. (boiling point of water)
225 F.	110 C.
250 F.	120 C.
275 F.	135 C.
300 F.	155 C.
325 F.	165 C.
350 F.	180 C.
375 F.	190 C.
400 F.	205 C.
425 F.	220 C.
450 F.	230 C.

NOTE: Most recipes follow approximate conversions for oven and deep-frying
temperatures. Examples above rule are approximate.

Volume Conversion

The liter is the basic unit of volume in the metric system. In this book, most recipes are converted into deciliters (dl) or centiliters (cl). One liter (1) equals 10 dl, 100 cl, or 1000 ml. Small amounts of liquid are measured in centiliters or milliliters. Table C-3 lists some common volume conversions.

Table

C-3. Volume Conversions

U.S.	Metric
1 tsp.	0.5 cl
1 tbsp. or 3 tsp.	1.5 cl
2 tbsp. or 1 oz. fluid	3 cl or 0.3 dl
2 oz. (fluid)	6 cl or 0.6 dl
3 oz.	9 cl or 0.9 dl
4 oz. or ½ cup	12 cl or 1.2 dl
8 oz. or 1 cup	25 cl or 2.5 dl
16 oz. or 2 cups	50 cl or 5 dl or 0.51
32 oz. or 1 qt.	100 cl or 10 dl or 1l
64 oz. or ½ gal.	200 cl or 20 dl or 2l
128 oz. or 1 gal.	400 cl or 40 dl or 4l
2 gal.	800 cl or 80 dl or 8l
3 gal.	1200 cl or 120 dl or 12l
4 gal.	1600 cl or 160 dl or 16l
5 gal.	2000 cl or 200 dl or 20l

NOTE: The above chart is used and accepted in the trade although the conversions are not exact. One quart equals. 0.95 l, but this figure is rounded to 1 l. The final products are not affected by these slight adjustments.

GLOSSARY

Anadromous Ascending rivers from the sea for breeding, such as shad and salmon.

Barquette A small, boat-shaped pie crust shell usually filled with hot or cold seafoods.

Beurre manié A mixture of equal weight of flour and butter used to thicken sauces.

Breaded Shrimp Peeled shrimp coated with breading. The product may be identified as fantail (butterfly) and round, with or without tail fins and last shell segment. Also known as portions, sticks, steaks, et cetera when prepared from a composite unit of two or more shrimp pieces, whole shrimp, or a combination of both without fins and shells.

Breading A commercial breading is a finely ground mixture, containing cereal products, flavorings, and other ingredients, that is applied to a product that has been moistened, usually with batter.

Brisling A small herring, resembling a sardine, that is cured and tinned for food especially in Norway.

Butterfly fillets The two skin-on fillets of a fish joined together by the belly skin.

Canapé An appetizer prepared on a base such as bread, crackers, or toast.

Canned fishery products Fish, shellfish, or other aquatic animals packed in cans, jars, or other containers, which are hermetically sealed and heat sterilized. Most, but not all, canned fishery products can be stored at room temperature for an indefinite time without spoiling.

Catadromous Living in fresh water and going to sea to spawn.

China cap A cone-shaped strainer or sieve.

Consumption of fishery products Estimated amount of commercially landed fish, shellfish, and other aquatic animals consumed in the United States. Estimates are on an edible weight basis.

Croutons Small pieces of fried or toasted diced bread used as a garnish in soups and other seafood dishes.

Cured fishery products Products preserved by drying, pickling, salting, and smoking. Does not include canned, frozen, irradiated, or pasteurized products. Dried products are cured by sun or air drying; pickled or salted products are preserved by applying salt, or by pickling (immersing in brine); smoked products are cured with smoke, sometimes in combination with drying or salting.

Duxelle Finely chopped mushrooms cooked with chopped shallots. Used primarily as part of stuffing for seafood.

En brochette On a skewer, like seafood en brochette.

Exvessel price Price received by fishermen for fish, shellfish, and other aquatic plants and animals landed at the dock.

Finnan haddie Smoked haddock.

Fish blocks Regular fish blocks are frozen blocks or slabs of fillets, or pieces of fillets, cut or sliced from fish. Minced fish blocks are frozen blocks or slabs of minced flesh produced by a meat and bone separating machine.

Fish fillets The sides of fish, either skinned or with skin on, cut lengthwise from the backbone. Most types of fillets are boneless or virtually boneless; some may be specified as "boneless fillets."

Fish portion A piece of fish flesh, generally of uniform size with a thickness of 3/8 inch or more, that does not conform to the definition of a fish stick. A fish portion is generally cut from a fish block.

Fish steak Cross section slices cut from large dressed fish. Steaks are usually 3/4 inch thick.

Fish stick An elongated piece of breaded fish flesh weighing not less than 3/4 ounce and not more than 1½ ounces, with the largest dimension at least three times that of the next largest dimension. A fish stick is generally cut from a fish block.

Fleuron Small, crescent-shaped baked puffed pastry used as garnish around prepared seafood dishes with sauces.

Forcemeat Chopped meats and seasonings used for stuffing or to make quenelles (dumplings).

Groundfish Broadly, fish that are caught on or near the sea floor. The term includes a wide variety of bottomfishes, rockfishes, and flatfishes. However, the National Marine Fisheries Service sometimes uses the term in a narrower sense. The term usually applies to cod, cusk, haddock, hake, pollock, and Atlantic ocean perch.

Julienne A method of cutting vegetables and fruit into fine long strips.

Landings, commercial Quantities of fish, shellfish, and other aquatic plants and animals brought ashore and sold. Landings of fish may be in terms of round (live) weight or dressed weight. Landings of crustaceans are usually on a live weight basis except for shrimp, which may be on a heads-on or heads-off basis. Mollusks are generally landed with the shell on, but in some cases only the meats are landed (as with scallops). Data for all mollusks are published on meat weight basis.

Liaison A thickening agent composed of heavy cream and egg yolks.

Marine fishing Fishing for finfish in oceans, bays, estuaries, and tidal portions of rivers. Marine fishing also includes the harvest of shellfish and other living aquatic organisms in these waters.

Matelote Fish stewed with wine, vegetables, and seasonings.

Mayonnaise collée A mixture of mayonnaise and aspic jelly; used to glaze cold foods.

Mirepoix A mixture of chopped onions, carrots, and celery.

Per capita consumption Consumption of edible fishery products in the United States, divided by the total population. In calculating annual per capita consumption, estimates of the resident population of the United States on July of each year are used.

Retail price The price of fish and shellfish sold to the final consumer by food stores and other retail outlets.

Round (live) weight The weight of fish, shellfish, or other aquatic plants or animals as taken from the water; that is, the complete or full weight as caught.

INDEX

474   Index

476   Index